Origins of the Right of Self-Defence in International Law

International Law in Japanese Perspective

Series Editors

Yuji Iwasawa and James Crawford

VOLUME 12

The titles published in this series are listed at *brill.com/iljp*

Origins of the Right of Self-Defence in International Law

From the Caroline *Incident to the United Nations Charter*

By

Tadashi Mori

Translated by

Jonathan Bloch

BRILL
NIJHOFF

LEIDEN | BOSTON

Library of Congress Cataloging-in-Publication Data

Names: Mori, Tadashi, 1970-, author.
Title: Origins of the right of self-defence in international law : from the Caroline Incident to the United Nations Charter / By Tadashi Mori ; Translated by Jonathan Bloch.
Description: Leiden : Brill Nijhoff, 2018. | Series: International law in Japanese perspective ; 12 | Includes bibliographical references and index. | Identifiers: LCCN 2017052800 (print) | LCCN 2017052893 (ebook) | ISBN 9789004355002 (E-book) | ISBN 9789004354975 (hardback : alk. paper)
Subjects: LCSH: Self-defense (International law)--History. | United Nations--Charters.
Classification: LCC KZ4043 (ebook) | LCC KZ4043 .M675 2018 (print) | DDC 341.5--dc23
LC record available at https://lccn.loc.gov/2017052800

Typeface for the Latin, Greek, and Cyrillic scripts: "Brill". See and download: brill.com/brill-typeface.

ISSN 0929-7111
ISBN 978-90-04-35497-5 (hardback)
ISBN 978-90-04-35500-2 (e-book)

This book is printed on acid-free paper and produced in a sustainable manner.

Contents

Preface IX
List of Abbreviations XIII

Introduction 1

PART 1
Re-formation of Perspectives

1 **Framework of the Conventional Debate** 11
A Bowett: Three Issues and One General Statement 14
B Brownlie: Re-formulation of Bowett's General Statement 17
C Beyond the Framework of Debate Set by Brownlie 20
1 *Influence of this Framework over Current Arguments* 20
2 *Beyond the Consensus Framework* 22

2 **Great Confusion over the Right of Self-Defence: The *Caroline* Incident Revisited** 25
A Divisions over the *Caroline* Incident 26
B Background to the Divisions: The Necessity Doctrine and the Self-Defence Doctrine 30
1 *Necessity Doctrine* 30
2 *Self-Defence Doctrine* 32
3 *Difference in the Function of the Right of Self-Defence* 35
C Differences in the Concepts: Self-preservation Doctrine 36
1 *Self-preservation Doctrine* 36
2 *Limits of the Self-preservation Doctrine* 38
D Perspectives 39

PART 2
Two Distinct Concepts

3 **The Right of Self-Defence before World War I** 43
A State Practice 43
1 *Justification for the Violation of the Territory of Another State* 45
2 *Justification for the Violation of the Flag-State Jurisdiction of Another State* 55

B Doctrine 69
1 *Mid-19th Century* 71
2 *Late-19th Century and Later* 75
C Policing Concept of the Right of Self-Defence 79

4 **The Right of Self-Defence as it Developed in the Inter-war Period** 82
A The Basic Function of Self-Defence: Resistance to Acts of Aggression 84
1 *The Covenant of the League of Nations (1919)* 85
2 *The Protocol for the Pacific Settlement of International Disputes (1924)* 88
3 *Rhineland Pact (Locarno Treaties) (1925)* 90
4 *The Pact of Paris (1928)* 92
5 *Summary of Section A* 94
B Scope of the Inter-war Right 95
1 *The Problem of Defining Aggression* 97
2 *The Existence of Limits: League of Nations Practice* 110
3 *Vague Boundaries* 119
4 *Precursor of Collective Self-Defence, and the Preconditions for Its Operation* 124
C Significance of the Inter-war Period's Conception of Self-Defence: Self-Defence as Defensive War 136

PART 3
The Pre-1945 Right of Self-Defence

5 **The Relationship between the Two Conceptions of Self-Defence** 141
A Coexistence of the Two Conceptions of the Right of Self-Defence 143
1 *The Pact of Paris and Protection of Nationals Abroad* 144
2 *The League of Nations Codification Conference* 161
3 *The US-Mexico Mixed Claims Commission* 163
B The Relationship between the Two Conceptions of Self-Defence 165
1 *The Right of Self-Defence in Customary International Law and Treaty Law* 167
2 *Violations of Territory and Resort to War* 169
3 *From Outlawry of War to Prohibition of the Use of Force* 174
C 'Outlawry of War' and the Two Conceptions of the Right of Self-Defence 180

6 **The Right of Self-Defence in the *Travaux Préparatoires* of the United Nations Charter** 181
A Formulation of the Non-use of Force Principle 183
1 *The Formulation Process* 184
2 *From the Moscow Declaration to the Dumbarton Oaks Proposals* 186
3 *Deliberations at the San Francisco Conference* 194
4 *Conclusions of Section A* 205
B The Perception of the Right of Self-Defence as Policing Measures 206
1 *Internal Discussions of the US Department of State* 207
2 *From Dumbarton Oaks to San Francisco* 210
3 *Theoretical Status of the Policing Conception of Self-Defence* 211
C 'Insertion' of the Right of Self-Defence as Defensive War 214
1 *From Dumbarton Oaks to San Francisco: The Two Contexts in Which the Right of Self-Defence was Discussed* 215
2 *The Birth of Article 51* 219
3 *Collective Self-Defence against Armed Attack and Individual Self-Defence against Aggression* 223
D The Meaning of the Right of Self-Defence in the Drafting Process of the UN Charter 228

Conclusion 232

Bibliography 245
Index 272

Preface

What *is* the right of self-defence in international law?

The question running though this book arose in the process of getting a handle on arguments concerning the legal character of the multinational force assembled for the Gulf War (1990–1991). Were its activities an exercise of the right of collective self-defence? Or an operation for collective security? It piqued my interest to see that participants in the vibrant debates of that time meant different things by 'self-defence'. In Japan at this time, constitutional arguments on collective self-defence and participation in collective security operations also grew more intense, conveying an urgent sense of the need to make clear the meaning of such terms in international law.

It was in this state of mind that I resolved to look thoroughly into the question of what the conception of a right of self-defence actually entailed. The importance of such an inquiry into essentials was later pointed up by the confusion evident in arguments on the right of self-defence against terror attacks on the United States of 2001.

It was in 1997 that I took up the study of the right of self-defence in earnest, after my appointment as a Research Associate at the Institute of Social Science, University of Tokyo. From the beginning, I was uneasy with the positioning of the *Caroline* incident as a precedent establishing the right of self-defence. This feeling of unease took shape in my article, 'Karoraingo Jiken ni okeru Jieiken no Kino (The "Right of Self-defence" in the *Caroline* Case)' ([1999] 50 Shakai Kagaku Kenkyu (Journal of Social Science (University of Tokyo)) 69–99 (*in Japanese*)), in which I articulated a view of two rights of self-defence which proved to be the viewpoint and structure that would govern my later enquiry, and ultimately the study presented here. The problem always before me has been to clarify the historical development of the legal conception of a 'right of self-defence'; I feel now as if that problem has led me, irrespective of any competing intentions I may have formed, to the presentation offered in these pages.

How far my efforts have been successful is for readers to judge. Whether my account of historical development in the years covered by this volume has any real significance, moreover, will be proven only as I proceed to research developments since the Second World War. Awaits me a great labor.

The present work is a translation into English of an updated version of my *Jieiken no Kiso* (*Right of Self-defence in International Law: From the* Caroline *Incident to the United Nations Charter*) published by the University of Tokyo Press, in Japanese, in March of 2009.

•••

Research is lonely work, but one does not do it alone.

In the short space permitted here, I wish to offer my thanks for the many people whose guidance and help have seen this work to completion.

•••

Professor Wakamizu Tsutsui set me on the path of a student of international law. The work itself, moreover, owes much to the good fortune of an association with this master in the study of the right of self-defence. From Professor Akira Kotera, my supervisor since the second year of my master's course, I learned much, in both formal and informal settings. From conception to completion, through development and drafting, this study has been greatly sustained by his wise advice. It fills me with great regret that Professor Kotera, who passed away in February of 2014, will not see this volume. During my residence at Oxford University, though he was under no obligation whatever to do so, Professor Vaughan Lowe (now of Essex Court Chambers), continually offered comments and encouragement on the work I pursued there, which formed the basis of this study.

Professor Soji Yamamato not only offered comment that cut to the heart of this study, but schooled me in what international law is all about. He, too, passed away before he could see the study completed, in September 2013. Professor Yasuaki Onuma pounded into me the rigor with which one must pursue one's scholarship. Professor Naoya Okuwaki, meanwhile, taught me that the depth of research is in the end the depth of the researcher. It is only now that many of my teachers' lessons hit home.

Professor Yuji Iwasawa not only reviewed my doctoral thesis but also kept me constantly aware of the work's interpretative significance. From Professor Junji Nakagawa, at the Institute of Social Science of the University of Tokyo, I received the gift of three years in which to devote myself entirely to this study. Had I not been offered those three years, I would not have been able to attempt a study of a theme so vast as the right of self-defence. Professor Akio Morita invited me to the wonderful research environment of Tokyo Metropolitan University and thereafter advised me continually on all manner of problems. Professors Hisakazu Fujita, Yozo Yokota, and Kazuhiro Nakatani, through their lectures and seminars, taught me the diversity of approaches possible to my field.

I was also supported in pursuing my study by the opportunities I was given to present and discuss my work in such forums as the Japanese Society of International Law and the Japanese Association of World Law, and by the comments and criticisms offered by many scholars in such forums. Another opportunity to rethink was given by the scholars from other fields whose comments and questions at my dissertation defense showed me the limitations of my approach. A further stimulus to deepen my study was provided by the arguments and discussions I enjoyed with many colleagues of my cohort. In that context I recall particularly the vibrant discussions I had, immediately on entering their ranks, with Kazuhiko Hayashida. May he rest in peace.

•••

In the Graduate Schools for Law and Politics, University of Tokyo, I was blessed with wonderful faculty and fellow-students. The University of Tokyo's Institute of Social Science gave me three years, as a research associate, in which to bury myself in my study. At Tokyo Metropolitan University, I was able to start my life as an instructor surrounded by colleagues passionate in their research and teaching. In the midst of immense challenges confronting the university, I was most generously allowed to enter a two-year resident fellowship abroad. The Oxford University Faculty of Law gave me tremendous intellectual stimulation, and at Merton College there I was blessed with many friends, including friends from other fields. That I have been surrounded by exceptional colleagues and students since first being made an instructor at the University of Tokyo's Graduate Schools for Law and Politics I can only regard as pure good luck.

Without the help of document repositories and archives in the United States and the United Kingdom, this study could not have been carried out. In order to visit them and use these resources, the support of the Japan Society of the Promotion of Science (Grants-in-Aid for Scientific Research and Overseas Research Fellowships) and the Nomura Foundation was essential. To the staff of such archival institutions I am indebted for all manner of aid.

For his help with publication of this work I am ever grateful to Professor Iwasawa. For their help at the final stage of editing this volume I am thankful to Ingeborg van der Laan and Saskia van der Knaap of Brill. To Mishio Saito of University of Tokyo Press, which published the Japanese version of this study, I offer thanks for agreeing so readily to publication of an English translation. Publication of this study was supported by Egusa Foundation for International Cooperation in the Social Sciences.

An English version of this work would not have been possible without the dedication and skill of its translator, Jonathan Bloch, whose kind interest in its arguments and fine rendering thereof have fortified my desire to bring it out. In the final copyediting of the manuscript I have had the assistance of Jun Okada, Satomi Shintani, Yusuke Kaide, Natsuko Sumi, and Kimihiko Okano.

•••

I offer my sincerest thanks to all the many people who have contributed to this study, including all those whom I am unable to name in this brief space. When I reflect on how many people have supported me, I understand how greatly I am blessed. I pray that I will discharge in my research and teaching the responsibility laid upon me by this good fortune.

In memoriam *Akira Kotera*.
May, 2017, Hongo, Tokyo

Tadashi Mori

List of Abbreviations

AJIL	American Journal of International Law
AJIL Suppl	Supplement to the American Journal of International Law
Australian Yb Int'l L	Australian Yearbook of International Law
BFSP	British and Foreign State Papers
BYIL	British Yearbook of International Law
Cambridge LJ	Cambridge Law Journal
Canadian Yb Int'l L	Canadian Yearbook of International Law
Chicago J Int'l L	Chicago Journal of International Law
Cong Rec	Congressional Record. Proceedings and Debates of the Congress of the United States of America
Cornell Int'l LJ	Cornell International Law Journal
EJIL	European Journal of International Law
Harvard J Int'l L	Harvard Journal of International Law
ICJ Rep	Reports of Judgments, Advisory Opinions and Orders of the International Court of Justice
ICLQ	International and Comparative Law Quarterly
ILM	International Legal Materials
Int'l Affairs	International Affairs
Int'l Conciliation	International Conciliation
Int'l Lawyer (American Bar Ass'n)	International Lawyer (American Bar Association)
J Conflict & Security L	Journal of Conflict and Security Law
League of Nations OJ	League of Nations Official Journal
League of Nations OJ Spec Suppl	League of Nations Official Journal Special Supplement
Leiden J Int'L L	Leiden Journal of International Law
PCIJ Rep Series A/B	Permanent Court of International Justice, Judgments, Orders and Advisory Opinions
Proc Am Soc'y IL	Proceedings of the American Society of International Law
RCADI	Recueil des Cours (Académie de Droit International de la Haye)
Rev Québécoise DI	Revue Québécoise de Droit International
Rev Gén DI Pub	Revue Géneralede Droit International Public
Rev Int'l Studies	Review of International Studies
RIAA	Reports of International Arbitral Awards
San Diego Int'l LJ	San Diego International Law Journal

Wisc Int'l LJ	Wisconsin International Law Journal
Wyoming LR	Wyoming Law Review
Yale J Int'l L	Yale Journal of International Law
Yale LJ	Yale Law Journal
Yb Int'l L Comm'n	Yearbook of International Law Commission

Introduction

What is the right of self-defence in international law?

This study examines a long-running conflict over the right of self-defence[1] in contemporary international law, focusing on the historical development of the concept of the right of self-defence from the mid-19th century to the establishment of the United Nations in 1945.

Regulation of the Use of Force in International Law and the Right of Self-Defence

Legal regulation of the use of force in international society has been a *raison d'être* of international law. The problem of how to regulate the use of force or recourse to war by states has, in turn, been among the most vital concerns in the study of international law.[2] While the scope of matters with which

1 Merely to speak of 'the right of self-defence' invites controversy, as it is not universally accepted that any such 'right' exists. Indeed, Article 21 of the Draft Articles on Responsibility of States for Internationally Wrongful Acts, adopted by the International Law Commission (ILC) of the United Nations in 2001, refers simply to 'self-defence', rather than to a 'right of self-defence'. This omission was not accidental. Roberto Ago, who as special *rapporteur* to the ILC from 1963 to 1979 took the leading role in the formulation of the article provisionally adopted in 1980, quite explicitly states: 'we think it wrong to treat self-defence ... as a "right", and hence to speak of a "right of self-defence"'. (R Ago 'Addendum to the Eighth Report on State Responsibility: The Internationally Wrongful Act of State, Source of International Responsibility (Part I) (Concluded)' [1980] 2–1 Yb Int'l L Comm'n 53) However, the commentary provided by the ILC on Article 21 as finally adopted states, 'Article 51 of the Charter of the United Nations preserves a State's "inherent right" of self-defence ... [A] State exercising its inherent right of self-defence as referred to in Article 51 of the Charter is not, even potentially, in breach of Article 2 (4)'. (J Crawford *The International Law Commission's Articles on State Responsibility* (CUP Cambridge 2002) 166).

Ago's argument stems from his understanding of what a 'right' entails: 'The term "right" ... indicates a "claim" which the law ... accords to a subject vis-à-vis other subjects, of whom he may rightfully require a specific performance or a specific conduct'. (Ago (n 1) 18) However, this understanding of rights may not be valid in all circumstances (see Chapter 3.B.2); indeed, if we hope to understand the 'right of self-defence' in contemporary international law, the meaning of 'right' within this phrase must be examined, not assumed.

Where possible, I follow Article 51 of the United Nations Charter and refer to 'the right of self-defence'. When discussing scholarly or other documents that refer only to 'self-defence', I preserve that usage.

2 S Tabata *Kokusaiho* (*International Law*) (new edn Yuhikaku Tokyo 1973) vol 1, 17–18 (*in Japanese*); Y Onuma *Senso Sekininron Josetsu* (*Introduction to the Issues of Responsibility for War*) (University of Tokyo Press Tokyo 1975) 3 (*in Japanese*). See also I Brownlie

 | DOI 10.1163/9789004355002_002

international law is concerned has expanded over time, and continues to grow apace with the interdependence of international society (globalisation),[3] this problem has not lost thereby any of its importance.[4]

If the problem gives international law importance and vitality, however, it also threatens international law's viability. At stake is not merely how best to regulate the use of force but whether regulating it meaningfully is even possible. Scepticism regarding the effectiveness of such legal regulation of the use of force is easily transformed into doubt about whether international law in this area can be meaningfully said to exist, and even into denial of the relevance of international law to 'the fundamental issues upon which the peace and welfare of nations depend'.[5]

In contemporary international law, use of force by states is generally prohibited. Article 2, paragraph 4, of the United Nations Charter provides that '[a]ll Members shall refrain in their international relations from the threat or use of force against the territorial integrity or political independence of any state, or in any other manner inconsistent with the Purposes of the United Nations'. However, to this prohibition of the use of force the Charter provides two main exceptions: use of force sanctioned by the Security Council (Chapter VII); and use of force in the exercise of the right of self-defence (Article 51), which is the focus of this study.

In order for the general prohibition of the use of force to be effective, the scope of the right of self-defence as one of the main exceptions to the prohibition must be defined. Otherwise, the general prohibition either has no real meaning[6] or is 'too broad to be of much guidance' to the action of states.[7] So much was clear in 1970, when Thomas Franck pronounced the death of Article 2(4) of the UN Charter, largely on the grounds that 'through practice, the exceptions have overwhelmed the rule and transformed the system';[8]

'The United Nations Charter and the Use of Force, 1945–1985' in A Cassese (ed) *The Current Legal Regulation of the Use of Force* (Martinus Nijhoff Publishers Dordrecht 1986) 491–493.

3 Eg O Schachter *International Law in Theory and Practice* (Kluwer Boston 1995) 1.

4 Brownlie (n 2) 491–493.

5 HJ Morgenthau 'Diplomacy' [1946] 55 Yale LJ 1080. See also HJ Morgenthau *Politics Among Nations* (5th edn Knopf New York 1973) 281; GF Kennan *Realities of American Foreign Policy* (OUP London 1954) 38.

6 DW Bowett *Self-Defence in International Law* (Manchester University Press Manchester 1958) 4.

7 R Higgins *The Development of International Law through the Political Organs of the United Nations* (OUP Oxford 1963) 167.

8 TM Franck 'Who Killed Article 2(4)?' [1970] 64 AJIL 811. See also L Henkin 'The Reports of the Death of Article 2(4) Are Greatly Exaggerated' [1971] 65 AJIL 544.

and, indeed, was stated more plainly in 1961: '[t]he meaning of the term "self-defence" has remained the most vital issue relating to the legal regulation of the use of force by States'.[9]

Importance of the Right of Self-Defence

In the post-Cold War era, the importance of the right of self-defence, and of subjecting it to scrutiny, have only been enhanced. Since the end of the Cold War, states have frequently resorted to force while claiming self-defence as justification. With regard to their missile attacks on Sudan and Afghanistan on 20th August 1998, for example, the United States maintained that they had exercised the right of self-defence in the face of a series of armed attacks on embassies and citizens of the United States.[10] After the terrorist attacks on the World Trade Center and the Pentagon on 11th September 2001, the United States again claimed the right of self-defence in undertaking major military action in Afghanistan.[11]

International society, of course, has not accepted these invocations of the right of self-defence without objection. Both states and scholars have criticised the claims – sometimes simply questioning whether the facts surrounding the use of force satisfied the conditions justifying action in self-defence, but often raising a more basic doubt: whether there exists in international law a common understanding of the concept of the right of self-defence.[12] How to define or understand the right of self-defence, which constitutes one of the main

---

9 I Brownlie 'The Use of Force in Self-Defence' [1961] 37 BYIL 183.

10 'Letter Dated 20 August 1998 from the Permanent Representative of the United States of America to the United Nations Addressed to the President of the Security Council' S/1998/780 (20 August 1998). See also 'Letter Dated 21 August 1998 from the Minister of State at the Ministry of Foreign Affairs of the Sudan Addressed to the President of the Security Council' S/1998/786 (21 August 1998). See eg R Wedgwood 'Responding to Terrorism' [1999] 24 Yale J Int'l L 559–576.

11 'Letter Dated 7 October 2001 from the Permanent Representative of the United States of America to the United Nations Addressed to the President of the Security Council' S/2001/946 (7 October 2001). See eg WM Reisman 'In Defense of World Public order' [2001] 95 AJIL 833–835; JI Charney 'The Use of Force against Terrorism and International Law' [2001] 95 AJIL 835–839; TM Franck 'Terrorism and the Right of Self-Defense' [2001] 95 AJIL 839–843; C Greenwood 'International Law and the "War against Terrorism"' [2002] 78 Int'l Affairs 301–317; European Journal of International Law Discussion Forum 'The Attack on the World Trade Center: Legal Responses' <http://www.ejil.org/forum_WTC/index.html>.

12 See articles cited at n 10, n 11 and n 19 of this chapter.

exceptions to the general prohibition of the use of force, remains a most vital issue concerning the regulation of the use of force by states.[13]

Conflict over Prerequisites of the Right of Self-Defence

The right of self-defence in contemporary international law is set down in Article 51 of the United Nations Charter, which provides that '[n]othing in the present Charter shall impair the inherent right of individual or collective self-defence if an armed attack occurs against a Member of the United Nations…'. Although the prerequisite for exercising the right of self-defence appears to be defined categorically (i.e. the occurrence of an armed attack against a member state), an age-old conflict, on precisely this question of what can establish the use of force as an exercise of the right, remains unresolved. Conflict persists between a restrictive and a permissive interpretation of this necessary condition.[14]

Under the restrictive interpretation, the right of self-defence can be exercised only when an armed attack occurs against the territorial integrity or political independence of a state.[15] By contrast, the permissive interpretation holds that the right is broader than that, and can in fact be exercised against 'aggression other than an armed attack'.[16] The permissive interpretation allows for self-defence in the form of protection of nationals abroad and for anticipatory self-defence.[17] Issues arising over 'the scope of the right of self-defence, especially as to whether anticipatory or "preemptive" self-defence and protection of nationals are lawful, are much discussed and date back to the creation of the United Nations'.[18] On these questions, a 'grande confusion'[19] has aptly been said to reign. Charles de Visscher's complaint from 1917 is not out of place today:

---

13 Brownlie (n 9) 183.

14 See The Institute of World Polity *The Law of Limited International Conflict* (Georgetown U Washington DC 1965) 23–26.

15 Eg I Brownlie *International Law and the Use of Force by States* (OUP Oxford 1963); J Žourek 'La notion de légitime défense en droit international' [1975] 56 Annuaire (Institut de Droit Interntional) 1–69; MAM Genoni *Die Notwehr im Völkerrecht* (Schulthess Polygraphischer Verlag Zürich 1987); LA Sicilianos *Les réactions décentralisées à l'illicite* (LGDJ Paris 1990).

16 DW Bowett 'Book Reviews: International Law and the Use of Force by States. By Ian Brownlie' [1964] 13 ICLQ 1107.

17 Eg Bowett (n 6); CHM Waldock 'The Regulation of the Use of Force by Individual States in International Law' [1952] 81 RCADI 451–517.

18 C Gray *International Law and the Use of Force* (3rd edn OUP Oxford 2008) 114.

19 Žourek (n 15) 2. After the terrorist attacks on 11th September 2001, the issue of whether 'an armed attack' provided for in Article 51 of the Charter covers not only an attack by states

> Dans le droit international, la notion de la légitime défense est une question fort mal élucidée. Il régne à cet égard des confusions nombreuses qui ont jeté un certain discrédit sur la conception elle-même et qui conduisent parfois à faire douter de la possibilité de son application dans ce domaine.[20]

Lack of Historical Scrutiny

This study seeks to help clear up this 'grande confusion' by examining the long-standing dispute between the restrictive and permissive interpretations through a historical perspective on the development of the concept of the right of self-defence from the mid-19th century to 1945. The current literature is more concerned with analysis of state practice *since* 1945 – understandably, given the foundational importance of the United Nations Charter to any definition of the preconditions for exercising the right of self-defence in contemporary international law.

The reason this study takes a historical perspective is best explained through an examination of the framework of the conventional debate. This examination, of the topics and grounds of argument that generally dominate today's

---

but also attacks by non-state actors including terrorist groups, has become a major controversy. See articles cited at n 10 and n 11 of this chapter; T Becker *Terrorism and the State* (Hart Oxford 2006); D Jinks 'State Responsibility for the Acts of Private Armed Groups' [2003] 4 Chicago J Int'l L 83; J Kammerhofer 'The Armed Activities Case and Non-State Actors in Self-Defence Law' [2007] 20 Leiden J Int'l L 89; SD Murphy 'Terrorism and the Concept of Armed Attack in Article 51 of the UN Charter' [2002] 43 Harvard J Int'l L 41–51; T Ruys and S Verhoeven 'Attacks by Private Actors and the Right of Self-Defence' [2005] 10 J Conflict & Security L 289–320; G Travalio and J Altenburg 'Terrorism, State Responsibility and the Use of Military Force' [2003] 4 Chicago J Int'l L 97; C Tams 'Note Analytique: Swimming with the Tide or Seeking to Stem It' [2005] 18 Rev Québécoise DI 275; JJ Paust 'Use of Armed Force against Terrorists in Afghanistan, Iraq, and Beyond' [2002] 35 Cornell Int'l LJ 533. More recently, D Bethlehem 'Self-Defense against an Imminent Attack or Actual Armed Attack by Nonstate Actors' [2012] 106 AJIL 770; D Akande and T Liflánder 'Clarifying Necessity, Imminence, and Proportionality in the Law of Self-Defense' [2013] 107 AJIL 563; D Tladi 'The Nonconsenting Innocent State: The Problem with Bethlehem's Principle 12' [2013] 107 AJIL 570; M Hmoud 'Are New Principles Really Needed? The Potential of the Established Distinction between Responsibility for Attacks by Nonstate Actors and the Law of Self-Defense' [2013] 107 AJIL 576; D Bethlehem 'Principles of Self-Defense – A Brief Response' [2013] 107 AJIL 579. This issue has added to the 'grande confusion' over the concept of the right of self-defence. While this study does suggest a perspective on this contemporary issue, it does so on the basis of its focused approach to the prior problem of the division between the restrictive and the permissive interpretation.

20 C de Visscher 'Les lois de la guerre et la théorie de la nécessité' [1917] 24 Rev Gén DI Pub 74.

debate, will be offered in the next chapter. It is worth noting here, however, how little the debate has looked to history for guidance in recent years and how obvious the prima facie case for doing so is.

The lack of historical perspectives is one of the striking points in contemporary studies on the right of self-defence. Christine Gray, one of the most eminent scholars in this field in our time, has in her truly important work, *International Law and the Use of Force*, paid no attention to historical development, declaring herself that her 'book will examine the use of force since the Charter; the focus will be on state and UN practice under the Charter'.[21]

In addition, since the end of the Cold War, especially since the terrorist attacks of 9/11, numerous authors have argued that the law of the United Nations Charter concerning the regulation of the use of force by states is dead[22] or has changed.[23] Such arguments tend to assume that, as far as the right of self-defence is concerned, the restrictive interpretation came into force with the Charter. Had the restrictive interpretation been the accepted governing law under the United Nations Charter, the case for claiming that the law had been abandoned would be clear. However, as Jane Stromseth shrewdly suggests, '[r]igid textualist interpretations of the Charter [i.e. the restrictive interpretation] may well be dead, but it is not clear that they were ever really alive'.[24] Before declaring that, or how, the law has changed, we should be able to say what the supposedly defunct law was – in particular, whether the restrictive interpretation was in fact valid when the Charter was written.

The lack of historical perspective is not a phenomenon peculiar to the current literature. The historical development of the right of self-defence, i.e., both the *travaux préparatoires* of the United Nations Charter and the preceding century of developments that led up to the preparatory work, has been subjected to no thorough re-examination since the 1960s. As will be shown in the next chapter, it has apparently been thought since the debate of the early 1960s that nothing remains to be examined in this history.

However, many relevant documents have become available only since that time, including background papers for the negotiations at the San Francisco Conference of 1945, where the United Nations Charter was adopted. Not yet fully studied by current writers, these recently released documents will in time

21 Gray (n 18) 7.

22 Eg MJ Glennon 'Why the Security Council Failed' [2003] 82(3) Foreign Affairs 16–35.

23 Eg M Byers 'The Shifting Foundations of International Law: A Decade of Forceful Measures against Iraq' [2002] 13 EJIL 21–42.

24 J Stromseth 'Law and Force after Iraq: A Transitional Moment' [2003] 97 AJIL 633.

provide new perspectives on the formative process of relevant provisions of the Charter. Moreover, taking a historical approach now will shed new light on material already familiar within contemporary debates.

Recent International Cases

Up to the beginning of this century, cases in international law concerning the use of force, including the right of self-defence, were very few. The *Case concerning Military and Paramilitary Activities in and against Nicaragua*[25] of 1986 and the *Advisory Opinion on the Legality of the Threat or Use of Nuclear Weapons*[26] of 1996 represent the only decision and opinion by the International Court of Justice produced in the twentieth century that deal directly with the question of the right of self-defence.[27] Since the beginning of this century, however, the ICJ has issued two decisions and one advisory opinion regarding this problem: a decision on the *Case concerning Oil Platforms*[28] of 2003, an advisory opinion on *the Legal Consequences of the Construction of a Wall in the Occupied Palestinian Territory*[29] of 2004, and a decision in the *Case concerning Armed Activities on the Territory of the Congo*[30] of 2005. Further, in 2005 the Eritrea-Ethiopia Claims Commission issued a partial award[31] in which the right of self-defence was examined.

All of these decisions and opinions regarded the occurrence of an armed attack as a prerequisite for exercising the right of self-defence; it seems that they adopted the restrictive interpretation.

However, they did not bring an end to the age-old conflict over the precondition. Not only have these decisions and opinions been subjected to harsh criticism,[32] suggesting that the restrictive interpretation is far from

25 *Case concerning Military and Paramilitary Activities in and against Nicaragua* (*Nicaragua v United States of America*) (Merits) [1986] ICJ Rep 14.

26 *Legality of the Threat or Use of Nuclear Weapons* (Advisory Opinion) [1996] ICJ Rep 226.

27 In the *Case concerning Corfu Channel*, the ICJ dealt with the issue of the use of force but not of the right of self-defence. *Case concerning Corfu Channel* (*United Kingdom of Great Britain v People's Republic of Albania*) (Merits) [1949] ICJ Rep 4.

28 *Case concerning Oil Platforms* (*Islamic Republic of Iran v United States of America*) (Merits) [2003] ICJ Rep 161.

29 *Advisory Opinion concerning the Legal Consequences of the Construction of a Wall on the Occupied Palestinian Territory* (Advisory Opinion) [2004] ICJ Rep 136.

30 *Case concerning Armed Activities on the Territory of the Congo* (*Democratic Republic of Congo v Uganda*) (Merits) [2005] ICJ Rep 168.

31 *Federal Democratic Republic of Ethiopia v State of Eritrea* (*December 19, 2005*) [2006] 45 ILM 430–435.

32 See Gray (n 18) 132–136, 143–147, 177–180.

settled doctrine; they have not settled the questions raised by the *Nicaragua case*,[33] which, while seemingly adopting the restrictive interpretation, put the meaning of the doctrine into question. In the *Nicaragua* case, the ICJ distinguished armed attack from 'less grave forms' of the use of force, holding that while the former may justify acts of individual or collective self-defence, the only responses justified by the latter are 'proportionate counter-measures'.[34] True, this framework seems to settle the question of what can satisfy the precondition for exercising the right of self-defence: an armed attack and nothing else. But it introduces a concept that calls out for clarification, 'proportionate counter-measures' in response to 'less grave forms' of the use of force.

In neither the *Nicaragua case* nor the *Oil Platforms case* does the ICJ provide such clarification. In particular, we find little guidance on whether a military response can be considered a proportionate counter-measure to any use of force not rising to the high standard of 'armed attack', or on how counter-measures involving any use of force can be squared with the non-use of force principle of Article 2(4) of the Charter.[35] The Eritrea-Ethiopia Claims Commission is also silent on this issue. Current rulings in international law, then, have not resolved the 'grande confusion' concerning the right of self-defence. Indeed, removed from an informing historical context, these rulings themselves are rather obscure in meaning.

As stated above, attempting to lay out the logic of our current conceptions of the right of self-defence will lead us to enquire into the historical development of those conceptions. Through this enquiry, we may hope to attain a point of view from which we can see beyond our 'grande confusion'. Toward this end, the next chapter seeks to make clear the inherited structure in which debate on the right of self-defence has been carried out.

---

33 *Case concerning Military and Paramilitary Activities in and against Nicaragua* (n 25) [1986] ICJ Rep 101 para 191.

34 Ibid 127 para 249.

35 See the separate opinion of Judge Simma in the *Oil Platforms case* (*Case concerning Oil Platforms* (n 28) 331–333 (Separate Opinion of Judge Simma)).

PART 1

Re-formation of Perspectives

CHAPTER 1

Framework of the Conventional Debate

The framework of conventional debate over the preconditions for the exercise of the right of self-defence, I would argue, was effectively constructed through the controversy carried out between Derek W. Bowett and Ian Brownlie in the late 1950s and the early 1960s.

Bowett and Brownlie

As mentioned in the Introduction, there has been a long-standing dispute over the restrictive and the permissive interpretations of the preconditions for the exercise of the right of self-defence in contemporary international law. As correctly pointed out by R. St. John Macdonald,[1] one of the best statements of the restrictive interpretation is that offered by Ian Brownlie, and among the best advocates of the permissive interpretation remains Derek Bowett.[2]

These two distinguished scholars are important not only because each is a leading exponent of his position but also because, as will be discussed in Section C.1, the debate between them, which began in the late 1950s and developed in the early 1960s, has established the framework of controversy over the issue of the scope of the right of self-defence, the framework within which most current writers develop their arguments. It is essential to recall and to understand the debate they waged.

Interpretation of the Text of the United Nations Charter

One of the key points dividing Bowett and Brownlie is, naturally, the interpretation of the text of the United Nations Charter, especially Article 2, paragraph 4, and Article 51. Brownlie argues that Article 51 of the Charter imposes restrictions on the right of self-defence formerly existing in customary international law and limits the exercise of that right of self-defence to response to an armed attack. As grounds for his contention, he lays particular stress on the phrase 'if an armed attack occurs' in this article. Applying the principle of effectiveness in interpretation of treaties,[3] he argues that the

1 RStJ Macdonald 'The Nicaragua Case: New Answers to Old Questions?' [1986] 24 Canadian Yb Int'l L 145 n 53–54.

2 See also C Gray 'The Use of Force and the International Legal Order' in MD Evans (ed) *International Law* (4th edn OUP Oxford 2014) 628.

3 R Jennings and A Watts (eds) *Oppenheim's International Law* (9th edn Longman London 1996) vol 1, 1271–1275.

 | DOI 10.1163/9789004355002_003

provision is meaningless unless read to exclude the exercise of the right of self-defence in other cases. But 'the decisive consideration',[4] in his argument, is that since the use of force is generally prohibited in the Charter (Article 2(4)), it is intended that any use of force should be authorized by the United Nations; since the right of self-defence is an exception to the prohibition, it should be interpreted narrowly.[5]

In contrast, Bowett contends that the Charter leaves the customary right of self-defence unimpaired. As the basis for his interpretation, he refers to the phrase 'the inherent right' in Article 51 and points out that at the San Francisco Conference it was stated that the 'use of arms in legitimate self-defence remains admitted and unimpaired'.[6] He also criticised Brownlie's interpretation of the significance of the phrase 'if an armed attack occurs', arguing that it is used 'illustratively rather than exhaustively'.[7] Against Brownlie's argument from the principle of effectiveness, Bowett contends that Article 51 is, like many provisions of other treaties, a declaration of existing rights inserted 'to avoid any uncertainty which might be caused by [its] omission'[8] and thus, that the article is not made meaningless if it is not read to prohibit the exercise of the right of self-defence except in response to an armed attack.

These divergent interpretations of the Charter's text are unlikely ever to converge. It is difficult to resolve the disagreement by any means more satisfactory than attributing it to the fact that 'the wording of the relevant UN Charter articles [is] full of ambiguity'[9] and 'almost every phrase in … Article 51 is open to more than one interpretation'.[10] If this understanding is correct, it

---

4 I Brownlie *International Law and the Use of Force by States* (Clarendon Press Oxford 1963) 273.

5 I Brownlie 'Recent Appraisals of Legal Regulation of the Use of Force' [1959] 8 ICLQ 718–719; Brownlie (n 4) 272–273.

6 DW Bowett *Self-Defence in International Law* (Manchester University Press Manchester 1958) 182–187, esp 185. See also JL Brierly *The Law of Nations* (6th edn CHM Waldock (ed) OUP Oxford 1963) 417. Regarding the controversy over the significance of this statement at that Conference, see n 193 in Chapter 6.

7 DW Bowett 'The Use of Force for the Protection of Nationals Abroad' in A Cassese (ed) *The Current Legal Regulation of the Use of Force* (Martinus Nijhoff Publishers Dordrecht 1986) 40.

8 DW Bowett 'Book Reviews: International Law and the Use of Force by States. By Ian Brownlie' [1964] 13 ICLQ 1107. See also Brierly (n 6) 417–418.

9 R Higgins *Problems and Process* (OUP Oxford 1994) 239.

10 Ibid 240.

appears unlikely that any interpretation entirely based on the text itself will prove conclusive.

Right of Self-Defence in Pre-1945 Customary International Law and the UN Charter

In addition to the interpretation of the text, the debate between Bowett and Brownlie centres on whether or not Article 51 restricted the right of self-defence that existed in pre-1945 customary international law.[11] If the pre-1945 understanding of the right of self-defence is not, as Malanczuk calls it, '[t]he most crucial question concerning self-defence in modern international law',[12] it is certainly one of the most crucial; and it is in any case the crux of the debate between Bowett and Brownlie. As Macdonald states, this is the point 'on which [these] two distinguished publicists are able to come to exactly opposite views on identical material'.[13]

However, this issue has not received substantial attention recently. Instead, as noted in Introduction, most current authors have tended to focus on state practice since 1945. It is valid to contend that '[g]iven this fundamental disagreement on the proper interpretation of the UN Charter, State practice since 1945 is crucial for an understanding of the scope of the right of self-defence'.[14] From the viewpoint of interpretation of treaties, too, focusing on state practice since 1945 is only natural, as reference to 'any subsequent practice in the application of the treaty' is part of 'a general rule of interpretation' of treaties.[15] Moreover, it can be argued that the analysis of the right of self-defence that existed in pre-1945 customary international law is not even examination of the 'preparatory work' for concluding the Charter of the United Nations, recourse to which is admitted as a supplementary means of interpretation.[16] It is fair to doubt whether analysis of pre-1945 understandings has anything to do with the interpretation of treaties now in force.

---

11 Brownlie (n 4) 272.

12 P Malanczuk 'Countermeasures and Self-Defence as Circumstances Precluding Wrongfulness in the International Law Commission's Draft Articles on State Responsibility' in M Spinedi and B Simma (eds) *United Nations Codification of State Responsibility* (Oceana Publications New York 1987) 244. See also S Yamamoto *Kokusaiho* (*International Law*) (2nd edn Yuhikaku Tokyo 1994) 732 (*in Japanese*).

13 Macdonald (n 1) 145.

14 Gray (n 2) 628.

15 Article 31 of the Vienna Convention of the Law of Treaties.

16 Article 32 of the Vienna Convention of the Law of Treaties.

However, as Article 31(3)(b) of the Vienna Convention provides, 'any subsequent practice in the application of the treaty' is meaningful only when it 'establishes the agreement of the parties regarding its interpretation'. Whether or not state practice regarding the right of self-defence since 1945 has established 'the agreement of the parties' to the Charter on this issue is a matter of controversy. It is well known that Gray and Franck, both of whom based their argument on the examination of state practice since 1945, reached almost opposite conclusions over the interpretation of the Charter provisions relating to the use of force and the right of self-defence.[17] Evidently, if state practice is to provide the grounds for resolving dispute, we stand in need of an appropriate perspective from which to analyse state practice.

Determining whether or not Article 51 has restricted the right of self-defence that existed in pre-1945 customary international law will not deliver the decisive interpretation of the relevant Charter articles. Rather, what this task promises is to provide a perspective from which state practice since 1945 can be analysed. Now, it is by no means obvious what the pre-1945 right of self-defence amounted to. On this question, many problems remain to be resolved. But to the extent that we can characterise this pre-1945 right we will attain a firmer basis for evaluating subsequent state practice. Here we have the focus of this study.

In order to clarify the problems to be discussed, we need to consider the arguments which Bowett and Brownlie offered, and, further, to make clear the structure of their debate. Following the order of publication of these scholars' respective major works,[18] Bowett's argument will be examined first.

A Bowett: Three Issues and One General Statement

Three Issues

As we noted in Introduction, divisions regarding the right of self-defence centre on its scope.[19] Whether we refer to the right of self-defence under the United Nations Charter or to the right of self-defence as it existed in and before 1945, the question of scope can be said to have three aspects: the scope of *die*

17 C Gray *International Law and the Use of Force* (3rd edn OUP Oxford 2008); T Franck *Recourse to Force* (CUP New York 2002).

18 The book of Bowett was published in 1958 (see n 6) and that of Brownlie in 1963 (see n 4).

19 Gray (n 17) 114.

Rechtsgüter,[20] or the substantive rights which can be protected by the right of self-defence (i.e. whether territorial integrity and political independence are the only substantive rights covered under the right of self-defence or whether some other rights to be protected also exist); the scope of the prior conduct against which the right of self-defence can be exercised (i.e. whether the right can be exercised only against an armed attack or also against a use of force below the threshold of an armed attack); and the scope of time (i.e. whether anticipatory self-defence is lawful or the right of self-defence can be exercised only after an armed attack occurs).[21] Bowett discusses each of these three areas separately; but, since his and Brownlie's differences on the issue of the scope of time are not, in fact, particularly serious,[22] this study will explore the first two issues only.

Rechtsgüter and Prior Conduct

The main argument which Bowett developed in his book concerns the scope of the *Rechtsgüter*. Part I of his book is entitled 'The Substantive Rights for which Self-Defence is a Permissible Means of Protection'. As such substantive rights, he examines and lists the rights of territorial integrity, political independence, defence of state security on the high seas, protection of nationals, and defence of economic interests.[23] On this issue, he does not make any distinction between the right of self-defence existing in and before 1945 and the right of self-defence under the Charter.

The scope of prior conduct is also an issue on which Bowett clearly states that he cannot share Brownlie's view.[24] Bowett emphasizes that the right of self-defence is legitimately invoked not only against armed attack but also against other 'forms of aggression'.[25] He argues:

> It is well recognized that an armed attack is by no means the only form of aggression, of imperilling a state's rights so that it may be compelled to resort to the exercise of a right of self-defence. The identification of

20 H Neuhold W Hummer and C Schreuer (eds) *Österrichisches Handbuchs des Völkerrechts* (Manzsche Verlags- und Universitätsbuchhandlung Wien 1983) vol 1, 267.

21 Eg Gray (n 17) 114.

22 On the issue of anticipatory self-defence, see ibid 160–165.

23 Bowett (n 6) 29–114.

24 Bowett (n 8) 1107. The other issue on which Bowett cannot agree with Brownlie is, as suggested above, that of anticipatory self-defence. (ibid)

25 Ibid.

> aggression and an armed attack is a gross simplification of a complex problem…[26]

He contends that the right of self-defence can be exercised against 'the various forms of indirect aggression such as assistance to revolting minorities'[27] and others.

General Statement

It should be noted that, in addition to his arguments on three distinct aspects of the scope of the right of self-defence, Bowett offers a general statement concerning the right of self-defence: 'The essence of self-defence is a wrong done, a breach of a legal duty owed to the State acting in self-defence'[28] and, '[t]he right of self-defence lies against conduct by states which is delictual as being in breach of a duty established by international law'.[29]

In this way, he emphasizes the wrongfulness of the prior conduct against which the right of self-defence can be exercised. This formulation of the right of self-defence, with the emphasis placed on the wrongfulness of the prior conduct, was shared by other leading contemporary advocates of the permissive interpretation.[30] The reason for this formulation seems to be that they intend to distinguish self-defence from self-preservation.[31] Bowett indeed states that 'by this pre-condition of delictual conduct on the part of the state against which action is taken, self-defence can be distinguished from self-preservation'.[32] On this point, it can be argued that the 'permissive' interpretation is intended to be 'restrictive' on the exercise of the right of self-defence, as distinguished from the right of self-preservation.

However, contrary to Bowett's intention, it is this emphasis on the wrongfulness of the prior conduct that Brownlie focuses on when he presents a counter-argument to Bowett.

---

26 Bowett (n 6) 192.

27 Ibid.

28 Ibid 9.

29 Ibid 269.

30 CHM Waldock 'The Regulation of the Use of Force by Individual States in International Law' [1952-ii] 81 RCADI 496; R Higgins *The Development of International Law through the Political Organs of the United Nations* (OUP Oxford 1963) 199.

31 Bowett (n 6) 9. Bowett even regards self-preservation as a non-legal concept. He states, 'It is doubtful whether self-preservation can have any meaning as a legal concept apart from a generic term of self-defence, self-help, and necessity; its appeal lies in the realm of ideology rather than of law'. (ibid 10)

32 Ibid 10.

B Brownlie: Re-formulation of Bowett's General Statement

Counter-argument to Bowett

Brownlie published his primary book in this area, *The Use of Force by Individual States and International Law*,[33] in 1963, five years after the publication of Bowett's *Self-Defence in International Law*.[34] Brownlie's book advances a counter-argument to Bowett; as will be discussed later, Brownlie's argument has subsequently become dominant, with regard to the precondition for the right of self-defence in contemporary international law. Put differently, it can be said that Brownlie established the framework of the debate on this question through a criticism of Bowett, and that it is within this framework that Brownlie's position has come to seem the stronger. Therefore, in order to re-examine this issue, it is essential to identify *how* he built up a counter-argument to Bowett.

Prior Conduct

On the scope of the prior conduct against which the right of self-defence can be exercised, Brownlie's contention is ambiguous: he does not address the issue directly. When he discusses the right of self-defence in the period from 1920 to 1939, he does not seem to distinguish between an armed attack and the use of force.[35] Indeed, summarizing the discussion, he concludes that 'resort to force in individual or collective self-defence is a reaction to an actual or imminent *resort to force* in the years 1930 to 1939'.[36] A 'resort to force' may be either an armed attack or simply a use of force. On the other hand, with regard to the right of self-defence under the Charter, he makes a distinction between these two notions: 'It is not to be assumed ... that every unlawful use of force will involve an armed attack...'.[37] However, he does not elucidate his reason for contending that self-defence under the Charter is a reaction only to armed attack, and not, as in the inter-war period, to a use of force short of an armed attack.

Moreover, his definition of 'armed attack' is itself ambiguous. Although most contemporary literature has considered indirect aggression not to be included in his definition of armed attack,[38] he himself, nearly 40 years after the

33 Brownlie (n 4).
34 Bowett (n 6).
35 Brownlie (n 4) 231–250.
36 Ibid 250. (emphasis added)
37 Ibid 365.
38 Eg Bowett (n 8) 1107; The Institute of World Polity (ed) *The Law of Limited International Conflict* (Georgetown University Washington DC 1965) 153 n 30.

publication of his primary work, asserts that his book did 'not take a narrow view of the general concept of armed attack' and in fact argued that indirect aggression occasionally would constitute an armed attack.[39] If this assertion is accepted, his definition of armed attack can include at least a part of what Bowett refers to as 'forms of aggression other than an armed attack'.[40]

Rechtsgüter

Regarding the scope of the *Rechtsgüter*, Brownlie either focuses on the change after 1945 or relies on a general argument. He contends, for example, that defence of state security on the high seas (one of those rights which Bowett argues can be protected by self-defence) was 'almost entirely discredited' through the development of the law after 1945 and thus was put outside the scope of protection.[41] That he should argue in this way is natural, assuming that his intention was to clarify the law of self-defence as it stood in 1963, when he published his book. However, as we will see later, his main argument is that, in 1945, at the time of the establishment of the United Nations Charter, the right of self-defence in customary international law could be exercised only when 'an armed attack occurs', as provided in Article 51 of the Charter. While stressing the change in the concept of the right of self-defence that occurred in the period from 1920 to 1939, Brownlie does not show us what the scope of the *Rechtsgüter* was, or how it changed, in that period.

In order to reject some other rights which Bowett argues can be protected by self-defence, Brownlie relies on the general argument that, in the era of the League of Nations, the right of intervention or self-help came to be prohibited.[42] With regard to the right of protection of nationals and of economic interests, he accepts that '[i]ntervention by armed forces to protect nationals was a

---

39 I Brownlie '*International Law and the Use of Force by States* Revisited' [2000] 21 Australian Yb Int'l L 27. It is true that Brownlie, in *International Law and the Use of Force by States*, touches on the issue of indirect aggression. However, the emphasis of his argument there seems to be placed on the contention that 'a right to resort to force against various forms of indirect aggression cannot be derived from Article 51 if the requirement of proportionality is strictly observed'. (Brownlie (n 4) 279) In this sense, his explanation 40 years after the publication of his book is not very persuasive. See Y Arai-Takahashi 'Shifting Boundaries of the Right of Self-Defence' [2002] 36 Int'l Lawyer (American Bar Ass'n) 1100 n 123.

40 Brownlie's understanding of the indirect aggression that would constitute an armed attack is still narrower than Bowett's, which includes even 'operations by a State designed merely to support revolutionary groups within the "defending" State'. (Bowett (n 8) 1107)

41 Brownlie (n 4) 308.

42 Ibid 281–301.

common occurrence in the period before 1914'[43] but he emphasizes that 'those instruments expressly prohibiting intervention both before and after 1945 may be considered to have rendered intervention for the protection of nationals illegal'.[44] However, it should be noted that 'those instruments' to which he refers simply prohibit intervention in general; they do not expressly forbid the protection of nationals in particular.[45]

In this way, he does not examine the question of which particular rights could be protected in and before 1945.[46] This attitude is consistent throughout his discussion. However, as Brownlie himself accepts that the right of protection of nationals, for example, could be protected by self-defence before 1914,[47] it appears necessary to examine whether or not this particular right was done away with during the inter-war era.

Counter-argument to Bowett's General Statement

Brownlie's main, unambiguous argument, however, is directed against Bowett's general statement of the right of self-defence: that '[t]he essence of self-defence is a wrong done, a breach of a legal duty owed to the State acting in self-defence'.[48] Brownlie accepts that Bowett means to distinguish self-defence from self-help, which in fact Bowett emphasizes in his book.[49] Brownlie contends, however, that 'this definition of self-defence in such a way to include the protection of certain rights makes it difficult and probably impossible to distinguish from self-help'[50] and, further, that 'this concept of the defence of essential rights seems in the last resort to differ little from the concept of self-preservation'.[51] In other words, Brownlie stresses that the concept of the right

43 Ibid 290.

44 Ibid 298.

45 See Chapter 5.A.1.

46 This is well summarized by Malanczuk, stating that '[a]ccording to the prevailing view, art. 51 restricts the customary right to self-defence and allows the use of armed force only to counter an "armed attack" *without taking into consideration the importance of the interests or rights of a State threatened by another one*'. (Malanczuk (n 12) 244. (emphasis added))

47 The appropriateness of this understanding of the protection of nationals abroad will also be discussed in Chapter 5.A.1.

48 Bowett (n 6) 9.

49 Ibid 8–25. Nevertheless, Bowett also states, confusingly enough, 'The right of self-defence in international law is one form of self-help'. (ibid 269) This statement may justify the way in which Brownlie understands his argument.

50 Brownlie (n 5) 715–716.

51 Ibid 716. See also Brownlie (n 4) 255–256.

of self-defence advanced by Bowett cannot be distinguished from the notion of self-help or of self-preservation. However, Brownlie does not elucidate the basis for his contention.

Brownlie's interpretation of Bowett's general statement about the right of self-defence does not seem to capture Bowett's intention and perhaps can be deemed a *re*-formulation of his statement. By basing his argument upon this understanding and indicating that the use of force for self-help or for self-preservation became prohibited in the period between 1920 and 1945, Brownlie rebuts Bowett's thesis as a whole,[52] with great success.

In other words, in addressing the questions of whether the right of self-defence can be exercised in an event other than the occurrence of an armed attack against the territorial integrity or the political independence of a state, i.e. the issues of the scope of the *Rechtsgüter* and of prior conduct, Brownlie bases his position on the prohibition of the use of force for self-help or self-preservation in the inter-war period. This is indeed the crux of the Brownlie's counter-argument.[53] And this is the framework of debate which Brownlie established; it is in this framework that Brownlie's argument has been overwhelmingly accepted by subsequent literature.

C Beyond the Framework of Debate Set by Brownlie

1 *Influence of this Framework over Current Arguments*

Strong and Lasting Influence

Considerable attention should be given to the structure of the debates between Bowett and Brownlie, especially the one based upon the re-formulation of the former's argument by the latter, because this framework has dominated the subsequent controversy over the precondition for the right of self-defence. Indeed, many writers discuss the right of self-defence from the angle of whether Article 51 of the Charter restricts it to the event of an armed attack or still permits self-help.[54]

---

52 Eg Brownlie (n 5) 715–716.

53 This approach can be clearly found also in his argument regarding the legality of anticipatory self-defence. One of his reasons for denying it derives from his understanding that '[t]o permit anticipatory action may well be to accept a right which is wider than that of self-defence and akin to that of self-preservation'. (Brownlie (n 4) 259–260)

54 Eg J Combacau 'The Exception of Self-Defence in U.N. Practice' in A Cassese (ed) (n 7) 25. See also BO Bryde 'Self-Defence' in R Bernhardt (ed) *Encyclopedia of Public International Law* (Elsevier Amsterdam 2000) vol 4, 363; PM Dupuy 'L'invocation de la légitime defénse dans la justification des états' in JF Guilhaudis and M Torrelli (eds) *Force armée*

However, it should be noted that whether Article 51 of the Charter restricts the right to the event of an armed attack and whether this provision still permits self-help are not the same question. Although, as generally understood, the use of force for self-help is prohibited under the Charter, this does not necessarily lead to the conclusion that the use of force in self-defence is restricted to the occurrence of an armed attack. The right of self-defence might be exercisable in the event of 'aggression other than an armed attack'[55] if the use of force in this event can be distinguished from the use of force for self-help.

Over-attachment to the framework established by Brownlie is obvious in some current arguments on the issue of whether the right of self-defence can be exercised against a use of force short of armed attack (i.e. on the scope of the prior conduct). Current writers often contend, in Randelzhofer's words, that 'the crucial point [is] whether Art. 51 has restricted self-defence to the case of an attack, or whether there is a general right of self-defence, apart from Art. 51'.[56] And for such writers, 'a general right of self-defence' is understood as the customary right of self-defence that existed in and before 1945, the content and scope of which 'are unclear and extend far into the spheres of self-help'.[57] This issue is, possibly beyond his intention, still being discussed within the framework set by Brownlie.

Emphasizing the importance of the framework of the debate established by Brownlie does not imply that no current writers focus on the various issues included in the scope of the right of self-defence. Jaroslav Žourek, for example, discusses the problems of '[b]iens dont l'attaque fait naître l'etat de légitime défense', '[s'il] permis de recourir à la légitime défense contre des emplois de la force autres que l'aggression armée', and '[l]a question de la légitime défense préventive', as distinct from one another.[58] Indeed, most writers deal with these issues.[59] Nevertheless, the question they usually examine remains precisely that formulated by Randelzhofer: 'whether Art. 51 has restricted self-defence to the case of an attack, or whether there is a general right of self-defence, apart

et diplomatie (Nijhoff Dordrecht 1985) vol 2, 134; MAM Genoni *Die Notwehr im Völkerrecht* (Schulthess Polygraphischer Verlag Zürich 1987) 157.

55 Bowett (n 8) 1107.

56 A Randelzhofer 'Article 51' in B Simma (ed) *The Charter of the United Nations: A Commentary* (2nd edn OUP Oxford 2002) 791.

57 Ibid 793.

58 J Žourek 'La notion de légitime défense en droit international' [1975] 56 Annuaire (Institut de Droit International) 54–57, 62–64.

59 See eg Gray (n 2) 601–605.

from Art. 51'.[60] Within this framework, Brownlie's argument has been overwhelmingly persuasive.

2 *Beyond the Consensus Framework*

Conventional Framework and the 'Grande Confusion' over the Right of Self-Defence

The dominance of Brownlie's argument, however, does not necessarily mean that there is no longer any disagreement regarding the preconditions for the right of self-defence in contemporary international law. On the contrary, it has been pointed out that a 'grande confusion règne à ce sujet'[61] and it is even said that '[t]his long-standing disagreement between states on interpretation of the UN Charter [concerning the scope of the right of self-defence] seem[s] beyond resolution'.[62] As noted above, Charles de Visscher's lament of 1917 remains disturbingly apt:

> Dans le droit international, la notion de la légitime défense est une question fort mal élucidée. Il règne à cet égard des confusions nombreuses qui ont jeté un certain discrédit sur la conception elle-même et qui conduisent parfois à faire douter de la possibilité de son application dans ce domaine.[63]

Re-examination of the Framework

Given that current discussions of the right of self-defence conducted within the framework set by the debate between Bowett and Brownlie have not come close to dispelling our 'grande confusion', it seems essential to question the appropriateness of this framework. In particular, two points require detailed consideration.

One is whether Brownlie's reformulation of Bowett's general statement of the right of self-defence is appropriate. As it is this reformulation that underlies Brownlie's argument (and, of course, much of our current debate), finding this reformulation problematic would call us to reevaluate Brownlie's argument as a whole. But this would not imply that Bowett's general statement

---

60 Randelzhofer (n 56) 791. See also Gray (n 2) 628, which states, 'As a matter of treaty interpretation, the debate centres on whether Article 51 is an exhaustive statement of the right to self-defence or whether there is a wider customary law right of self-defence beyond the right to respond to an armed attack'.

61 Žourek (n 58) 2.

62 Gray (n 17) 166.

63 C de Visscher 'Les lois de la guerre et la théorie de la nécessité' [1917] 24 Rev Gén DI Pub 74.

should be endorsed; on the contrary, it would mean that Bowett too stands in need of reconsideration, in terms other than those which Brownlie left us.

The other questions to be examined are whether the right of self-defence that existed in and before 1945 was legitimately exercised only against armed attack or also against 'aggression other than an armed attack'; and what the *Rechtsgüter* are. These are questions on which Brownlie did not properly argue, and we will not attain clear answers to them simply by appealing to the fact that the use of force for self-help or self-preservation was prohibited in the inter-war period. Accordingly, these issues must be examined separately.

Inter-war Period

A key to these two points can be found in the criticism made by Brownlie against those advancing the permissive interpretation. He argues that those writers 'assume that the customary law became static by 1920 or earlier, and ignore the possibility that the customary right may have received some more precise delimitation in the period between 1920 and 1945'.[64] Indeed, where the restrictive interpretation stresses the importance of developments in the inter-war period, the permissive interpretation emphasizes the continuity of the customary right of self-defence from the mid-19th century to 1945 (and later).[65] In other words, the conflict between the permissive and the restrictive interpretations over the pre-1945 right of self-defence turns in part on the question of whether, for the purposes of discussion, greater importance should be attached to the developments in the pre-World War I era or to those in the inter-war era. If we can speak of 'the right of self-defence that existed before World War I' and 'the right of self-defence as it developed in the inter-war period', it can be argued that the controversy concerns the problem of how to define the content of each and of how to understand the relationship between the two.

19th Century, Inter-war Period, and the Adoption of the United Nations Charter

This question is closely associated with the aforementioned structure of the debate between Bowett and Brownlie. Criticizing Bowett, Brownlie contends that '"self-defence" in the classical law [of the 19th century] was a term which was regarded by States as interchangeable with "self-preservation", "necessity" and "intervention"';[66] he stresses the importance of the developments in the inter-war period and argues that the use of force for self-help or for

64 Brownlie (n 4) 274. See also Brownlie (n 5) 720; Brownlie (n 39) 23–25.

65 Implicitly, Bowett (n 6) 29–114. More explicitly, Waldock (n 30) 461–499; Higgins (n 30) 198–199.

66 Brownlie (n 5) 720. See also Brownlie (n 4) 231.

self-preservation was prohibited *in the period from 1920 to 1945*.[67] According to Brownlie, emphasizing the importance of the right of self-defence that existed before World War I or asserting that the customary right of self-defence continued from the mid-19th century to and beyond 1945 makes it 'probably impossible to distinguish [self-defence] from self-help'[68] or from self-preservation. In this way, the issue of whether greater importance should be attached to the developments of the pre-World War I era or to those of the inter-war era leads up to the crux of his argument.

This problem carries within it other questions. Firstly, a careful examination should be made as to whether Brownlie's understanding of the right of self-defence that existed before World War I is correct. In fact, ambiguity still surrounds the right existing before the First World War: is Bowett's understanding of the right of self-defence before World War I appropriate?; how about Bowett's general statement?; and what about Brownlie's re-formulation of Bowett's statement or Brownlie's understanding of the pre-World War I right? If the pre-1919 right of self-defence is found to be at odds with Bowett's and Brownlie's characterization of that right, it will be necessary to reexamine its relation with the right of self-defence that existed in the inter-war period and, furthermore, to reconsider the issue of what the right of self-defence was that obtained in and before 1945. This, of course, is precisely the issue on which the debate between the two eminent scholars centres.

Structure of this Book

Hence, in order to resolve these questions and to define the right of self-defence existing in and before 1945, we need first to detach ourselves from the conventional framework of the debate (which we will attempt in Chapter 2), then to characterise the right of self-defence that existed before World War I (Chapter 3) and the right of self-defence as it developed in the inter-war period (Chapter 4), and to clarify the relationship between the conceptions prevailing in these two periods (Chapter 5). Following this exploration, we will be in a position to discuss the *travaux préparatoires* of the United Nations Charter and to present an improved interpretation of the preconditions for exercising the right of self-defence provided in Article 51 of the Charter when it was adopted in 1945 (Chapter 6).

---

67 Brownlie (n 5) 720; Brownlie (n 4) 274; Brownlie (n 39) 23–25.

68 Brownlie (n 5) 716.

CHAPTER 2

Great Confusion over the Right of Self-Defence: The *Caroline* Incident Revisited

This chapter will provide a standpoint from which to view the issues of how to define the right of self-defence that (may have) existed before World War I and the right of self-defence as it developed in the inter-war period, and of how to elucidate the relationship between these two concepts. This standpoint will be reached by a review of the literature on the right of self-defence, with particular attention to each writer's treatment of the *Caroline* incident (1837–1842) – more specifically, each writer's view of whether this incident can be regarded as a precedent for the right of self-defence in contemporary international law.

Why the *Caroline* Incident?

For those who do and for those who do not regard the *Caroline* incident as establishing a precedent for the right of self-defence in contemporary international law, this incident has been a particular focus of debate in relation to the right of self-defence.[1] Moreover, differing perceptions of the incident seem to reflect broader differences among competing conceptions of the right of self-defence. The incident is thus useful for characterizing a writer's notion of self-defence and provides a sort of key to the general issues considered in this chapter.[2]

1 J Žourek 'La Notion de Légitime Défense en Droit International' [1975] 56 Annuaire (Institut de Droit International) 20.

2 However, it should be noted that the issue of whether or not the *Caroline* incident can be regarded as a precedent for the right of self-defence in contemporary international law must be distinguished from the question of whether or not the so-called Webster Formula can be applied to self-defence in contemporary international law. This formula, so named for having been advanced by the US Secretary of State Daniel Webster, requires that self-defence be justified by a necessity 'instant, overwhelming, leaving no choice of means, and no moment for deliberation' ('Mr Webster to Mr Fox, April 24, 1841' in K Bourne (ed) *British Documents on Foreign Affairs: Reports and Papers from the Foreign Office Confidential Print, Part I From the Mid-Nineteenth Century to the First World War, Series C North America, 1837–1914* (University Publications of America 1986) vol 1 (McLeod and Maine, 1837–1842), 159) and has been regarded as the precondition for exercising the right of self-defence in traditional international law. (See eg R Higgins *The Development of International Law through the Political Organs of the United Nations* (OUP Oxford 1963) 198; CHM Waldock 'The Regulation of the Use of Force by

DOI 10.1163/9789004355002_004

In addition to this theoretical concern, the *Caroline* incident merits our attention by its historical significance. As is well known, self-defence was regarded as one of the elements justifying the recourse to war in the just war doctrine as developed during the 17th and 18th centuries.[3] However, as in the 19th century the just war doctrine collapsed and the view that states had the right or prerogative of resort to war prevailed, the concept of the right of self-defence in this context lost its legal significance: legal justification of the resort to war did not require invoking the right of self-defence.

Though the *Caroline* incident occurred in the mid-19th century, a right of self-defence was nevertheless invoked as legal justification. Self-defence thus seems to have retained some role in justification of state activity. By examining what, in this incident, the right of self-defence was held to justify, we attain a key for understanding the notion of self-defence at work in the 19th century.

A Divisions over the *Caroline* Incident

The *Caroline* Incident

The *Caroline* incident arose during the Canadian rebellion of 1837 against British rule. While the rebels were not in the ascendant within the main territory of British Canada, there was wide support for the rebellion, as well as strong anti-British feeling, on the US side of the border area. The US government tried but failed to discourage such support.[4]

During the rebellion, the *Caroline*, an American steamboat, was hired by the rebels to bring munitions and troops from US territory to Navy Island in British Canada. This island lies on the Niagara, the river forming the border between the United States and British Canada, and was occupied by the rebels at that time. The *Caroline* was attacked by British troops on the morning of 29th December 1837, when it was moored at the US port of Schlosser in the State of New York. After a brief struggle, the *Caroline* was set on fire and cut adrift

Individual States in International Law' [1952-ii] 81 RCADI 477) Even if the *Caroline* incident is not regarded as a precedent for self-defence, one can still argue that the Webster Formula holds. (See DW Bowett *Self-Defence in International Law* (Manchester University Press Manchester 1958) 59–60; contra I Brownlie 'International Law at the Fiftieth Anniversary of the United Nations' [1995] 255 RCADI 203) The scope of the application of this formula should be examined separately.

3 SA Alexandrov *Self-Defense against the Use of Force in International Law* (Kluwer Law International The Hague 1996) 1–18.

4 KR Stevens *Border Diplomacy : The Caroline and McLeod Affairs in Anglo-American-Canadian Relations, 1837–1842* (University of Alabama Press Tuscaloosa Ala London 1989) 1–17.

from the shore, plunging in Niagara Falls. At least one American was killed and twelve went missing.[5]

The United States government immediately complained about the destruction of the *Caroline* and the death of US citizens. In reply, the British government contended that the destruction of the *Caroline* was justified by 'the necessity of self-defence and self-preservation'. The United States thereupon demanded that the British government present a convincing case that conditions for establishing the 'necessity of self-defence' had been met. After these initial exchanges of views, this issue was not discussed until 1841, following the arrest of Alexander McLeod on charges of murder and arson in connection with the events of 29th December 1837. The controversy was then renewed. Great Britain claimed that conditions establishing the 'necessity of self-defence' had been fulfilled while, at the same time, expressing regret that 'some explanation and apology for this occurrence was not immediately made'.[6] In the end, though the United States did not agree that the conditions had been met, she was satisfied to find that the British government accepted the conditions for the necessity of self-defence she presented and expressed regret. Accordingly, in 1842, the US government finally agreed to a settlement of the dispute.[7]

Divisions

Disagreements over the *Caroline* incident have been remarkably sharp.[8] It is, on the one hand, regarded as the '*locus classicus* of the *law* of self-defence';[9] but, on the other, it is asserted, 'Il faut ici redresser l'opinion si couramment

5 With regard to the British recognition of facts leading to the destruction of the *Caroline*, see 'Sir Francis Head, Lieutenant Governor of Upper Canada, to Henry S. Fox, British Minister to the United States, January 8, 1838, annexed to the letter from Henry S. Fox, British Minister to the United States, to John Forsyth, Secretary of State of the United States, February 6, 1838' in WR Manning (ed) *Diplomatic Correspondence of the United States; Canadian Relations 1784–1860* (Carnegie Endowment for International Peace Washington 1943) vol 3 (1836–1848), 416–419. As to that of the United States, see 'Mr Stevenson to Viscount Palmerston, May 22, 1838' in Bourne (ed) (n 2) 31–32.

6 'Lord Ashburton to Mr Webster, July 28, 1842' in ibid 335.

7 RY Jennings 'The *Caroline* and McLeod Cases' [1938] 32 AJIL 82–91; JB Moore *A Digest of International Law* (Government Printing Office Washington 1906) vol 2, 409–414. See also Chapter 3.A.1.(b).

8 See C Gray *International Law and the Use of Force* (3rd edn OUP Oxford 2008) 148–149. The *Caroline* has recently been 'raised' and then 'sunk' again. See T Kearley 'Raising the Caroline' [1999] 17 Wisc Int'l LJ 325; MB Occelli '"Sinking" the *Caroline*: Why the Caroline Doctrine's Restrictions on Self-Defense Should Not be Regarded as Customary International Law' [2003] 4 San Diego Int'l LJ 467.

9 Jennings (n 7) 92. This article, which was written in 1938, is still very influential and often cited as authoritative. For example, Byers cites it in support of the claim that 'the modern law

répandue, d'après laquelle la fameuse affaire de la Caroline, …constitue une illustration de l'utilisation de la légitime défense…'.[10]

Each of these perceptions of the *Caroline* incident is based on a certain understanding of the right of self-defence; the incident can be regarded as a precedent for the right of self-defence in contemporary international law only when it fits a writer's notion of this right. In this sense, divided perceptions of the incident reflect the 'grande confusion'[11] over the right of self-defence. At the same time, each writer's notion of the right of self-defence in contemporary international law is itself derived from his understanding of various historical questions, including: whether there was any right of self-defence before World War I; what, if it did exist, was the right of self-defence that existed in the 19th century; whether it changed afterwards and, if so, how; and what relationship the pre-World War I right of self-defence has with the right of self-defence as it developed in the inter-war period. When positions are taken on these questions, the *Caroline* incident is used as support for all of them. In this sense, it is one of the main factors accounting for the abovementioned confusion over the right of self-defence.

Conflict over the Right of Self-Defence and the *Caroline* Incident

The permissive and restrictive interpretations of the preconditions of exercising the right of self-defence sharply contrast with each other in the accounts they offer of the *Caroline* incident.

Proponents of the permissive interpretation generally regard the *Caroline* incident as a precedent establishing the right of self-defence (the 'self-defence' doctrine). They contend that the right of self-defence existed before the First World War, that the *Caroline* incident is one of the most important precedents defining that right, and that the right of self-defence remained basically unchanged in the inter-war period. They emphasize the continuity of the conception of the right from the mid-19th century through the inter-war period and to the present.[12]

---

of self-defence was born' in the *Caroline* incident. (M Byers 'Terrorism, the Use of Force and International Law after 11 September' [2002] 51 ICLQ 406).

10 PM Dupuy 'L'invocation de la légitime défense dans la justification des états' in JF Guilhaudis and M Torrelli (eds) *Force armée et diplomatie* (Nijhoff Dordrecht 1985) vol 2, 135.

11 Žourek (n 1) 2.

12 Waldock (n 2) 451–517; R Higgins *The Development of International Law through the Political Organs of the United Nations* (OUP Oxford 1963). Bowett's argument is similar to that of Waldock and Higgins in the sense that he argues for the permissive interpretation and does not attach much importance to any development in the inter-war period, but his perception of the *Caroline* incident is not unambiguous. On the one hand, he regards the

By contrast, proponents of the restrictive interpretation generally do not accept the *Caroline* incident as a precedent for the right of self-defence in contemporary international law. However, interpretations of the incident also reveal a division between two doctrines within the restrictive school: the doctrines of 'necessity' and of 'self-preservation'.

The 'necessity' doctrine regards the *Caroline* incident as a precedent for a 'state of necessity' justification rather than for the right of self-defence. It argues that the right of self-defence attained its significance in international law for the first time in the inter-war period, as a result of the outlawry of war in that era. Accordingly, this doctrine accepts neither the existence of a distinct right of self-defence before World War I nor, therefore, the relevance of the *Caroline* incident as a precedent establishing a right of self-defence.[13] For its part, the 'self-preservation' doctrine accepts that the right of self-defence existed in the 19th century and regards the *Caroline* incident as a precedent for the right of self-defence of that time. However, it maintains that, in the 19th century, the right of self-defence was indistinguishable from that of self-preservation and stresses that, with the outlawry of war in the inter-war period, the concept of self-defence became more distinct. Thus, the self-preservation doctrine rejects the relevance of the *Caroline* as a precedent establishing the right of self-defence in contemporary international law.[14]

In this way, it is suggested that the remarkably sharp disagreements over the perceptions of the *Caroline* incident stem from differences (referred to in Chapter 1) with regard to whether greater importance should be attached to developments of the pre-World War I era or to those of the inter-war era. The self-defence doctrine regards the developments in the 19th century as crucial, but proponents of the doctrines of necessity and self-preservation prefer to emphasize the importance of developments from 1920 to 1945.

---

incident as an illustration of the 'right of necessity' (Bowett (n 2) 59–60, esp 60); on the other, he also treats it as an instance of self-defence. (ibid 189)

13 R Ago 'Addendum to the Eighth Report on State Responsibility: The Internationally Wrongful Act of State, Source of International Responsibility (Part 1) (Concluded)' [1980] 2–1 Yb Int'l L Comm'n 61–63; K Nagy *Le problème de la légitime défense en droit international* (Acta Universitatis Szegediensis Szeged 1992) 5–18; LA Sicilianos *Les réactions décentralisées à l'illiciet* (LGDJ Paris 1990) 28–29, 40–44; Dupuy (n 10) 134–142; P Malanczuk 'Countermesures and Self-Defence as Circumstances Precluding Wrongfulness in the International Law Commission's Draft Articles on State Responsibility' in M Spinedi and B Simma (eds) *United Nations Codification of State Responsibility* (Oceana Publications New York 1987) 241–243; J Crawford *The International Law Commission's Articles on State Responsibility* (CUP Cambridge 2002) 179–180.

14 I Brownlie *International Law and the Use of Force by States* (Clarendon Press Oxford 1963) 40–44, 231–235, 247–250; Žourek (n 1) 10–37.

What is in dispute, however, is not simply the historical development of the right of self-defence. Contending histories of this development are derived from more fundamental divisions among contending writers' conceptions of the right of self-defence. As mentioned earlier, whether or not the *Caroline* incident can be regarded as a precedent for the right of self-defence depends on the writer's notion of what this right consists of.

In the following sections, the origin and implications of these divisions will be examined. First, we will examine two distinct notions of the right of self-defence that are presumed respectively by the necessity doctrine and the self-defence doctrine (Section B). The self-preservation doctrine will then be examined as a reflection of these distinct notions of the right of self-defence; and this will provide a key to a sharper definition of their distinguishing characteristics and to clarifying the relationship between them (Section C). With this key in hand, we will then review the significance of these distinct concepts in relation to the Bowett-Brownlie debate (Section D).

B Background to the Divisions: The Necessity Doctrine and the Self-Defence Doctrine

As Brownlie stresses,[15] doctrines from the mid-19th to the early-20th century mainly treated the *Caroline* incident under the rubric of the right of self-preservation.[16] However, from the end of the 19th century to the years following the First World War, because of growing scepticism about fundamental rights of States, of which the right of self-preservation is one,[17] the demand arose for a reconsideration of the significance of the *Caroline* incident in relation to the right of self-preservation. Contending assessments of the incident were apparent from the outset of this review.

1 *Necessity Doctrine*

Domestic-Law-based Dichotomy and Unlawful Prior Attack

The necessity doctrine was first proposed shortly after the end of World War I.[18] This doctrine made a distinction between the right of self-defence and

---

15 Brownlie (n 14) 43.

16 The significance of this fact will be discussed in Chapter 3.

17 With regard to the impact of denial of the fundamental right of state on this issue, see eg D Anzilotti *Cours de droit international* (G Gidel (tr) Librairie de Recueil Sirey Paris 1929) 508.

18 Eg K Strüpp *Das Völkerrechtliche Delikt* (W Kohlhammer Stüttgart 1920) 153–154. See also Anzilotti (n 17) 507; R Ago 'Le délit international' [1939] 68 RCADI 541.

the state of necessity. This distinction rested on a difference in the legality of prior conduct: the right of self-defence was regarded as exercisable against unlawful attack, while the state of necessity was not considered dependent upon any unlawful prior conduct by a State.[19] In the terms of this dichotomy,[20] the necessity doctrine held that as no unlawful prior attack by the United States against Great Britain had taken place in the *Caroline* incident, the incident involved state of necessity rather than an exercise of the right of self-defence.

Thus, the necessity doctrine considered the right of self-defence to be exercisable only against unlawful attack. On this basis, proponents of the doctrine argued that the right of self-defence had not been recognised in general international law in the period before World War I, during which resort to war was generally permitted, and that the right of self-defence emerged, as special international law, only after certain kinds of wars had come to be prohibited by treaties, such as the Covenant of the League of Nations (1919) and the Pact of Paris (1928).[21] According to this view, the right of self-defence was recognised only in the context of the outlawry of war and was regarded as 'une notion nouvelle en droit international'.[22] In other words, the right of self-defence was seen as an exception to the prohibition of the recourse to war and as related to 'la légitimité de la guerre' only.[23] In this context, unlawful attack, which was considered to be the prior conduct necessary for exercising the right of self-defence, was nothing more than recourse to war prohibited by treaties; and what could be justified as an exercise of the right of self-defence was simply the resort to war or use of force against the unlawful attack.

---

19 Strüpp (n 18) 124; P Fauchille *Traite de droit international public* (Rousseau Paris 1922) vol 1, 421.

20 This dichotomy started to be contested before the First World War. For example, von Franz von Liszt introduced this domestic-law-based dichotomy into international law in 1898, stating '[d]ie strafrechtlich und privatrechtlich anerkannten Begriffe der Notwehr und des Notstandes schließen auch für das Gebiet des Völkerrechts die Rechtswidrigkeit der begangenen Verletzung aus'. (vF von Liszt *Das Völkerrecht* (O Haering Berlin 1898) 128) Since the end of the 19th century, while the notion of the right of self-preservation started to fade, the doctrine of state responsibility was formed. When, in the latter doctrine, circumstances precluding wrongfulness were claimed, writers tried to introduce from domestic laws into international law concepts of self-defence and of the state of necessity. (eg Strüpp (n 18) 120–121. See also Anzilotti (n 17) 506–515; H Kelsen 'Unrecht und Unrechtsfolge im Völkerrecht' [1932] Zeitschrift für Öffentliches Recht 560–568; Ago (n 18) 537–545)

21 Anzilotti (n 17) 506–507; Kelsen (n 20) 562–564; Ago (n 18) 539–540. But see also von Liszt (n 20) 128; Strüpp (n 18) 200 n 1.

22 É Giraud 'La théorie de la légitime défense' [1934] 49 RCADI 715.

23 See J Basdevant 'Règles générales du droit de la paix' [1936] 58 RCADI 539 n 3.

Necessity Doctrine Today

Contemporary writers committed to the necessity doctrine support this argument. Roberto Ago, for example, in his report on State responsibility to the International Law Commission, points out that both self-defence and acts taken under the state of necessity are 'acts in response to an imminent danger'[24] but holds that the difference between them stems from the existence or non-existence of prior illegal conduct. He states:

> the State vis-à-vis which another State adopts a form of conduct inconsistent with an international obligation without having any excuse other than "necessity" is a State which has committed no international wrong against the State taking the action. By contrast, the State against which another State acts in "self-defence" is itself responsible for the threat to that other State.[25]

Moreover, he contends in his report that the concept of self-defence had, or could have, no place in the pre-World War I international legal order in which war was not prohibited and further argues: 'it was not until the legal conscience of States had to react to the horrors and disastrous consequences of the First and Second World Wars that the preconditions for the admission of the notion of "self-defence" *stricto sensu* into international law were created'.[26] Thus it can be argued that 'le Pacte de la Société des Nations interdisant la guerre dans certains cas a introduit la notion de la légitime défense';[27] and that the *Caroline* incident, which occurred long before the establishment of the League of Nations, 'relèvent d'un cadre juridique differént',[28] which is obviously the state of necessity.

2 *Self-Defence Doctrine*

Dichotomy and Unlawful Armed Attack

The same dichotomy, between self-defence and the state of necessity, the two distinguished by the existence or non-existence of unlawful prior conduct, has been adopted by some who regard the *Caroline* incident as a precedent

24 Ago (n 13) 53 para 88.
25 Ibid.
26 Ibid 52 para 82.
27 Nagy (n 13) 15.
28 Sicilianos (n 13) 29.

for the right of self-defence.[29] When one relies on this dichotomy, the issue as to whether one can regard this incident as a precedent for self-defence depends on the question of whether there was any unlawful prior conduct by the United States. However, that no such prior conduct was claimed by the British government[30] seriously undermines this argument.

By contrast, interestingly, most who in the inter-war era regarded the *Caroline* incident as a precedent for the right of self-defence did not rely on that dichotomy and thus did not hold unlawful prior conduct to be a precondition for the exercise of the right of self-defence.[31] Kaufmann, for example, made this view clear by stating that 'à l'encontre des représailles qui présupposent des actes illicites, le droit de légitime défense ne présuppose qu'une lésion ou un danger de lésion ou un danger de lésion d'intérêts'.[32] While some other writers proposed aggression[33] or attack[34] as preconditions for self-defence, they did not assume that that prior conduct should be unlawful. They were thus able to present the *Caroline* incident as establishing a precedent for the right of self-defence, without asking whether any unlawful prior conduct had occurred.

However, the scope of the prior conduct, i.e. whether the prior conduct for self-defence must be unlawful or not, is not the only point on which this doctrine of self-defence differed from the necessity doctrine. The doctrines differed also on the question of what actions the right of self-defence justified. The self-defence doctrine, indeed, stressed that 'la légitime défense ne tempère pas seulement ce caractère illicite lorsqu'il a été établi par traité, *elle tempère aussi d'autres règles*';[35] and understood the right of self-defence as

---

29 C de Visscher 'Les lois de la guerre et la théorie de la néccssité' [1917] 24 Rev Gén DI Pub 76; M Bourquin 'Règles générales du droit de la paix' [1931] 35 RCADI 220 n 1; A Ross *A Textbook of International Law* (Longman London 1947) 244, 248–249.

30 R Taoka *The Right of Self-Defence in International Law* (The Institute of Legal Study, Osaka University of Economics and Law Osaka 1978) 19–22. See also Chapter 3.A.1.(b).

31 Basdevant (n 23) 539–541; WGF Phillimore 'Droits et devoirs fondamentaux des états' [1923] 1 RCADI 51; CG Fenwick *International Law* (George Allen & Unwin London 1924) 143–144; T Baty *The Canons of International Law* (John Murray London 1930) 97; E Kaufmann 'Règles générales du droit de la paix' [1935] 54 RCADI 579–580; JL Brierly 'Règles générales du droit de la paix' [1936] 58 RCADI 126–129; Jennings (n 7) 82.

32 Kaufmann (n 31) 581.

33 Brierly (n 31) 127–128.

34 Jennings (n 7) 91; Fenwick (n 31) 142.

35 Basdevant (n 23) 541. (emphasis added) Thus, the difference between the concept of self-defence in international law and that of self-defence in domestic laws was emphasized. He stated:

extending to 'la légitimité de la guerre'.[36] The right of self-defence was held to justify a variety of otherwise impermissible actions, such as: 'l'usage de la force sur le territoire d'un autre État';[37] violation of '*par exemple*, la règle du respect du territoire';[38] violation of 'the sovereignty of another [State]';[39] 'the temporary invasion of the territory of a neighboring state';[40] 'a trivial invasion of the sovereignty of another';[41] 'de dépasser la frontière';[42] and 'intervention'.[43]

Self-Defence Doctrine Today

However, this understanding of the right of self-defence is not shared by current arguments that regard the *Caroline* incident as a precedent for the right of self-defence.[44] It lasted only until just after the adoption of the United Nations Charter. Subsequently, the issue of what the right of self-defence justifies was gradually forgotten: the right of self-defence has been regarded only as an exception to the prohibition of the use of force provided for in Article 2(4) of the Charter, i.e. as a justification of the use of force. As discussed in Chapter 1,

---

"L'exception de légitime defense a sa place dans toutes le legislations internes that anciennes que modernes. …

…on sera aisément enclin à transporter ce principe [de légitime défense] à ordre international.

Mais un examen plus attentive fait apparaître combien il est délicat de faire cette transposition. Dans l'ordre interne, ce principe joue en matière pénale; or, le droit pénal n'existe pas dans les rapports entre États. Dans l'ordre interne, ce principe est mis en application par le juge; dans les rapports internationaux, le juge n'intervient qu'à titre exceptionnel et, en pratique, rarement. Dans l'ordre interne, la légitime défense vient tempérer la règle que la violence entre individus est *a priori* illicite parce que l'État a le monopole de la contrainte; dans l'ordre international, la violence n'est pas *a priori* illicite, et la légitime défense ne tempère pas seulement ce caractère illicite lorsqu'il a été établi par traite, elle tempère aussi d'autres règles (par exemple, la régle du respect du territoire). Dans l'ordre international, la défense légitime ne paraît pas être aussi strictement limitée dans son objet et sa durée que dans l'ordre interne. (ibid 540–541)".

36 Ibid 539 n 3.

37 Brierly (n 31) 128.

38 Basdevant (n 23) 541. (emphasis added)

39 The Earl of Birkenhead *International Law* (6th edn R Moelwyn-Hughes (ed) JM Dent & Sons London 1927) 80.

40 Fenwick (n 31) 130.

41 Baty (n 31) 96.

42 Phillimore (n 31) 50.

43 Jennings (n 7) 82, 92; Kaufmann (n 31) 580 n 1.

44 See, as an exception, Bowett (n 2) 24.

the subject of debate regarding the right of self-defence has been limited in its scope.

For example, James L. Brierly, in the fourth edition of *The Law of Nations*, published in 1949, states:

> A state, like an individual, may protect itself against *an attack*, actual or threatened. This right is expressly affirmed in the Charter of the United Nations ... The principle of self-defence is clear, though its application to specific facts may often be a matter of difficulty. But a particularly clear example of *an intervention* justified on this ground is afforded by the incident of the steamer *Caroline* in 1837.[45]

Here, the right of self-defence is regarded as exercisable against 'an attack' in order to justify 'an intervention'; and the *Caroline* incident is referred to as a precedent. In contrast, while the sixth edition of the same book, published in 1963, edited by Waldock, regards the *Caroline* incident as being commonly considered to be 'the best statement of the conditions for ... [the] exercise [of the right of self-defence]'[46] and allows for 'forcible self-defence against unlawful acts of force not amounting to an armed attack',[47] it defines the issue of the right of self-defence as an exception to the prohibition of the use or threat of armed force,[48] and states that the subject of controversy is 'the precise scope of the right of self-defence under the law of the Charter'.[49]

3 *Difference in the Function of the Right of Self-Defence*

Thus the differences between the necessity and the self-defence doctrines, especially in the inter-war period, were striking; they concerned not only the scope of the prior conduct but also the function of the right of self-defence, i.e. what actions the right of self-defence justified. The necessity doctrine regards the right of self-defence as a justification for resorting to the use of force, and not for anything else. Advocates of the self-defence doctrine in that period, in contrast, deemed the right of self-defence as justifying violation not only of the prohibition of war but also of 'other rules'. The two doctrines, in other words, worked with quite different conceptions of what 'self-defence', or the self-defence problem, amounted to.

45 JL Brierly *The Law of Nations* (4th edn OUP Oxford 1949) 291. (emphasis added)
46 JL Brierly *The Law of Nations* (6th edn CHM Waldock (ed) OUP Oxford 1963) 405.
47 Ibid 418.
48 Ibid 415.
49 Ibid 416.

These differences as to the function of the right of self-defence are not fully appreciated in the current literature.[50] Current arguments usually focus on the scope of the right of self-defence, especially the scope of prior conduct. Recognizing and understanding the distinct notions at work, however, is key to resolving the 'grande confusion'; where the same word is used to refer to quite different things, confusion, after all, is a natural result. In the following section, we turn to the self-preservation doctrine. This doctrine, which takes the differences between the two distinct concepts into account, may help us to sharpen our understanding of the concepts and the relationship between them.

C Differences in the Concepts: Self-preservation Doctrine

1 *Self-preservation Doctrine*

That no clear distinction between self-defence and self-preservation had been formulated at the time of the *Caroline* incident, and that doctrinal argument in the following decades had treated the incident as a matter of self-preservation, had already been pointed out in the inter-war period.[51] It was after World War II, however, that the lack of a self-defence/self-preservation distinction was made grounds for denying that the incident had established any right of self-defence valid in contemporary international law.[52]

Change of Context in Which the Right of Self-Defence was Discussed

After the Second World War, the self-preservation doctrine treated the *Caroline* incident as an example of 'some attempts [during the 19th century] to restrict the right to go to war'.[53] It was careful, however, to deny that the incident had carved out a 'self-defence' justification valid in the post-World War II period. Brownlie, for example, maintained that '[s]elf-defence was regarded either as synonymous with self-preservation or as a particular instance of it'[54] and accordingly that 'to regard any form of action formerly held to be self-defence, at a time when self-defence was a phrase regarded as interchangeable with "self-preservation" and "necessity", as within a surviving "customary right", is

50 Ryoichi Taoka is one of the writers who are most conscious of this distinction. See Taoka (n 30) 151–153. See also Bowett (n 2) 24.

51 Jennings (n 7) 91.

52 Brownlie (n 14) 43, 274; Žourek (n 1) 18–24.

53 Brownlie (n 14) 42.

54 Ibid 43.

a very arbitrary process'.[55] This line of argument is taken because, while the right of self-preservation was 'vague and comprehensive'[56] and justified any action to ensure national security,[57] 'the law relating to the use of force had [in the inter-war period] reached the most significant stage of development and the right of self-defence frequently appeared in *contexts* in which it was related to the use of force'.[58]

In other words, even though the right of self-defence was interchangeable with the right of self-preservation at that time, the *Caroline* incident can be regarded as an instance of the right of self-defence that existed in the 19th century. However, it has lost its significance as a precedent for the right of self-defence in contemporary international law, since the outlawry of war in the inter-war period changed the context in which the right of self-defence was discussed. That is to say, this change in the perceptions of the *Caroline* incident followed the change in the contexts in which self-defence was discussed.

Change of the Contexts and the Function of the Right of Self-Defence

However, it should be noted that this change in context does not relate only to the scope of the prior conduct necessary for the exercise of the right of self-defence. Brownlie, one of the most important proponents of this self-preservation doctrine, states that 'in the period of the League the right of self-defence commonly appeared in *the context of the use of force*. It was essentially a reaction by a state against the use or threat of force by the armed forces of another state'.[59] This refers to prior conduct, 'the use or threat of force by the armed forces of another state'. But he goes on to say, '[t]he essence of such a right was proportionality to the threat offered and this would create a presumption that *force* was only lawful as a reaction against force'.[60] Here, 'the context of the use of force' refers not only to the prior conduct necessary for self-defence – 'the use or threat of force by the armed forces of another state' – but also to the function, i.e. what is justified by the right of self-defence – 'force'. According to the self-preservation doctrine, then, the right of self-defence in

55 Ibid 274.
56 Eg ibid 241.
57 Ibid 42.
58 I Brownlie 'Recent Appraisals of Legal Regulation of the Use of Force' [1959] 8 ICLQ 720. (emphasis added) See also R Kolb 'La légitime défense des états au XIXe siècle et pendant l'époque de la Société des Nations' in R Kolb (ed) *Commentaire sur le Pacte de la Société des Nations* (Bruylant Bruxelles 2014) 1298–1330.
59 Brownlie (n 14) 252. (emphasis added)
60 Ibid. (emphasis added)

the 19th century and the right of self-defence in the inter-war period differed in their respective functions, not merely in the scope of the prior conduct. If the doctrine is correct on this point, it poses the question whether we should consider the 19th century right of self-defence a substantially different conception from that of the inter-war period.

2 *Limits of the Self-preservation Doctrine*

Let us look more closely, then, at the two 'contexts' in which the right of self-defence was discussed and consider how appropriate it is to describe their relationship as one taking the place of the other.

Contexts in Which the Right of Self-Defence was Discussed

As the above quotations from Brownlie[61] obviously indicate, the context in which the right of self-defence as it developed in the inter-war period was discussed relates to war or the use of force: the right of self-defence justifies the recourse to war or the use of force against the same. This understanding of the right of self-defence is the same as that at work in the necessity doctrine.

How, then, to characterize the context of the other conception of the right of self-defence, under which the *Caroline* incident is taken as precedent establishing the legitimacy of any action taken to ensure national security?[62] This context is less obvious. However, in order to define the relationship between these two contexts, it is important to notice that Brownlie regards the self-defence of the 19th century as self-help.[63] He argues that the right of self-defence was equated with not only the right of self-preservation but also the right of self-help.[64] The distinction between the right of self-preservation and the right of self-help, for Brownlie, was also obscure.[65] Further, indicating the confusion between the right of self-defence and the right of self-preservation, he states that the right of self-defence,[66] 'defined in terms of self-help',[67] 'involved action to prevent or redress violation of legal rights'.[68]

61 Esp Brownlie (n 58) 720; Brownlie (n 14) 252.

62 Ibid 42.

63 Ibid 231.

64 Ibid.

65 Ibid 256–257.

66 Brownlie uses the term 'legitime defence' as interchangeable with the right of self-defence. (see ibid 231)

67 Ibid.

68 Ibid.

Relationship between the Contexts

With regard to the relationship between these two contexts, Brownlie characterizes it as a change from one to the other. He does not find this change, however, in explicit normative standards but rather in state practice. In the inter-war period, he says, the right of self-defence 'appeared in the context of the use of force'.[69] 'The right of legitimate defence, defined in terms of self-help', he explains, 'could hardly exist without considerable modification in the period of the League Covenant',[70] and he contends that state practice 'gives the strongest indication that ... force was justified only in reaction against some armed attack or threat of force'.[71]

From the discussion above, it follows that the self-preservation doctrine merits respect for pointing out that the right of self-defence that existed before World War I and the right of self-defence as it developed in the inter-war period are distinct from each other. However, while suggesting the importance of a grasp of the relationship between these two concepts, the doctrine does not examine that relationship closely and, as a result, leaves the relationship ambiguous.

D Perspectives

As we have seen, behind the contending interpretations of the *Caroline* incident lie different conceptions of 'self-defence'. As the self-preservation doctrine indicates, the notion of the right of self-defence supported by the self-defence doctrine on the one hand and that supported by the necessity doctrine on the other differ from each other as to what the right justifies and as to the context in which each of them is discussed.

It is important that we do not assume that these distinct conceptions are simply contending doctrines. It may be more accurate and more useful to view them as describing distinct components of the right of self-defence in international law. The concept of the right of self-defence that (may have) existed before the First World War, of which the *Caroline* incident is an illustration, and that of the right of self-defence as it developed in the inter-war period, may

69 Ibid 252.

70 Ibid 231.

71 Ibid 232. Stone criticizes Brownlie for taking treaties from the League period as his main source of evidence for state practice. See J Stone 'Book Review' [1965] 59 AJIL 402 (reviewing Brownlie (n 14)).

themselves differ from each other both in their functions and in the context in which each of them is discussed.

If we take a perspective allowing for the possibility of two conceptions of self-defence that may coexist, we see immediately that the conventional debate over the preconditions for exercising the right of self-defence poses a choice between two alternatives: an emphasis on the continuity of the right from the mid-19th century to 1945 (the permissive interpretation) or the stress on the importance of developments in the period 1920 to 1945 (the restrictive interpretation). This choice seems unavoidable if we imagine the two conceptions of the right of self-defence as two interpretations of the same thing, i.e. the right of self-defence as a justification for the use of force against another state.

This dichotomous view is natural to the current literature, as this literature has been concerned simply with the scope of the right of self-defence, understood as an exception to the prohibition of the use of force. The deadlock in which the literature finds itself, however, should lead us to question whether it makes more sense to treat contending notions of self-defence as contending interpretations of a single right or to think of two conceptions of self-defence as existing side-by-side in international law, differing in function and context. In other words, it seems necessary to question whether the fact that 'the right of self-defence frequently appeared in contexts in which it was related to the use of force'[72] signifies that a wider right of self-defence, which had been discussed in a different context, ceased to exist.

The perspective that allows for the possibility of two distinct concepts of self-defence invites us to examine closely the relationship between the right that arguably existed before World War I and the right as it developed afterwards, and the validity of a choice between these two conceptualized rights. Before addressing the relationship, however, it is necessary to define each concept of self-defence better than we have done to this point. The next part (Part 2) takes up this task of definition.

---

72 Brownlie (n 58) 720.

PART 2

Two Distinct Concepts

CHAPTER 3

The Right of Self-Defence before World War I

This chapter will consider the problem of how to define the right of self-defence that existed before World War I, by closely examining both state practice (Section A) and doctrine (Section B). Particular attention will be given to the recognised function of the right and to the context in which it was discussed.

A State Practice

Incidents and Cases to be Examined

In order to define the function and the context of the pre-World War I right of self-defence, it is vital to choose which incidents and cases to examine, since one's concept of self-defence depends on the cases one takes as precedents. While different writers and different eras may consider different cases, the following incidents are commonly invoked: the seizure of the Danish fleet by British forces (1807), the Amelia Island incident (1817), the US–Mexico border incidents (1836–1919), the *Caroline* incident (1837–1842), and the *Virginius* incident (1873); as is the recurring issue of protection of nationals abroad.

This section, rather than selecting cases to fit into a particular understanding of the right of self-defence, will try to draw out the contemporary understanding of the right of self-defence at work in cases in which States in fact asserted that right. From this viewpoint, this section will look into the US–Mexico border incidents, the *Caroline* incident, the *Virginius* incident, and the *Bering Sea Fur Seal* Arbitration (1893). While the *Bering Sea* Arbitration has rarely been referred to in writings on the right of self-defence, this case seems essential to any discussion of the pre-World War I right of self-defence, as it is the only arbitration case in which the right of self-defence was argued intensively.

On the other hand, the Danish fleet and Amelia Island incidents will not be examined here, since, as Taoka has pointed out, 'there is no evidence that the parties asserted the right of self-defence and argued over those assertions'.[1]

1 R Taoka *Kokusaihojo no Jieiken* (*Right of Self-defense under International Law*) (2nd edn Keiso-shobo Tokyo 1981) 30 (*in Japanese*). The Danish fleet incident will be discussed in Section B.2 of this chapter.

The Amelia Island Incident needs some explanation here. Amelia Island is the southernmost island of a chain of barrier islands stretching from North Carolina to Florida, in the United States, and lies at the mouths of the Nassau River and the St. Mary's River, off the

 | DOI 10.1163/9789004355002_005

In addition, the relationship of the protection of nationals abroad to the concept of the pre-World War I right of self-defence will be discussed in Chapter 5.A.1. The protection of nationals abroad, as noted in Chapter 1, has been one of the main arenas of contention over the scope of the right of self-defence and has often been cited as an example of the right of self-defence in the 19th century. However, this subject requires more careful examination than the space of this chapter allows, and will thus be discussed separately.

Viewpoints to Examine

In examining the incidents and the arbitration case described above, I would like to devote particular attention to the relationship between the concept of the right of self-defence and the concept of war. As described in Chapter 2, the concept of the right of self-defence as it developed in the inter-war period is understood as relating to the legitimacy of war. By contrast, it is generally understood that states in the 19th century had a recognised right or prerogative of going to war,[2] and thus did not need to rely on the right of self-defence as

coast of Florida near the boundary of the State of Georgia. This incident happened in 1817, when Florida was a Spanish territory and Georgia was a state of the United States. Thus, at that time, the island was situated near the border between the United States and the Spanish colony, on the side of the latter. In 1817, this island was seized by a band of buccaneers, who indiscriminately preyed on the commerce of Spain and the United States. The Spanish government was not able or willing to drive them off and the nuisance became so dreadful that immediate action was required. Thus, James Monroe, then President of the United States, sent a vessel of war, which destroyed the works and vessels of the marauders and expelled them from the island. (F Wharton *A Digest of the International Law of the United States, Taken from Documents Issued by Presidents and Secretaries of State, and from Decisions of Federal Courts and Opinions of Attorney-General* (2nd edn Government Printing Office Washington 1887) vol 1, 222; JB Moore *A Digest of International Law* (Government Printing Office Washington 1906) vol 2, 406–408) In fact, in relation to this incident, the President of the United States referred 'a principle of self-defence' and 'the right of self-defence' in at least two speeches to the US Congress in 1818. (JD Richardson *A Compilation of the Messages and Papers of the Presidents 1789–1897* (Government Printing Office Washington 1896) vol 2, 32, 41) However, to the best of my knowledge, these terms were not used in the diplomatic negotiations between the United States and Spain over this incident. (See W Lawrie and WS Franklin *American State Papers: Documents, Legislative and Executive, of the Congress of the United States from the First Session of the Fourteenth to the First Session of the Seventeenth Congress, Inclusive: Commencing March 4, 1815, and Ending May 8, 1822* (Gales and Seaton Washington 1834) vol 4, 130, 183–184, 292, 450, 463–464, 478) In any case, given the clear similarity between this and the *Caroline* incident, detailed consideration of this case would not substantially change the following discussion.

2 I Brownlie *International Law and the Use of Force by States* (Clarendon Press Oxford 1963) 19–26; Y Dinstein *War, Aggression and Self-Defence* (5th edn CUP Cambridge 2011) 75–77.

justification. If the pre-World War I right of self-defence was thus not understood or used as justification for war, it should have had another function and been discussed in another context.

What, then, did the right of self-defence justify, if not the resort to war? This question provides a starting point for clarifying the function and the context of the right of self-defence before World War I. This exploration will be followed by an examination of how state practice was reflected in doctrine and how the concept of the (pre-World War I) right of self-defence was formulated (Section B).

1 *Justification for the Violation of the Territory of Another State*

(a) The US–Mexico Border Incident (1836)

From the early-19th century to the beginning of the 20th century, the United States and Mexico frequently conducted military expeditions across each other's borders in pursuit of hostile Native Americans. These troubles were regarded as one of the most difficult issues between these two countries.[3] While such violations of each other's territory were an oft-recurring irritant throughout this period,[4] only one incident, which took place in 1836 and in which the right of self-defence was discussed, will be examined here.

Facts

On 20 April 1836, in a time of intensifying agitation for the independence of Texas from Mexico, US secretary of state John Forsyth conferred with Manuel Eduardo de Gorostiza, the Mexican Minister to the United States. Forsyth stated to de Gorostiza that orders would be given to troops of the United States to take such positions as would enable them 'to preserve the territory of the United States and Mexico from Indian outrage and the territory of the United States from any violation by the Mexicans, Texians or Indians'.[5] He also attempted to assure de Gorostiza of the United States' benign intent:

---

3 RD Gregg *The Influence of Border Troubles on Relations between the United States and Mexico 1876–1910* (The Johns Hopkins Press Baltimore 1937) 14.

4 Moore (n 1) 418–425. More generally on the border issues, see HW Baade 'American-Mexican Boundary Disputes and Cooperation' in R Bernhardt (ed) *Encyclopedia of Public International Law* (Elsevier Amsterdam 1992) vol 1, 136–144.

5 'Memorandum of a Conference between John Forsyth, Secretary of State of the United States, and Manuel Eduardo de Gorostiza, Mexican Minister to the United States, April 20, 1836' in WR Manning (ed) *Diplomatic Correspondence of the United States: Inter-American Affairs 1831–1860* (Carnegie Endowment for World Peace Washington 1937) vol 8 (Mexico 1831–1848 (Mid-Year)), 45.

> Should the troops in the performance of their duty be advanced beyond the point Mexico might suppose was within the territory of the United States, the occupation was not to be taken as an indication of any hostile feeling or of a desire to establish a possession or claim not justified by the Treaty of Limits[6] [between the United States and the United Mexican States]. The occupation would be precautionary and provisional, and would be abandoned … whenever the disturbances in that region should cease.[7]

Forsyth understood that de Gorostiza had agreed with him at the conference[8] but, later, de Gorostiza stated to Forsyth that his government had not recognised the US troops' right to enter the territory of Mexico.[9]

This problem came to a head in July 1836. 'Incorrectly informed that the Indians in Texas were planning trouble',[10] American troops entered Mexican territory. In response to a protest by the government of Mexico,[11] the US argued that their action was justified by 'the great principle of self preservation'[12] and 'the immutable principles of self defence'.[13] Mexico did not accept this US contention but in its reply did recognize 'the principle of self-defence'.[14]

---

6 'Treaty of Limits between Mexico and the United States, signed at Mexico City, 12 January 1828' in C Parry (ed) *The Consolidated Treaty Series* (Oceana Publications New York 1969) vol 78 (1827–1828), 35–42; 'Treaty of Amity, Settlement and Limits between Spain and the United States, signed at Washington, 22 February 1819' in ibid vol 70 (1819–1820), 1–30.

7 'Memorandum of a Conference between Forsyth and de Gorostiza' (n 5) 45–46.

8 'John Forsyth, Secretary of State of the United States, to Powhatan Ellis, Unites States Chargé d'Affairs at Mexico City, December 10, 1836' in Manning (ed) (n 5) 71.

9 'Manuel Eduardo de Gorostiza, Mexican Minister to the United States, to John Forsyth, Secretary of States of the United States, April 23, 1836' in Manning (ed) (n 5) 313–314.

10 JM Callahan *American Foreign Policy in Mexican Relations* (Macmillan Company New York 1932) 83.

11 'Manuel Eduardo de Gorostiza, Mexican Minister to the United States, to John Forsyth, Secretary of State of the United States, September 10, 1836' in Manning (ed) (n 5) 349–350.

12 'Asbury Dickins, Acting Secretary of State of the United States, to Manuel Eduardo de Gorostiza, Mexican Minister to the United States, October 13, 1836' in Manning (ed) (n 5) 67. Relying on 'the great principle of self preservation' suggests that the distinction between the right of self-preservation and that of self-defence was obscure. However, after this particular letter, self-preservation was not invoked at all but self-defence was consistently cited by both the governments of Mexico and the United States.

13 'Forsyth to Ellis, December 10, 1836' (n 8) 73.

14 'Manuel Eduardo de Gorostiza, Mexican Minister to the United States, to Asbury Dickins, Acting Secretary of State of the United States, October 15, 1836' in Manning (ed) (n 5) 370.

Relationship to the Concept of War

In attempting to justify US Actions, Forsyth emphasised a decoupling of 'the immutable principles of self defence' and the concept of war. Invading Mexican territory to prevent hostile moves against the United States by Native Americans, he argued, 'rests upon principles of the law of nations entirely distinct from those on which war is justified – upon the immutable principles of self defence…'.[15]

If this decoupling is counterintuitive to a late-20th century mind, following Forsyth's discourse a bit further helps to draw out the logic. In his argument, self-defence justifies 'decisive measures of precaution to prevent irreparable evil to our own or to a neighbouring people';[16] while on the other hand, war could be waged, according to a treaty between the US and Mexico,[17] only after the frontier area had been violated, one government had demanded redress from the other, and it had waited for the demand to be refused.[18] 'To make war upon Mexico for this involuntary failure to comply with her obligations', Forbes reasoned, 'would be equivalent to an attempt to convert her misfortunes into crimes, her inability to guilt'.[19]

In other words, 'misfortunes' and 'inability' lead to measures in self-defence; but 'crimes' and 'guilt' can trigger war. Here, according to Forsyth, 'misfortunes' referred to the fact that a third party, not the Mexican government, caused the injuries against American people and 'inability' meant her lack of ability to prevent those injuries. He suggested that, if, on the other hand, the injuries had been caused by the Mexican government itself, the latter would have been regarded as a criminal and guilty, and then the United States could have made war against Mexico.[20]

Significance of the Right of Self-Defence

In the diplomatic exchange over this incident, the concept of self-defence was clearly contrasted with that of war. The 'principle of self defence' in this incident was not a justification for war; what did it justify, in response to what, and in defense of what?

15 'Forsyth to Ellis, December 10, 1836' (n 8) 73.

16 Ibid.

17 Article 34 of the Treaty of Amity, Commerce and Navigation between Mexico and the United States, signed at Mexico City, 5 April 1831. (Parry (ed) (n 6) vol 81 (1830–1831), 408)

18 'Forsyth to Ellis, December 10, 1836' (n 8) 73.

19 Ibid.

20 Ibid.

Justification for the Violation of the Territory of Another State

The point at issue in this incident was the invasion and temporary occupation of Mexican territory by US troops.[21] The principles of self-preservation and self-defence were invoked, and accepted, as justifications for such actions.

In a letter to Asbury Dickins, the Acting Secretary of State of the United States, on 10 October 1836, de Gorostiza complained that '[t]he honor and rights of my Country are … greatly compromised *by the violation of its territory and subsequent occupation* of Nacogdoches by the troops of the United States'.[22] In response, Dickins stated that Mexico, under the aforementioned border treaty with the United States, had an obligation to prevent Native Americans in its territory from entering the United States. However, he stated, '[i]f, by failure of Mexico to fulfil her part of the obligation, it becomes necessary for the United States to occupy a portion of the contiguous Mexican territory, in order to be able to perform that duty, they have, from that necessity, the right to do so'.[23] Moreover, he added that the right was 'founded on the great principle of self preservation, which, as it constitutes the first and highest duty of all states, forms the very essence of the law of nations'.[24] He went on to argue:

> The present inability of Mexico to restrain the Indians within her territory from hostile incursions upon the citizens of the United States, if they should once be engaged in hostility near the frontier, and the barbarous character of their warfare which respects neither the rights of nations nor of humanity, renders it imperative on the United States to adopt other means for the protection of their citizens. What those means should be, must depend upon the nature of the danger. Should that require the temporary occupation of posts beyond the frontier, the duty of self preservation gives them the right to such occupation.[25]

In reply, although he did not concede that the principle could be applied to this particular incident, de Gorostiza agreed that the violation of the territory

21 See eg 'Memorandum of a Conference, April 20, 1836' (n 5) 45; 'de Gorostiza to Forsyth, April 23, 1836' (n 9) 313.

22 'Manuel Eduardo de Gorostiza, Mexican Minister to the United States, to Asbury Dickins, Acting Secretary of State of the United States, October 10, 1836' in Manning (ed) (n 5) 367. (emphasis added)

23 'Dickins to de Gorostiza, October 13, 1836' (n 12) 66.

24 Ibid 67. It was considered that 'the great principle of self preservation' enabled the US government to take 'a necessary measure of self defence'. (ibid)

25 Ibid.

of another state under certain circumstances could be justified by 'the principle of self-defence'.[26]

Necessity and the *Rechtsgüter* of Self-Defence

Next, it is necessary to examine in response to what situation, in protecting what *Rechtsgüter*, 'the principle of self-defence' was held to justify the violation of the territory of another state.

Before its troops crossed into the territory of Mexico, the US had stated that the violation of territory would be justified '[i]n case of necessity'.[27] However, from that time, the US repeatedly indicated that Mexico was unable to prevent hostile acts by Native Americans from Mexican territory upon US citizens within US territory; the United States stressed that the inability on the part of the Mexican government to prevent these incursions 'renders it imperative on the Unites States to adopt other means for the protection of their citizens'.[28] In other words, the *Rechtsgüter* of self-defence were the life and property of the US citizens and its necessity was found in the fact that the territorial government could not prevent private entities from inflicting injuries on those citizens.

By way of response, de Gorostiza stated:

> This principle [of self-defence] would never have been allowed ... unless in a case of absolute necessity, when the danger is imminent, when it cannot be avoided by any other means, and when the injury apprehended is infinitely greater than that which we are about to occasion.[29]

Concerning this incident, then, there was no agreement between the United States and Mexican governments either on the lawfulness of the US actions or on the preconditions for the application of 'the principle of self-defence'. However, there was indeed agreement on the function of self-defence, as justification for the violation of the territory of another state under certain circumstances.

---

26 'de Gorostiza to Dickins, October 15, 1836' (n 14) 369–370. Compare with 'Manuel Eduardo de Gorostiza, Mexican Minister to the United States, to Asbury Dickins, Acting Secretary of State of the United States, September 27, 1836' in Manning (ed) (n 5) 364.

27 'John Forsyth, Secretary of State of the United States, to Manuel Eduardo de Gorostiza, Mexican Minister to the United States, May 3, 1836' in Manning (ed) (n 5) 47.

28 'Dickins to de Gorostiza, October 13, 1836' (n 12) 67.

29 'de Gorostiza to Dickins, October 15, 1836' (n 14) 370.

It should also be noted that, with regard to the necessity of self-defence, Mexico proposed criteria similar to the Webster Formula[30] which was later presented in the *Caroline* incident; and that the US emphasized the inability of the territorial state to prevent private entities, Native Americans in this instance, from inflicting injuries on another state. Although these two factors relating to the preconditions for actions undertaken in self-defence had been proposed by Mexico and the United States respectively, with neither state relating the two factors to each other, the link between these factors was drawn in the cases we will consider next.

(b) The *Caroline* Incident (1837–1842)[31]

Relationship to the Concept of War

With regard to the relationship of 'the necessity of self-defence' to the concept of war in the *Caroline* incident, it is necessary to be aware that the incident brought the two states, Great Britain and the United States, to the brink of war. The tension between them was heightened following the arrest of Alexander McLeod in November 1840, who had bragged about taking part in the destruction of the boat. In consequence, Andrew Stevenson, the US Minister to Great Britain, repeatedly wrote to his government about the prospect of war between the two states and the need to make preparations for war.[32] Henry S. Fox, British Minister to the United States, wrote in a similar vein to the British government.[33] In these circumstances, the operative concept of self-defence distinguished action based on that concept from a resort to war, in two ways.

Firstly, self-defence was contrasted with war from the viewpoint of the state against which it was exercised. After the *Caroline* incident had been settled, John Tyler, the president of the United States, stated in his address to Congress, on the *Caroline* incident, 'When border collisions come to receive the sanction, or to be made on the authority of either government, general war must be the

30 See text to n 46 of this chapter.

31 With regard to the facts, refer to Section A of Chapter 2.

32 'Andrew Stevenson, United States Minister to Great Britain, to Daniel Webster, Secretary of State of the United States, April 7, 1841' in WR Manning (ed) *Diplomatic Correspondence of the United States; Canadian Relations 1784–1860* (Carnegie Endowment for International Peace Washington 1943) vol 3 (1836–1848), 626; 'Andrew Stevenson, United States Minister to Great Britain, to Daniel Webster, Secretary of State of the United States, June 18, 1841' in ibid 639.

33 'Mr Fox to Viscount Palmerston, January 10, 1841' in K Bourne (ed) *British Documents on Foreign Affairs: Reports and Papers from the Foreign Office Confidential Print, Part I From the Mid-Nineteenth Century to the First World War, Series C North America, 1837–1914* (University Publications of America Maryland 1986) vol 1 (McLeod and Maine, 1837–1842), 110.

inevitable result'. However, he allowed that 'a case of most urgent and extreme necessity', i.e. a case of necessity of self-defence, constituted an exception to this rule.[34]

Secondly, self-defence was contrasted with war from the viewpoint of the state that exercised it. Viscount Palmerston, the British Secretary of State for Foreign Affairs, wrote to Andrew Stevenson, the US Minister to Great Britain, stating that when the government of New York State had proved unable to prevent the rebellion (which had been operating from its territory) from harming British Canada, and unable to stop its preparation, that government had either intentionally sanctioned the rebels or lost its authority over the border districts. In the former case, he wrote, the British government would have a right to resort to 'war against war'; in the latter case, even though it would have no right to make war, Britain would have a right to repress the rebellion, on her own, in the territory of the United States.[35]

This distinction became a more sophisticated legal argument in 'A Letter'[36] by Robert Phillimore to Lord Ashburton, the British Special Envoy to the United States. This letter directly considered the *Caroline* incident and discussed the right of self-defence in depth. Phillimore argued that, since the US government apparently had known the situation in the border districts (rallies of the rebels against British Canada), the US failure to ameliorate the situation showed either that the United States had not thought it proper to repress the rebellion, or that it had intended to do so but been physically unable to carry out its intention. He then contended that, in the first case, Great Britain would have been authorized to make war against the United States and, in the second, Britain might have repressed the rebellion in the territory of the United States by invoking the 'duty of self-defence'.[37] The case in which the right of self-defence

34 'Extract from Message of President, at the close of the year 1841' *cited* in RJ Phillimore *A Letter to the Right Honourable Lord Ashburton, Suggested by the Questions of International Law, Raised in the Message of the American President* (J Hatchard and Son London 1842) 81–82.

35 'Viscount Palmerston to Mr Stevenson, August 27, 1841' in Bourne (ed) (n 33) 185–190.

36 Phillimore (n 34). Although the letter was written before the settlement of this incident, it is unclear how much this letter influenced British policy. However, it deserves considerable attention as detailed and contemporary legal analysis of the incident.

37 Ibid 17–24, esp 21. Even in the 19th century, 'duty of self-defence' was not a widely used expression. However, considering that self-preservation was then regarded as 'not only a right with respect to other states, but a duty with respect to its own members' (H Wheaton *Elements of International Law with a Sketch of the History of the Science* (Carey, Lea & Blanchard Philadelphia 1836) 81), self-defence can also be deemed a State's duty with respect to its nationals. On the duty of self-preservation, see also R Phillimore

could be exercised was clearly distinguished from the case in which resort to war would have been justified.

In addition to this distinction based on different attitudes of the US government, Britain also distinguished justifiable war and justifiable self-defence based on the function and context of action in self-defence.

It is to be noted here that Britain exercised self-defence not against invasion or the use or threat of force by the United States, but against the rebellion by Canadians and Americans who acted from US territory. The *Caroline* became a target since it was hired for the rebellion. In addition, self-defence was not regarded as a justification for an attack against the United States. According to British perspectives, the attack against the *Caroline* was not one against 'a Vessel of the United States' and 'could not be considered a hostile movement against the U. States Govt.'.[38] The concept of self-defence in this incident was thus distinct from the concept of war, with regard both to its function and to the context in which it was discussed.

Significance of the Right of Self-Defence

If self-defence in this incident was neither against an act of war nor invoked as justification for resort to war, then what was the right of self-defence held to justify, in response to what, and in protecting what *Rechtsgut*?

Justification for the Violation of the Territory of Another State

The destruction of the *Caroline* within the territory of the United States raised two legal issues: injury to the property of the boat owner, and violation of US territory.[39] It is the former issue that was the focus of the initial phases of the diplomatic negotiation following the destruction of the boat in 1837. The US government first demanded redress for '[t]he destruction of the property, and the assassination, of citizens of the United States on the soil of New York'.[40]

Commentaries upon International Law (WG Benning London 1854) vol 1, 225; M de Vattel *Le droit des gens ou principes de la loi naturelle* (edn of 1758 Carnegie Institute Washington DC 1916) vol 1, 1–2, 23, 26.

38 'Deposition of J. Radenhurst, Aide-de-Camp to Colonel Allen N. MacNab, Canadian Commander, Enclosed with the Letter from Lord Palmerston, British Secretary of State for Foreign Affairs, to Andrew Stevenson, United States Minister to Great Britain, August 27, 1841' in Manning (ed) (n 32) 648–649.

39 Besides these, the assassination of US citizens was also raised in the beginning. ('John Forsyth, Secretary of State of the United States, to Henry S. Fox, British Minister to the United States, Jan. 5, 1838' in Manning (ed) (n 32) 32) However, little attention was paid to this issue and it was not referred to afterwards.

40 Ibid.

In reply, Henry S. Fox, British Minister to the United States, argued that, because of the 'extraordinary state of things',[41] the British authorities had been impelled to pursue and destroy the *Caroline*, '*wheresoever* they might find her'.[42] At this stage, both governments discussed the destruction of the boat but did not focus on the question of whether the incident happened within the territory of British Canada or of the United States.

However, when Andrew Stevenson, the US Minister to Great Britain, responded to this contention of Fox's, he focused on the issue of the violation of territory in addition to damages to be paid. In his letter to Palmerston, he not only demanded reparation but also described the British action as 'a manifest act of hostile and daring aggression upon the rights and sovereignty' of the United States and stressed the inviolability of the territory of independent states.[43] In response to this contention, the British government made no reply for more than three years. However, when this incident was addressed by the two countries again after the arrest of McLeod in 1840, the issue of the territorial violation came to the fore.

In parallel with narrowing down the points at issue to the matter of territorial violation, the concept of the right of self-defence was gradually defined as a justification for such violation. This understanding of self-defence is evident in the instruction from Lord Aberdeen, British Secretary for Foreign Affairs, to Lord Ashburton, the British Special Envoy to the United States. According to Aberdeen, 'any just ground of complaint, or claim for compensation [for the destruction of the *Caroline*] on the part of the Owner [of the vessel]' was 'utterly untenable'.[44] 'There remains, however', he stated, 'the violation of the independent Jurisdiction of the United States'; and on that problem, he advised, '[t]he [United States] believe, in truth, that it admits but of one plea of justification – the plea of self defence'.[45]

This understanding of self-defence is also apparent in the so-called Webster formula. In the letter to Fox of 24th April 1841, Daniel Webster, the US Secretary of State, stated:

---

41 'Henry S. Fox, British Minister to the United States, to John Forsyth, Secretary of State of the United States, Feb. 6, 1838' in Manning (ed) (n 32) 423.

42 Ibid. (emphasis added)

43 'Mr Stevenson to Viscount Palmerston, May 22, 1838' in Bourne (ed) (n 33) 30–34.

44 'Lord Aberdeen, British Secretary of State for Foreign Affairs, to Lord Ashburton, British Special Envoy to the United States, Feb. 8, 1842' in Manning (ed) (n 32) 692.

45 Ibid. See also 'Lord Ashburton, British Special Envoy to the United States, to Lord Aberdeen, British Secretary of State for Foreign Affairs, April 25, 1842' in Manning (ed) (n 32) 704.

> It will be for that Government to show a necessity of self-defence, instant, overwhelming, leaving no choice of means, and no moment for deliberation. It will be for it to shew, also, that the local authorities of Canada, even supposing the necessity of the moment authorized them to enter the territories of the United States at all, did nothing unreasonable or excessive[.][46]

As clearly shown in these passages, the necessity to be shown was nothing but 'the necessity ... to enter the territories of the United States'.[47]

Necessity and the *Rechtsgüter* of Self-Defence

If this understanding is correct, we face the following question: under what circumstances, in protecting what *Rechtsgut*, was the violation of territory justified by the claim of self-defence? The self-preservation doctrine's view of the *Caroline* incident holds that justification of the exercise of the right of self-defence rested upon ambiguous criteria, such as 'the security or safety of the state'.[48] It is true that, as Brownlie points out, the so-called Webster formula itself is 'no more informative than the crude formula that there must be a necessity to act'.[49] However, in the diplomatic negotiations between them, both states attempted to make this formula more concrete and precise.

Before presenting his formula, Webster stated:

> the extent of this right is a question to be judged of by the circumstances of each particular case; and when its alleged exercise has led to the commission of hostile acts within the territory of a power at peace, nothing less than a clear and absolute necessity can afford ground of justification.[50]

That is to say, Webster argued that stricter criteria applied to the exercise of the right of self-defence when such exercise involved the violation of the territory of another state than in other cases.

---

46 'Mr Webster to Mr Fox, April 24, 1841' in Bourne (ed) (n 33) 159.

47 Ibid. See also 'Mr Webster to Lord Ashburton, July 27, 1842' in Bourne (ed) (n 33) 332; 'Lord Ashburton to Mr Webster, July 28, 1842' in Bourne (ed) (n 33) 332–335; 'Mr Webster to Lord Ashburton, Aug. 6, 1842' in Bourne (ed) (n 33) 346–347.

48 Brownlie (n 2) 42.

49 I Brownlie 'The Use of Force in Self-Defence' [1961] 37 BYIL 265. See text to n 46 of this chapter.

50 'Mr Webster to Mr Fox, April 24, 1841' (n 46) 156.

In reply, the British government consistently contended that such a condition had been fulfilled as the US government had not discouraged or was unable to prevent the acts of rebellion within its own territory.[51] Ashburton indeed argued that a state had a right to defend itself when 'cannon are moving and setting up in a battery which can reach you, and are actually destroying life and property by their fire; if you have remonstrated for some time without effect, and see no prospect of relief'.[52] Thus, the *Rechtsgüter* of the right of self-defence were defined as the life and property of citizens; and the necessity for self-defence was found in the fact that the state within whose territory the right had been exercised was not able, on its own, to prevent the rebellion from harming another state.

In short, it is suggested that the right of self-defence in the *Caroline* incident was regarded as a justification for the violation of a state's territory by another state insofar as the former state could not prevent the injury to persons or property of citizens of the latter.[53]

2 *Justification for the Violation of the Flag-State Jurisdiction of Another State*

(a) The *Virginius* Incident (1873–1874)

Facts[54]

On 31st October 1873, the steamer *Virginius*, flying the American flag, was overtaken by a Spanish man-of-war on the high seas. The *Virginius* was taken to Santiago de Cuba and, after a summary trial by court-martial, on a charge of piracy, fifty-three persons on board were condemned to death and shot. The condemned included Americans, British subjects and Cubans. The rest of the people on board were held as prisoners. The charge of piracy appears to have

51 'Sir Francis Head to Mr Fox, Jan. 8, 1838' in Bourne (ed) (n 33) 15; 'Mr Fox to Viscount Palmerston, Jan. 13, 1838' in Bourne (ed) (n 33) 19; 'Henry S. Fox to John Forsyth, Feb. 6, 1838' (n 41) 422–423.

52 'Lord Ashburton to Mr Webster, July 28, 1842' (n 47) 333.

53 This understanding of the *Caroline* incident is not entirely new. See B Cheng *General Principles of Law as Applied by International Courts and Tribunals* (Stevens & Son London 1953) 87; J Delivanis *Le légitime défense en droit international public moderne* (JGDJ Paris 1971) 13–15, 16–17; W Meng 'The Caroline' in Bernhardt (ed) (n 4) 537–538; T Kearley 'Raising the *Caroline*' [1999] 17 Wisc Int'l LJ 325, 328–329.

54 Moore (n 1) 895–903; [1873–1874] 65 British and Foreign State Papers (hereinafter BFSP) 223–229; GT Curtis *The Case of the Virginius, Considered with Reference to the Law of Self-Defence* (Baker, Voorhis & Co New York 1874) 3–20; R Taoka *The Right of Self-defense in International Law* (Institute of Legal Study, Osaka University of Economics and Law Osaka 1978) 27–30.

been based upon the fact that the vessel was engaged in conveying arms, ammunition and men to aid the insurrection against Spanish colonial rule in Cuba.

Soon after the incident, Great Britain sent a man-of-war to Santiago and demanded that no further executions of British subjects take place until the case had been investigated by higher authorities. Great Britain admitted that the seizure of the vessel and the detention of the people on board were justified as self-defence, but condemned the execution of the British subjects as not justified by the immediate necessity of self-defence. The dispute between Great Britain and Spain was resolved at the end of 1874 when Spain agreed to compensate the families of the British subjects who had been on board and were executed.

In contrast, the United States condemned not only the execution of the American subjects on board, but also the seizure of the American ship on the high seas. Thus the United States demanded:

> the restoration of the *Virginius*, and the release and delivery to the United States of the persons captured on her who have not already been massacred, and that the flag of the United States be saluted in the port of Santiago, and the signal punishment of the officials who were concerned in the capture of the vessel and the execution of the passengers and crew.[55]

In response to this demand, Spain released the vessel and the American detainees to the United States. The demand for a salute to the US flag was withdrawn when Spain proved that the vessel was not eligible to carry the US flag. The dispute was finally resolved in March 1875 when Spain agreed to pay compensation to the company owning the vessel and the families of the Americans who had been executed.

Relationship to the Concept of War

In this incident, the relationship of self-defence to war was not explicitly discussed. However, with regard to the seizure of the *Virginius*, the United States argued that '[*n*]*o state of war existed*, conferring upon a maritime power the right to molest and detain upon the high seas a documented vessel' and emphasized that '*in time of peace*, ...any visitation, molestation, or detention of such vessel by force, or by the exhibition of force, on the part of a foreign

55 Moore (n 1) 896.

power, is in derogation of the sovereignty of the United States'.[56] The American argument suggests that the seizure of the vessel neither happened in time of war nor brought a state of war into being. Certainly, the right of self-defence was not deemed a justification of war.

Significance of the Right of Self-Defence

If, as just mentioned, it was not held that an exercise of the right of self-defence implied a state of war, then it is necessary again to ask what action the right of self-defence justified, in response to and in defence of what.

Justification for the Violation of the Flag-State Jurisdiction of Another State

This case presented two actions requiring justification: the seizure of the *Virginius* and the execution of the people on board. An attempt was made to justify the former as an act of self-defence or self-preservation.[57]

Great Britain drew a clear distinction between the two acts:

> [the British government did] not take the ground of complaining of the seizure of the Virginius, nor of the detention of the passengers and crew.... Much may be excused ... in acts done under the expectation of instant damage in self-defence by a nation as well as by an individual. But after the capture of the Virginius and the detention of the crew was effected, no pretence of imminent necessity of self-defence could be alleged.[58]

On the other hand, the argument of the United States was not clear on this point. Indeed, some literature contrasted the US attitude, which consistently condemned the seizure of the vessel, with the British attitude, which accepted the seizure as an act of self-defence.[59] However, the United States did not rebut the contention that the seizure was, or could be, justified by the right of self-defence or of self-preservation. In response to Spain's contention that

56 F Wharton *A Digest of the International Law of the United States* (2nd edn Government Printing Office Washington 1887) vol 3, 148–149. (emphasis added)

57 In this incident, the British government referred to the term 'self-defence' but the US and Spanish governments to the words both 'self-defence' and 'self-preservation'.

58 Cited in WE Hall *A Treatise on International Law* (2nd edn Clarendon Press Oxford 1884) 252.

59 Typically ibid 251; CHM Waldock 'The Regulation of the Use of Force by Individual States in International Law' [1952] 81 RCADI 465.

the seizure of the vessel was justified by 'the right of self-preservation',[60] the United States in fact argued that '[i]t is not necessary ... to assent to or to deny the justice of this proposition in the extreme case and with ... the great limitations'.[61] Moreover, the United States went on to state that the right of self-preservation did not provide any state with the jurisdiction to try the case and that, 'had Spain, after [the] capture [of the *Virginius*], restored her and her passengers and crew to the United States, to be dealt with according to their laws, the appropriateness of the [contention of the right of self-preservation] would appear to be more manifest'.[62] The United States did not entirely deny that the seizure of the *Virginius* on the high seas was, or might have been, justified by the right of self-preservation.

The attitudes of both Great Britain and the United States suggest the sense in which the seizure of the *Virginius* was an issue of international law: whether a Spanish claim of self-defence or of self-preservation might justify violation of the freedom of the high seas, particularly the freedom of navigation. This is implied by the fact that the seizure of the vessel was condemned for having been done not within Spanish territorial waters but on the high seas. Hamilton Fish, the Secretary of State of the United States, made this point clear by summarizing the Spanish contention as arguing that 'this right of transportation [on the high seas] may be subordinated by the necessities of self-preservation in the government which is contending with an insurrection'.[63] Now, the freedom of the high seas can be expressed as the exclusive jurisdiction of a flag-state over vessels on the high seas;[64] the violation of the former is nothing other than the violation of the latter. Thus, it is also possible to define the right of self-defence in this instance as a justification for the violation of the flag-state jurisdiction of another state.

Necessity and the *Rechtsgüter* of Self-Defence

The issue becomes, then, under what circumstances and in protecting what *Rechtsgüter* the violation of flag-state jurisdiction would be justified by

60 'Admiral Polo de Bernabé to Mr Fish, February 2, 1874' in *Foreign Relations of the United States 1875* (Government Printing Office Washington 1875) vol 2 (hereinafter [1875–2] FRUS), 1177.

61 'Mr Fish to Admiral Polo de Bernabé, April 18, 1874' [1875–2] FRUS 1192.

62 Ibid.

63 Ibid.

64 T Treves 'High Seas' in R Bernhardt (ed) *Encyclopedia of Public International Law* (Elsevier Amsterdam 1995) vol 2, 707.

the claim of self-defence. On this point, as key to establishing 'necessity of self-defence', Great Britain emphasized 'the expectation of instant damage'.[65] She distinguished the seizure of the vessel from the execution of the people on board and accepted that the seizure might well have been judged necessary 'under the expectation of instant damage' but argued regarding the executions, that 'no pretence of imminent necessity of self-defence could be alleged'.[66]

For her part, Spain contended that she had acted in self-defence to prevent injury to herself from the *Virginius*, the United States having failed to prevent that ship from departing New York with intention to aid the Cuban insurrection. Indeed, Spain complained that:

> the United States have not prevented the organization, the departure, and the active prosecution of the different hostile enterprises against Cuba in which the Virginius was an agent. The United States answer that they took efficacious measures toward preventing her departure from New York, and to this Spain ... insists that [the fraudulent documents issued by the collector of customs at that port] show the very reverse of having taken efficacious measures of prevention[.][67]

In the *Virginius* incident, in short, the principle was advanced, and not controverted, that 'the necessity of self-defence' justified the violation of the freedom of the high seas, particularly that of navigation, or the violation of flag-state jurisdiction, when the flag-state could not prevent the insurrection using vessels against another State. In other words, the concept of self-defence which we have seen applied to action on land was extended to the high seas. However, it is to be noted that self-defence did not justify the trial or the execution of the people on board. The function of the right of self-defence was thus limited.

On the other hand, in this incident, it is not clear what was regarded as the *Rechtsgut* of the right of self-defence. While it echoes the *Caroline* incident in assuming the relevance of rebellion, it seems to deem as the *Rechtsgüter* the maintenance of a colony rather than, as in the *Caroline* incident, the life and property of a state's own citizens.

---

65 Hall (n 58) 252.

66 Ibid.

67 'Admiral Polo de Bernabé to Mr Fish, February 2, 1874' (n 60) 1160–1161. On the other hand, the United States did not indicate their understanding about the circumstances under which the right of self-preservation could be exercised, since, as mentioned above, they argued that it was not necessary to assent to or to deny such a proposition.

(b) The Bering Sea Arbitration (1893)

Facts[68]

The territory of Alaska and its neighbouring islands in the Bering Sea was ceded by the Emperor of Russia to the United States in 1867. The United States subsequently enacted a series of laws for the purpose of the protection of the fur seal in that area. However, the fur seal in those islands was brought to the brink of extinction as a result of British sealing schooners' catching fur seals on the high seas surrounding the islands. In response, the US authorities in 1886 seized some British vessels on the high seas, about sixty or seventy miles from the closest land, for the offence of hunting and killing seals in that part of the sea, and punished the masters and crews of those ships. The United States also seized some other vessels in 1887.

The United States in 1887 called upon concerned states, including France, Great Britain, Japan and Russia, to cooperate with the US government in the protection of the fur-seal fisheries in the Bering Sea. Although the United States received favourable responses from those countries, negotiations were suspended in May 1888; at the request of the Canadian government, the British government refused to agree to such cooperation. In response to this British decision, the US government hardened its policy. In 1889 US authorities seized British vessels operating in the fur-seal fisheries on the high seas and placed them in detention.

Britain's protest against the seizure of these ships led to diplomatic negotiations with the United States, which did not resolve the dispute. A treaty of arbitration was thereupon signed in February 1892 and the dispute between these two states 'concerning the jurisdictional rights of the United States in the waters of Bering's Sea, and concerning also the preservation of the fur seal in, or habitually resorting to, the said sea, and the rights of the citizens and subjects of either country as regards the taking of fur seal in, or habitually resorting to, the said waters'[69] was submitted to a tribunal of seven arbitrators, two of whom were to be nominated by the President of the United States, two by Her Britannic Majesty, and one each by the President of France, the King of Italy, and the King of Sweden and Norway. While five questions were submitted to the tribunal for judgement, the only question that related to our enquiry was the fifth: 'Has the United States any right, and if so, what right of protection or

68 JB Moore *A Digest of International Law* (Government Printing Office Washington 1906) vol 1, 890–923; JB Moore *History and Digest of the International Arbitrations to Which the United States Has Been a Party* (Government Printing Office Washington 1898) vol 1, 755–957; W Williams 'Reminiscences of the Bering Sea Arbitration' [1943] 37 AJIL 562.

69 Moore (n 68 (*A Digest of International Law*)) 905.

property in the fur seals frequenting the islands of the Untied States in Bering Sea when such seals are found outside the ordinary three-mile limit [of the territorial waters]?'[70]

The tribunal convened in February 1893 and gave its judgment on 15th August of the same year. On the fifth question, the United States claimed the right of protection based on the right of self-defence. Great Britain offered a counter-argument chiefly based on the absence of necessity of self-defence and of the substantive rights that could be protected by the right of self-defence.

The argument of the United States on the right of protection of the fur seal in Bering Sea was not accepted by the tribunal. With only the two judges named by the President of the United States dissenting, the tribunal determined that 'the United States [had] not any right of protection or property in the fur-seals frequenting the islands of the United States in Bering Sea, when such seals are found outside the ordinary three-mile limit'.[71]

As no claim of self-defence was affirmed, and, importantly, as the reasoning for the decision of the tribunal was not written down,[72] it is not possible to delineate sharply the concept of the right of self-defence defined by the judgment itself. This has led to the view that the *Bering Sea* Arbitration has 'only minor value for the purpose of studying the meaning and scope of the right of self-defence'.[73] However, in their written statements and oral arguments, the parties to the dispute discussed the concept of the right of self-defence at great length, making it possible at least to discern and compare *their* notions of the right of self-defence. Therefore, far from being unimportant, this case is highly significant in clarifying the concept of the right of self-defence that existed before World War I.

---

70 Ibid 906. The other questions were:

"1. What exclusive jurisdiction in the sea now known as the Bering's Sea, and what exclusive rights in the seal fisheries therein, did Russia assert and exercise prior and up to the rime of the cession of Alaska to the United States?

2. How far were these claims of jurisdiction as to the seal fisheries recognized and conceded by Great Britain?

3. Was the body of water now known as the Bering's Sea included in the phrase 'Pacific Ocean', as used in the Treaty of 1825 between Great Britain and Russia; and what rights, if any, in the Bering's Sea were held and exclusively exercised by Russia after said Treaty?

4. Did not all the rights of Russia as to jurisdiction, and as to the seal fisheries in Bering's Sea east of the water boundary, in the Treaty between the United States and Russia of the 30th March, 1867, pass unimpaired to the United States under that Treaty? (ibid 905)"

71 Ibid 913.

72 Williams (n 68) 583.

73 Taoka (n 54) 51.

Relationship to the Concept of War

In this case, there was *prima facie* confusion about the relationship of the concept of the right of self-defence to the concept of war. This is because Great Britain formulated the concept of war in a broader sense than was usually understood.

Charles Russell, the British Attorney-General, contrasted the rights obtaining in time of peace and those obtaining in time of war and argued that the United States had asserted the latter where only the former could be claimed:

> The fundamental fallacy ... is found in the proposition advanced in the Argument of the United States that a State has in time of peace a right under international law, and in its full rights of self defence and self-preservation, to do on the high seas whatever it may conceive to be necessary to protect its property or its interests. ...It makes the rights in time of peace the same as the rights in time of war.[74]

Against this, the US delegate contended that the right of self-defence could be exercised even in time of peace, arguing, for example:

> It has been said that the right of search is confined to a time of war. That assertion proceeds upon the ground that only in time of war can the necessity for it arise. No one has ever claimed that the right should be denied in time of peace, if an equal necessity for it exists. And when such necessity has been regarded as existing, the right has been asserted.[75]

At first sight, the arguments of these two states seem to assume the dichotomy between the law of peace and that of war, and to be in sharp conflict with each other over the possibility of the exercise of the right of self-defence in time of peace. The differences between the two states, however, were not so

---

74 'Oral Argument of Sir Charles Russell, Q.C.M.P., Her Britannic Majesty's Attorney-General, on Behalf of Great Britain' in *Proceedings, Proceedings of the Tribunal of Arbitration, Convened at Paris under the Treaty between the United States of America and Great Britain Concluded at Washington February 29, 1892, for the Determination of Questions Between the Two Governments concerning the Jurisdictional Rights of the United States in the Waters of Bering Sea* (Government Printing Office Washington 1895) (hereinafter *Proceedings*) vol 13, 295.

75 'Argument of the United States' in *Proceedings* (n 74) vol 9, 161.

wide. This is clear from the understanding of the *Caroline* incident, which both states regarded as a precedent for the right of self-defence.

James C. Carter, US counsel, referred to the *Caroline* incident in arguing that 'there is no truth in the assertion that the exercise by a nation of the right of self-defence ... is confined to times of war. ...The right exists in time of peace just as well',[76] and in the *Caroline* incident, he noted, there was 'no condition of war'.[77] In other words, the US delegate defined a time of peace as the absence of a state of war between states.[78]

On the other hand, although he also referred to the *Caroline* incident, Russell argued that 'the justification [for the British action in the *Caroline* incident] was a justification based upon a belligerent right'.[79] However, the conflict in which Britain was a belligerent, in his argument, was not between Britain and the United States, but rather that which 'the people of New-York had begun ... against Her Majesty's Canadian Provinces'.[80] Moreover, while he once contended that the Amelia Island incident[81] was 'found to have been in effect belligerency',[82] Russell changed his argument when Judge Hannen asked whether it was against the people in the island that war was waged.[83] Russell admitted that the United States 'did not treat this party [in the island] as a real belligerent ... [but] rather as a case of land pirates' and that '[i]t was rather an act of military execution than of belligerency' or, phrased differently, an act of 'quasi-belligerency'.[84] Finally, he argued that the US action in the Amelia Island incident was, 'whether war was formally declared or informally declared, ...in the nature of belligerent acts, directed to putting down the persons who were assuming, without authority, jurisdiction, and who were committing acts ... of land piracy'.[85]

76 'Oral Arguments of James C. Carter Esq., on Behalf of the United States' in *Proceedings* (n 74) vol 12, 247.

77 Ibid 246.

78 See also 'Oral Argument of Hon. Edward J. Phelps, on Behalf of the United States' in *Proceedings* (n 74) vol 15, 215.

79 'Oral Argument of Sir Charles Russell' (n 74) 307.

80 Ibid 306.

81 See n 1 of this chapter.

82 'Oral Argument of Sir Charles Russell' (n 74) 303.

83 Ibid 304.

84 Ibid.

85 Ibid 305. See also ibid 310–311.

It is apparent that both states posited the same situation as justifying the exercise of the right of self-defence: a state suffering from rebellion or armed groups acting from neighbouring states.

Nevertheless, Great Britain defined this situation as a time of war while the US held that it may obtain as well in time of peace. These differences are derived from the disagreement over the necessity of self-defence and the substantive rights that could be protected by the right of self-defence. Indeed, Russell argued that 'the genuine emergency of danger', in which the right of self-defence could be exercised, could be found only in belligerency. He stated that 'belligerent rights rest on the genuine emergency of danger, which is the true basis of all exceptional acts of self-defence, or of self-preservation'.[86] The United States, on the other hand, understood the necessity of self-defence more broadly. They contended that 'the right of self-defence is not confined to the mere defence of the existence of the nation, as from an enemy that threatens its conquest or its destruction. It extends to every interest of the nation that is worth protecting'.[87]

Therefore, it can be argued that Great Britain defined the situation in which the right of self-defence could be exercised as a time of war, since they intended to emphasize the narrow interpretation of the necessity of self-defence, whereas the United States defined the situation as a time of peace in order to stress its broader interpretation. In this sense, while the differences between them appear to be considerable, both states understood a state of affairs in which the right of self-defence could be exercised to be different from a state of war.

This understanding was also shared by the judges. The president of the court, indeed, explicitly regarded the destruction of the *Caroline* as 'rather an act of military execution than of belligerency'.[88] Moreover, even the delegates of the British government had to admit that the act of self-defence had been distinguished from that of belligerency. Agreeing to this understanding presented by the president, Russell stated, 'That may be so – quasi-belligerency, in point of fact, I suppose'.[89]

Significance of the Right of Self-Defence

If in this *Bering Sea* case the situation in which the right of self-defence could be exercised was thus distinguished from a state of war between states, then

86 Ibid 295.

87 'Oral Argument of Hon. Edward J. Phelps' (n 78) 128.

88 'Oral Argument of Sir Charles Russell' (n 74) 304.

89 Ibid.

it is necessary to define what actions the right of self-defence justified; and, in response to what, and in protecting what *Rechtgüter*, it was exercised.

Justification for the Violation of the Flag-State Jurisdiction of Another State

In order to examine the function of the right of self-defence as recognized in this case, it is useful to take a look at the understanding shared by the two states of the function of the right of self-defence that was found in incidents which they regarded as precedents, including the *Caroline* incident. This is useful because the United States argued that the concept of the right of self-defence that had been established in these precedents could be applied to this case.[90] In its use of the doctrines of the time, indeed, the United States defined the right of self-defence in the *Caroline* incident in such a way as to justify the 'otherwise gross violation of the territory of a friendly nation'.[91]

According to the United States, the concept of the right of self-defence thus defined was applicable to the case at hand: as in the *Virginius* incident, the US maintained, that concept should be understood as a justification for the violation of the freedom of the high seas. The United States clearly stated:

> The ground upon which the destruction of the seal is sought to be justified, is that the open sea is free; and that since this slaughter takes place there, it is done in the exercise of an indefeasible right in the individuals engaged in it; that the nation injured can not defend itself on the sea, and therefore upon the circumstances of this case can not defend itself at all, let the consequences be what they may.
>
> The United States Government denies this proposition. While conceding and interested to maintain the general rule of the freedom of the sea, ...it asserts ... that the right of self-defence on the part of a nation is a perfect and paramount right, to which all others are subordinate, and which upon no admitted theory of international law has ever been surrendered; ...that in the time, the place, the manner, and the extent of its execution, it is limited only by the actual necessity of the particular case; that it may, therefore, be exercised upon the high seas, as well as upon the land, and even upon the territory of other and friendly nations, provided only that the necessity for it plainly appears; and that whenever an important and just national interest of any description is put in peril for the

90 'Argument of the United States' (n 75) 172.

91 Ibid 153. See Sub-section 1.(b) of this section. See also, on the US–Mexico Border incident, 'Argument of the United States' (n 75) 154.

> sake of individual profit by an act upon the high seas, ...the nation will be entitled to protect itself against the injury, by whatever force may be reasonably necessary, according to the usages established in analogous cases.[92]

It is apparent that the violation of the territory of another state and that of the freedom of the high seas were treated as effectively equivalent by the United States. However, there is a *prima facie* difference between them. In the case of a territorial violation, as in the *Caroline* incident, even though a state exercised force within the territory of another state not at war with it, the exercise of force was not itself regarded as necessarily comprehended within the exercise of the right of self-defence. By contrast, in the case of the violation of the freedom of the high seas, it seems that the use of force itself was more consciously regarded as essential to the exercise of the right. Indeed, US counsel Carter stated that 'whenever a nation finds it necessary to employ acts of force upon the high seas in order to protect its own rights or the rights of its citizens, it has the right to employ such acts of force'.[93]

However, this difference is only to be expected; it stems from the respective natures of the violation of territory and the violation of the freedom of the high seas. While an incursion into the territory of another state matters by itself, an incursion into the high seas does not. In the latter case, indeed, no 'incursion' can take place without the use of force. Moreover, 'acts of force' on the high seas do not imply recourse to war or the use of force of any substantial magnitude; the incursion into the high seas in this case was nothing other than the seizure of the fishing vessels. Carter referred to the exercise of force but stated:

> the United States has the right to seize [a vessel engaged in pelagic sealing] and capture her; that is to say, it has the right to employ necessary force for the purpose of protecting, in the only way in which it can protect, its property in the seals, or its property interest in the industry which it maintains upon the islands.[94]

Indeed, the freedom of the high seas, particularly in this instance that of fishery, would be violated only when a state seizes, or attempts to seize, vessels of another state engaged in fishing; and the seizure of, or attempts to seize,

92 Ibid 140.

93 'Oral Argument of James C. Carter, Esq.' (n 76) 102.

94 Ibid 253.

vessels of another state usually involves the exercise or demonstration of force. Therefore, if the right of self-defence justified the violation of the freedom of the high seas or the violation of the flag-state jurisdiction of another state, this concept of the right of self-defence could entail the only an exercise of force strictly limited to the seizure of vessels.

Necessity and the *Rechtsgüter* of Self-Defence

On the question of under what circumstances the violation of the freedom of the high seas was justified by the claim of the right of self-defence, the argument of the United States was consistently ambiguous. The United States position that 'in the time, the place, the manner, and the extent of its execution, [the right of self-defence] is limited only by the actual necessity of the particular case'[95] says nothing more than that 'there must be a necessity to act'.[96]

The British delegates discussed 'the necessity of self-defence' more specifically and concretely. As mentioned earlier, they once argued that the basis of the right of self-defence was 'the genuine emergency of danger' and that such an emergency could be found only in belligerency.[97] Moreover, they understood the Webster formula[98] in the *Caroline* incident from the viewpoint of whether or not prior diplomatic protest might have sufficed to prevent the harm feared:

> The occasions for acts of self-defence, or self-preservation, are occasions of emergency – sudden emergency – occasions when there is no time, … – when there is no time for deliberation, no time for contrivance, no time for warning, no time for diplomatic expostulation. …And … in such a case as the present, where there was *no* such instant overwhelming necessity of self-defence, where there *was* time for device of means, where there *was* time for deliberation, where there *was* time for diplomatic expostulation and representation, that it is idle to try to treat this case as a case of necessary self-defence or self-preservation. …[T]here was, before the seizures began, no representation made to Great Britain by the United States that she regarded this as a matter of national interest by which, right or wrong, they were determined to stand.[99]

95 'Argument of the United States' (n 75) 140.

96 Brownlie (n 49) 265. See also 'Oral Argument of James C. Carter, Esq.' (n 76) 247; 'Oral argument of Hon. Edward J. Phelps' (n 78) 128.

97 See n 82 of this chapter and the corresponding text.

98 See n 46 of this chapter and the corresponding text.

99 'Oral argument of Sir Charles Russell' (n 74) 299–301.

Against this, the United States countered that, although '[i]t might be said that the Government of the United States might make the conduct of these Canadian pelagic sealers … the subject of complaint to Great Britain herself', the complaint would have been pointless. The US emphasized that 'there is no way in which a nation can protect its rights upon the high seas other than by the employment of force'.[100]

On the question of the *Rechtsgüter* of the right of self-defence, too, the argument of the United States was not clear; but it can be argued that for *Rechtsgüter*, the United States proposed economic interests. On the one hand, the United States defined the *Rechtsgüter* very broadly: 'every interest of the nation that is worth protecting'.[101] On the other, they offered the narrower formulations 'its own rights or the rights of its citizens',[102] 'their revenue'[103] and 'its property in the seals, or its property interest in the industry in which it maintains upon the islands'.[104] However, these formulations of the *Rechtsgüter* were harshly criticized by Great Britain[105] and were not accepted by the Tribunal.

In light of the above discussion, it can be argued that there was a common understanding between these two states that the right of self-defence could justify the violation of the freedom of the high seas, i.e. the violation of the flag-state jurisdiction of another state under certain circumstances.[106] Nor did the tribunal reject this understanding. Judge Harlan's opinion on this point affirmed it, at least in principle:

> the commonest and simplest form in which the doctrine of self-preservation is illustrated is in cases where a nation employs force

100 'Oral Argument of James C. Carter, Esq.' (n 76) 253.

101 'Oral Argument of Hon. Edward J. Phelps' (n 78) 128.

102 'Oral Argument of James C. Carter, Esq.' (n 76) ibid 102.

103 Ibid 247.

104 Ibid 253.

105 'Case Presented on behalf of the Government of Her Britannic Majesty to the Tribunal of Arbitration' in *Proceedings* (n 74) vol 4, 103; 'Oral Argument of Sir Charles Russell' (n 74) 295.

106 In a dispute between Great Britain and Russia over the seal fishery in the North Pacific, which arose in 1892 and was resolved in 1894, Russia argued that the seizure of seal-fishing vessels on the high seas was justified by the claim of self-defence. ('M. Chichkine to Sir R. Morier, Le 6/18 Avril, 1893' in [1893–1894] 86 BFSP 229) Although Great Britain took a cooperative stance towards the protection of fur seal by Russia, it is unclear whether Great Britain accepted Russia's claim of self-defence. (eg 'The Earl of Rosebery to Sir R. Morier, March 17, 1893' in [1893–1894] 86 BFSP 225–226)

> beyond its own limits, either on the high seas or within the limits of another state, in order to meet a threatened attack upon its existence or a threatened invasion of its territory.[107]

However, as the tribunal rejected the United States contention that the right could be exercised in this particular instance, what might constitute sufficient *Rechtsgüter* and preconditions of its exercise was left obscure.

B Doctrine

This section will examine the doctrine on the right of self-defence advanced from the mid-19th to the early-20th century. As we did in discussing state practice, we will carry out this examination with particular regard to the conceptual relationship between self-defence and war, on the one hand, and on the other between self-defence and self-preservation; the focus will be on the function of the right of self-defence and the context in which it was discussed.

Relationship to the Concept of War

The relationship of the right of self-defence to war was not explored intensively by writers in this period. However, there was a commonly accepted understanding that the exercise of the right of self-defence was not identical to recourse to war but had its own significance. On this point, William E. Hall emphasised a disjunction between the right of self-defence and the concept of war, arguing that the violation of the territory of another state, which he considered justifiable by a claim of the right of self-defence, did not imply any hostile intention against that state:

> a violation of [the territory of another state in self-defence] is not hostile in intention, it may indeed be committed with the express object of preventing occurrences which would lead to war, and it is not directed against the state, or against persons or property belonging to it because they belong to it, but against specific ill-doers because of their personal acts; it therefore differs in very important respects from ordinary acts of war[.][108]

107 'Opinion of Mr Justice Harlan' in *Proceedings* (n 74) vol 1, 195.

108 Hall (n 58) 245 n 1. See also Curtis (n 54) 36.

In addition, while it is true that some other writers regarded the violation of the territory of another state in self-defence as 'imperfect war', they in fact also took the view that it did not constitute or imply a state of war.[109]

Relationship to the Concept of the Right of Self-preservation

By contrast, discussion was remarkably intense on the relationship between the right of self-defence and the right of self-preservation. An examination of doctrine on this point is important because, as discussed in Chapters 1 and 2, the perception that the right of self-defence of the 19th century was not distinguished from the right of self-preservation provides Brownlie with the basis of his argument, especially his counter-argument against Bowett.

As mentioned earlier, it is true that '[m]any works on international law both before and after the *Caroline* case regarded self-defence as an instance of self-preservation and subsequently discussed the *Caroline* under that rubric'.[110] It has also been argued that the right of self-preservation is 'applicable when action is necessary for the security or safety of the state',[111] and even that '[i]n the last resort almost the whole of the duties of states are subordinated to the right of self-preservation'.[112] From these two propositions, it appears that one can draw a conclusion that the pre-World War I right of self-defence allowed states to disregard any obligation when to do so was necessary for national security. Indeed, the self-preservation doctrine on the *Caroline* incident, which has been discussed in Chapter 2 and one of whose most important proponents is Brownlie, understood the 19th century right of self-defence in this way.

However, while in studies of that time the right of self-defence was indeed discussed under the rubric of 'the right of self-preservation', the former was, as will be argued below, distinguishable from the latter. The right of self-defence was understood to have its own distinctive significance and function. Moreover, it is when the right of self-preservation was narrowed in the late-19th and early-20th century that the conception of the right of self-defence came to be

109 H Halleck *International Law; or, Rules Regulating the Intercourse of States in Peace and War* (HH Bancroft & Co San Francisco 1861) 96; C Calvo *Le droit international théorique et pratique précédé d'un exposé historique des progrès de la science du droit des gens* (3rd edn Guillaumin et Cie Paris 1880) vol 1, 311; P Pradier-Fodéré *Traité de droit international public* (A Durand et Pedone-Lauriel Paris 1885) vol 1, 412–414. See also the different views on this point of the American and British delegations in the *Bering Sea* Arbitration (A.2(b)).

110 Brownlie (n 2) 43.

111 Ibid 42.

112 Hall (n 58) 244.

clearly articulated. Understanding the right of self-preservation operative in the pre-World War I period requires that we see the points of contrast between that right and the right of self-defence. For this purpose, the doctrine to be examined will be divided into two: the doctrine of the mid-19th century (from the late-1830s, when the *Caroline* incident occurred, to 1880) and the doctrine of the late-19th century and later.[113]

1 *Mid-19th Century*

Measures Taken within a State's Own Territory and Extra-territorial Defence

In the early-19th century, the right of self-preservation was regarded as 'one of the most essential and important, and that which lies at the foundation of all the rest'[114] of the fundamental rights of states. The concept of the fundamental rights of states in international law is originally found in the mid-18th century and was well systematized in the late-18th and the early-19th century. In the mid-19th century, it was dominant.[115]

Doctrine in the mid-19th century generally conceived the right of self-preservation to justify some measures within a state's territory and other measures outside it. Every state was entitled to take measures '*within* her own dominions'[116] to protect her safety, including the organization of military and naval forces and the construction of fortifications. At the same time, a state was justified in taking 'precautionary measures *without* these limits, and even in transgressing the borders of her neighbour's territory'.[117] These measures were called 'Extra-territorial defense'.[118]

---

113 It is considered that the position of the right of self-preservation in the theory of international law changed around 1880. See L Oppenheim *International Law* (Longmans, Green, and Co New York 1905) vol 1 (Peace), 158.

114 H Wheaton *Elements of International Law with a Sketch of the History of the Science* (Carey, Lea & Blanchard Philadelphia 1836) 81.

115 A Nussbaum *A Concise History of the Law of Nations* (2nd edn Macmillan Company New York 1962) 152, 183. See also G Gidel 'Droits et devoir des nations' [1925] 10 RCADI 537–599.

116 R Phillimore *Commentaries upon International Law* (WG Benning & Co Law Booksellers London 1854) vol 1, 227.

117 Ibid.

118 HW Halleck *Elements of International Law and Laws of War* (JB Lippincott & Co Philadelphia 1866) 59. See also AW Heffter *Das Europäische Völkerrecht der Gegenwart* (Berlag von EH Schroeder Berlin 1844) 50–52; JL Klüber *Droit des gens moderne de l'europe* (new edn MA Ott (ed) Librairie de Guillaumin et Cie Paris 1861) 58–65; T Twiss *The Law of Nations*

It is in this right of extra-territorial defence that the pre-World War I right of self-defence finds its origin. Indeed, the *Caroline* incident, the incident most frequently referred to by writers of the 19th-century, was cited as an example of extra-territorial defence. Therefore, in order to clarify the conception of the right of self-defence that existed before World War I, the difference between the right of extra-territorial defence and the right to take measures within a state's own territory needs to be more closely examined.[119]

Relationship to Other States' Rights

Firstly, these two rights differed in their relationship to the rights of other states. A state's rights in its own territory were considered as not infringing the rights of other states, and as controlled 'by the equal and corresponding Rights of other Nations'.[120] On the other hand, the right of extra-territorial defence was considered to conflict with other states' right to territorial inviolability. When these two rights collided with each other, it was generally understood that the right of extra-territorial defence prevailed. Thus, Phillimore continues directly:

> For International Law considers the Right of Self-Preservation as prior and paramount to that of Territorial Inviolability, and, where they conflict, justifies the maintenance of the former at the expense of the latter right.[121]

Considered as Independent Political Communities (Longman, Green, Longman & Roberts London 1861) 144–145, 148–150; C Calvo *Le droit international théorique et pratique* (2nd edn A Durand et Pedone-Lauriel Paris 1870) vol 1, 258–260.

119 Writers of the early-19th century did not even discuss the right of extra-territorial defence under the rubric of the right of self-preservation. Compare respectively GF de Martens *Précis du droit des gens moderne de l'europe fondé sur les traités et l'usage* (2nd edn Librairie de Dieterich Gottingue 1801) 186 (§117) with GF de Martens *Précis du droit des gens moderne de l'europe* (new edn MC Vergé (ed) Guillaumin Paris1858) vol 1, 303–304 (§117), and Wheaton (n 114) 81–82 with H Wheaton *Wheaton's Elements of International Law* (5th English edn C Phillipson (ed) Stevens & Sons London 1916) 87–91. However, see JL Klüber *Droit des gens moderne de l'europe* (Librairie de JG Cotta Stuttgart 1819) vol 1, 78–79. Even in the mid-19th century, Halleck argued against the inclusion of this right in the right of self-preservation. (Halleck (n 109) 94–96) He only understood the right of self-preservation as the right of states to take measures within their own territory. These facts themselves indicate the essential distinction between these two rights.

120 Twiss (n 118) 144–145. See also Phillimore (n 116) 225–226.

121 Ibid 227. See also Heffter (n 118) 51; Klüber (n 119) 64; Twiss (n 118) 149.

Conditions for the Exercise of Each Right

Secondly, the right of extra-territorial defence differed from the right to take measures within a state's own territory in the preconditions for its exercise. In the case of the latter right, the condition was understood broadly. While different writers might find different measures within the right, they commonly understood that states could exercise this right, and take any measures pursuant to that right that might be necessary 'for the security of National Independence'.[122] Further, they commonly held that such measures 'do not affect the independence of other nations'.[123] In contrast, the precondition for the exercise of the right of extra-territorial defence was formulated more narrowly. This right was considered to justify the violation of a state's territory by another state only when the former state could not prevent harm to the latter. It is to be noted that this condition is consistent with the condition discussed in the previous section in connection with the *Caroline* incident. This is entirely to be expected since this condition was formulated based on the *Caroline* incident.

Indeed, referring to the *Caroline* incident, Phillimore stated:

> [when] the territory of one nation is invaded from the country of another, – whether the invading force be composed of the refugees of the country invaded, or of subjects of the other country, or of both – ... if the cause be the feebleness of [the government of the country from which the invasion has come], the invaded country is warranted in redressing her own wrong, by entering the territory, and destroying the preparations of war therein made against her[.][124]

By contrast, it seems that Travers Twiss defined the conditions for extra-territorial defence and for taking measures within a state's own territory in a more vague way: 'When the safety of the State is at stake, the Right of Self-Preservation may warrant a Nation in extending its precautionary measures beyond the limits of its own dominions, and even in trespassing with that object on a neighbour's territory'.[125] However, he in fact limited the legitimate exercise of the right to the case in which 'the Nation to which the territory belongs is unable or unwilling to defend [the territory]'[126] and thus to prevent harm to another state.

---

122 Twiss (n 118) 144.

123 Phillimore (n 116) 225. See also Klüber (n 119) 59; Halleck (n 109) 92; Calvo (n 118) 258.

124 Phillimore (n 116) 230.

125 Twiss (n 118) 149.

126 Ibid 150. See also Calvo (n 118) 259–260.

Conditions for the Exercise of the Right and the Relationship to Rights of Other States

The understanding that measures a state might take within its own territory did not infringe on other states' rights was the crucial basis for distinguishing the conditions for exercising the self-preservation right on a state's own territory and the conditions for exercising that right on the territory of another state. Phillimore made this clear in a succinct formulation: 'All means *which do not affect the independence of other nations* are lawful for this end [of self-preservation]'.[127] Preconditions for exercising the right of extra-territorial defence were understood to be relatively narrow because that right was understood to collide with, to prevail over and thus to infringe, the rights of other states.

Extension to the High Seas

It should also be noted that, in the mid-1870s, after the *Virginius* incident, some writers argued that the right of extra-territorial defence applied to cases in which a state seized on the high seas ships under another state's jurisdiction. George Curtis defined the right of self-defence in the *Caroline* incident as 'a very important exception to the absolute inviolability of national territory'.[128] On this basis, he argued that the so-called Webster formula[129] should be applied to the seizure by Spain of the *Virginius* and that 'the right of self-defence … may be exercised on the ocean'.[130] Thus he claimed that the scope of application of the right of self-defence extended beyond the land to the high seas.

Caroline Incident in the Context of Extra-territorial Defence

In summary, while it is true that in the mid-19th century the *Caroline* incident was discussed in the context of the right of self-preservation, this does not mean that the *Caroline* incident was presented as illustrating some general right to do whatever might be necessary for a state's security. The right of self-preservation itself comprised two distinct concepts, and the right of self-defence recognized in the *Caroline* and the *Virginius* incidents was one of them: the right of extra-territorial defence. Permissible exercise of this right of extra-territorial defence was conditional and restricted. As shown in the *Caroline* incident and others, it could be exercised by a state only when another territorial or flag state was unprepared or unable to prevent harm to the former.

127 Phillimore (n 116) 225. (emphasis added)
128 Curtis (n 54) 31.
129 See text to n 46 of this chapter.
130 Curtis (n 54) 38.

2 *Late-19th Century and Later*

Right of Self-preservation as the Right of Extra-territorial Defence

From the late-19th to the early-20th century, the concept of the right of self-preservation changed:[131] the right came to be defined simply as the right of extra-territorial defence. The right of self-preservation was no longer taken to imply the right to take measures within a state's own territory;[132] this latter right came to be considered a mere consequence of the freedom of states, which was derived from their independence, and thus to require no grounding in a right of self-preservation. By contrast, most writers focused on the right of extra-territorial defence, the justification for the exercise of force by a state to defend itself within the territory of another state or on the high seas.[133] John Westlake, for example, distinguished between the right to take measures within a state's own territory and the right of extra-territorial defence, as follows:

> When a fully sovereign state employs force in its own territory, or on the high seas on board a ship which carries its flag as belonging to itself or to its subjects, or when by its laws it threatens its subjects with punishment on their return for their acts committed abroad, its independence is internationally its sufficient warrant. For the sovereignty of a state extends over its subjects, over its territory, and over the ships which carry its flag on the high seas; and full sovereignty is independence. But when a state employs force in the territory of another state, or on the high seas on board a ship which carries the flag of another state as belonging to it or to its subjects – or when it attempts by threats to restrain the freedom of action of another state within the territory of the latter, or that of subjects of another state elsewhere than within its own territory or on high seas under its own flag – the state so acting or threatening must find its jurisdiction in some other principle.

---

131 See text to n 113 of this chapter.

132 See as an exception Pradier-Fodéré (n 109) 412–414. Moreover, some of the new editions of the books published before 1880 discussed the right to take measures within the territory as a category of the right of self-preservation. See Calvo (n 109) 309–310; P Fiore *Nouveau droit international public suivant les besoins de la civilisation moderne* (2nd edn C Antoine (tr) A Durand et Pedone-Lauriel Paris 1885) vol 1, 391.

133 In the late-19th century, most writers discussed, in addition to the violation of the territory of another state, the violation of the flag-state jurisdiction on the high seas. See Hall (n 58) 250–252; J Westlake *Chapters on the Principles of International Law* (CUP Cambridge 1894) 117–118.

> The principle commonly put forward on such occasions is that of self-preservation[.][134]

Danish Fleet Incident (1807)

When the right of self-preservation became understood merely as the right of extra-territorial defence, some writers argued that the notion of extra-territorial defence included the prevention not only of harm caused by private persons but also of harm caused by a state. Some writers began to argue that the right of extra-territorial defence justified the seizure of the Danish fleet by the British force in 1807.

Hall describes the background to this incident. At the time, Denmark possessed a considerable fleet but no army capable of withstanding a potential attack from France. With Napoleon Bonaparte conquering much of Europe, the taking of the Danish fleet by France would have placed France in position for an attack on Ireland and descent upon the coast of England and Scotland. The French forces were within easy striking distance and the British government expected that they would soon move into action. To address this danger, Britain demanded that the Danish fleet be delivered into their custody. Denmark chose to regard this action as hostile, and war ensued. After several weeks of conflict, the Danish forces surrendered and their fleet was confiscated by the British navy.[135]

There is a significant difference between this incident and the other precedents discussed above. In the *Caroline* and the *Virginius* incidents, a state exercised the right of self-defence in order to prevent harm caused by private persons operating from within the territory of another state or from ships on the high seas under the flag-state jurisdiction of another state. In contrast, in the Danish fleet incident, extra-territorial action was taken against the threat posed by the potential availability of Denmark's fleet as a tool of hostility.[136] That is to say, the action was taken against (potential) harm by a state, not at the hands of private persons.

For the Danish fleet incident to be justified by the right of extra-territorial defence, the concept of extra-territorial defence needed to be expanded. However, interestingly, although this incident took place in 1807, it was not referred to as a precedent for extra-territorial defence by writers of the mid-19th century, including Phillimore, Twiss and Halleck. Hall seems to have been the first to

134 Westlake (n 133) 110–111.

135 Hall (n 58) 248–250.

136 Ibid.

describe the incident as an exercise of the right of extra-territorial defence,[137] and most of the writers who found it justified by the right of self-preservation or of self-defence were British.[138] Furthermore, it should be noted that, in this instance, war ensued as a result of the British demand; the seizure of the Danish fleet was thus effected in a state of war. This made the Danish fleet incident entirely different from the other incidents examined in the previous section. Taking these factors into account, the argument that the concept of extra-territorial defence expanded in this incident is difficult to support.[139]

Condition for the Exercise of the Right of Extra-territorial Defence

The Danish fleet incident notwithstanding, it can be argued that, as in the mid-19th century, the right of extra-territorial defence was considered exercisable when one territorial state or one flag-state could not prevent harm from befalling another or when the latter state did not have time to wait for the former to take the measures necessary to prevent such harm from befalling it.[140]

Restriction of the Right of Self-preservation

As the right of self-preservation came to be understood merely as the right of extra-territorial defence, it also came under more severe legal restriction. In fact, the right of self-defence came to be understood as the right of self-preservation restricted in this sense. John Westlake indeed contrasted 'The

137 It is certainly not easy to identify the first person to make this argument. However, I have not been able to find anyone who argued thus before Hall. In addition, other writers cited Hall as their source. Oppenheim, for example, who treated the incident as establishing a precedent for the right of self-preservation in his book of 1905, stated, 'I follow Hall's ... summary of the facts'. (Oppenheim (n 113) 179. See also AG Heffter *Le Droit International de l'Europe* (4th edn FH Geffchen (ed) J Bergson (tr) HW Müller Berlin 1883) 73 n 3).

138 Eg Hall, Oppenheim and Westlake (n 133) 119–120. Heffter's *Le droit international de l'europe,* which was annotated by F. Heinrich Geffecken, pointed out that the lawfulness of the British action in this incident was argued by 'les auteurs Anglais, tel que Mr Hall'. (Heffter (n 137) 73 n 3)

139 As noted in Section A of this chapter, 'there is no evidence that the parties [to this incident] asserted the right of self-defence and argued over those assertions'. (Taoka (n 1) 30) Although the term 'self-defence' can be found in the proclamation by the Commanders in Chief of the British Forces ('Proclamation by the Commanders in Chief of His Majesty's Forces by Sea and by Land, 16th August 1807' in *Papers Presented to the House of Commons, Relating to the Surrender of the Danish Fleet & c.* (London 1808) 3), the character of the proclamation, which was directed not to the Danish government but to the inhabitants of the area where the fleet moored, is obscure.

140 Westlake (n 133) 114–115; Oppenheim (n 113) 178–179; Hall (n 58) 245.

Alleged Inherent Right of Self-preservation'[141] with 'The True International Right of Self-preservation'[142] and rejected the idea that states could take any and all measures necessary for their security. Moreover, he argued that '[w]hat we take to be pointed out by justice as the true international right of self-preservation is merely *that of self-defence*'[143] and cited cases including the *Caroline* and the *Virginius* incidents as exemplifying the right of self-defence defined in this way.[144] Lassa Oppenheim presented a similarly restricted view of the right of self-preservation:

> It is frequently maintained that every violation is excused as long as it was caused by the motive of self-preservation, but it becomes more and more recognised that violations of other States in the interest of self-preservation are excused in cases of *necessity* only. Such acts of violence in the interest of self-preservation are exclusively excused as are necessary in self-defence[.][145]

Change in the Position of Self-preservation in the Theory of International Law

In addition to this tendency toward restricting the right of self-preservation, we should note a change in the position of the right of self-preservation in the theory of international law. In the mid-19th century, as we have seen, the right of self-preservation was understood to be one of the fundamental rights of states – so fundamental, in fact, that when it collided with other states' right to territorial inviolability, it was held to prevail.[146] However, from the late-19th to the early-20th century, this conception came to be criticised as favourable to the arbitrary use of power by strong states and as seriously injuring the sovereignty of others.[147] From such considerations, self-preservation became regarded as a somewhat abstract 'principle' or as an 'excuse', rather than as a fundamental right of states. Westlake argued:

---

141 J Westlake *International Law* (CUP Cambridge 1904) Part I (Peace), 296.

142 Ibid 299.

143 Ibid. (emphasis added)

144 Ibid 299–300, 167–168.

145 Oppenheim (n 113) 178.

146 See text to n 121 of this chapter.

147 Eg Calvo (n 109) 311. This criticism was also directed against the whole theory of fundamental rights of states.

> [S]ince the cases in which the right of self-preservation is alleged are precisely those in which it would clash with the right of independence, which is equally asserted by the advocates of abstract rights, it follows that no rules, but confusion, must result from recognising either right as absolute.[148]

Oppenheim also pointed out:

> If every State really had a *right* of self-preservation, all the States would have the duty to admit, suffer, and endure every violation done to one another in self-preservation. But such duty does not exist. On the contrary, although self-preservation is in certain cases an excuse recognised by International Law, no State is obliged patiently to submit to violations done to it by such other State as acts in self-preservation, but can repulse them. It is a fact that in certain cases violations committed in self-preservation are not prohibited by the Law of Nations. But they remain nevertheless violations and can therefore be repulsed. Self-preservation is consequently an excuse, because violations of other States are in certain exceptional cases not prohibited when they are committed for the purpose and in the interest of self-preservation, although they need not patiently be suffered and endured by the States concerned.[149]

This change in the position of the right of self-preservation theoretically predicted a re-evaluation of the *Caroline* incident, which was conducted intensively from the beginning of the 20th century to the inter-war period.

C Policing Concept of the Right of Self-Defence

The Policing Concept of the Right of Self-Defence

Our examination of several incidents has revealed that the pre-World War I right of self-defence was contrasted with resort to war. It was neither a response to war nor a justification for resorting to war. Rather, the right of self-defence was considered justification for the violation of a state's territory or its flag-state jurisdiction by another state, when the former state could not prevent harm to the latter by private persons operating from within its territory

---

148 Westlake (n 133) 112.

149 Oppenheim (n 113) 177–178.

or from ships on the high seas under its flag-state jurisdiction. Its *Rechtsgüter* was generally considered to be the life and property of a state's own citizens. In this sense, the pre-World War I right of self-defence can be called a 'policing concept of the right of self-defence'.

Pre-World War I Self-Defence and the Doctrine

From the mid-19th to the early-20th century, doctrine generally accepted this understanding of the right of self-defence. To be sure, incidents such as the *Caroline* were discussed under the rubric of the right of self-preservation. However, the right of self-defence held to have been established in those incidents was neither regarded as indistinguishable from the right of self-preservation, which was regarded as vague and comprehensive, nor considered to prevail over rights of other states. As a justification for the violation of the territory and the flag-state jurisdiction of other states, the right of self-defence had its own significance and function. The distinction between the right of self-defence and the right of self-preservation, which was seen as vague and comprehensive, became clearer when the latter came to be restricted from the late-19th century.

If the position of the right of self-preservation in international law changed, so did that of the right of self-defence. In the mid-19th century, the right of self-defence was considered a subsection of the right of self-preservation, one of the fundamental rights of states; thus, it was deemed a right. With the late-19th century criticism of the theory of fundamental rights of states gaining strength, however, the right of self-defence came to be generally regarded as a principle or an excuse, rather than as a right.

From the mid-19th to the early-20th century, then, the concept of the right of self-preservation changed drastically. Unfortunately, this change is little noted in the current literature on the right of self-defence.

Differences in Context

The function of the right of self-defence before World War I, in short, was justification for the violation of the territory or the flag-state jurisdiction of other states.[150] It related to the context of the inviolability of territory and the

150 The function could be even defined as 'abating a nuisance'. (JB Scott 'The American Punitive Expedition into Mexico' [1916] 10 AJIL 339) The analogy in international law of this concept of US tort law must be examined carefully. (T Baty *The Canons of International Law* (John Murray London 1930) 98–99; CG Fenwick *International Law* (George Allen &

freedom of the high seas. The pre-World War I right thus differed essentially from the right of self-defence that relates to the context of the use of force.

Unwin London 1924) 152) However, when we take into account that the right of self-defence in international law is often argued by analogy with self-defence in domestic criminal law, this argument provides a clear contrast between the right analogised from these criminal laws and the pre-World War I right of self-defence. See also Delivanis (n 53) 13–17; Meng (n 53) 538; Kearley (n 53) 325–330.

CHAPTER 4

The Right of Self-Defence as it Developed in the Inter-war Period

This chapter seeks to clarify the conception of self-defence constructed during the inter-war period. Toward this end, it considers first what the contemporary understanding of self-defence makes of developments of that period.

The Restrictive Interpretation and Its Reading of the Inter-war Period

As noted in Chapter 1, the restrictive and permissive interpretations of the preconditions for exercising the right of self-defence differ greatly in their views of the importance of inter-war developments. The permissive interpretation sees little significance in this period, emphasizing instead the continuity between the legally enshrined conception of self-defence that has existed since 1945 and the corresponding conception supposed to have governed from the mid-19th century. The restrictive interpretation, on the other hand, finds great importance in a redefinition effected in the inter-war years, which is held to have limited the right of self-defence to 'reaction to an actual or imminent resort to force'.[1]

A reading of the inter-war period through the lens of the restrictive interpretation of the right of self-defence leads to two important claims. The first is that the right of self-defence in the interwar period no longer included the 19th-century right, a right defined 'in terms of self-help'.[2] At the same time, it provides a basis for Brownlie's contention that '[i]t is not surprising that the draftsmen of the United Nations Charter should define [the right of self-defence] in Article 51 by reference to the occurrence of an "armed attack"'.[3]

As we will see in Section A below, the restrictive interpretation's view of the inter-war right of self-defence as limited to 'reaction to an actual or imminent resort to force' is tenable, at least with respect to the basic function of the right of self-defence as defined by treaties and draft treaties of the interwar period

1 I Brownlie *International Law and the Use of Force by States* (Clarendon Press Oxford 1963) 250.

2 Ibid 231.

3 Ibid 256. The drafting history of the United Nations Charter itself will be examined in Chapter 6.

 | DOI 10.1163/9789004355002_006

concerning the legal prohibition of war. We will also see, however, that we must be cautious before affirming on that basis either of the above contentions.

'Resort to Force' and 'Armed Attack'

There is a difference between claiming that self-defence consists in a 'reaction to an actual or imminent resort to force' and claiming that the right of self-defence can be exercised only where armed attack has occurred. 'Resort to force' and 'armed attack' are not two names for the same thing. Brownlie himself states clearly that '[not] every unlawful use of force will involve an armed attack ' in the Article 51 sense of the latter term.[4] This distinction poses a question to which Brownlie provides no clear answer: if during the inter-war period self-defence was conceived as 'reaction to an actual or imminent resort to force', why does Article 51 refer not to 'use of force' but instead to the narrower 'armed attack'?

Bowett seizes on the gap between these two concepts to argue that neither before nor after 1945 was armed attack the precondition for exercising the right of self-defence. Emphasizing the distinction between 'armed attack' and 'aggression', Bowett argues that '[t]he identification of aggression and an armed attack is a gross over-simplification of a complex problem'.[5] Bowett, however, can hardly be said to have formulated his distinction between these phenomena on the basis of close study of state practice of the inter-war period.

Neither the advocates of the restrictive interpretation, then, nor those who argue for the permissive interpretation, seem to have considered very thoroughly the scope of preconditions justifying the exercise of the right of self-defence established in the inter-war period. In this chapter, we will try to gain a fuller picture of the right of self-defence which the inter-war period put in place. After clarifying the basic function of self-defence recognized in the inter-war period (in Section A), we will proceed to consider, from a number of perspectives, the problem of the scope of preconditions for the exercise of the right (in Section B).

Relationship between the Right of Self-Defence as Developed in the Inter-war Period and the Pre-World War I Right

As a final preliminary before examining the inter-war period directly, we must note that even if we accept that the inter-war period defined self-defence as 'reaction to an actual or imminent resort to force', it does not quite follow, as

4 Ibid 365.

5 DW Bowett *Self-Defence in International Law* (Manchester University Press Manchester 1958) 192.

the restrictive interpretation would have it, that the customary right of self-defence established in the 19th century ceased thereafter to exist. As we saw in Chapter 3, contra the restrictive interpretation's emphasis on the similarity between self-defence and self-preservation as understood before World War I, these two conceptions were in that period quite distinct. Further, as shown in Chapter 2, the claim of a sharp break between pre- and post-World War I conceptions of the right of self-defence is not based on close consideration of the relationship between pre- and post-War norms around this concept. It is based, rather, on observation of a fragment of inter-war state practice, the fact that in this period the right of self-defence was typically discussed in the context of the use of force. Reconsidering state practice over the two periods, with the problem in mind of how to characterise the normative relationship between them, will likely yield a different set of conclusions. This reconsideration will be presented in Chapter 5.

A The Basic Function of Self-Defence: Resistance to Acts of Aggression

This section seeks to clarify the basic function assigned to the right of self-defence[6] in the inter-war period through a consideration of treaties and draft treaties produced in the process of outlawing war under the League of Nations.[7]

---

6 To be sure, as Stone has correctly pointed out (J Stone 'Book Review (reviewing Brownlie (n 1))' [1965] 59 AJIL 400), the term 'right of self-defence' was not consistently used in preference to such phrases as 'legitimate defence' and 'legitimate self-defence', and it cannot be assumed that all of these terms referred to exactly the same concept. However, they were not used in such a way as to suggest any intended difference in meaning. The English version of the Rhineland Agreement, for example, used 'legitimate defence' simply as a translation of the French 'légitime défense'. It is also worth noting the view that the conception of self-defence occupied different positions in continental and British legal systems, which are reflected in different countries' understandings of the right of self-defence in international law. See H Nakanishi 'Kokusai Chitsujo wo meguru Ho to Seiji ni kansuru Ikkosatsu (A Study about Law and Politics over the International Order)' in *Kyoto Daigaku Hogakubu Soritsu Hyakushunen Kinen Ronbunshu* (*A Festschrift in Celebration of Kyoto University Faculty of Law's Centennial Anniversary of Foundation*) (Yuhikaku Tokyo 1999) vol 2, 515–543 (*in Japanese*).

7 The view exists that the origins of the inter-war period's conception of the right of self-defence lies in the late-19th century right of neutrals to resist violations of their neutrality by belligerent states. (See eg A Verdross 'Règles générales du droit international de la paix' [1929] 30 RCADI 482 n 25) This view takes violations of neutrality as illegal assault, on an analogy between the right of self-defence in international law and legitimate defence in

Development of the Outlawry of War

In the 19th century, states were considered to have a general right or freedom to resort to war.[8] Early in the 20th century, a number of treaties were concluded prohibiting recourse to war or hostility in certain cases, such as the Convention on the Limitation of the Employment of Force for the Recovery of Contract Debts (the Drago-Porter Convention)[9] and the bilateral Bryan treaties[10] which the US concluded with many states in 1913 and 1914. Outlawry of war in earnest, however, began only in the wake of the cataclysm of World War I. In the inter-war period, a large number of treaties restricting or prohibiting recourse to war were agreed, some of which came into force and some of which did not. These treaties and draft treaties, while restricting or prohibiting war, also recognised, whether explicitly or tacitly, a right of self-defence which signatories might exercise. A study of these documents should do much to clarify the basic function of the right of self-defence discussed in this context of efforts to outlaw war. Among the most important of these documents are: the Covenant of the League of Nations (1919), the Draft Treaty of Mutual Assistance (1923), the Protocol for the Pacific Settlement of International Disputes (1924), the Locarno Treaties (1925), the Pact of Paris (1928) and the draft Act Relating to the Definition of the Aggressor (1933).

1 *The Covenant of the League of Nations (1919)*

The Covenant and the Outlawry of War

The Covenant of the League of Nations was concluded as part of the Treaty of Versailles which ended the Great War.[11] In its preamble, the High Contracting Parties accepted 'obligations not to resort to war'. As is well known, however, the outlawry of war in the League Covenant had several gaps. While Article 10 obligated the signatories 'to respect and preserve as against external aggression the territorial integrity and existing political independence of all Members', it did not prohibit war more generally. Though it established a moratorium

domestic law. This view, however, is sufficiently rare that we can safely consider only the conception of self-defence discussed in the context of outlawing war under the League.

8 Brownlie (n 1) 19–26; Y Dinstein *War, Aggression and Self-Defence* (5th edn CUP Cambridge 2011) 75–79.

9 W Benedek 'Drago-Porter Convention (1907)' in R Bernhardt (ed) *Encyclopedia of Public International Law* (Elsevier Amsterdam 1992) vol 1, 1102–1103.

10 HJ Schlochauer 'Bryan Treaties (1913/1914)' in ibid 509–511.

11 With regard to the drafting history of the Covenant, see H Miller *The Drafting of the Covenant* (GP Putnam's Sons New York 1928); F Couveinhes-Matsumoto 'Les travaux préparatoires' in R Kolb (ed) *Commentaire sur le Pacte de la Société des Nations* (Bruylant Bruxells 2014) 7–78.

during which no Member country would resort to war in the event of a dispute with another Member, it did not go so far as to prohibit resort to war after the moratorium's expiration.

Again, while Article 12, paragraph 1 provided that 'if there should arise between [Members] any dispute likely to lead to a rupture they will submit the matter either to arbitration or to judicial settlement or to enquiry by the Council' (or, in other words, prohibited resort to war prior to submitting a dispute for resolution)[12], Article 15, paragraph 7 provided that

> If the Council fails to reach a report which is unanimously agreed to by the members thereof, other than the Representatives of one or more of the parties to the dispute, the Members of the League reserve to themselves the right to take such action as they shall consider necessary for the maintenance of right and justice.

Similarly, while Article 12, paragraph 1 stated that Members must 'in no case to resort to war until three months after the award by the arbitrators or the judicial decision, or the report by the Council', this merely called for a sort of cooling-off period; it did not prohibit resort to war thereafter. The Covenant prohibited resort to war, in fact, only where a party to a dispute had complied with either a decision rendered on the dispute by an approved tribunal (Article 13, paragraph 4) or a Council report approved by all Members of the League (Article 15, paragraph 6).[13]

It is possible to regard the Covenant as not so much attempting a total prohibition of war as distinguishing lawful from unlawful war.[14]

The Covenant of the League of Nations and the Right of Self-Defence

The Covenant said nothing about a right of self-defence. It was generally understood, however, that signatories reserved that right.[15] Wehberg, for

---

12 H Wehberg 'Le problème de la mise de la guerre hors la loi' [1928] RCADI 163. Formulating the requirement in this way reflected an understanding of war as the ultimate means of resolving conflict.

13 On the structure of the Covenant's outlawing of war, see Wehberg (n 12) 163–164; Brownlie (n 1) 55–65; A Randelszhofer 'Use of Force' in R Bernhardt (ed) *Encyclopedia of Public International Law* (Elsevier Amsterdam 2000) vol 4, 1248.

14 AM Rifaat *International Aggression* (Almqvist & Wiksell Internationa Stockholm 1979) 45, 78; R Kolb 'De la S.D.N. à l'O.N.U. en matière de maintien de la paix' in Kolb (ed) (n 11) 1349–1358.

15 Brownlie (n 1) 61; Bowett (n 5) 124; K Nagy *Le problème de la légitime défense en droit international* (Acta Universitatis Szegediensis Szeged 1992) 21; D Anzilotti *Cours de droit international* (G Gidel (tr) Librairie de Recueil Sirey Paris 1929) 506; A Cavaglieri 'Règles

example, stated plainly that '[d]'après le Pacte, la guerre défensive n'est jamais interdite'.[16] This was tacitly assumed throughout the attempts made in the League era, which we will consider below, to outlaw war; and explicitly confirmed in the process of amending the Covenant to bring it into harmony with the 1928 General Treaty for Renunciation of War as an Instrument of National Policy (the Kellogg-Briand Pact, also called the Pact of Paris).[17]

The relationship of self-defence to the Covenant, then, was a matter of the relationship of the right of self-defence to the prohibition of war. Indeed, it was precisely the fact that the Covenant outlawed war, albeit only partially, that arguably provided a rationale for the right of self-defence in international law:[18]

> Tant que la guerre, bien qu'elle pût paraître moralement condemnable, était juridiquement licite, il n'y avait pas place pour les notions juridiques d'agression et de légitime defense. Le Pacte de la Société des Nations, en interdisant dans certains cas la guerre, a introduit dans le droit international la notion de légitime defense.[19]

As the resort to war became in some cases unlawful, so at the same time was the legitimacy of the right of self-defence, in the sense of 'la guerre défensive' or 'la defense militaire d'un pays',[20] confirmed.

Self-Defence and Outlawry of War – Further Development

If the Covenant of the League did not mention self-defence, we will see below that the work of filling in its 'gaps' would make the basic function of self-defence clearer. In the effort to make the prohibition of war more absolute, it was necessary to formulate explicitly the exceptions under which war could be permitted; as one of those exceptions, self-defence would come to be discussed in more concrete terms.

---

générales du droit de la paix' [1929] 26 RCADI 556; É Giraud 'La théorie de la légitime défense' [1934] 49 RCADI 715; R Ago 'Le délit international' [1939] 68 RCADI 540.

16 Wehberg (n 12) 164. See also Brownlie (n 1) 61.

17 'Amendment of the Covenant of the League of Nations in Order to Bring It into Harmony with the Pact of Paris (Report Submitted by the Sub-Committee)' in [1931] 94 League of Nations OJ Spec Suppl 146.

18 See Chapter 2, Section B.2.

19 Giraud (n 15) 715. See also R Kolb 'La légitime défense des états au xixe siècle et pendant l'époque de la Société des Nations' in Kolb (ed) (n 11) 1315–1328.

20 Wehberg (n 12) 164.

2 *The Protocol for the Pacific Settlement of International Disputes (1924)*

The Draft Treaty of Mutual Assistance

The opening salvo in the fight to fill in the Covenant's gaps was the Draft Treaty of Mutual Assistance, proposed to the Fourth Assembly of the League of Nations.[21] The Draft Treaty announced that a war of aggression constituted an international crime, obligated signatories not to commit that crime, and provided for assistance of a country subjected to such a war. The drafters stopped short of referring to 'self-defence', however,[22] and strong opposition to the Draft resulted, in any case, in its rejection by the Assembly.[23]

---

21 For the text of this Draft Treaty, see 'Report Submitted by the Third Committee to the Assembly' in [1923] 13 League of Nations OJ Spec Suppl 403. Useful sources for overviews and assessments of the Draft Treaty include League of Nations *Ten Years of World Co-operation* (Secretariat of the League of Nations Geneva 1930) 55–65; FP Walters *A History of the League of Nations* (OUP Oxford 1952) 216–230; and T Ueda *Chiikiteki Anzen Hosho no Shiteki Kenkyu* (*Historical Study of Regional Security*) (Yamakawa Tokyo 1989) 42–45 (*in Japanese*). Also see T Sogawa 'Shudanteki Jiei: Iwayuru US Formula no Ronriteki Kozo to Genjitsuteki Kino (Collective Self-defence: Logical Structure and Actual Function of So-Called US Formula)' in T Sogawa (ed) *Kokusai Seiji Shiso to Taigai Ishiki* (*International Political Thought and Foreign Consciousness*) (Sobunsha Tokyo 1977) 461–466 (*in Japanese*).

It is worth describing briefly the background to the Draft Treaty. Article 16 of the League Covenant provided for sanctions against any Member who should 'resort to war in disregard of its covenants under Articles 12, 13, or 15'. Although the question of how this clause should be enforced was discussed at the first General Assembly, a resolution taken by the Second General Assembly confirmed that each Member state would decide for itself whether any of these provisions had been violated. With application of the Article 16 sanction provisions thus left to individual Members, the effectiveness of the League's security system was severely compromised. A movement arose to improve the Covenant's enforcement provisions and thus to ensure assistance to countries faced with Covenant-violating war. At the same time, the need for ensuring assistance adequate to maintenance of Members' security against unlawful war was pointed out in connection with Article 8 provisions relating to disarmament. Drafting of a mutual assistance treaty was accordingly proposed to the Third Assembly, and a draft was presented to the Fourth Assembly.

22 If the term was not used, it can nevertheless be argued that the concept of self-defence established in the inter-war period had already been accepted in the argument concerning this draft treaty.

23 For Member country reactions to the Draft Treaty, see 'Treaty of Mutual Assistance: Replies from Governments' in [1924] 26 League of Nations OJ Spec Suppl 129–168. See also Rifaat (n 14) 54; and BB Ferencz *Defining International Aggression* (Oceana New York 1975) vol 1, 13–14.

Protocol for the Pacific Settlement of International Disputes

Following this failure, the Fifth Assembly recommended acceptance of the Protocol for the Pacific Settlement of International Disputes (also called the Geneva Protocol), based on a joint report by Czech foreign minister Edvard Benes and Greece's representative to the League, Nikolaos Politis. In its basic conception, the Protocol called for (1) an absolute prohibition of aggressive war; (2) establishment of a collective security system requiring the signatories jointly to impose sanctions, including military force, against aggressors; (3) introduction of compulsory procedures for settling international disputes; and (4) a general obligation to limit and reduce armaments.[24] Though highly praised as a great step toward the peaceful resolution of international disputes and the outlawing of war,[25] the Protocol never came into force, failing to overcome the opposition of Britain and others and be ratified by the requisite number of countries.[26] While the text of the Protocol itself does not refer to 'self-defence', the right of self-defence was explicitly discussed and accepted by the subcommittee report on which the Protocol was based; and this report represents the typical understanding of the right of self-defence as it developed in the inter-war period.

The Right of Self-Defence as Resistance to Aggressive War

As noted above, the absolute prohibition of aggressive war was one of the defining concepts of the Geneva Protocol. Indeed, it prohibited all war among signatories 'except in case of resistance to acts of aggression or when acting in agreement with the Council or the Assembly of the League of Nations in accordance with the provisions of the Covenant and of the present Protocol'.

---

24 'Protocol for the Pacific Settlement of International Disputes' in [1924] 23 League of Nations OJ Spec Suppl 498–502; FAF von der Heydte 'Geneva Protocol for the Pacific Settlement of International Disputes (1924)' in R Bernhardt (ed) *Encyclopedia of International Law* (Elsevier Amsterdam 1995) vol 2, 529–530. See also H Wehberg 'Le Protocole de Genève' [1925] 7 RCADI 1; DH Miller *The Geneva Protocol* (Macmillan Company New York 1925); PM Brown 'The Geneva Protocol' [1925] 19 AJIL 338. On the background to the adoption of the Protocol, PJN Baker *The Geneva Protocol for the Pacific Settlement of International Disputes* (PS King London 1925).

25 JW Garner 'The Geneva Protocol for the Pacific Settlement of International Disputes' [1925] 19 AJIL 123. See also C Eagleton 'The Attempt to Define Aggression' [1930] 264 Int'l Conciliation 577, 602; Brownlie (n 1) 70.

26 Britain's opposition, widely seen as a critical factor behind this failure, has been attributed to her unease with the imposition of the Protocol's compulsory procedures and to a fear of being drawn into wars unrelated to her national interests. (WR Bisschop 'The Locarno Pact' [1925] 11 Transactions of the Grotius Society 86–87)

(Article 2) That what the Protocol was meant to prohibit was aggressive war alone, Politis stated plainly:

> The general principle of the Protocol is the prohibition of aggressive war.
>
> …
>
> The prohibition affects only aggressive war. It does not, of course, extend to defensive war. The right of legitimate self-defence continues, as it must, to be respected. The State attacked retains complete liberty to resist by all means in its power any acts of aggression of which it may be the victim.[27]

As Politis's commentary above makes clear, the Geneva Protocol was understood to have the function of permitting 'defensive war' or 'resistance to aggression'. It framed a right of self-defence within the context of prohibition of aggressive war.

3 *Rhineland Pact* (*Locarno Treaties*) (1925)

The Locarno Treaties

In the wake of the failure to strengthen world security through the Geneva Protocol, which aimed at a fortified system of universal collective defence, the view gained currency that treaties among particular nations promised more progress. This position was articulated most forcefully by Britain, whose government held:

> that the best way of dealing with the situation is … to supplement the Covenant by making special arrangements in order to meet special needs[,] … by knitting together the nations most immediately concerned, and whose differences might lead to a renewal of strife, by means of treaties framed with the sole object of maintaining, as between themselves, an unbroken peace.[28]

27 'Arbitration, Security and Reduction of Armaments: General Report submitted to the Fifth Assembly on behalf of the First and Third Committees by M. Politis (Greece), Rapporteur for the First Committee, and M. Benes (Czechoslovakia), Rapporteur for the Third Committee' in [1924] 24 League of Nations OJ Spec Suppl 121.

28 'Statement by the representative of Great Britain' in [1925] 6 League of Nations OJ 450. See also Bisschop (n 26) 85–91.

Effort on these lines culminated in the Locarno Treaties, signed 16 October 1925. Among these five treaties, annexed to the Final Protocol of the Locarno Conference convened from 5 October, the so-called 'Rhineland Pact', by which Germany, Belgium, France, Britain, and Italy exchanged guarantees of mutual security, is particularly important for this study.[29] The core elements of this Pact were (1) an absolute prohibition of any attack or invasion; (2) an obligation to assist a country subjected to any such aggression that might fail to be deterred; and (3) an obligation to resolve international disputes peacefully.[30]

The Right of Self-Defence as Resistance to Attack, Invasion, or Resort to War

Under Article 2 of the Rhineland Pact, 'Germany and Belgium, and also Germany and France, mutually undertake that they will in no case attack or invade each other or resort to war against each other'. This Article immediately lays out a self-defence exception, however: 'This stipulation shall not, however, apply in the case of: ... The exercise of the right of legitimate defence, that is to say, resistance to a violation of the undertaking contained in the previous paragraph'.[31] As in the Geneva Protocol, then, a right of self-defence is presented in the context of a prohibition of aggression; an exception to a general

29 The four other treaties were arbitration agreements which Germany concluded with Belgium, Czechoslovakia, France, and Poland. Concluded at the same time were French treaties mutual assistance treaties with Poland and Czechoslovakia. See 54 League of Nations Treaty Series (hereinafter LNTS) 289–363.

30 On the Locarno Treaties and the Rhineland Pact in particular, see Bisschop (n 26) 79–115; C Fenwick 'The Legal Significance of the Locarno Agreements' [1926] 20 AJIL 108–111; Wehberg (n 12) 194–206; W Morvay 'Locarno Treaties (1925)' in R Bernhardt (ed) *Encyclopedia of Public International Law* (Elsevier Amsterdam 1997) vol 3, 242–245; Ueda (n 21) 53–69.

31 This is not the only exception recognised by Article 2. Article 2(2) allows military action pursuant to Article 16 of the Covenant of the League of Nations, and Article 2(3) allows action taken pursuant to a decision by the Assembly or the Council of the League of Nations or in violation of Article 15, paragraph 7 of the Covenant. A 'flagrant breach of Articles 42 or 43' of the Treaty of Versailles, pertaining to 'the assembly of armed forces in the demilitarised zone' established by that treaty was also specified as a condition justifying resort to war. (Article 2(1)) Furthermore, as the Locarno Treaties did not define 'aggression' as clearly as did the Geneva Protocol, the uncertainty that existed prior to these treaties over what would justify recourse to war persisted. (See Eagleton (n 25) 604) This point will be discussed further in Section B.1.(d) of this chapter.

prohibition is advanced which justifies resistance to invasion, aggression, or resort to war.

4 *The Pact of Paris (1928)*

The inter-war movement toward outlawing war would culminate in the Pact of Paris, concluded in August 1928 to come into force in July 1929.[32] This treaty originated in French foreign minister Briand's proposal of a bilateral French–US treaty renouncing war. The US, however, hoping rather for a multilateral treaty joining all the major powers, would take the lead in drafting the Pact. This treaty is frequently called the Kellogg-Briand Pact, after France's foreign minister and Frank Kellogg, the US secretary of state.

The central conceptions of this treaty were an absolute prohibition of the resort to war (Article 1) and an obligation on all signatories to settle their disputes by peaceful means (Article 2). By the end of 1929, 57 countries (about 80 percent of the countries of the world) had ratified the treaty; by the end of 1938 it had been ratified by 63 (almost 90 percent). Moreover, with the conclusion by Latin American states in October 1933 of the Saavedra Lamas Treaty, a treaty closely matching the Pact of Paris in its fundamental content, nearly all the countries of the world came to assume essentially the same obligation of renouncing war.[33]

Recognition of the Right of Self-Defence

The Pact of Paris, comprising but two short substantive Articles, contains no provisions on a right of self-defence *per se*. However, during negotiations over the Pact, many countries, including the US, the primary drafter of the text, repeatedly stated that the right of self-defence would be reserved to the treaty's signatory states. That a right of self-defence existed was widely accepted. British foreign minister Austen Chamberlain, for example, stated this belief plainly:

> After studying the wording of article 1 of the United States draft, His Majesty's Government do not think that its terms exclude action which a State may be forced to take in self-defence. Mr. Kellogg has made it

32 CD Wallace 'Kellogg-Briand Pact' in R Bernhardt (ed) (n 24) 76–79. See also the sources cited by Wallace. For a useful narrative of the events culminating in the conclusion and adoption of this Pact, see Y Onuma *Senso Sekininron Josetsu* (*Introduction to the Issues of Responsibility for War*) (University of Tokyo Press Tokyo 1975) 84–88 (*in Japanese*).

33 A total of 69 of the world's 71 countries. 'Rights and Duties of States in Case of Aggression: Draft Convention, with Comment, Prepared by the Research in International Law of Harvard Law School' [1939] 33 AJIL Suppl 824.

> clear … that he regards the right of self-defence as inalienable, and His Majesty's Government are disposed to think that on this question no addition to the text is necessary.[34]

Scope and Function of Self-Defence

In a June 1928 note to other signatory governments, Kellogg stated that explicit reference in the Pact to a right of self-defence would create difficulties similar to those posed by attempting to include in the Pact a definition of 'aggression'. The definitions of aggression and self-defence, he said, were two sides of the same coin.[35] He thus suggested that against aggression the right of self-defence might be exercised. He also stated that the right of self-defence 'is inherent in every sovereign state and is implicit in every treaty. Every nation is free at all times and regardless of treaty provisions to defend its territory from attack or invasion'.[36]

These statements of the Secretary of State are often taken as expressing an official view of the US government,[37] and upon this supposition some contemporaries asserted that the right of self-defence reserved to signatories of the Pact was exercisable only against uses of force that violated the Pact's provisions.[38] In this context, the right of self-defence has been understood as an exception to an absolute prohibition of the resort to war or as justification for resorting to war.

---

34 'Sir Austen Chamberlain to Mr. Houghton, May 19, 1928' in DK Adams (ed) *British Documents on Foreign Affairs: Reports and Papers from the Foreign Office Confidential Print, Part II From the First World to the Second World War, Series C North America, 1919–1939* (University Publications of America Maryland 1995) vol 18, 132. See also 'The Japanese Minister for Foreign Affairs (Tanaka) to the American Ambassador (MacVeagh)' in The Department of State *Treaty for the Renunciation of War; Text of the Treaty, Notes Exchanged, Instruments of Ratification and of Adherence and Other Papers* (Government Printing Office Washington 1933) 48–51; 'The British Secretary of State for Foreign Affairs (Chamberlain), on behalf of the Union of South Africa, to the American Chargé (Atherton)' in ibid 55–56; 'Note of the Government of the United States to the Governments of Belgium, Czechoslovakia, France, Germany, Great Britain, Irish Free State, Italy, Japan and Poland, Delivered at the Respective Foreign Offices, June 23, 1928' in ibid 57.

35 'Note of the Government of the United States, June 23, 1928' (n 34) 57.

36 Ibid.

37 M Yanagihara 'Iwayuru "Musabetsu Sensokan" to Senso no Ihoka (The "Idea of Non-Discriminating War" in Japan and the Doctrine of Carl Schmitt)' [2001] 20 Sekaiho Nenpo (Yearbook of World Law) 27 (*in Japanese*).

38 SC Stratis *Le pacte générale de renonciation à la guerre* (M Rivière Paris 1931) 150; M Descamps 'Le droit international nouveau; l'influence de la condamnation de la guerre sur l'évolution juridique internationale' [1930] 31 RCADI 469–471; Brownlie (n 1) 239–241.

This is arguably but one aspect of the right of self-defence reserved to states under the Pact of Paris. The US Senator Claude Swanson, in defending the treaty on the Senate floor, certainly implied as much. In a statement addressing French concerns, Kellogg had stated, among other things, that the treaty would in no way impair any state's right to defend its territory. Against the suggestion that this mention of a state's territory restricted the right of self-defence to actions necessary to defend that territory against attack or invasion, Swanson advanced the view that 'naming the territory ... is simply an illustration and ... a minor illustration can not repeal or abolish the general term relating to self-defence'.[39]

In Chapter 5, we will consider in greater detail the implications of the right of self-defence recognised in the Pact of Paris. For the moment, we need only to bear in mind that, at a minimum, this Pact joined the other treaties of the inter-war period which we have considered in treating self-defence within the context of absolute prohibition of resort to war and recognising self-defence as justification for resorting to war against attack or invasion of a state's territory.

5 *Summary of Section A*

Throughout the efforts to outlaw war in the inter-war period, a right of self-defence was consistently acknowledged and progressively established as a meaningful conception. The conception was discussed in a context of outlawing war or aggression, and the right of self-defence was understood to possess

39 [1928–1929] 70 Cong Rec 1181. See also, ibid 1122–1123. Kellogg and the treaty's Senate supporters had at once to answer the criticism that the treaty unduly restricted the right of self-defence and the opposite criticism, that in leaving every country to decide for itself what its self-defence required, the treaty restricted the right not at all. (See eg RS Morris 'The Pact of Paris for the Renunciation of War: Its Merits and Effect in International Law', [1929] 33 Proc Am Soc'y IL 88, 90–91) Kellogg did indeed maintain that every country must determine whether resort to war was necessary for its own defence. ('Note of the Government of the United States, June 23, 1928' (n 34) 57) Crucially, however, Kellogg added that '[i]f [the country claiming self-defence] has a good case, the world will applaud it and not condemn it; but a nation must answer to the tribunal of public opinion as to whether its claim of the right of self-defense is an adequate justification for it to go war'. ([1928–1929] 70 Cong Rec 1063) To be sure, Kellogg did not propose to establish a formal body charged with assessing claims of self-defence, and this can perhaps be judged a defect in the treaty. It does not follow, however, that each country ultimately had the right to judge the legitimacy of its own self-defence claims; and Kellogg certainly rejected that position. The thesis that the treaty did not remove all claims of self-defence from the realm of justiciable questions is well argued by H Lauterpacht *The Function of Law in the International Community* (Clarendon Press Oxford 1933) 178–180. Section B.2 of this chapter will address this matter in the context of considering practice under the League.

the function of justifying resistance, or defensive war, as against aggressive acts. The *Rechtsgut* of self-defence was simply the safety of the nation. This understanding of the right of self-defence recognised by the treaties and draft treaties of the period was widely accepted by contemporary commenters.[40]

The inter-war right of self-defence was thus thoroughly different from that which existed before the war. What, then, was the relationship between the pre-war and inter-war conceptions of self-defence? Did the former simply disappear with the advent of the latter? Before addressing this question directly in Chapter 5, it is worth considering in more detail the scope of the inter-war conception of the right of self-defence.

B Scope of the Inter-war Right

As noted at the beginning of this chapter, doctrine on the scope of preconditions for exercising the inter-war right of self-defence was not developed in much detail. Brownlie acknowledges this: 'The state practice does not provide any precise definition of aggression, attack, resort to force, *et cetera*'.[41] He maintains, however, that state practice nevertheless did place significant limits on the exercise of the right of self-defence, which he frames is a variety of ways. 'A feature common to the treaty practice relating to obligations of non-aggression and the like…' he writes, 'is the preoccupation with the use of force, particularly attack or invasion'.[42] Elsewhere, he writes that 'when

40 Anzilotti (n 15) 507; H Kelsen 'Unrecht und Unrechtsfolge im Völkerrecht' [1932] 12 Zeitschrift für Öffentliches Recht 481, 562–564; Giraud (n 15) 712–787. See also L Oppenheim *International Law* (5th edn H Lauterpacht (ed) Longmans, Green & Co London 1935) vol 2, 157–160. Considering the right of self-defence strictly in the context of outlawry of war, as the inter-war commentators generally did, and focusing only on the right of self-defence as defined in the treaties and draft treaties of the period, was not the only course available. This is clear given what we have learned about the conception of self-defence at work in the *Caroline* and other incidents, as we have seen in Chapter 2 and especially in Section A of that chapter. If the *Caroline* incident is understood as establishing a precedent pertaining to a state of necessity, the right of self-defence at work there is framed as a matter of defensive war or resistance to aggression. But the right of self-defence for which the incident established a precedent can also be seen more broadly. The relationship between the broader and narrower conceptions is discussed in Chapter 2. A above, and will be further considered in Chapter 5 below, especially in its Sections A and B.

41 Brownlie (n 1) 232.

42 Ibid 247.

justified use of force was defined in state practice it was frequently in terms of legitimate defense against armed attack, or threat thereof',[43] and that 'apart from Article 16 [of the Covenant], force was justified only in reaction against some armed attack or threat of force'.[44]

These claims are correct, as far as they go. It must be noted, however, not only that they do not rest on any detailed examination of inter-war state practice, but also that the scope of actions that might fall comfortably enough under these descriptions to justify action in self-defence is extremely broad, extending from armed attack to statements of intent to resort to force and even to providing support to an aggressor state.

In so far as Brownlie seeks to demonstrate only that the 19th century right of self-defence had ceased to exist in the inter-war period, his cursory review of common features of the period's treaties and his argument from general tendencies of the period are appropriate.[45] It suffices for his argument to emphasize the difference between the inter-war tendency and the 19th century right of self-defence, which he considered to have been 'defined in terms of self-help'.[46] However, Brownlie makes his reading of the prior conduct problem a basis of his argument that the right of self-defence under the UN Charter is restricted to cases of armed attack,[47] and this raises a difficulty. As is clear from the list of actions justifying self-defence which Brownlie himself presents, the inter-war right of self-defence was not in fact limited to cases of armed attack. As Brownlie acknowledges, the scope of the self-defence right in the inter-war treaties encompassed a variety of acts other than armed attack, and, moreover, varied by treaty. The problem of preceding acts thus calls for more detailed inquiry.

Structure of this Section

We begin by considering the problem of how to define aggression (in Subsection 1). As we have seen, justifiable self-defence under the League Covenant was generally considered to amount to resistance to aggression. Aggression, however, was not clearly defined. The scope of precedent acts justifying the exercise of self-defence was thus unfortunately vague, as we will see in Subsections 2 and 3. In Subsection 4, however, we will note, in connection with the inter-war precursor of the right of collective self-defence, that certain acts were definitely recognised as within the scope of precedent acts. That the

43 Ibid 231–232.

44 Ibid 232.

45 This issue will be discussed further in Chapter 5.

46 Brownlie (n 1) 231.

47 Ibid 255–256.

notion of precedent acts did have recognised meaning, even if the notion was far from well defined, is key to understanding the preconditions to the exercise of self-defence under the United Nations Charter. That, however, will be discussed in Chapter 6.

1 *The Problem of Defining Aggression*

As the right of self-defence under the League Covenant was generally understood as the right to resist aggression, the need arises to consider what was meant by 'aggression'. As was said at the time, 'to ask what is legitimate defense is to ask who is the aggressor'.[48] On the latter question, of course, depended the actions which other countries were obliged to take; formulating a clear definition of aggression was thus considered absolutely essential.

This, however, was recognised as 'one of the greatest, if not the greatest, obstacles to all plans for the control of war'.[49] Different treaties defined this all-important term differently, and in some treaties the very attempt to define it was abandoned.[50]

If the major inter-war treaties and draft treaties on the outlawry of war present no common, generally accepted definition of aggression, then to describe such consensus as may have existed, and to clarify differences among alternative contemporary understandings, we can ask what approaches to overcoming the definitional problem were attempted, what these implied regarding the scope of precedent acts, and how the definitional problem was discussed.

(a) The Covenant of the League of Nations

Article 10 of the Covenant read as follows:

> The Members of the League undertake to respect and preserve as against external aggression the territorial integrity and existing political independence of all Members of the League. In case of any such aggression or in case of any threat or danger of such aggression the

48 Eagleton (n 25) 611. See also Giraud (n 15) 747; Oppenheim (n 40) 159; JT Shotwell *War as an Instrument of National Policy and Its Renunciation in the Pact of Paris* (Harcourt New York 1929) 207.

49 Eagleton (n 25) 583.

50 For general arguments on the inter-war definition of aggression, see MW Komarnicki 'La définition de l'agresseur dans le droit international moderne' [1949] 75 RCADI 1–68; Ferencz (n 23) 6–36; Rifaat (n 14) 41–102; C Rousseau *Le droit des conflits armés* (Pedone Paris 1983) 575–581.

> Council shall advise upon the means by which this obligation shall be fulfilled.

The focus was thus obviously placed on 'aggression'. This does not mean, however, that 'aggression' was made the preceding act that would establish military action as an exercise of the right of self-defence. As we have noted, the Covenant did not refer explicitly to self-defence; and even if we say that self-defence was understood as 'defensive war' or the defence of the nation by military means, it is difficult to find evidence of a conscious attempt to define the preceding acts that would make military action defensive. As no preceding actions were defined that might justify a claim of self-defence, even 'aggression' was not assigned this function.

Moreover, as has been frequently pointed out, 'aggression' in the Covenant was not defined.[51] This is not to say that the term as it appears in the Covenant had no meaning; its use in Article 10 was intended to give legal significance to this term, which had been used in diplomacy and treaties since before the Great War but not as designating a properly legal concept. The Covenant effectively defined aggression as involving the violation of a state's territorial integrity or political independence and provided that the Council should recommend measures to be taken in the event of such violation or the 'threat or danger' thereof occurring.[52]

Nevertheless, it must be recognized that 'aggression' does not appear in the Covenant outside of Article 10. The later provisions on maintenance and restoration of peace, including the Article 16 provisions on sanctions against violations of the Covenant, refer rather to 'war'. Article 10 was accordingly criticised as standing in no clear relation to the provisions of Articles 11 through 15, and it would be difficult to argue that 'aggression' was given any strict legal definition, at least at the time of the Covenant's drafting.[53]

(b) The Draft Treaty of Mutual Assistance

In the drafting of this first attempt to fill gaps in the League Covenant by treaty,[54] the definition of aggression was taken up as one of the most important problems to be addressed.

---

51 Eagleton (n 25) 590.

52 Rifaat (n 14) 46, 3–38. See also J Ray *Commentaire du Pacte de la Société des Nations selon la politique et la jurisprudence des organs de la Société* (Sirey Paris 1930) 343–346.

53 Eagleton (n 25) 590. See also Rifaat (n 14) 46; Ray (n 52) 362–363.

54 See n 21 of this chapter.

The League Council's 'Complete Discretion'

The Draft Treaty declared that 'aggressive war is an international crime'[55] and prohibited signatory countries from engaging in it (Article 1). It also committed signatories to provide aid to a country subjected to aggressive war (Article 2). In the event of hostilities arising among two or more countries, the League Council was to determine which country or countries had suffered aggression and whether the country or countries suffering aggression could demand assistance (Article 4).[56]

As the system of mutual assistance constructed by the treaty was to be set in motion by determinations of the Council,[57] the definition of aggression and the determination of aggressor were matters of great importance. The draft treaty contained no such definition, however, and by way of guidance said only that no country complying with a unanimous recommendation of the Council or a judgment of the Permanent Court of International Justice or the Permanent Court of Arbitration, and no country that had not violated another's territorial integrity or political independence, would be considered an aggressor. This sparse guidance, meanwhile, was more than was provided by the earlier draft submitted by the Temporary Mixed Commission for the Reduction of Armaments,[58] which simply passed over the problem

55 'Report Submitted by the Third Committee to the Assembly' (n 21) 403. See also League of Nations (n 21) 55–56.

56 These determinations were to be made within four days of the matter being brought to the Council and by unanimous consent of the Council without including the votes of the belligerents themselves and of countries who had concluded security treaties with any of the belligerents to be disregarded (Article 4).

57 On the treatment of cases in which aid is provided prior to Council authorization, see subsection 4.(a) of this section below.

58 This commission was established alongside the Permanent Advisory Commission on Military, Naval, and Air Questions as a forum for discussion of disarmament. The Permanent Advisory Commission was established May 19th, 1920, pursuant to Article 9 of the League Covenant, and was tasked with advising the Council on implementation of Article 8 and, indirectly, of Article 16 of the Covenant, and with preparing League policy on disarmament. It was composed of army, navy, and airforce representatives appointed by League Member countries. The Temporary Mixed Commission was established by the Council, pursuant to the recommendation of the First Assembly, to consider disarmament questions not solely from the technical standpoint addressed by the Permanent Advisory Commission, but also from political, social, and economic perspectives, and comprised not only members of the Permanent Advisory Commission and similar official representatives but also individuals serving on the basis of their own expertise. See F Knipping, H von Mangoldt and V Rittberger *The United Nations System and Its Predecessors* (OUP Oxford 1997) vol 2, 287–296.

altogether.[59] In the Permanent Advisory Commission on Military, Naval, and Air Questions,[60] the difficulty of defining aggression and the need to indicate this difficulty in the treaty text were emphasised.[61]

The draft of the Temporary Mixed Commission was revised by the Third Subcommittee and the resulting revised Draft Treaty of Mutual Assistance was submitted to the Assembly. In the meantime, however, a special committee was established to consider the problem of how to define 'aggression'. This special committee, while noting that it would be desirable to define what constitutes aggression, declared it impracticable.[62] This is not to say that the attempt to define the term was completely abandoned. Recognizing that in many cases invasion constituted aggression, the special committee proposed that where military forces of one country invaded territory of another the invading country be presumed to have engaged in aggression; and certain acts it treated as clearly amounting to aggression, such as large scale attacks on territory and sneak attacks using poison gas in an another country's airspace.[63] Nevertheless, on the general definitional question, the special committee stated that 'it would seem impossible to decide even in theory what constitutes an act of aggression'[64] and that 'even supposing that such a definition were possible, there would still be difficulty in determining when an act of aggression within the meaning of this definition has actually taken place'.[65] Declaring it evident that no simple definition of aggression could be formulated and no simple standard offered for determining whether aggression had actually occurred in any specific case, the special committee concluded that '[i]t is therefore clearly

59 'Report of the Temporary Mixed Commission for the Reduction of Armaments' in [1923] 16 League of Nations OJ Spec Suppl 103, 105.

60 See n 58 of this chapter.

61 'Report of the Temporary Mixed Commission for the Reduction of Armaments' (n 59) 116–118. This was not adopted as a collective view of the Permanent Advisory Commission. The British delegation was unable to secure the necessary instructions from their national government, Italy's delegation stated that it could not discuss an agreement on merely a portion of the Temporary Commission's report, and other countries also declined to endorse a joint statement. The view cited here was the joint view of the representatives of Belgium, Brazil, France, and Sweden.

62 'Commentary on the Definition of a Case of Aggression, Drawn up by a Special Committee of the Temporary Mixed Commission' in [1923] 16 League of Nations OJ Spec Suppl 183.

63 Ibid 183–184.

64 Ibid 183.

65 Ibid 184.

necessary to leave the [League] Council complete discretion' in determining which country was the aggressor.[66]

In discussions of the Draft Treaty of Mutual Assistance, however, League Member countries made it clear that they had no intention of granting the Council, a political body, discretion over such vital questions in the absence of any clear standards to be applied in its determinations. This was one of the reasons why the Draft Treaty was not adopted by the Assembly.[67]

Two Distinct Aspects of the Definition Problem

Although the Draft Treaty of Mutual Assistance did not solve the problem of defining aggression, and was not adopted in any case, the special committee's Commentary deserves attention for having shown clearly not one problem but two: the problem of defining 'aggression', first of all, but also the distinct though related problem of certifying that aggression had occurred, or designating an aggressor country. As we will see, the identification of these interacting difficulties provides a perspective from which to understand later inter-war period discussions on how the term should be defined.

(c) The Protocol for the Pacific Settlement of International Disputes

Identifying Aggressors by 'Automatic Procedure'

The Geneva Protocol, adopted by the Assembly in 1924, took an approach to designating aggressors diametrically opposed to that attempted in the Draft Treaty of Mutual Assistance. Denying discretion to the Council, it adopted an 'automatic procedure'.

At the outset of discussions on the Geneva Protocol, the plan was to task the Council with identifying aggressor countries. Drafters changed course, however, as the problem arose of whether Council determinations should be made unanimously or by majority vote. Both of these formulas were seen to carry

66 Ibid. The special committee did offer several elements for the Council to consider in making this judgment: '(1) economic or industrial mobilization by a country either within its own territory or through individuals or associations outside its territory; (2) covert mobilization of military forces through the formation or use of paramilitary forces, or through declarations of the danger of war employed as pretexts or excuses for entering into hostilities; (3) attack by one country against another from air or sea or employing chemical weapons; (4) the presence of one country's military forces in another country's territory; (5) refusal of either of the countries to withdraw their armed forces behind a line or lines indicaed by the League Council; and (6) clearly aggressive policy taken by one country against another with refusal of peaceful means of dispute settlement.' (ibid 185)

67 Eagleton (n 25) 596. See also 'Annex E: Report of the British Delegates relating to the Protocol for the Peaceful Settlement of International Disputes' in Miller (n 24) 249.

serious difficulties: if unanimity were to be required, a single country could block a necessary designation of aggressor, while under a majority rule a country that opposed an aggressor designation would have to apply sanctions in violation of its own judgment. The only way of overcoming these difficulties, it was concluded, was to adopt automatic standards, such that wherever certain conditions were met a country would be presumed to be an aggressor.[68]

Interestingly, the General Report prepared in preparation for the Geneva Protocol stated that 'the definition of aggression itself is a relatively easy matter'.[69] Its justification for this remarkable statement was that 'it is sufficient to say that any State is the aggressor which resorts in any shape or form to force in violation of the engagements contracted by it either under the Covenant [of the League of Nations] ... or under the [Geneva] Protocol'.[70] The Report undercut this apparent insouciance, however, by noting that 'to ascertain the existence of aggression is a very difficult matter', as it is often difficult to determine who first resorted to force in violation of treaty obligations.[71]

It was for this very reason that tasking the Council with aggressor determination was considered and rejected, and the automatic procedure formula adopted.[72] Under this procedure, any country resorting to war would be presumed an aggressor,

> when a resort to war is accompanied:
>
> By a refusal to accept the procedure of pacific settlement or to submit to the decision resulting therefrom;
>
> By violation of provisional measures enjoined by the [League] Council...;
>
> Or by disregard of a decision recognising that the dispute arises out of a matter which lies exclusively within the domestic jurisdiction of the other party and by failure or by refusal to submit the question first to the Council or the Assembly.[73]

It would be possible to overturn this presumption by a unanimous judgment of the Council.[74]

---

68 'General Report' (n 27) 127. See also Miller (n 24) 244.

69 'General Report' (n 27) 127.

70 Ibid.

71 Ibid.

72 Ibid.

73 Ibid.

74 Ibid.

Difficulties Posed by the Automatic Procedure

The automatic procedure was thus adopted to avoid the dangers posed by entrusting the aggressor designation to the Council: mistaken designations of aggression and failure of aggression to be designated as such. By adopting this procedure, however, the Geneva Protocol did not resolve all difficulties.

For one, as many pointed out, while rejection of peaceful settlement was made an indicator of aggression, it is often unclear at what moment or stage in a dispute a country can be said definitively to have rejected or failed to comply with a peaceful settlement.[75] Moreover, as it is not simply the rejection of peaceful settlement but the resort to war that makes a country an aggressor, it is necessary to determine which country resorted to war first.

(d) The Rhineland Pact (Locarno Treaties)

Abandoning the Attempt to Define Aggression

As we have seen, intense interest in the definitional problem led to the introduction in the Geneva Protocol of an automatic procedure of designating aggressors. In contrast, '[d]uring the Locarno meetings no one paid much attention to the question of trying to define aggression'.[76] In fact, the Rhineland Pact placed less weight on the concept of aggression *per se* than did the Draft Treaty of Mutual Assistance and Geneva Protocol or Article 10 of the League Covenant. The Rhineland Pact signatories' primary promise, after all, was that they would 'in no case attack or invade each other or resort to war against each other'. (Article 2) While the Pact did say (Article 4, paragraph 3) that a 'flagrant breach' of Article 2 of the Pact or of Article 42 or 43 of the Versailles Treaty might 'constitute an unprovoked act of aggression', it was silent on the question of what might make such a violation sufficiently 'flagrant'.

British–French Discussions

Avoidance of the aggression problem in the Locarno Treaties was not the result of a lack of awareness. Though the Locarno Treaties generally did without the term 'aggression' and referred instead to treaty violations, they can be said to have employed 'a distinction ... between simple aggression and flagrant aggression';[77] and in the process of concluding the treaties, the problem of defining aggression was discussed, especially by Britain and France, in

75 Eagleton (n 25) 600; Wehberg (n 12) 98–101; Miller (n 24) 57–59; Baker (n 24) 126.

76 Ferencz (n 23) 19. See also Rifaat (n 14) 58.

77 Eagleton (n 25) 603. See also B Broms 'The Definition of Aggression' [1977] 154 RCADI 307; Rifaat (n 14) 57.

connection with the conditions triggering assistance for a country subjected to aggression, and in the form of the problem of designating aggressor countries.

On this matter, Britain initially argued consistently for entrusting the designation of aggressors to the League Council, as in Britain's initial treaty draft and in a memorandum of 11 July from the foreign minister to France's ambassador.[78] In response, France distinguished between technical or minor violations (simple aggression) and major violations (flagrant aggression), and argued that in the latter case the provision of assistance should not wait on a judgment of the Council.[79] Britain ultimately accepted this French position.[80]

Determination by the Council

On the significance of the simple/flagrant distinction in terms of preconditions for assistance to countries subjected to aggression, discussion is reserved for later in this chapter.[81] What should be noted here is that neither 'simple' nor 'flagrant' was given any precise definition.[82] The judgment of whether simple aggression had occurred was left to the Council, but no criteria for reaching such judgment were presented; if the Council was 'satisfied' that a violation had occurred, the signatory countries were to come to the aid of the country against whom the violation had been committed (Article 4, paragraph 2). In the case of 'flagrant' aggression, a signatory country was to 'satisfy' *itself* that the violation had been committed (Article 4, paragraph 3); with no objective criteria given for making such a judgment, much was left to signatories' subjective judgment. To be sure, the Council was to issue 'findings' and 'recommendations' in the latter case (Article 4, paragraph 3), but these were similarly not subject to specified criteria. As Eagleton noted, '[t]he definition of aggression

78 'French views regarding British draft of mutual guarantee, 10th July, 1925 [CR9216/459/18]' in *The National Archives, Kew* (formerly *Public Record Office, Kew*) (hereinafter *PRO*) *FO 371/10746*. See also Ueda (n 21) 59.

79 'Anglo-French negotiations regarding proposed treaty of mutual guarantee, 23rd July, 1925 [C9801/459/18]' in *PRO, FO 371/10736*.

80 'Anglo-French negotiations regarding proposed draft Treaty of Mutual Guarantee, 11th August, 1925: Notes of a Conversation which took place at the Foreign Office on August 11, 1925, at 3 p.m., between Representatives of Great Britain and France [C10610/459/18]' in *PRO, FO 371/10738*; 'Anglo-French negotiations regarding proposed draft Treaty of Mutual Guarantee, 12th August, 1925: Notes of a Conversation which took place at the Foreign Office on August 12, 1925, at noon, between Representatives of Great Britain and France [C10611/459/18]' in ibid. Note, however, that under this scheme the parties were to comply with a Council judgment after the fact

81 Subsection 4.(b) in this section.

82 Eagleton (n 25) 604.

is not so clear as in the [Geneva] Protocol; on the contrary, many of the older uncertainties reappear'.[83]

(e) The Pact of Paris

Definition Problem Abandoned

The challenge of defining aggression was abandoned in the negotiation stages of this Pact concluded in 1928. The word does not appear in the Pact, and a conscious effort was made to avoid naming aggressive war as prohibited; what the Pact prohibited was war 'as an instrument of national policy' (Article 1). Among other grounds advanced for not attempting to define aggression was that presented by Frank Kellogg, in connection with the question of whether explicit mention should be made of a right of self-defence, which the United States insisted during negotiations all states inherently enjoyed:

> Express recognition by treaty of this inalienable right, however, gives rise to the same difficulty encountered in any effort to define aggression. It is the identical question approached from the other side. Inasmuch as no treaty provision can add to the natural right of self-defence, it is not in the interest of peace that a treaty should stipulate a juristic conception of self-defence since it is far too easy for the unscrupulous to mold events to accord with an agreed definition.[84]

How the question of whether to employ a conception of aggression was viewed in the formulation of the Pact can be viewed even more clearly in the US–French disagreement over whether the Pact should specifically prohibit wars of aggression.

The US–France Dispute

As noted earlier,[85] the Pact of Paris was originally conceived as a French–US treaty renouncing war. The draft submitted by France proposed that France and the US 'solemnly declare ... that they condemn recourse to war and renounce it respectively as an instrument of their national policy towards each other'.[86] The US preferring to seek a multilateral treaty,[87] France called for such

---

83 Ibid.

84 'Note of the Government of the United States, June 23, 1928' (n 34) 57.

85 Section A.4. of this chapter.

86 'Draft of Pact of Perpetual Friendship between France and the United States, Submitted June 20, 1927' in Department of State (n 34) 9–10.

87 'The Secretary of State (Kellogg) to the French Ambassador (Claudel), December 28, 1927' in ibid 11–12.

a treaty to pledge renunciation of 'all war of aggression'.[88] In response, Secretary of State Kellogg questioned why France now proposed restricting prohibited war to wars of aggression and expressed his hope that the language of the original draft forbidding war 'as an instrument of national policy' would be restored.[89] Kellogg expanded on his concerns in a later memorandum:

> If [a treaty outlawing war] were accompanied by definitions of the word 'aggressor' and by exceptions and qualifications stipulating when nations would be justified in going to war, its effect would be very greatly weakened and its positive value as a guaranty of peace virtually destroyed.[90]

Whether the differences between France and the US on this point had much real legal significance was doubted even by participants in the exchange.[91] James Barrington Hurst, legal advisor of the British foreign office, complained to his French counterpart Fromageot that he could not understand how the move from a bilateral to a multilateral treaty necessitated introduction of the term 'aggression'.[92] Fromageot explained that while there was in fact no difference between prohibiting wars of aggression and prohibiting war as an instrument of national policy, Belgium and Czechoslovakia had reacted fiercely to the French government's bilateral treaty proposal of June, 1927, arguing that it would render meaningless the obligation under the Locarno treaties to assist countries subjected to aggression.[93] A memorandum of British foreign secretary Chamberlain similarly held there to be no theoretical difference between the alternative expressions;[94] France's and America's insistence on their respective preferred phrasings he attributed to France's commitment under the Rhineland Pact to submit to the judgments of the League Council and to America's decided unwillingness to be bound by decisions of the League.[95]

88 'The French Ambassador (Claudel) to the Secretary of State (Kellogg), le 5 janvier, 1928' in ibid 13–14.

89 'The Secretary of State (Kellogg) to the French Ambassador (Claudel), January 11, 1928' in ibid 15–17.

90 'The Secretary of State (Kellogg) to the French Ambassador (Claudel), February 27, 1928' in ibid 23. For a more detailed treatment of this exchange, addressing its political background, see Onuma (n 32) 84–88.

91 Onuma (ibid) sees in it a great sensitivity to US domestic political pressures.

92 'United States arbitration treaties etc., Jan. 30th, 1928 [A691/1/45]' in *PRO FO 371/12789*.

93 Ibid.

94 'Memorandum by the Secretary of State for Foreign Affairs: The Franco-American Draft Pact of Mutual Friendship' in Adams (ed) (n 34) 80–81.

95 Ibid 80, 82.

Rejection of Council Judgment

The US refusal to employ the concept of aggression in defining either the scope of action prohibited by the Pact under negotiation or the conditions for exercising the right of self-defence under that Pact was thus not due simply to the difficulty of defining the concept; what the US refused to accept was the device frequently employed in this period of entrusting to the League the judgment of whether aggression had occurred.[96]

(f) The Act Defining Aggressor

'An Absolutely Rigid Definition of Automatic Application'

In stark contrast to the Rhineland Pact and the Paris Pact, a proposed Act Defining Aggressor was an attempt to define the term precisely.[97] This Act was submitted to the League of Nation Conference for the Reduction and Limitation of Armaments of 1933 as a report by the Committee on Security Questions.[98] Article 1 listed the following acts which would constitute aggression: (1) declaration of war on another state; (2) armed invasion of another state's territory with or without a declaration of war; (3) attack on territory, vessels, or aircraft of another state; (4) naval blockade; and (5)

> provision of support to armed bands formed in [a State's] territory which have invaded the territory of another State, or refusal, notwithstanding the request of the invaded State, to take in its own territory all the measures in its power to deprive those bands of all assistance or protection.[99]

Article 2, meanwhile, provided that '[n]o political, military, economic or other considerations may serve as an excuse or justification for the aggression referred to in Article 1'.[100] The Act thus clearly defined aggression and made clear that the determination of an aggressor depended entirely on the question of which state first took any of an enumerated set of actions. The framework

---

96 Eagleton complained that the Pact of Paris, in failing to define either self-defence or aggression and leaving each country to judge for itself which label fit a particular case, restored the lamentable ante-bellum status quo in which any war could be defended as a war in self-defence. (Eagleton (n 25) 609)

97 AN Mandelstam *Le conflit Italo-Éthiopien devant la Société des Nations* (Sirey Paris 1937) 330–346.

98 'Report of the Committee on Security Questions (Conf. D/C G 108)' in League of Nations *Conference for the Reduction and Limitation of Armaments, Conference Documents* (Series of League of Nations Publications, IX. Disarmament, 1935 IX 4) vol 2, 679–685.

99 Ibid 683.

100 Ibid.

it set forth was quickly labelled 'an absolutely rigid definition of automatic application'.[101]

Calls for a More Flexible Approach

The system proposed by the draft Act was opposed by a number of countries, including Great Britain, who called for a more flexible approach. Britain argued that the Act's definition would work only in 'perfectly simple cases',[102] precisely those in which any country and any international organisation would correctly designate the aggressor even without a definition to rely on. 'It was the doubtful and difficult cases', the British government argued, 'in which the question of definition was so exceptionally important, and it was precisely in such cases that ... a definition of this sort was not only of doubtful utility but might be positively injurious'.[103] It was thus Britain's view that any definition should be flexible and that where a country carried out an enumerated act of aggression, an international organisation bearing the responsibility to designate an aggressor should take into account all relevant circumstances in making its judgment.[104]

Difficulties in Designating Aggressors

It should also be noted that having a definition of aggression at one's disposal does not free one of the difficulties involved in identifying an aggressor. If the designation of aggressor depends on who first committed an aggressive act, it is by no means easy, in many cases, to determine who that was. For that

101 League of Nations *Records of the Conference for the Reduction and Limitation of Armaments, Series B* (*Minutes of the General Commission*) vol 2 (December 14th 1932–June 29th 1933) (Series of League of Nations Publications, IX. Disarmament, 1933 IX 10), 513. See also League of Nations, *Records of the Conference for the Reduction and Limitation of Armaments, Series D* (*Minutes of the Political Commission*) vol 5 (February 27th 1932-March 10th 1933) (Series of League of Nations Publications, IX. Disarmament, 1936 IX 8), 49, 54.

102 League of Nations *Records of the Conference for the Reduction and Limitation of Armaments, Series B* (*Minutes of the General Commission*) vol 2 (December 14th, 1932–June 29th, 1933) (n 101), 513.

103 Ibid.

104 Ibid 513–514. See also League of Nations *Conference for the Reduction and Limitation of Armaments, Preliminary Report on the Work of the Conference, Prepared by the President, Mr. Arthur Henderson* (Conf. D 171 (1)) (Series of League of Nations Publications, IX. Disarmament, 1936 IX 3) 40; 'Provisional Minutes of the Sixty-Fifth Meeting, Geneva, May 25, 1933 – (Received in Foreign Office, June 7)' in PJ Beck (ed) *British Documents on Foreign Affairs: Reports and Papers from the Foreign Office Confidential Print, Part II From the First to the Second World War, Series J The League of Nations, 1918–1941* (University Publications of America Maryland 1992) vol 4 (The Question of Disarmament, 1932–1933), 233–236.

reason, the Committee on Security Questions report, into which the draft Act was incorporated, also proposed the formation as necessary of a Commission for Establishing the Facts of an incident of aggression.[105] Such a Commission would have freed the Council from the difficult problem of determining who had committed aggression, but this simply means that any Commission would have had to confront the difficulties itself.

(g) Summary of Subsection 1
The Difficulty of Defining Aggression

From the above account of attempts to define aggression, we can see, first of all, that in the inter-war period no generally accepted definition existed.[106] Different treaties employed different definitions, and some treaties abandoned the task completely.

The definition proposed in the draft Act was adopted by some later treaties.[107] It is difficult to say, however, that the definition ever gained general acceptance. Arthur Henderson, president of the Disarmament Conference, noted as much in his *Preliminary Report on the Work of the Conference*, prepared as 'a short chronological record of the proceedings of the Conference, a summary of its technical work on specific problems and a general review of the results achieved'.[108] The views of participants on the definition problem had been divided, he said, between a group seeking a strict and precise definition and one seeking more flexibility. 'The consultation' between these two groups, he wrote, 'has not so far led to any general agreed definition of the aggressor'.[109]

That no consensus existed on the definition of aggression should make us wonder what it means to say that the inter-war right of self-defence was (or was in part) a right to resist aggression. The statement may be correct, but a general

105 'Report of the Committee on Security Questions (Conf. D/C G 108)' (n 98) 682–685.

106 See Brownlie (n 1) 104, 353.

107 Esp 'Convention de définition de l'aggression (signé 3 Juillet 1933)' 147 LNTS 68; EA Korovine 'The U.S.S.R. and Disarmament' [1933] Int'l Conciliation 351–354. See also 'Treaty of Arab Brotherhood and Alliance between the Kingdom of Saudi Arabi and Iraq (signed 2 April 1936)' 174 LNTS 132–133; 'Traité de non-agression entre le Royaume d'Afghanistan, le Royaume de l'Irak, l'Empire de l'Iran et la République Turque (signé 8 Juillet 1937)' 190 LNTS 22, 24.

108 League of Nations *Conference for the Reduction and Limitation of Armaments, Preliminary Report on the Work of the Conference, Prepared by the President, Mr. Arthur Henderson* (n 104) 9.

109 Ibid 40. See also League of Nations, *Records of the Conference for the Reduction and Limitation of Armaments, Series B* (*Minutes of the General Commission*) vol 2 (December 14th, 1932-June 29th, 1933) (n 101) 513.

definition of the preceding acts that could be said to constitute aggression and thus to justify the exercise of the right of self-defence proved extremely difficult to attain. The inter-war right of self-defence, seemingly so sharply limited and defined, was in truth an exceptionally difficult conception to formulate.

Two Approaches

Secondly, two basic approaches to overcoming the difficulties of definition can be observed. One was to seek precision of definition (as in the draft Act Defining Aggressor) or institute an automatic process of aggressor-identification (as in the Geneva Protocol). The other was either to abandon the definition task (as in the Draft Treaty of Mutual Assistance) or to define aggression quite generally or flexibly and leave determination of whether aggression has occurred to the discretion of some institution, typically the League Council (as in the Rhineland Pact).[110]

A relationship also appears between strictness of definition and process of designating aggressors under these two approaches. In order for aggressors to be designated without recourse to the discretionary judgment of a designating body, an absolutely clear definition is necessary; where the designating body is granted discretion, a flexible definition will suffice (is needed, in fact).

Remote Effects of the Definitional Problem

The difficulties that confronted attempts to define aggression would directly influence arguments on the precursor to the right of collective self-defence (which are treated in Subsection 4 of this section below). As we will see in Chapter 6, the framework of the UN Charter should also be viewed from this perspective.

2 *The Existence of Limits: League of Nations Practice*

As we saw in Subsection 1, throughout the inter-war period the operative definition of aggression was far from clear. This does not mean, however, that self-defence, understood in terms of resistance to aggression, was an infinitely elastic concept. Under the League, claims of self-defence were often rejected.

---

110 Giraud (n 15) 747–787. These two approaches correspond to alternative formulae that would be employed in UN-era attempts to define aggression: definition by enumeration and definition in general terms. These efforts would ultimately lead to a General Assembly resolution defining aggression. (UNGA Res 3314 (XXIX) (14 December 1974)) See BB Ferencz 'Aggression' in R Bernhardt (ed) (n 9) 58–63; GG Fitzmaurice 'The Definition of Aggression' [1952] 1 ICLQ 137, 141–143. It should be noted that the Pact of Paris fits well into neither category; on the significance of that anomaly, see n 96 of this chapter.

There were also numerous cases in which a belligerent's use of military force was judged unlawful though it was unclear whether the belligerent had even asserted a right of self-defence.[111] The existence of limits to the currency of self-defence claims can be confirmed by consideration of a number of cases in which the League rejected self-defence claims either advanced by belligerents or taken up by the League on its own initiative: the Manchurian Incident (1931), the Italy-Ethiopia Conflict (1935), and the Marco Polo Bridge Incident (1937).

(a) The Manchurian Incident

Facts[112]

On the evening of 18 September 1931, an explosion destroyed track of the South Manchuria Railway near Mukden (now Shenyang, in Liaoning Province).[113]

---

111 In the Peru-Colombia Leticia dispute of 1932 and 1933, the League found unambiguously that Colombian territory was invaded by Peruvians, Colombian officials ejected from their posts, and the invading Peruvians supported by Peruvian military authorities. ('Report of the Council, Provided for in Article 15, Paragraph 4, of the Covenant, Submitted by the Committee of the Council' in [1933] 14 League of Nations OJ 599–609, esp 608.) The case is also treated in LH Woolsey 'The Leticia Dispute between Colombia and Peru' [1933] 27 AJIL 317–324; LH Woolsey 'The Leticia Dispute between Colombia and Peru' [1935] 29 AJIL 94–99; and Walters (n 21) 536–540.

Similarly, the Soviet Union was judged clearly to have violated Article 12 of the League Covenant in its 1939–1940 war with Finland. ('Report of the Assembly, Provided for in Article 15, Paragraphs 4 and 10, of the Covenant, Submitted by the Special Committee of the Assembly' in [1939] 20 League of Nations OJ 531–542, esp 540) This case is also treated by Walters (n 21) 804–810; A Klein 'Finland' in A Toynbee and VM Toynbee (eds) *The Initial Triumph of the Axis* (OUP London 1958) 59–95; and L Gross 'Was the Soviet Union Expelled from the League of Nations?' [1945] 39 AJIL 35–44.

112 The literature on this incident is large. Valuable treatments of the facts of the case can be found in Walters (n 21) 465–499; WW Willoughby *The Sino-Japanese Controversy and the League of Nations* (Greenwood Press New York 1935); GM Gathorne-Hardy *A Short History of International Affairs, 1920–1939* (4th edn OUP Oxford 1950) 309–321; and MO Hudson *The Verdict of the League: China and Japan in Manchuria* (World Peace Foundation Boston 1933).

113 Chinese and Japanese accounts of the incident and the conditions preceding it are outlined in the so-called Lytton Report (League of Nations *Appeal by the Chinese Government, Report of the Commission of Enquiry* (C 663 M320 1932 VII) (Series of League of Nations Publications, VII. Political, 1932 VII 12) 67–70). This Report noted that prior to the incident tensions had existed between Japanese and Chinese forces in the area, and stated that the Japanese military action of September 18 and 19 followed carefully prepared plans for action to be taken in the event of hostilities arising between the two countries' armies. The Report also emphasised that while an explosion had indeed damaged the rail line, the damage was slight. (ibid 71)

The Japanese army, which was guarding the railway, decided that preventive military measures were needed, and dispatched units beyond the rail zone to nearby cities, which proceeded to occupy cities including Mukden, Changchun, Andong, and Gonkou. The government of China on 21 September appealed to the League Council for action pursuant to Article 11 of the Covenant. On 22 September, the Council President urged both countries' governments to refrain from action that might worsen the situation, and a Council resolution of 30 September urged normalization of relations between Japan and China. Thereafter, however, Japan expanded the scope of its activities, establishing the nominally independent country of Manchukuo in March, 1932.

In the midst of the worsening situation, the League dispatched a Commission of Enquiry (the 'Lytton Commission') to ascertain the facts. Following receipt of the Commission's report,[114] the Assembly of the League entrusted a Special Committee to consider the matter. The report of this special committee, which unambiguously censured the government of Japan, was approved by the Assembly on 24 February 1933.[115]

The Japanese Government's Position and the Judgment of the League

From the first, Japan justified its actions as self-defence. Japan's representative in the Assembly asserted that:

> In face of the situation created by the systematically vexatious manner in which the Chinese authorities deal with our essential rights and interests, the command of the Japanese troops considered it indispensable, after the incident of September 18th, to take legitimate defensive action[.][116]

The Lytton Report rejected this position. After noting that damage from the explosion had not been severe enough to prevent the train from Chanchung

114 Ibid.

115 'Report Provided for in Article 15, Paragraph 4, of the Covenant, Submitted by the Special Committee of the Assembly in Execution of Part III (Paragraph 5) of the Resolution of March 11th, 1932, and Adopted by the Assembly on February 24th, 1933 (A (Extr) 22 1933 VII)' in [1933] 112 League of Nations OJ Spec Suppl 56–76.

116 [1931] 12 League of Nations OJ 2317. See also ibid 2343, 2347; 'Text of Memorandum Sent from the Japanese to the Chinese Government, dated October 9, 1931 (C 690 M 296 1931 VII)' in [1931] 12 League of Nations OJ 2482; 'Letter from the Japanese delegation to the Secretary-General of the League of Nations regarding the Incident at Chinchow, October 12, 1931 (C 704 M 310 1931 VII)' in [1931] League of Nations OJ 2504.

arriving on schedule, the Report addressed the more general issue plainly: 'The military operations of the Japanese troops during [the night of September 18th] ... cannot be regarded as measures of legitimate self-defence'.[117]

In the observations which the Japanese government submitted to the League on the Report, Japan particularly condemned this element of the Report's conclusions. Citing the views of the United States, Great Britain, France, and Germany expressed in negotiations on the Pact of Paris, Japan described the conclusion as one that should astound any signatory of that Pact and argued that as it had been repeatedly confirmed that as the decisive judgment regarding the right of self-defence ultimately rested the country exercising it, only Japanese commanders on the ground were qualified to determine whether their actions were measures taken in self-defence. Noting the Lytton Report's acknowledgment that Japanese commanders may have believed themselves to be taking measures in self-defence, Japan insisted on the subjective character of judgments regarding the exercise of self-defence.

Japan's argument also reached back to the 'Webster formula', arguing that the conditions of that excellent statement of the right of self-defence had clearly been fulfilled in Mukden: With Japan's interest, its status in East Asia, threatened by attack from vastly numerically superior Chinese forces, it had had to respond and without the time or space necessary for full deliberation on what might be the best response possible.

The report of the special committee, which was adopted by the Assembly, gave very short shrift to these arguments.[118] Though the possibility cannot be denied that Japanese commanders on the night of 18th September believed themselves to be acting in self-defence, the Report concluded, the Assembly could consider neither the actions of the Japanese military forces as a whole of that night, in Mukden and elsewhere in Manchuria, nor the actions taken by Japan's army thereafter, to be measures taken in self-defence. Nor, it was added, could Japan evade its obligation under Article 12 of the Covenant to submit the dispute to the Council.[119]

---

117 League of Nations *Appeal by the Chinese Government, Report of the Commission of Enquiry* (n 113) 71. Continuing directly, the Report did allow that 'officers on the spot may have thought they were acting in self-defence'. (ibid)

118 'Report provided for in Article 15, Paragraph 4, of the Covenant, Submitted by the Special Committee of the Assembly in Execution of Part III (Paragraph 5) of the Resolution of March 11th, 1932, and Adopted by the Assembly on February 24th, 1933 (A (Extr) 22 1933 VII)' (n 115) 56–76.

119 Ibid 72.

The Conception of the Right of Self-Defence at Work in the League's Judgment

On what basis the Lytton Report or the later Report of the Special Committee concluded that Japan's military actions could not be regarded as an exercise of the right of self-defence is not entirely clear. The Lytton Report's emphasis on the slightness of the damage from the 18th September explosion suggests a rejection of Japan's claims based on the non-existence of preceding acts sufficient to warrant a claim of self-defence. There are suggestions in the records of the Assembly's consideration of the Lytton Report, however, that the problem was rather a deficit of proportionality in the measures Japan took.[120]

In any case, neither Report lays out the basis of its conclusions; it is thus impossible to say with any precision how the right of self-defence was understood. It is clear, however, even if this was not explicitly stated, that Japan's contention that only a country party to a conflict was competent to judge the necessity and proportionality of acts taken in self-defence, was rejected.[121] In other words, the League quite definitely denied that the exercise of self-defence might be removed from all possible limitations based on the subjective judgment of a belligerent country.

(b) The Italo–Ethiopian War

Facts[122]

Italian hopes of making Ethiopia a colony dated back to the 19th century.[123] Under Mussolini and against the backdrop of the global economic crisis, these arose again in the 1930's, and plans were advanced for the project. On 5 December 1934, the Italian and Ethiopian armies clashed in the 'Wal Wal incident' near the hazy border between Ethiopia and Italian Somaliland, resulting

120 Eg 'Records of the Special Session of the Assembly Convened in virtue of Article 15 of the Covenant at the Request of the Chinese Government, Vol. III' in [1933] 111 League of Nations OJ Spec Suppl 36, 46.

121 Ibid 44.

122 The facts of this case are treated by T Mori 'Italia-Echiopia Senso (Italo-Ethiopian War)' in Kokusaiho Gakkai (Japanese Soc'y of Int'l L) (ed) *Kokusai Kankeiho Jiten* (*Encyclopedia of International Law*) (2nd edn Sanseido Tokyo 2005) 26 (*in Japanese*); Walters (n 21) 623–691; AE Zimmern *The League of Nations and the Rule of Law, 1918–1935* (Macmillan London 1936); AJ Toynbee *Abyssinia and Italy* (*Survey of International Affairs* 1935, vol 2) (OUP London 1936); Gathorne-Hardy (n 112) 392–418; Mandelstam (n 97); A Serup *L'article 16 du Pacte et son interprétation dans le conflit Italo-Ethiopien* (Rousseau Paris 1938).

123 The First Italo-Ethiopia War broke out in 1889. It ended in Italian failure in 1896.

in many deaths. Ethiopia from an early stage in the conflict announced its intention to submit to arbitration in the matter, and formally applied to the Council in January, 1935.

League deliberations on the conflict moved slowly. Italy requested that the Council delay considering the matter, announcing that it would seek a peaceful solution under a bilateral arbitration treaty with Ethiopia. Great powers Britain and France, meanwhile, seeking to avoid a decisive confrontation with Italy, did not push the League to move more urgently.

An arbitral judgment was rendered on 3 September 1935, which assigned responsibility to neither side. The matter was taken up the next day in the Council, but deliberation was removed to the Assembly at Ethiopia's request. On the 25th of September, Ethiopia notified the Secretary-General that to avoid giving a pretext for aggression it had withdrawn its forces to 30 kilometers from the border, and requested that monitors be sent.[124] On the 28th, the Emperor of Ethiopia gave the order for mobilization.[125] On 3 October, Italy commenced its attack on Ethiopia.

Position of the Italian Government and the League's Judgment

Italy asserted to the Council that as a result of the policies of Ethiopia's emperor, it had been forced to 'take the necessary measures of defence'.[126] The Ethiopian policies of which Italy complained were the order of mobilization and the withdrawal of forces behind the frontier, the latter of which Italy condemned as a strategic move. On 7 October, Italy presented its actions to the Council as merely the exercise of 'her right of legitimate defence'.[127]

A committee established by the council to investigate the matter reported on 7 October that Italy had resorted to war in violation of Article 12 of the League Covenant.[128] All members of the Council (other than representatives of the belligerents) declared their agreement with the report's conclusions.[129] In the Assembly, 50 of 54 countries supported the Council's conclusions.[130]

---

124 'Telegram, Dated September 25th, 1935, from His Majesty the Emperor of Ethiopia to the Secretary-General (C 384 M 192 1935 VII)' in [1935] League of Nations OJ 1602.

125 'Telegram, Dated September 28th, 1935, from His Majesty the Emperor of Ethiopia to the President of the Council (C 400 M 197 1935)' in [1935] 16 League of Nations OJ 1603.

126 'Telegram, Dated October 3rd, 1935, from the Italian Government to the Secretary-General, October 3rd, 1935 (C 404 M 200 1935 VII)' in [1935] 16 League of Nations OJ 1603.

127 [1935] 16 League of Nations OJ 1218.

128 'Dispute between Ethiopia and Italy: Report of the Council Committee, October 7th, 1935 (C 417 1935 VII)' in [1935] 16 League of Nations OJ 1223–1225.

129 Ibid 1225.

130 Walters (n 21) 656.

The Conception of the Right of Self-Defence Operative in the League's Judgment

Italy's claims of self-defence were thus rejected. Unfortunately, the conception of self-defence on which Italy had relied was unclear, and the notion of self-defence was not actually taken up by the committee report. What the report emphasized was the obligation under the Covenant to seek peaceful resolution of disputes:

> Members of the League are not entitled, without having first complied with the provisions of Articles 12, 13, and 15, to seek a remedy by war for grievances they consider they have against other Members of the League. The adoption by a state of measures of security on its own territory and within the limits of its international agreements does not authorise another state to consider itself free from its obligations under the Covenant.[131]

This conclusion can be read to mean that the taking of measures for security is not sufficient justification for a claim of self-defence.

(c) The Marco Polo Bridge Incident

Facts[132]

On the night of 7 July 1937, Japanese and Chinese forces clashed near the Marco Polo Bridge, about fifteen kilometers southwest of Beijing.[133] Such skirmishes were common at the time, and it was thought that this one would be resolved at the local command level. The field of battle, however, proceeded to expand.

In September of that year, China's government decided to appeal to the League of Nations. Seeking to gain the support of the United States, however, who had not joined the League, China took its case not to the Council or the Assembly, but to the Far-East Advisory Committee. In this body, which was established in connection with the Manchurian Incident of 1931 and had not been active since, the United States was represented.[134] A subcommittee

131 [1935] 16 League of Nations OJ 1224.

132 For good accounts of the facts, see Walters (n 21) 731–738; and Gathorne-Hardy (n 112).

133 Japanese and Chinese views of conditions that day are outlined in 'First Report of the Sub-Committee of the Far-East Advisory Committee, Adopted by the Committee on October 5th and by the Assembly on October 6th, 1937 (A 78 1937 VII)' in [1937] 177 League of Nations OJ Spec Suppl 38.

134 See Walters (n 21) 734–735 on the cautious attitude taken by the US in this case.

prepared two reports, both of which were adopted by the Committee[135] and thereafter by the Assembly.[136] Japan, which had already quit the League, rejected the Committee's call to participate in deliberations, saying that Japan and China should themselves resolve the problem between them.[137] As a result, Japan's views were not put clearly before the League; they are represented in the subcommittee reports by means such as quotations from remarks of the prime minister or foreign minister in the Japanese Diet.

The League's Judgment

The sub-committee's first report states that Japan's actions, prima facie violations of its obligations under the Nine-Power Treaty of 1922 and the Pact of Paris, could be justified only in so far as they could be shown to have been measures necessary for self-defence (including defence of Japanese forces and citizens legally on Chinese territory).[138] As the expression of Japan's claim of self-defence, a quotation was presented from a 5th September address by Prime Minister Konoe.[139] In his remarks, Konoe stated: 'I am of the firm belief that to have launched a decisive strike against such a country was in accord with our right of self-defence and in the interest of justice'.[140]

This position, of course, was rejected by the sub-committee report:

> After examination of the facts laid before it, the Committee is bound to take the view that the military operations carried out by Japan against China by land, by sea, and by air are out of all proportion to the incident that occasioned the conflict; that such action [of Japan] can be justified neither on the basis of existing legal instruments nor that of the right of self-defence, and that it is in contravention of Japan's obligations

---

135 'Report of the Far-East Advisory Committee and Resolution Adopted by the Assembly on October 6th, 1937 (A 79 1937 VII)' in [1937] 177 League of Nations OJ Spec Suppl 35.

136 [1937] 169 League of Nations OJ Spec Suppl 125, 148–149.

137 [1937] 177 League of Nations OJ Spec Suppl 36.

138 'First Report of the Sub-Committee of the Far-East Advisory Committee, Adopted by the Committee on October 5th and by the Assembly on October 6th, 1937 (A 78 1937 VII)' (n 133) 40.

139 Ibid 41. The quotation is ostensibly from an English translation of remarks by the foreign minister, Hirota. The original Diet transcript in Japanese, however, suggests that it was the prime minister, Konoe, who actually made the remarks. See *Kampo* (*Official Gazett*) (Extra News 6th September 1937 (The 72nd Shorthand Report of Parliamentary Proceedings of Empire Council, the Lords of Peers, vol 2)) (*in Japanese*).

140 Ibid. Reproduced here is the English translation found in the subcommittee report.

> under the Nine-Power Treaty of February 6th, 1922, and under the Pact of Paris...[141]

The Conception of the Right of Self-Defence in the League's Judgment

While the subcommittee, and the Assembly, clearly found Japan to have violated treaty obligations, it is difficult to say that the conception of self-defence adopted by the League in this case was made clear. Japan itself never presented a claim of self-defence, and the only statement of its views on the matter considered by the League was a translated remark made on the floor of the Diet. What 'self-defence' was understood to mean in the report is quite indeterminate. We can say little more than that, given the report's characterization of Japan's actions as 'out of all proportion' to the initial incident, the claim of self-defence can perhaps be considered as rejected based on the principle of proportionality.

(d) Summary of Subsection 2

Claims of self-defence offered to the League were often rejected. That 'aggression' was never clearly defined, despite the inter-war understanding of self-defence as resistance to aggression, does not mean that no limits to the actions that could be taken in self-defence were in fact recognised.

Nevertheless, the scope of recognised self-defence, as shown in the cases considered above, was hardly made very clear. The most clearly indicated basis for precluding a self-defence claim with respect to the Marco Polo Bridge incident was a lack of proportionality in Japan's actions; so too in the earlier Manchurian incident was proportionality a focus of the League's judgment.[142] In the Manchurian incident, we see alongside the principle of proportionality a suggestion that a very small explosion will not suffice as a preceding act justifying the use of force in self-defence. In the case of the Italo-Ethiopian War, we find, notably, a suggestion that measures for security taken within a state's own territory will similarly not serve as a sufficient condition.

---

141 'First Report of the Sub-Committee of the Far-East Advisory Committee, Adopted by the Committee on October 5th and the by the Assembly on October 6th, 1937 (A 78 1937 VII)' (n 133) 42.

142 On the importance of the principle of proportionality for limiting the exercise of the right of self-defence in international law of the inter-war period, see K Nemoto 'Jieikenkoshi ni okeru Hitsuyosei-Kinkyusei Gensoku (Nessesity and Proportionality Principles of Self-Defence)' in S Murase (ed) *Jieiken no Gendaiteki Tenkai* (*The Right of Self-defence in the Contemporary Context*) (Toshindo Tokyo 2007) 59–87 (*in Japanese*).

These are, however, mere suggestions, drawn not from any general argument on the conception of self-defence but merely found in the context of judgments on particular cases. Our ability to identify clear bounds of the scope of self-defence based on such suggestions is limited. If in these cases a small explosion or security measures taken on a state's own territory were found not to be within the scope of acts justifying the action in self-defence, we can hardly say that they would not serve that function in other cases; we are not left with a general principle.

In the next subsection of this section, we will consider this problem of the limits to the scope of self-defence from a broader perspective.

3 *Vague Boundaries*

In an attempt to make clearer the scope of preceding actions that could justify a claim of self-defence in the inter-war period, we will consider in Subsubsection (a) below a category of actions in which we might hope to find a sort of lower boundary. As an example of such relatively minor provocations, we will consider the relationship of self-defence to frontier incidents. In Subsubsection (b), I would like to pursue the question a bit further by looking into the ambiguities that arise around that lower boundary from the principle of proportionality.

(a) Frontier Incidents

Frontier Incidents and the Right of Self-Defence

'Frontier incidents' are typically, by definition, small armed skirmishes.[143] Because they are small, in both scale and effects, the question of whether they come within the scope of preceding actions justifying the use of force in self-defence promises to bring us within sight of a lower boundary of adequate preceding acts.[144]

---

143 Brownlie (n 1) 366.

144 In *Nicaragua v United States of America*, the International Court of Justice employed the concept in this way, distinguishing a frontier incident from armed attack in scale and effects and holding that while an armed attack may justify exercise of the right of self-defence, a mere frontier incident will justify not self-defence but only a more narrowly circumscribed response. (*Case concerning Military and Paramilitary Activities in and against Nicaragua* (*Nicaragua v United States of America*) (Merits)) [1986] ICJ Rep 103–104. See also C Gray *International Law and the Use of Force* (3rd edn OUP Oxford 2008) 177–183. The ICJ, in other words, located frontier incidents beneath our lower boundary, holding that they will not justify an exercise of the right of self-defence. This case, decided in 1986, is obviously far outside the scope of our enquiry; it is mentioned here only for the sake of

Under the League of Nations, the question of the relationship of frontier incidents to self-defence was in fact addressed, in the case of a Greco-Bulgarian frontier incident of October 1925.

The Greco–Bulgarian Frontier Incident

On 19 October 1925, an exchange of gunfire occurred between border guards of Bulgaria and Greece. It is unclear which side fired first. At first, the incident seemed no more than a minor skirmish such as frequently occurred around the border between the two countries. On this occasion, however, the incident escalated. By the 22nd, Greek forces extending some 16 miles along the frontier crossed several miles into Bulgarian territory.[145]

On the 22nd, Bulgaria appealed to the League to take the necessary measures without delay pursuant to Articles 10 and 11.[146] The next day, the acting president of the Council called on both countries to cease hostilities and withdraw their forces; at the same time, he convoked a special meeting of the Council for 26 October,[147] which promptly resolved that the belligerent countries withdraw their forces as urged by the acting president and that observers of the completed withdrawal be dispatched from other states.[148] After war was averted by both countries complying with the demand for withdrawal, the facts of the incident and the question of who bore responsibility were discussed in the Council.

The Greek and Bulgarian Claims

Both countries claimed to have acted in self-defence. 'The aggressors who have violated and occupied without any provocation a foreign territory', Greece argued, 'are the Bulgarians'.[149] Greece also maintained that 'all the measures

---

illustrating the question of whether and how frontier incidents can point to the limits of the scope of preceding acts.

145 'Report of the Commission of Enquiry into the Incidents on the Frontier between Bulgaria and Greece (C 727 M 270 1925)' in [1926] 7 League of Nations OJ 197–203; J Garner, 'Settlement of the Graeco-Bulgarian Dispute' [1926] 20 AJIL 337; G Scott *The Rise and Fall of the League of Nations* (Hutchinson London 1973) 126–127.

146 'Telegram from the Bulgarian Minister for Foreign Affairs to the Secretary-General, dated Sofia, October 22nd, 1925' in [1925] 6 League of Nations OJ 1696.

147 'Telegram from the Acting President of the Council to the Greek and Bulgarian Government, Paris, October 23rd' in [1925] 6 League of Nations OJ 1696–1697.

148 [1925] 6 League of Nations OJ 1699–1700.

149 Ibid 1705.

which the [Greek] military command has been compelled to take are nothing but measures of legitimate defence'.[150] For its part, Bulgaria argued:

> At the time when the incident arose, the whole of [the] frontier district was guarded only by three Bulgarian companies. In these circumstances, it is not possible to speak of any aggression on the part of Bulgaria, who, on the contrary was in a state of legitimate self-defence.[151]

The League's Judgment

A commission of enquiry established by the Council gave a clear assessment of the actions of both armies.[152] The commission rejected Greece's claims, concluding that by occupying part of Bulgaria's territory Greece had violated the Covenant.[153] Bulgaria, the commission judged, had acted in accord with the Covenant. If a few Bulgarian soldiers had entered Greek territory, as Greece claimed, their crossing a few yards over the frontier did not amount to a violation of Greece's territorial integrity.[154]

The commission of enquiry can be seen as believing that in the event of a border incident, it was permissible to resist an attack by means within the scope of actions necessary under the circumstances at hand.[155] The commission did not *per se* base its judgment on the concept of 'legitimate defence' or 'legitimate self-defence', which both sides had invoked. Neither, however, did it reject the parties' claim that the right of self-defence could be exercised in a frontier incident. We must therefore acknowledge that the commission did not quite make clear the relationship between a frontier incident and the right of self-defence. Had it wished to do so, the commission might have identified a lower boundary of preceding acts justifying action in self-defence. In not expressing a view on this question, it left that lower boundary undefined.

---

150 'Telegram dated October 24th, 1925, from the Greek Minister for Foreign Affairs to the Secretary-General' in [1925] 6 League of Nations OJ 1697. See also [1925] 6 League of Nations OJ 1705–1707; [1926] 7 League of Nations OJ 111–117.

151 [1925] 6 League of Nations OJ 1703. See also [1926] 7 League of Nations OJ 108–111.

152 The report of this commission was accepted by the Council. See [1926] 7 League of Nations OJ 172–177.

153 'Report of the Commission' (n 145) 203.

154 Ibid.

155 Verdross (n 7) 484–485.

(b) The Principle of Proportionality

Proportionality and the Right of Self-Defence

The report of the commission of enquiry on the Greco-Bulgarian frontier incident, considered in Sub-subsection (a) above, is frequently cited as an application of the principle of proportionality.[156] In contemporary international law, the principle of proportionality performs a function of placing limits on actions which states claiming self-defence can take.[157] The principle was understood in this way in the inter-war period.[158] Brierly, for example, in 1936 maintained that while the right of self-defence allowed for a use of force necessary to avert or repel a threat, 'il ne l'autorise pas dans une mesure excessive par rapport à ce danger, et – il faut insister sur ce point – lorsqu'on a été oblige de commencer à se defender, il n'autorise pas à continuer l'usage de la force en vue de buts ultériurs après que le danger a cessé'.[159]

Proportionality and the Scope of Preceding Acts

Emphasizing the importance of proportionality, however, undercuts the intended basic function of the principle, the placing of limits on the exercise of the right of self-defence, by making obscure the scope of preceding acts that might justify its exercise.[160] A good illustration of this problem is provided by the report submitted by de Brouckère to the Preparatory Commission for the Disarmament Conference in 1926.[161] In this report, widely praised for its

156 Eg M Bourquin 'Le problème de la sécurité internationale' [1934] 49 RCADI 469, 479 n 3.

157 *Case concerning Oil Platforms* (*Islamic Republic of Iran v United States of America*) (Merits) [2003] ICJ Rep 183; Bowett (n 5) 269; Brownlie (n 1) 261–264; C Greenwood 'The Relationship between Ius ad Bellum and Ius in Bello' [1983] 9 Rev Int'l Studies 221–222; O Schacter *International Law in Theory and Practice* (Kluwer Law International Boston 1995) 153–155; Gray (n 144) 148–149. For a broad discussion of the principle of proportionality, see J Gardam *Necessity, Proportionality and the Use of Force by States* (CUP Cambridge 2004).

158 Anzilotti (n 15) 507; Bourquin (n 156) 479; E Kaufmann 'Règles générales du droit de la paix' [1935] 54 RCADI 580; Ago (n 15) 539.

159 JL Brierly 'Règles générales du droit de la paix' [1936] 58 RCADI 129.

160 Bowett (n 5) 269–270.

161 [1926] 6 Monthly Summary of the League of Nations 200–201, 295. Established by a Council resolution of December 12th, 1925 to consider a broad range of questions pertaining to disarmament in advance of the opening of the Disarmament Conference, the Preparatory Commission was made up of representatives of 33 countries, including not only Council member countries and other League member countries facing distinctive conditions with respect to disarmament for reasons of geography, but also a number of non-member countries, including Germany, the US, and the Soviet Union. (Knipping et al (n 58) 297–300)

insistence on the importance of the proportionality principle,[162] de Brouckère argues as follows:

> Every act of violence does not necessarily justify its victim in resorting to war. If a detachment of soldiers goes a few yards over the frontier in a colony remote from any vital centre; if the circumstances show quite clearly that the aggression was due to an error on the part of some subaltern officer; if the central authorities of the 'aggressor State' reprimand the subordinate concerned as soon as they are apprised of the facts; if they cause the invasion to cease, offer apologies and compensation and take steps to prevent any recurrence of such incidents – then it cannot be maintained that there has been an act of war and that the invaded country has reasonable grounds for mobilizing its army and marching upon the enemy capital ... In short, to borrow the felicitous phrase of the Treaty of Locarno, 'the country in question must be exercising the right of legitimate defence'.[163]

He added that a country could resort to war in self-defence only if 'it were the victim of a flagrant aggression of such a serious character that it would obviously be dangerous not to retaliate at once'.[164]

We should bear in mind, however, that even in de Brouckère's formulation, such flagrant aggression is not required for the exercise of the right of self-defence, though the measures taken in self-defence must not amount to resort to war:

> Legitimate defence implies the adoption of measures proportionate to the seriousness of the attack and justified by the imminence of the danger. If a country flagrantly exceeded these limits, even if it were affronted by some incident of little intrinsic importance, it would become in actual fact the real aggressor[.][165]

162 [1927] 8 League of Nations OJ 133–135; [1933] League of Nations OJ Spec Suppl 45; Giraud (n 15) 811; Kaufmann (n 158) 581; Komarnicki (n 50) 26; Brownlie (n 1) 261.

163 'Report by M. de Brouckère on Point 1 (b) of the Proposal Laid before the Preparatory Commission for the Disarmament Conference of the French Delegation' in League of Nations *Reports and Resolutions of the Subject of Article 16 of the Covenant* (*Memorandum and Collection of Reports, Resolutions and References prepared in Execution of the Council's Resolution of December 8th, 1926*) (A 14 1927 V) (Publications of the League of Nations, V. Legal, 1927 V 14) 69.

164 Ibid 69.

165 Ibid.

To be sure, de Brouckère's point is to warn against measures that go beyond the necessary response to an incident of aggression; but in this formulation does not an 'incident of little intrinsic importance' justify a proportionately slight response?

In any case, de Brouckère's report offers no guidance as to what counts as an incident of 'intrinsic importance', or as to how serious an act of aggression must be to call forth justified self-defence. The lower boundary of preceding acts remains elusive.

(c) Summary of Subsection 3

Like the definition of 'aggression', the concept on which the inter-war understanding of self-defence as resistance to aggression must turn, the lower boundary of preceding acts serious enough to justify claims of self-defence remains elusive, even after we have considered the jurisprudence surrounding the Greco-Bulgarian frontier incident and the principle of proportionality. Surely self-defence was not conceived as something that could be exercised in response to any and all actions. But in response to what actions the right of self-defence could or could not be exercised remained unclear in many respects.

4 *Precursor of Collective Self-Defence, and the Preconditions for Its Operation*

The ambiguities besetting the concepts of aggression and preceding acts would become a serious problem for efforts to formulate the precursor concepts to our contemporary understanding of collective self-defence, and would exert a powerful influence on the preconditions recognised in those inter-war predecessor concepts.

Precursor of Collective Self-Defence

Contemporary international law recognises not only an individual, but also a collective right of self-defence. The right of self-defence recognised in the 19th century was the right of an individual state, and, even if not explicitly characterised as such, so was the right established in the inter-war period, at least in so far as it was approached from the perspective of what a country directly subjected to aggression might do in exercising it.

The term 'collective self-defence' is generally understood to have been first used with the adoption in 1945 of the United Nations Charter,[166] Article 51 of which provides for both individual and collective self-defence. If we cut through a number of fine legal disputes and characterise the right of collective

166 J Delbrück 'Collective Self-Defence' in R Bernhardt (n 9) 656–657.

self-defence in a functional way,[167] as 'the legal basis on which a country that has not directly been subjected to aggression may join in an attack with a country that has',[168] then the inter-war treaties and draft treaties can be said to have established a precursor of the contemporary right.

In the inter-war period, as we have noted in some detail, the scope of preceding acts sufficient to establish self-defence as exercised by a single country was rather vague. Interestingly, the preceding acts which in this period were held to justify collective defence were defined more clearly. We must bear in mind, however, that the inter-war attempt to make them plain was spurred by the very difficulties we have noted in defining aggression and identifying aggressors.

The Monroe Doctrine and the Chamberlain Doctrine

A precursor of the right of collective self-defence is found by some in the Monroe Doctrine and the Chamberlain Doctrine, which the US and Britain respectively advanced in connection with the Pact of Paris.[169]

Commenting on the American draft of that Pact, Austen Chamberlain wrote that 'there are certain regions of the world the welfare and integrity of which constitute a special and vital interest for [Britain's] peace and safety' and that protection of such regions against attack 'is to the British Empire a measure of self-defence'.[170] The Monroe Doctrine was referenced in the US Senate's debate on ratification of the Pact of Paris, where it was argued that the doctrine would be accepted under the Pact as a measure of self-defence.[171] While the precise

---

167 T Mori 'Shudanteki Jieiken no Tanjo (Birth of the Right of Collective Self-Defence)' [2003] 102-1 Kokusaiho Gaiko Zassi (Journal of Int'l L & Diplomacy) 80 n 2 (*in Japanese*).

168 S Yamamoto *Kokusaiho* (*International Law*) (2nd edn Yuhikaku Tokyo 1994) 736 (*in Japanese*). Also see Bowett (n 5) 205–207; Brownlie (n 1) 328–331; A Cassese 'Article 51' in JP Cote et al (eds) *La Charte des Nations Unies* (3rd edn Economica Paris 2005) 1354; A Randelzhofer and G Nolte 'Article 51' in B Simma et al (eds) *The Charter of the United Nations: A Commentary* (3rd edn OUP Oxford 2012) vol 2, 1420; *Case concerning Military and Paramilitary Activities in and against Nicaragua* (*Nicaragua v United States of America*) (Merits) [1986] ICJ Rep 545 (dissenting opinion of Judge Jennings).

169 For treatment of the Monroe Doctrine and the Chamberlain Doctrine as precedents for the right of collective self-defence, see Bowett (n 5) 207–215; R Taoka *Kokusaihojo no Jieiken* (*Right of Self-defense under International Law*) (2nd edn Keisoshobo Tokyo 1981) 174–179 (*in Japanese*). A contemporary interpretation of the doctrines as a matter of 'defence of third parties' (*'la légitime defense d'autrui'*) is found in Descamps (n 38) 482–485. (See also Stratis (n 38) 160–172)

170 'Sir Austen Chamberlain to Mr. Houghton, May 19, 1928' (n 34) 132–133.

171 [1928–1929] 70 Cong Rec 1120, 1188.

meaning of the doctrine was hardly clear,[172] a US Department of State memorandum written prior to ratification also cast the doctrine as a matter of self-defence, calling it 'an ex parte statement by this Government that American countries are to be secure in their independence against European interference'[173] and noting that 'considerable interference would be an act of war'.[174]

It is hard to square an understanding of self-defence that comprises the Monroe Doctrine and the Chamberlain Doctrine with US Secretary of State Frank Kellogg's June 1928 definition of the right of self-defence, delivered publicly and in writing, as a country's freedom to defend its territory from attack.[175] The gap was papered over by the language of the Pact's preamble, the signatories proclaiming themselves:

> Convinced that all changes in their relations with each other should be sought only by pacific means and be the result of a peaceful and orderly process, and that any signatory Power which shall hereafter seek to promote its national interests by resort to war *should be denied the benefits furnished by this treaty*[.][176]

It was generally understood that the Chamberlain and Monroe Doctrines served as means of escaping obligations imposed by the Pact of Paris and restoring the freedom to wage war.[177] It should be noted, however, that this freedom

172 P Malanczuk 'Monroe Doctrine' in R Bernhardt (ed) (n 30) 460–464. See also Department of State *Memorandum on the Monroe Doctrine, Prepared by J Reuben Clark, Undersecretary of State, December 17, 1928* (Government Printing Office Washington DC 1930).

173 'Latin America and the Renunciation of War, Sept. 12, 1928 [711.0012 Anti-War/440]' in *National Archives at College Park, College Park, MD, RG 59, Decimal File 1910–1929, Box 6514*.

174 Ibid.

175 'Note of the Government of the United States, June 23, 1928' (n 34) 56–63 esp 57.

176 (Emphasis added) This point is treated in greater detail in Mori (n 167) 93–95. Contemporary views of the problem are succinctly laid out in R Taoka 'Fusen Joyaku no Igi (Significance of the Pact of Paris)' [1932] 1–2 Hogaku (Journal of L & Political Science (Tohoku University)) 153–155 (*in Japanese*). On the position of the Monroe Doctrine in international law, see Taoka (n 169) 177–179.

177 Oppenheim (n 40) 161 refers to the freedom of action possessed under international law prior to the conclusion of the Pact of Paris. A similar characterization is offered by M Yanagihara 'Senso Ihoka to Nihon (Outlawry of War and Japan)' in Kokusaiho Gakkai (Japanese Soc'y of Int'l L) (ed) *Anzen Hosho* (*Interational Security*) (Sanseido Tokyo 2001) 278 (*in Japanese*). If the Pact of Paris is understood as having abolished the international system of war *per se* (as in Descamps (n 38) 460–468; and le le Fur 'Le développement historique du droit international, de l'anarchie internationale à une communauté

was not a freedom to judge whether adequate cause for war had been given, but rather a freedom to decide whether to go to war and whether to resort to war rather than other measures.[178]

In any case, the Pact of Paris being concluded outside the League of Nations framework, the Chamberlain and Monroe Doctrines were intended to restore or preserve the freedom to engage in war without bearing directly on the League's system of collective security.[179]

Automatic Procedures for Aid to Countries Subjected to Aggression

A precursor to the right of collective self-defence can also be found within the League framework. As we have noted, a number of treaties and draft treaties of the inter-war era sought to fill in gaps in the League Covenant by strengthening the system of collective security. These treaties were intended to impose obligations on signatory countries to aid countries subjected to aggression and to take hostile acts against aggressors. Generally, the obligation to act under these treaties was to become effective upon a determination by the League Council that aggression had occurred and that aid should be provided to the victim of the aggression.

The Draft Treaty of Mutual Assistance and the Rhineland Pact, however, did not merely provide for such obligations but permitted a country to extend assistance, under certain circumstances, prior to a Council determination. Automatic procedures of calling forth assistance were a precursor of collective self-defence within the framework of the League and the existing inter-war security system.

The Draft Treaty of Mutual Assistance and the Rhineland Pact were conceived to work in close relation with the League Council. In that sense, they are more closely related than the Monroe and Chamberlain Doctrines to the problem that concerns us of understanding the right of self-defence recognised by the mainstream of international law of the time. We will consider below how these two agreements addressed the problem of the scope of preceding acts in relation to collective self-defence.

---

internationale organisée' [1932] 41 RCADI 536–540), no such freedom of action can be considered preserved. Oppenheim (n 40) 153 argues that the Pact was not intended to abolish war as such, as does Kaufmann (n 158).

178 Yanagihara (n 37) 21 n 12, citing T Sogawa, 'Karu Shumitto ni okeru "Senso Kannen no Tenkan" ni tsuite (Carl Schmitt's "Shift of Theory of War") (1)' [1953] 17-2 Hogaku (Journal of L & Political Science (Tohoku University)) 86 (*in Japanese*).

179 Mori (n 167) 95–96.

(a) The Draft Treaty of Mutual Assistance

Automatic Triggers of Collective Action

As we have seen, the Draft Treaty of Mutual Assistance,[180] prepared in 1923, proposed to prohibit 'aggressive war' (Article 1) and to impose obligations to assist countries subjected to aggression (Article 2). Designation of aggressors and determination of assistance to be provided against them were entrusted to the Council, and signatories were to comply with the Council's judgments (Articles 4 and 5). In the interest of seeing needed assistance provided quickly, however, the Draft Treaty made allowance for supplementary agreements by which particular signatories would commit to assisting each other in the event of aggression (Article 6).[181] Where aggression contemplated by such an agreement occurred, it was to be possible for collective measures to be taken automatically:[182] signatory countries were to act immediately to implement the agreements, providing assistance on their own judgment and without waiting for Council authorization (Article 8).[183] It is true that the conception of self-defence was not introduces.[184] Britain's representative to the Third Committee, however, stated: 'It could not be denied', he argued, 'that if a State were attacked it had *the right to defend itself*. A group of States should have *the same right* and should be able to take action before any decision on the part of the Council'.[185] The attempt here was to ground collective defence on the right of self-defence.

Arguments for and against Automatic Collective Action

The matter of automatic implementation of measures of collective defence called forth particularly intense debate in the drafting of the Treaty of Mutual Assistance. Opponents of such provisions argued that they were likely to hinder or undo the work of constructing collective security arrangements under the League and were incompatible with the League's essential character.[186] If the purpose of the League of Nations was to replace the pre-war system of

---

180 See n 21 of this chapter.

181 Under Article 6, the Council would consider whether such supplementary agreements were in accord with the League Covenant and the Treaty of Mutual Assistance.

182 [1923] 16 League of Nations OJ Spec Supp 43.

183 The Council was to be notified without delay of measures taken to implement such agreements, and the signatories were to comply with Council judgments (Article 8).

184 Sogawa (n 21) 465–466.

185 [1923] 16 League of Nations OJ Spec Suppl 44. (emphasis added)

186 'Report Submitted by the Third Committee to the Assembly' (n 21) 401; [1923] League of Nations OJ Spec Suppl 141 (showing the objections of the representative of the Netherlands), 30 (Japan), 43 (Italy).

military alliances with a system of collective security, it was argued, providing for automatic collective measures meant abandoning the system of collective security, resurrecting the dangerous system of military alliances, and so rendering meaningless whatever progress toward a better system had been made since the war.

The argument for automatic measures stressed the need for emergency action that might arise between the occurrence of aggression and the taking of action pursuant to Council determination.[187] Advocates also argued that it was best to leave the possibility of automatic action open as long as it was unclear whether the collective security framework to be put in place by the Treaty of Mutual Assistance would work effectively.[188]

Difficulty of Defining Aggression and Identifying Aggressors

The dispute over automatic measures appears at first glance a matter of whether collective security or formation of military alliances is the better policy for defending a country.[189] In reality, the dispute was born of another problem

187 'Report Submitted by the third Committee to the Assembly' (n 21); [1923] 16 League of Nations OJ Spec Suppl 44 (showing comments of France's representative).

188 This was argued, eg, by Portugal's representative. (ibid) These disputes over the relationship between collective measures and collective security anticipated those of the present day. See eg Gray (n 144) 189–192.

189 Collective security is typically defined as a formula whereby many countries, including countries in some degree opposed or hostile to each other, commit to refraining from the use of force against each other and, should any country break its promise, the others fight together to make the violator cease its aggressive behavior. (See eg S Tabata *Kokusaiho* (*International Law*) (2nd edn Iwanamishoten Tokyo 1966) 383 (*in Japanese*); Y Yamamoto 'Shudan Anzen Hosho (Collective Security)' Kokusaiho Gakkai (Japanese Soc'y of Int'l L) (ed) (n 122) 453 (*in Japanese*).) Collective security as an ideology appeared as a replacement for the policy of alliances, whereby a country counters aggression on the part of an enemy or potential enemy (assumed to exist) through joining in the fight with allies wherever the enemy country engages in aggression against any member of the alliance. See M Kosaka 'Shudan Anzen Hosho to Domei no Hensen (Transition of Collective Security and Alliance)' [1981] 258 Kokusai Mondai (International Affairs) 2–3 (*in Japanese*). Comparison with alliance systems brings out the following characteristics of collective security systems. (Delbrück (n 166) 646–649)

First of all, while alliances are externally oriented, in the sense that they are systems for resistance against hostile countries conceived as external to an alliance's membership, collective security arrangements have an internal orientation; they are frameworks for handling potential or latent aggressors within the collective itself. On the basis of this difference in orientation, collective security arrangements are conceived as working toward repression of drives to war, while alliances are held to be apt to provoke outbreaks and

we have already noted, the difficulty of defining aggression and identifying aggressors.[190] For example, in objecting to the introduction of automatic defence measures, Italy's representative argued that if collective measures were to be incorporated in spite of the difficulties of defining and designating aggression, the result might well be in practice that each country judges for itself whether aggression has occurred and is thus free to start a war which might draw in all of Europe or even all the world.[191]

Those who argued the necessity of introducing automatic measures did not make light of this risk. Britain's representative, for example, acknowledged the difficulties in defining and identifying aggression. He stressed, however, that the implementation of automatic measures, prior to a judgment of the Council, would be triggered only by 'flagrant' acts of aggression, with responses to less serious cases entrusted to the Council's judgment.[192]

This raises the question, of course, of what would count as 'flagrant'. France saw no great difficulty here: 'Though it is difficult to define specifically *all* cases of aggression, it is undoubtedly possible to specify the most flagrant

---

escalations of war. For a typical statement of this view, Y Matsui *Gendai Nihon no Kokusai Kankei: Anpo Taisei no Hoteki Hihan* (*International Relations of Contemporary Japan: Legal Criticism to the Japan–US Security Alliance*) (Keisoshobo Tokyo 1978) 15 (*in Japanese*). Secondly, in a collective security system, judgment on matters such as whether aggression has occurred, how serious and of what nature the aggression is, and what action should be taken, is institutionalized, entrusted to an organization rather than proceeding from a state's sovereign authority.

If the League of Nations was the first collective security system, its internal orientation was given clear expression in the Covenant (Article 16, paragraph 1). In light of events of the 1930s, however – Japan's and Germany's withdrawal from the league, the exclusion of the Soviet Union, and so forth – whether this orientation held consistently in practice is doubtful. Moreover, institutionalization of decisions surrounding the use of force by the Covenant was plainly incomplete; the negotiation of inter-war treaties under the League was an ongoing attempt to remedy this deficiency. At the same time, while institutionalization is obviously much stronger under the United Nations, the inward orientation of the organization as defined by the UN Charter (Article 39) is less clear than that presented by the Covenant of the League. (Yamamoto (n 168) 715)

190 [1923] 16 League of Nations OJ Spec Suppl 30 (statements by Japan's representative), 43 (Italy's). On the difficulty of defining aggression in the Draft Treaty of Mutual Assistance and contemporary actors' perceptions of the problem, see Section B.1.(b) of this chapter above.

191 [1923] 16 League of Nations OJ Spec Suppl 43.

192 Ibid 44. Britain and France also stressed that countries party to supplementary treaties of assistance would comply with any Council judgment on aggression issued following the initiation of automatic measures of collective defence. See n 181 above.

cases…'.[193] As noted in Subsection 1.(b) of this section, the special committee formed, in the course of the discussion on the Draft Treaty, to consider the problem of defining aggression, concluded that it was impossible to define aggression and that complete discretion in designating aggressors should be given to the League Council.[194] However, the committee also pointed out that the aggressor could be conclusively determined when one state carried out 'a large scale attack upon the territory of the other'[195] or 'a surprise attack by poison gas'.[196] There thus seemed to be at least some markers of 'flagrant' aggression.

Where Aggression is Flagrant

A revised draft of the Treaty incorporating a prohibition of automatic implementation of collective measures was rejected.[197] The taking of collective measures prior to a designation of an aggressor by the Council was thus recognised as permissible. This was done, however, in full awareness of the difficulties involved in defining and identifying the 'aggression' that would have to be present for automatic implementation of collective measures; automatic action was to be triggered only where aggression was flagrant. In other words, the conditions under which collective action might be taken prior to a Council decision were a restricted subset of the conditions under which the collective security system would act: 'aggression' might trigger the collective security action, but automatic action required that the aggression be 'flagrant'.

The principal *Rechtsgut* of the collective measures to be taken prior to Council judgment was national security. The measures were conceived as a policy for securing national security which the League framework of collective security could not be confidently trusted to ensure. It is striking that in discussions of this basic point, little attention seems to have been paid to the question whether the national security to be protected under this scheme was that of one's own nation or that of other nations.[198] What this reflects may be a contemporary understanding that the *Rechtsgut* of the collective measures included international peace and security.[199]

---

193 'Replies of the Governments on the Subject of the Draft Treaty of Mutual Assistance' [1924] 26 League of Nations OJ Spec Suppl 160.

194 'Report Submitted by the Third Committee to the Assembly' (n 21) 406–408.

195 Ibid 407.

196 Ibid.

197 16 League of Nations OJ Spec Suppl 45.

198 See Mori (n 167) 80 n 2.

199 This same point was perhaps made plainer in discussion of the Geneva Protocol, where the interests of a country facing aggression were understood to coincide with the general interest. See 'General Report' (n 27) 121.

(b) The Rhineland Pact (Locarno Treaties)

Automatic Collective Measures

As we have seen, the Rhineland Pact, one of the treaties signed following the Locarno Conference of 1925 by Germany, France, Belgium, Britain, and Italy, pledged Germany and Belgium, and Germany and France, from attacking, invading, or resorting to war against each other (Article 2), required any party claiming a violation of that prohibition to submit its case to the Council (Article 4, paragraph 1), and required the Council to notify the parties without delay of a finding that such violation had occurred, in which event all the signatories, including Britain and Italy, were obligated to come immediately to the aid of the country suffering attack (Article 4, paragraph 2).

The Pact provided for two exceptions to these obligations. The first was 'exercise of the right of legitimate defence' (Article 2): a country had the right of 'resistance to a violation' of a promise not to attack or invade it.[200] This right was to be exercised by the country subjected to attack or aggression, and was simply the right of that country to defend itself.

The second exception allowed for automatic implementation of collective defence, Article 4, paragraph 3 providing that 'In case of a flagrant violation of Article 2 … by one of the High Contracting Parties, each of the other Contracting Parties hereby undertakes immediately to come to the help of the Party against whom such violation … has been directed'. Flagrant violations were defined as unprovoked and involving the crossing of a frontier, outbreak of hostilities, or massing of forces in a demilitarised zone. What we want to note here is that it was only in the event of a 'flagrant' violation that the parties were to come to a victim country's assistance without waiting for the Council.[201]

Arguments for and against Automatic Collective Measures

As in the drafting of the Draft Treaty of Mutual Assistance, so in the drafting of the Rhineland Pact were the pros and cons of automatic collective measures hotly contested. In the latter case, the dispute was particularly intense between Britain and France, but as in the former case it was the difficulty of defining and designating aggression that fuelled argument.

Regarding the assistance which signatories were to provide to countries subjected to aggression, Britain was initially cool. A series of British drafts proposed that such assistance should come only once the Council had confirmed

200 The right could also be exercised in the event of 'flagrant breach' of Article 42 or 43 of the Treaty of Versailles.

201 Where such automatic action was taken, the parties were to comply with recommendations issued thereafter by the Council. (Article 4, paragraph 3)

violation of a relevant treaty provision.[202] The British attitude is captured in notes by foreign ministry legal advisor Cecil Hurst on the article concerning assistance: it 'constitutes a very drastic and far-reaching guarantee ... but recognises', he said, 'the part to be played by the Council of the League in that *the council's notification is a condition precedent to the guarantee being operative*'.[203]

France, on the other hand, from the first stressed the importance of urgent, immediate action and on that basis argued strongly that automatic measures of collective defence were needed. Britain's view on assistance, France held, would remove '*la plus grande partie de leur valeur*' from the proposed security guarantee.[204] Against this imputation, Britain argued that it was not in the general interest for collective action to proceed from what would be after all a particular country's allegation of violation: 'In the interest of all parties concerned and of the world at large, it must be established that the allegation is correct, and it is this duty which, under ... the British draft treaty, it is proposed to entrust to the Council of the League'.[205]

The two countries reached agreement on the points under dispute by distinguishing conditions in which automatic action would be possible and conditions in which assistance would be provided only pursuant to a Council decision. What France had been unable to accept was the view that collective action should 'subordinated *in all cases* to a decision of the Council of the League'.[206] Britain accepted France's call for automatic action to operate in certain cases:

> *In clear cases* where His Majesty's Government themselves admitted that there had been a violation of the frontier..., the guarantee should operate in advance of any decision by the Council. The public would

202 'Draft Security Pact suggested by Sir C. Hurst, May 12, 1925' in WN Medlicott and D Dakin (eds) *Documents on British Foreign Policy 1919–1939* (hereinafter DBFP) (Her Majesty's Stationary Office London 1986) First Series vol 27, 488–489; 'Draft suggested by Central Department as basis for a Security Pact, May 13, 1925' in ibid 496–498; 'Draft Security Pact, June 17, 1925' (enclosure in 'Notes by Sir C. Hurst on the Revised Draft Security Pact, June 17, 1925') in ibid 616–617; 'Anglo-French negotiations regarding proposed draft Treaty of Mutual Guarantee, 11th August, 1925; Annex (A) Proposed Treaty of Mutual Guarantee, Original British Text, July 3, 1925 [C10610/459/18]' in *PRO, FO 371/10738*.

203 'Notes by Sir C. Hurst on the Revised Draft Security Pact, June 17, 1925' in DBFP (n 202) 615.

204 'French views regarding British draft of mutual guarantee, 10th July, 1925 [C9216/459/18]' in *PRO, FO 371/10736*.

205 Ibid.

206 'Anglo-French negotiations regarding proposed treaty of mutual guarantee, 23rd July, 1925 [C9801/459/18]' in *PRO, FO 371/10736*. (emphasis added)

understand that in any case of doubt Great Britain should not be bound to come to her assistance before the Council's decision, but where the facts were admitted and the situation brooked no delay, the guarantee should operate.[207]

'Simple' and 'Flagrant' Aggression

Discussions between Britain and France yielded a distinction between 'simple' and 'flagrant' aggression,[208] and the draft of 12 August 1925 provided for automatic action in collective defence only in the latter case.[209] This draft was accepted without substantive change by legal advisors of the German, Belgian, French, and Italian governments meeting at London prior to the Locarno conference,[210] and later adopted without substantive change at the Locarno conference itself.[211]

Britain's cautious attitude toward automatic collective action obviously owed in part to unease over the imposition of obligations to take collective measures. At the same time, however, concern was understandable over how treaty violations that would call forth collective action were to be designated, as we have already noted. The limitation of automatic measures to flagrant treaty violations was an attempt to balance the need for emergency action against the difficulties inherent in designating aggression, and to balance the *Rechtsgut* of national security with the objective of international peace and security.

As we noted in discussing the Draft Treaty of Mutual Assistance, agreement on special treatment of 'flagrant' violations leaves unanswered the question what counts as 'flagrant'. Britain attempted to address this problem first by stressing the danger of allowing collective action to be undertaken at the discretion of countries party to a dispute, and thus the need for a neutral authority to judge allegations of treaty violations, and then by agreeing to limit

207 Ibid. (emphasis added)

208 Eagleton (n 25) 603; Broms (n 77) 307; Rifaat (n 14) 57.

209 'Anglo-French negotiations regarding proposed draft Treaty of Mutual Guarantee, 12th August, 1925: Annex (C) Proposed Treaty of Mutual Guarantee (including the Amendments provisionally agreed upon by Mr. Chamberlain and M. Briand on August 12, 1925) [C10611/459/18]' in *PRO, FO 371/10738*.

210 'Report by Sir C. Hurst on the Proceedings of a Meeting of Jurists held at the Foreign Office, September 1–4, 1925, in connection with the proposed Treaty of Mutual Guarantee' in *DBFP* (n 202) 754, 757–758.

211 'Proceedings of the Conference of Locarno and Records of Conversations connected therewith, October 5–16, 1925' in ibid 1078, 1084, 1086–1088, 1090–1091.

automatic action to cases of flagrant violations. But as we have noted,[212] the problem was fundamentally left unresolved: no objective standards were provided for determining whether a flagrant violation had been committed; indeed, scope was left for subjective judgments on the part of countries party to the agreement who would provide the assistance to be triggered by violations.

It is important to notice that, in addition to the distinction between the preconditions for automatic collective action (the precursor to collective self-defence) and those for assistance pursuant to a Council decision, the preconditions of automatic collective action also differ from those for action in self-defence by a particular country. Where the exercise of self-defence by a particular country requires simply a 'violation' of Article 2, automatic collective defence action requires a 'flagrant violation'.

(c) Summary of Subsection 4

As we have seen, a precursor to contemporary collective self-defence is visible in the treaty practice of the inter-war period as represented by the Draft Treaty of Mutual Assistance and the Rhineland Pact, both of which provided for military assistance to be extended to victim countries prior to a decision of the Council. In this respect, these treaties were supplementary to the system of mutual security directed to the *Rechtsgüter* of national security and of international peace and security. The form or name given this precursor was automatic action in collective defence, which was adopted after fierce argument that is traceable to earlier disputes over the difficulties involved in defining and identifying aggression.[213] Opponents of automatic implementation of collective measures emphasised these difficulties and argued that judgment by the Council was indispensable. Their concern was to prevent the danger of countries declaring aggression on their own discretion by requiring that any such declaration be made by the Council; and those who supported automatic collective measures were fully aware of the risk which opponents highlighted.

The difficulties were resolved by the restricting of conditions under which automatic collective measures could be implemented to cases of flagrant aggression. Among the implications of this solution is that the preconditions

212 Section B.1.(d) in this chapter.

213 We recall here that automatic measures were rejected in the drafting of the Geneva Protocol. It should be noted that what was rejected in the drafting of the Geneva protocol was an automatic procedure for designating aggression; the slightly different issue of emergency measures to be taken prior to Council decision seems not to have been a major focus of discussion. See Sogawa (n 21) 468–469.

for the exercise of the right of collective self-defence were more restrictively defined than both those for the implementation of collective security measures under the authority of the League and those for the exercise of self-defence by a single country. Measures under the latter two rubrics required simply aggression, which might or might not be judged flagrant. Restricting the scope of preceding acts to flagrant aggression was intended to limit the risk of discretionary designations of aggression and the risk inherent in automatic collective action of triggering the outbreak or escalation of wars. While these issues had been discussed in the formulation of the Draft Treaty of Mutual Assistance, they were explicitly addressed in the text of the Rhineland Pact.

C Significance of the Inter-war Period's Conception of Self-Defence: Self-Defence as Defensive War

The Policing Conception of Self-Defence and the Defensive War Conception of Self-Defence

As we have seen, the right of self-defence established in the inter-war period was generally discussed in terms of prohibition of resort to war or prohibition of aggression; self-defence was conceived as justifying resistance to acts of aggression. The *Rechtsgut* was the security of the nation concerned, but was conceived as covering also international peace and security, especially where the precursor to the right of collective self-defence was concerned.[214]

This contrasted with the pre-war conception of the right of self-defence, which was discussed in the context of territorial inviolability and freedom of the high seas: its function was to excuse the violation by one state of another state's territory or of a ship on the high seas under the flag of another state, in order to prevent or make cease a violation against the first state, where the other state was not able to suppress the violators on its own. The fundamental *Rechtsgut* of this pre-war right of self-defence was the protection of the lives and property of a state's nationals, though under certain circumstances and to a certain extent the *Rechtsgut* might be said to have covered also the nation's security.

214 As noted above (n 199 of this chapter), this international dimension to the *Rechtsgut* was in some way present even in cases of the exercise of the individual self-defence, in so far as it was accepted that the interests of a country subjected to aggression accord with the general interest.

If we can say that the pre-war right of self-defence conceived of self-defence as a 'policing' function, the inter-war period conceived of self-defence as defensive war.[215]

Legal Status of Policing and Defensive War Conceptions

Policing-type self-defence, widely recognized as a genuine right in the mid-19th century, had by the end of that century been recast in the more restrictive mold of an 'excuse'. The status of defensive war as a genuine right throughout the pre-war period is clearer; and the inter-war treaties outlawing war clearly prohibited not war undertaken in self-defence but only wars of aggression. The allowance for self-defence was repeatedly made quite explicit in the inter-war period. In the words of the subcommittee report cited earlier,[216] 'one point appears beyond dispute – namely, that ... in the Covenant of the League in its present form ... the prohibition of recourse to war [does not] exclude the right of legitimate self-defence'. With respect to the Geneva Protocol, the same categorical assurance was offered:

> The prohibition affects only aggressive war. It does not, of course, extend to defensive war. The right of legitimate self-defence continues, as it must, to be respected. The State attacked retains complete liberty to resist by all means in its power any acts of aggression of which it may be the victim.[217]

Article 2 of the Rhineland Pact created a clear exception to the obligation of the parties not to resort to war against each other: 'This stipulation shall not apply ... in the case of ... [t]he exercise of the right of self-defence'. With respect to the Pact of Paris, we need only recall the British foreign minister's statement: 'His Majesty's Government do not think that its terms exclude action which

---

215 It is not novel to suggest that the single term 'right of self-defence' has been used to refer to two quite distinct rights. Dinstein, for example, distinguishes '(individual) Self-defence in response to an armed attack *by* a State' and '(individual) Self-defence in response to an armed attack *from* a State'. (Dinstein (n 8) 242–277. (emphasis added) See also DP O'Connell *International Law* (Stevens & Sons, London, 1965) vol 1, 338–344; J Žourek 'La notion de légitime défense en droit international' [1975] 56 Annuaire (Institut de Droit International) 23; AV Lowe, 'Peace without Justice' in WE Butler (ed) *Perestroika and International Law* (Nijhoff Dordrecht 1990) 289–290.)

216 'Amendment of the Covenant of the League of Nations in Order to Bring It into Harmony with the Pact of Paris' (n 17) 146.

217 'General Report' (n 27) 121.

a State may be forced to take in self-defence'.[218] It is simply not the case that under the inter-war treaties all war was prohibited, and made an exception for defensive war alone; there was no question of prohibiting defensive war, which was clearly held to be a legitimate right of states.

The Right of Defensive War and the Definition of Aggression

The right of self-defence established in the inter-war era thus seems clearly defined. We must recall, however, that the definition at work rested on the conception of aggression, for which no generally accepted definition existed. There was, indeed, a widely shared impression that defining aggression and designating aggressors were fraught with difficulty. Aggression was the precondition for the exercise of the inter-war right of self-defence, but what was 'aggression'? As definition of the term proved extremely difficult and no widely accepted definition existed, we must recognise that definition of the preconditions of exercising the right of self-defence was equally elusive. Moreover, as discussions of the time concerning frontier incidents and proportionality suggest, definition of such preconditions could not rest on a common understanding of the lower bound of preceding acts, which remained quite undefined.

These definitional difficulties were addressed in concrete ways in discussions of the precursor of a right of collective self-defence, automatic collective defence actions. It is awareness of these difficulties, in fact, that explains the formula adopted of limiting the exercise of the precursor of the right of collective self-defence to cases of flagrant aggression. In light of the great ambiguities in the concept of aggression, the need was felt to limit the risk of discretionary declarations of aggression by particular countries, and, ultimately, the risk inherent in automatic implementation of measures of collective defence of provoking war or causing a conflict to escalate into another World War.

The difficulty of defining and designating aggression created a need to place limitations on the precursor of collective self-defence. Consciousness of this essential problem was quite acute in the process of drafting a United Nations Charter, as we will discuss in Chapter 6.

---

218 'Sir Austen Chamberlain to Mr. Houghton, May 19, 1928' (n 34) 132.

PART 3

The Pre-1945 Right of Self-Defence

CHAPTER 5

The Relationship between the Two Conceptions of Self-Defence

This chapter examines the relationship that existed in the inter-war period between the 19th century's policing conception of the right of self-defence and the conception established in the inter-war period of self-defence as defensive war.

Existing Views of this Relationship

As discussed in Chapter 1, Section B, a broad gap divides proponents of a permissive interpretation from proponents of a restrictive interpretation of the right of self-defence. The permissive interpretation defines the 19th century right as 'a general right of self-protection against a forcible threat to a State's legal rights'.[1] Defined in this way, its exercise does not require the occurrence or imminent threat of armed attack.[2] The permissive interpretation also holds that in the inter-war period this right was neither abolished nor limited, and, in fact, that it continues to exist as a matter of customary law even under the United Nations.[3]

The restrictive interpretation holds that the customary law right of self-defence effective when the United Nations was established in 1945 was such that it could be exercised only in the event of armed attack.[4] Aside from

1 CHM Waldock 'The Regulation of the Use of Force by Individual States in International Law' [1952] 81 RCADI 496. See also R Higgins *The Development of International Law through the Political Organs of the United Nations* (OUP Oxford 1963) 199.

2 Eg Waldock (n 1) 451–517; DW Bowett *Self-Defence in International Law* (Manchester University Press Manchester 1958).

3 Waldock (n 1) 476–477, 496–499; Bowett (n 2) 200.

4 Some proponents of the restrictive interpretation argue that while the preconditions were broader than this under the customary law, they were thus restricted by the UN Charter. PM Dupuy 'L'invocation de la légitime defénse dans la justification des états' in JF Guilhaudis and M Torrelli (eds) *Force armée et diplomatie* (Nijhoff Dordrecht 1985) vol 2, 140; K Yokota *Jieiken* (*Right of Self-defence*) (Yuhikaku Tokyo 1951) 44–67 (*in Japanese*); Y Takano *Kokusaiho Gairon* (*Treatise on International Law*) (rev edn Kobundo Tokyo 1985) vol 1, 186–189 (*in Japanese*).

 | DOI 10.1163/9789004355002_007

obligations of reporting to the Council, the customary law right, this interpretation holds, did not differ from that defined by the Charter.[5]

Among proponents of the restrictive interpretation, there are, broadly, two views on the relationship between the inter-war and the 19th century rights of self-defence. Some consider the pre-World War I right to have been as broad as presented by the permissive interpretation, but maintain that it was narrowed as the outlawry of war progressed in the inter-war period, such that by 1945, under the customary law 'force was justified only in reaction against some armed attack or threat of force'.[6] In defending this position, Brownlie directly rebutted the claim that the customary law right of self-defence was 'reserved' under the Pact of Paris, which is properly seen as the culmination of the campaign to outlaw war.[7]

The other school of thought within the restrictive interpretation holds that only with the inter-war prohibition of a certain category of wars was the right of self-defence recognised in international law, and accordingly denies that a right of self-defence existed at all prior to the First World War.[8] On this view, there can be no grounds for positing a relationship between the right of self-defence established in the interwar period and what can only loosely be termed a 19th century right of self-defence.

We saw in Chapter 3, however, that a right of self-defence, established by state practice, did exist in the 19th century. We also saw that this 19th century right was somewhat different in character from what is generally supposed: it was not 'a general right of self-protection against a forcible threat to a State's legal rights',[9] but a justification or excuse for violating the territory of another state or a ship on the high seas under the jurisdiction of another state, where the state whose territory or jurisdiction was violated was unable to prevent persons under its jurisdiction from doing injury to the state acting in

---

5 On the relationship between the duty to report to the Security Council and the customary international law, see A Randelzhofer and G Nolte 'Article 51' in B Simma et al (eds) *The Charter of the United Nations: A Commentary* (3rd edn OUP Oxford 2012) vol 2, 1424 n 193.

6 I Brownlie *International Law and the Use of Force by States* (Clarendon Press Oxford 1963) 232.

7 Ibid 240.

8 R Ago 'Addendum to the Eighth Report on State Responsibility: The Internationally Wrongful Act of the State, Source of International Responsibility (Part 1) (Concluded)' [1980] 2–1 Yb Int'l Comm'n 53; J Žourek 'La notion de légitime défense en droit international' [1975] 56 Annuaire (Institut de Droit International) 24–28; LA Sicilianos *Les réactions décentralisées à l'illicite* (LGDJ Paris 1990) 40–44.

9 Waldock (n 1) 496. See also Higgins (n 1) 199.

self-defence. A right of self-defence existed in the 19th century, but was radically different from that of the inter-war period, which was conceived in terms of resistance or defensive war against aggression.

Structure of this Chapter

If the foregoing is correct, then the relationship between the 19th century right of self-defence and that of the inter-war period can be understood in terms other than those provided by either the restrictive or the permissive interpretation. Accordingly, this chapter seeks to consider this relationship as it can be discerned through state practice and a number of lines of doctrine developed in the inter-war period. If the two conceptions of 'the right of self-defence' differ in nature, the possibility arises that they existed side-by-side in the inter-war period. Section A of this chapter explores and confirms this possibility. A finding of the coexistence of the two conceptions shows that the relationship between the two conceptions is not that of displacement of the older by the newer and thus reveals the need to ask afresh what that relationship was. We take up this question in Section B, asking how the inter-war outlawry of war influenced the right of self-defence that had existed since the mid-19th century.

A Coexistence of the Two Conceptions of the Right of Self-Defence

As argued in Part 2 of this work, the two concepts of self-defence before us differed in terms of the contexts in which they were discussed. As a result, fairly little argument of the inter-war period deals directly with their relationship. The period's silence on this topic also makes sense in light of the period's focus on outlawing war and the corresponding engagement with the problem of self-defence as justification for defensive war.

A number of arguments developed in the inter-war period, however, bring to the surface contemporary countries' understandings of the relationship. Little scholarly attention has been paid to these sources of evidence, or indeed to the very problem of how to characterise the relationship we aim to clarify. In Subsection 1, we will consider how, when resort to war was prohibited by the Pact of Paris, the protection of nationals abroad was justified. In Subsection 2, we will attempt to characterise the national understandings of the problem at work in the League of Nations Conference for the Codification of International Law of 1930. Finally, in Subsection 3, we will consider the 1930 US-Mexican Mixed Claims Commission.

1 *The Pact of Paris and Protection of Nationals Abroad*

(a) Protection of Nationals and the Two Conceptions of the Right of Self-Defence

(i) *Current Argument*

Self-Defence and the Protection of Nationals

The right of protection of nationals abroad can be defined as countries' right to use military force 'to rescue their own nationals whose lives or health are endangered in a foreign country'.[10] Whether the protection of nationals is a substantive right covered under the right of self-defence and whether in the exercise of the right of self-defence military force can be used for this purpose is an area of sharp contention between advocates of the restrictive and permissive interpretations.

Both camps agree, however, that before World War I the right of self-defence could be exercised to that end. Brownlie states plainly: 'Intervention by armed forces to protect nationals was a common occurrence in the period before 1914'.[11] 'The jurists of the nineteenth century', he says, 'universally considered as lawful the use of force to protect the lives and property of nationals'.[12] So it is that, as noted in Chapter 3, protection of nationals is often cited as an example of the right of self-defence in the 19th century.[13]

---

10 A Randelzhofer 'Use of Force' in R Bernhardt (ed) *Encyclopedia of Public International Law* (Elsevier Amsterdam 2000) vol 4, 1254. At present, opinion is bitterly divided on the lawfulness under international law of using force to protect nationals abroad, and among those who do consider it lawful, there are differences in the grounds on which they do so. While some ground the practice in a right of self-defence, others treat it as outside the range of acts prohibited by Article 2(4) of the UN Charter, others consider it justifiable on state-of-emergency grounds, and others still rest their defence on the incapacity of the UN. (A Randelzhofer and O Dörr 'Article 2(4)' in Simma et al (eds) (n 5) 226–228) On this point, valuable references include N Ronzitti *Rescuing Nationals Abroad through Military Coercion and Intervention on Grounds of Humanity* (Martinus Nijhoff Publishers Dordrecht 1985). As one of the latest arguments, see T Ruys *'Armed Attack' and Article 51 of the UN Charter* (CUP Cambridge 2010) 213–249. The focus in this work is the relationship between protection of nationals abroad and the right of self-defence before World War I. For an overview of the Japanese government's views on self-defence in relation to the protection of nationals, see M Asada 'Nihon to Jieiken (Japan and Right of Self-defence)' in Kokusaiho Gakkai (Japanese Soc'y of Int'l L) (ed) *Anzen Hosho* (*International Security*) (Sanseido Tokyo 2001) 40–46 (*in Japanese*).

11 Brownlie (n 6) 290.

12 Ibid 289. See also DW Bowett 'The Use of Force for the Protection of Nationals Abroad' in A Cessase (ed) *The Current Legal Regulation of the Use of Force* (Martinus Nijhoff Publishers Dordrecht 1986) 39; Waldock (n 1) 466–467; Ronzitti (n 10) 21.

13 Whether this was in fact part of the 19th century right of self-defence we will consider later in this chapter.

On whether such protection of nationals was justified by the right of self-defence in the inter-war period, the permissive and restrictive interpretations part ways. The restrictive interpretation holds that with the transformation of the conception of self-defence that occurred after World War I, the use of force to protect naturals ceased to be justified by the right of self-defence.[14] In contrast, the position of the permissive interpretation is stated by Bowett:

> There is ample evidence that, prior to 1945, States assumed the right to use force abroad for the protection of their nationals when their lives or their property were in imminent danger ... Moreover, there is also ample evidence to show that States regarded this right of protection as being essentially part of the more general right of self-defence.[15]

Significance of the Dispute

The current dispute over whether the right of self-defence could be exercised for the purpose of protecting nationals in the inter-war period mirrors the larger question of how to understand the relationship between the right of self-defence established in the 19th century and that established in the inter-war period. Asking how the protection of nationals was related to the right of self-defence in the inter-war period promises to clarify not only what the inter-war right of self-defence entailed but how it related to the preexisting right of the 19th century.

(ii) *Argument from the Mid-19th Century through the Inter-War Period*

Evolution of the Concept of the Right to Protect Nationals

Though it is now generally accepted that protection of nationals was justified prior to the World War I by the right of self-defence, assessing the validity of that common view calls for careful examination of the state practice and

14 Brownlie (n 6) 299.

15 Bowett (n 12) 39. Bowett argued, further, that the UN Charter preserves the customary law right of self-defence that existed before the Charter's adoption and, accordingly, that if protection of nationals was part of the right of self-defence before 1945 it surely has been since. (ibid 40; see also Waldock (n 1) 466–467, 503) Bowett took a slightly different view in 1957, however: though maintaining, as in 1986, that 'there is no doubt' that the use of force to protect nationals was lawful, he did not directly address the question of whether its lawfulness in the pre-World War I era was based on a right of self-defence but merely noted 'the identity of the conditions governing the right of protection and those governing any exercise of self-defence'. (DW Bowett 'The Use of Force in the Protection of Nationals' [1957] 43 Transactions of the Grotius Society 118)

doctrine of the time. It was not until after 1900 that the conception of protection of nationals as understood today was formed, and it is unlikely that protection of nationals was seen as a type of action in self-defence before 1914.

From the latter half of the 19th century until early in the 20th, 'protection of nationals' meant, at least in part, what today we call diplomatic protection.[16] The 19th century authority Hall, for example, after stating that 'States possess a right of protecting their subjects abroad which is correlative to their responsibility in respect of injuries inflicted upon foreigners within their dominions',[17] proceeded to clarify his meaning:

> the right, that is to say, to exact reparation for maltreatment of their subjects by a foreign government or its administrative agents if no means of obtaining legal redress through the tribunals of the country exist, or if such means as exist have been exhausted in vain; … and … the right to require that, as between their subjects and other private individuals, the protection of the state and the justice of the courts shall be afforded equally, and that compensation shall be made if the courts from corruption or prejudice or other like causes are guilty of serious acts of injustice.[18]

Similarly, when John Westlake examined 'The Protection of Subjects Abroad',[19] he mainly focused on the issue of the denial of justice.[20]

The focus on such diplomatic services in the conceptualization of protection of nationals reflected the fact that much of what countries actually did to protect nationals took that form. In reviewing case studies of the protection of nationals, we need to take this reality into account.

---

16 WK Geck 'Diplomatic Protection' in R Bernhardt (ed) *Encyclopedia of Public International Law* (Elsevier Amsterdam 1992) vol 1, 1045–1067.

17 WE Hall *A Treatise on International Law* (2nd edn Clarendon Press Oxford 1884) 254.

18 Ibid.

19 J Westlake *International Law* (CUP Cambridge 1904) Part I, 312.

20 Ibid 312–320. Moreover, even when the right to intervene for the protection of nationals was discussed in this period, what was meant was the right to claim damages after an injury to a country's nationals had been done. See Westlake (n 19) 320; L Oppenheim *International Law* (Longmans, Green & Co. London 1905) vol 1, 183. See also E Pittard *La protection des nationaux à l'étranger* (Imprimerie W Kündig & Fils Genève 1896) 250–258; A Mérignhac *Traité de droit public international* (LGDJ Paris 1905) 297–298.

Precedents and the Evolution of the Concept

Milton Offutt's *The Protection of Citizens Abroad by the Armed Forces of the United States,*[21] published in 1928, is an oft-cited source of detailed case studies in this area. That Offutt lists over 70 cases of the use of American forces for protection of nationals between 1813 and 1927 is taken to show how unexceptional such a use of force was in the state practice of the period.[22] The actions presented from the 1810s and 1820s, however, were reprisals against piracy, and most of the actions from the 1830s through the 1880s were taken to demand punishment or reparations for damages already incurred by US citizens. Cases of the protection of nationals in the sense in which we understand the concept do not appear regularly in the record until the 1890s, and did not occur with great frequency until the 1900s.[23]

Reflecting this change in state practice since the early 20th century, the concept of protection of nationals came to assume the form in which we recognise it. Frantz Despagnet's 1905 treatment of '*intervention pour la défense des nationaux*', for example, discussed not only such measures as reprisals in response to violations of nationals' rights, but also the right of a country, where a state refuses or fails to protect the country's nationals in its territory, to act in the place of the territorial state to defend those nationals.[24] In the 1899 edition of the same source, by contrast, Despagnet had not discussed the latter sort of protective action; his discussion of protection of nationals in that edition concerned rather the recovery of loans extended by nationals to foreign governments.[25]

A 1912 memorandum prepared for the Solicitor of the US Department of State reveals a dawning of awareness of the issue of using force to protect nationals abroad:

---

21 M Offutt *The Protection of Citizens Abroad by the Armed Forces of the United States* (Johns Hopkins Press Baltimore 1928).

22 See eg Brownlie (n 6) 290.

23 Ibid. See also *Right to Protect Citizens in Foreign Countries by Landing Forces* (Memorandum by the Solicitor) (Department of State, Division of Information, Series M, No. 14, printed and distributed October 5, 1912) 31–32. The rising trend of such actions from the 19th century to the outbreak of World War I can plausibly be linked to the development over that period of capital export. (See Offutt (n 21) 150–161; E Root 'The Basis of Protection to Citizens Residing Abroad' [1910] 4 AJIL 517–519).

24 F Despagnet *Cours de droit international public* (3rd edn Sirey Paris 1905) 216–220. See also Root (n 23) 517–528, esp 520–521.

25 F Despagnet, *Cours de droit international public* (2nd edn Sirey Paris 1899) 197–199.

> The precise question at issue is whether or not one state may, if necessary, use actual force (*i.e.*, use its army and navy) for and in behalf of and to secure the protection and security of the persons and property of its citizens resident or domiciled in another state in cases of sudden emergency where the other state fails, either through its unwillingness, its impotence, or from any other cause, to protect the citizens of the first state and their property from destruction.[26]

Theoretical Foundations

If the protection of nationals abroad came at the beginning of the 20th century to be understood in more or less its current sense, the theoretical foundations of this understanding were by no means clear. This ambiguity was enhanced by the coexistence of views treating such protection as mere 'imposition', in contrast with 'intervention' in the domestic political affairs of foreign states,[27] with views that based the right to protect nationals in the 'right of self-preservation'.[28] We certainly cannot say that the protection of nationals was universally considered as comprised within the right of self-defence.

We should note, however, that notwithstanding the state of theory at the time, the function of the protection of nationals was understood in the same way as the function of the right of self-defence recognised in the 19th century. As noted in Chapter 3, the pre-World War I right of self-defence was thought of as an excuse for the violation of a state's territory or of a vessel on the high seas under that state's jurisdiction, a justifiable means by which a country might prevent harm to itself where the state with jurisdiction over the territory or ships was unable to prevent people under its jurisdiction from doing it harm. Similarly, when the protection of nationals came to be understood in its current sense at the beginning of the 20th century, it was understood as justifying actions to protect a country's citizens in the territory of a state unable to

---

26 *Right to Protect Citizens* (n 23) 3. See also Root (n 23) 520–521. Prior to World War I, diplomatic protection and what we today think of as protection of nationals proper were not sharply differentiated from each other. Borchard, for example, writing in a volume published in 1915, discussed the use of military force for diplomatic protection, citing as purposes for such action the protection of American citizens in regions experiencing rebellion or unrest, as well as punishment or reparations for the killing or other violations of the rights of American citizens. (EM Borchard *The Diplomatic Protection of Citizens Abroad or the Law of International Claims* (Banks Law Publishing New York 1915) 448)

27 *Right to Protect Citizens* (n 23) 22–23; Borchard (n 26) 448–449. Waldock, incidentally, rejected this distinction as neither accurate nor necessary. (Waldock (n 1) 467)

28 *Regulations for the Government of the Navy of the United States* (Government Printing Office Washington DC 1909) 86–87.

afford them protection itself. The essential function of the right of protection of nationals, in other words, was simply justification of the violation of another state's territory. US Secretary of State Elihu Root, for example, held that:

> armed forces have often been landed from men-of-war for the protection of the life and property of their national citizens ... Such a course is undoubtedly often necessary, but *it is always an impeachment of the effective sovereignty of the government in whose territory the armed demonstration occurs*, and it can be justified only by ... the incapacity of the government of the country to perform its international duty of protection.[29]

The Conception of the Right to Protect Nationals in the Inter-War Period

In the inter-war period, 'protection of nationals' came to mean almost universally what it means today. While a strain of doctrine in the inter-war years denied the existence of a 'right' of protection of naturals,[30] the majority doctrinal position accepted it. The commenters in this majority can be broadly divided between those who considered the right of protection of nationals part of the right of self-defence[31] and those who sought its justification elsewhere.[32] Those who accepted the right of protection of nationals as part of the right of self-defence held that this right of self-defence had existed since before the War, understanding it as a justification for the violation of another country's territory. Alfred Verdross is a particularly conspicuous advocate of this view. Verdross distinguished '*Le droit de légitime défense*', defined as '*le droit de s'opposer par la force à un agression injuste, c'est-à-dire contraire à un règle du droit*',[33] from '*Actes d'auto-protection défensive autre que la légitime défense*', justified by the right '*de repousser des violations qui proviennent non de la part d'États*

29 Root (n 23) 521 (emphasis added); Borchard (n 26) 448–449.

30 SC Stratis *Le pacte générale de renonciation à la guerre* (M Rivière Paris 1931) 150–151; LE Le Fur 'Le développement historique du droit international' [1932] 41 RCADI 536–537; J Basdevant 'Règles générales du droit de la paix' [1936] 58 RCADI 547.

31 CG Fenwick *International Law* (Century New York 1924) 156–159; A Verdross 'Règles générales du droit international de la paix' [1929] 30 RCADI 487–488; T Baty *The Canons of International Law* (John Murray London 1930) 105–112; PB Potter 'L'intervention en droit international moderne' [1930] RCADI 647.

32 Offutt (n 21) 1–8; BC Rodick *The Doctrine of Necessity in International Law* (Columbia University Press New York 1928) 49–50; FS Dunn *The Protection of Nationals* (Johns Hopkins Press Baltimore 1932) 19; É Giraud 'La théorie de la légitime défense' [1934] RCADI 735–738.

33 Verdross (n 31) 481.

étrangers eux-mêmes mais simplement de leur territoire ou d'un domaine assimilé à ceux-ci'.[34] For Verdross, the right to protect nationals was encompassed by the latter.[35] Verdross's '*Le droit de légitime défense*' and his right '*Actes d'autoprotection défensive autre que la légitime défense*' correspond respectively to what we have described as the inter-war period's right of self-defence and the right of self-defence that existed before the War and continued to exist thereafter. In other words, the fact that Verdross treats the right of protection of nationals as a matter of justification of violations of a state's territory tells us that in his view this right was comprehended under the right of self-defence that had existed since the 19th century.

(iii) *The Pact of Paris and the Two Conceptions of Self-Defence*

As noted in Chapter 4, Section A.4, when the Pact of Paris was concluded in 1928, it was generally accepted that the right of self-defence was reserved to the signatory countries. Regarding the scope and function of that reserved right, it is often noted that in his memorandum to the original signatories US secretary of state Frank Kellogg stated that '[e]very nation is free at all times and regardless of treaty provisions to defend its territory from attack or invasion'.[36]

This statement, in fact, has often served as grounds for understanding the right of self-defence established by the Pact, and thus the right of self-defence (or of 'legitimate defence') of the interwar period, as the right of resorting to force 'against some armed attack or threat of force'.[37]

At least three countries, however – the US, Britain, and Japan – continued to maintain, after the conclusion of the Pact, that action to protect nationals was permitted. We will consider the understandings employed by these countries in some detail below. If we bear in mind that the right of self-defence advanced as justification for such action was the right of self-defence that existed before the War, examination of the framing of protection of nationals within these countries' understandings will help to clarify a number of issues. How was protection of nationals to be justified in relation to the Pact of Paris? Was it justified as an exercise of the right of self-defence? Was it held to be permissible

34 Ibid 485–486.

35 Ibid 487–488. Note that Verdross treated the *Caroline* incident as illustrating this latter right.

36 'Note of the Government of the United States to the Governments of Belgium, Czechoslovakia, France, Germany, Great Britain, Irish Free State, Italy, Japan and Poland, Delivered at the Respective Foreign Offices, June 23, 1928' in Department of State *Treaty for the Renunciation of War: Text of the Treaty, Notes Exchanged, Instruments of Ratification and of Adherence and Other Papers* (Government Printing Office Washington DC 1933) 57.

37 Brownlie (n 6) 232. See also ibid 239–241.

not as self-defence but on other grounds? How, in either case, was the right of self-defence defined? In presenting such questions, a focus on these countries' understandings of the status of protection of nationals under the Pact of Paris affords an opportunity to examine the relationship between the 19th century and inter-war conceptions of the right of self-defence and thus to clarify what the inter-war right of self-defence entailed.

(b) Protection of Nationals and the Pact of Paris

Process of the Pact's Formation

By 1939, almost 90 percent of the world's countries and regions[38] had become Pact of Paris signatories. The original signatories numbered fifteen, of which six had been involved from the beginning of the process of shaping its content: the United States, France, Britain, Germany, Italy, and Japan. Once these six had reached a basic agreement, to which they and the other nine signed on, the other countries were urged to accept the proposed treaty.

Of the six countries closely and actively involved in the initial drafting stages, the US, Britain, and Japan believed that protection of nationals would be permitted after the Pact came into force. How Germany, Italy, and France thought about this question is not clear. These three countries seem not to have offered any official statement of views on the question, and a close review of the notes which the US (and France to a lesser extent) exchanged with other countries on their accession to the treaty shows that no country explicitly addressed the issue.[39] Our consideration of signatories' views is thus limited by necessity to the three countries on record: the US, Britain, and Japan.

(i) *Japan*

Protection of Nationals as Covered by the Right of Self-Defence

Japan's government was cognizant of the issue of protection of nationals relatively early in the process of concluding the Pact of Paris. The matter was discussed in the process of preparing a response to the US treaty draft of 13th April, 1928.[40] In its draft response of 23rd May, Japan held the right of

38 Sixty-three of the 71 countries of the time. ('Rights and Duties of States in Case of Aggression: Draft Convention with Comment, Prepared by the Research in International Law of the Harvard Law School' [1939] AJIL Suppl 284)

39 'Notes Exchanged between the United States and the Governments which were Invited to Adhere – Instruments of Adherence' in Department of State (n 36) 109–306.

40 'Dai-ichiji Teian nitaisuru Kaitoan (Dai-ichi-an – Dai-juyon-an) (Draft Reply to the First Proposal (1st–14th Draft))' in M Yanagihara (ed) *Kokusaiho Senrei Shiryoshu (1) Fusen Joyaku (Document Collection of International Law Precedents (1) Pact of Paris)* (Shinzansha Tokyo 1996) vol 1, 182–190 (*in Japanese*).

self-defence to 'include, where appropriate, protection of the life and property of nationals abroad'.[41] Further, the topic was treated in detail in a memorandum of May 1929, just two months before Japan's ratification of the treaty, prepared by the Ministry of Foreign Affairs Asia Bureau, 'Jieiken ni tsuite (On the Right of Self-defence').[42]

This memorandum considered three issues, in the following order: 'whether dispatch of troops to protect Japanese subjects abroad constitutes self-defence', 'whether defence of Japan's interests in Manchuria is self-defence', and 'the basis for maintenance of order in Manchuria'. Protection of nationals was considered under the first of these, but on all three questions the conclusion was that the legitimacy of Japanese action should be asserted in connection with the right of self-defence.

This implies, of course, that protection of nationals was to be justified by the right of self-defence. The conception of 'self-defence' invoked, it is also clear, was so broad and elastic as to have no legal meaning and to remove the reasoning from the realm of legal analysis. However, it is important to note that, as we will see below, even as Japan's government advanced this catholic view, it was in fact aware of clear differences in the self-defence justifications required by the three issues.

---

41 Ibid 182.

42 'Jieiken nitsuite (1929 (Showa 4-nen) Ajia-kyoku Dai-ichi-ka) (On Right of Self-defence (1929) Asian Affairs Bureau 1st Devision)' in Yanagihara (n 40) 361–366 (*in Japanese*). This memorandum is examined particularly closely in M Yanagihara 'Senso Ihoka to Nihon (Outlawry of War and Japan)' in Kokusaiho Gakkai (Japanese Soc'y of Int'l L) (ed) (n 10) 277–278. On the general question of how Japan understood the right of self-defence under the Pact of Paris there exist a number of fine studies. Representative assessments of the Japanese government's views hold, for example, that 'they had less to do with a notion of self-defence than with something close to the 19th century notion of self-preservation ... and were such as to render meaningless the Pact of Paris's outlawry of war' (Y Matsui 'Nihon Gunkokushugi no Kokusaihoron (International Law Theory under Japanese Militarism)' in Tokyo Daigaku Shakai Kagaku Kenkyujo (Institute of Social Science, University of Tokyo) (ed) *Senji Nihon no Hotaisei* (*Legal System of Japan in Time of War*) (University of Tokyo Press Tokyo 1979) 375 (*in Japanese*)); or that 'they were like a magic wand that would fully account for any and all actions Japan might take in future' (T Matsuda 'Senso Ihoka to Nihon (Outlawry of War and Japan)' [1981] 79–5 Kokusaiho Gaiko Zassi (Journal of Int'l L & Diplomacy) 78 (*in Japanese*). See also Yanagihara (n 42) 277–279) It is thus worth emphasizing that our focus here is not Japan's view of the place of self-defence under the Pact of Paris as a whole, but the narrower question of how Japan understood the right of self-defence in relation to the protection of nationals.

A Tripartite Division of Cases

The government's view that protection of nationals was an exercise of the right of self-defence was made clear in both doctrine and practice.[43] For the moment, we will defer consideration of the government's views on this question.

On the question of whether defence of Japan's interests in Manchuria amounted to self-defence, the memorandum was less straightforward. It acknowledged, first, that on a standard interpretation of the right of self-defence, justification was not obvious:

> The notion that defence of our interests is justified by the right of self-defence is very widely accepted, and the national interests we are entitled to defend are broader than simply the lives and property of Japanese subjects. *It does not necessarily follow, however, from the [doctrine of self-defence], that the defence of our interests is an exercise of the right of self-defence.*[44]

The memorandum goes on to maintain, however, that as Britain, the US, and France had 'recognised' distinctive Japanese interests in Manchuria, 'the taking of appropriate measures in defence of those interests *is an exercise of self-defence by Japan based upon an acceptance of those interests which we regard as granted by the Great Powers*'.[45] In other words, Japan's government decided to seek the self-defence justification of its actions in an 'acceptance' of its special interests by the Great Powers – an 'acceptance', moreover, which Japan was to 'regard' as having been granted. This formulation shows clearly that Japan was well aware that it lacked sufficient grounds for claiming a right of self-defence consistent with the standard understanding of that concept.

As for justification of Japan's actions for 'maintenance of order' in Manchuria, the memorandum presented that as even more difficult to ground in the right of self-defence. The argument advanced was that 'the action of a nation depends on that nation's strength and is not fully bound by existing international law' and that 'in Manchuria, given our distinctive status in that region, *we believe* that our actions for maintenance of public order *are justified based on the right of self-defence*'.[46] Acknowledging that 'existing international law'

43 'Jieiken nitsuite (On Right of Self-defence)' (n 42) 361. See 'Gimon Gito (Simulation Questions and Answers)' in Yanagihara (n 40) 431 (*in Japanese*).

44 'Jieiken nitsuite (On Right of Self-defence)' (n 42) 362. (emphasis added)

45 Ibid 363. (emphasis added)

46 Ibid 364. (emphasis added)

would not provide a self-defence justification, the memorandum appealed to some 'right of self-defence' outside of any such right acknowledged in international law; this was a plain confession of the weakness of Japan's legal claim.[47]

The Asia Bureau memorandum thus 'presented a judgment that not only the deployment of troops for the protection of imperial subjects in China or the defence of national interests in Manchuria, but also the policing of Manchuria, was possible on the basis of the right of self-defence'.[48] What the Japanese government understood as the right of self-defence 'was clearly exceptionally broad'.[49] Japan accepted, however, that as a matter of positive international law, neither the defence of distinctive Japanese interests in Manchuria nor its policing actions there could be justified as an exercise of the right of self-defence.

In contrast, that the deployment of troops for the protection of Japanese imperial subjects was, in the Japanese government's view, justifiable by the right of self-defence as commonly understood is suggestive of its view of what the positive law right of self-defence meant in relation to the Pact of Paris, and brings to the fore the question of precisely how Japan's government saw the relationship between self-defence and the protection of nationals in the process of concluding and ratifying the Pact.

The Conception of 'the Right of Self-Defence'

How, then, did the memorandum characterise 'the right of self-defence' as commonly understood? And how was protection of nationals framed in relation to that understanding?

'Based on the parts of Sakutaro Tachi's *Kokusai Koho* concerning the right of self-defence',[50] the memorandum defined the right of self-defence as 'an extraordinary right that comes into operation where a nation's institutions or

---

47 See Yanagihara 'Senso Ihoka (Outlawry of War)' (n 42) 277–278.

48 Ibid 277.

49 Matsuda (n 42) 78.

50 'Jieiken ni tsuite (On Right of Self-defence)' (n 42) 361. The memorandum suggests that its analysis is based on a particular source, the *Kokusai Koho* (*Public International Law*) by Sakutaro Tachi. What source this is, however, is not completely clear. The memorandum does not specify the edition of this work that is cited. A work of this title by this author exists (published by the Tokyo Hogakuin, year unknown), but the passages identified by the citations do not agree with the text quoted. On the other hand, there is a work entitled *Heiji Kokusai Koho* (*Peacetime Public International Law*) (published by Chuo University, year unknown), the inner title page of which identifies the work as 'the 1917 edition'. Whether this date reference indicates a year of publication is unclear. Now, the rear title page of this volume suggests that *Heiji Kokusai Koho* (*Peacetime Public International Law*) was printed together with a volume on wartime public international law, *Senji Kokusai*

subjects are subject to imminent harm and justifies as the exercise of that right conduct which would otherwise be a violation of another nation's rights'.[51] The memorandum also laid out five preconditions for the exercise of the right.[52] On the basis of this definition and these preconditions, the memorandum concluded that 'dispatch of troops for the purpose of protection of imperial subjects in China' was justifiable as 'self-defence'.[53] The memorandum also cites Tachi's *Nairan to Kokusaiho,*[54] Borchard's *The Diplomatic Protection of Citizens Abroad or the Law of International Claims,*[55] and the views of the American delegate to the Havana Conference in 1928.[56]

On the issue we seek to address, the relationship of the right of self-defence invoked in this context to the 19th century right of self-defence and the right of self-defence established in the inter-war period, the memorandum is not clear. When it says that the right of self-defence will justify actions that would otherwise be violations of another state's rights, it does not say what violations of other states' rights are contemplated.

Insofar as the memorandum relied on Tachi, however, we can plausibly say that the memorandum refers to the pre-War right. As an example of the exercise of the right of self-defence, Tachi cites the *Caroline* incident;[57] and Tachi characterises the issue at stake in that incident as 'the violation of territory

---

Koho. This volume does contain passages nearly identical to the quotations found in the memorandum.

51 'Jieiken ni tsuite (On Right of Self-defence)' (n 42) 361. This definition matches that in Tachi (n 50 (*Heiji Kokusai Koho*)) 46.

52 'Jieiken ni tsuite (On Right of Self-defence)' (n 42) 361. The five preconditions were: '(1) subjection of a nation, its institutions, or its subjects to harm or imminent threat thereof; (2) unavoidability of the action (urgent necessity of employing the means in question, other means being inadequate to the purpose of protecting from harm); (3) limitation of actions taken in self-defence to the acts necessary to that purpose; (4) that the harm or threatened harm not be due to unlawful action on the part of the nation (or of its institutions) taking action in self-defence; and (5) that the harm or threatened harm be due to unlawful action on the part of the nation against whom action in self-defence is taken or on the part of institutions of said nation, or that the harm or threatened harm be such that it is the responsibility of the nation against whom self-defence is invoked to prevent it'.

53 Ibid.

54 S Tachi *Nairan to Kokusaiho* (*Internal Strife and International Law*) (Nihon University Tokyo 1912) (*in Japanese*).

55 Borchard (n 26).

56 Quoted in Brownlie (n 6) 293.

57 Tachi (n 50 (*Heiji Kokusai Koho*)) 47.

of … the United States'.[58] This suggests that Tachi's understanding of the right of self-defence comprehended the right existing from the 19th century,[59] and thus that the memorandum's appeal to the right of self-defence in connection with protection of nationals was an appeal to that earlier right.[60]

(ii) *Britain*

The Pact of Paris and Protection of Nationals

With respect to Britain's position on the right of self-defence in the formation of the Pact of Paris, attention has been focused on the 'Chamberlain Doctrine' announced 19th May, 1928.[61] How the protection of nationals figured in Britain's understanding of self-defence has been almost universally ignored.[62] Britain evinced acute awareness of the issue, however, from the outset of negotiations on the treaty, considering in detail the problem of protection of nationals as early as March, 1928, the month prior to the US release of its treaty draft;[63] and the issue would remain a major point of British concern.

Britain consistently maintained that action in protection of nationals would not be prohibited by the Pact of Paris. This was not to say that the Pact would not limit or influence such action. A Foreign Ministry minute laying out issues to be considered, while maintaining that the full right to take 'police measures' would be preserved, accepted that '[p]ropaganda or agitation not involving a direct threat to life or property [of nationals abroad] could not well be suppressed by the threat of armed force after signature of the treaty'.[64]

---

58 Ibid 48.

59 How Tachi conceived of the right of self-defence established in the inter-war period and its relationship to the pre-War right we will consider in Section B of this chapter.

60 See, however, n 82 of this chapter.

61 See Chapter 4, Section B.3.

62 Protection of nationals was hardly a matter of no relevance for the Chamberlain Doctrine, as is indicated by British concerns over turbulence in what Britain called 'special regions'. ('Memorandum on the Draft Treaty for the Renunciation of War, with particular reference to the Question of the "Special Regions" mentioned in Paragraph 10 of the British Note of May 19, 1928' in DK Adams (ed) *British Documents on Foreign Affairs: Reports and Papers from the Foreign Office Confidential Print, Part II From the First to the Second World War, Series C North America, 1919–1939* (University Publications of America Maryland 1995) vol 18 (Arbitration, Arms Control and Pact of Paris, 1927–1929), 159–162; 'Position created by treaty for renunciation of war, 11th Sept. 1928 [A6444/1/45]' in *The National Archives, Kew* (formerly *Public Record Office, Kew*) (hereinafter PRO), FO 371/12800)

63 'Franco-United States proposals for treaty to outlaw war, 5th March 1928 [A1815/1/45]' in *PRO, FO 371/12794*.

64 'Foreign Office Minute, Proposed treaty for renunciation of war, 7th June, 1928 [A 3886/1/45]' in *PRO, FO 371/12793*.

Protection of Nationals as 'Police Measures'

Interestingly, Britain's government distinguished the justification for using military action to protect nationals from the right of self-defence.[65] Britain would understand protection of nationals as distinct from self-defence, and 'police measures' for the former purpose, it held, would be justifiable.[66] These police measures it understood as action 'short of an actual resort to war'.[67] In other words, protection of nationals was not 'self-defence' and would be justifiable under the treaty because it would not rise to the level of war.

As this formulation suggests, Britain, during the process leading to conclusion of the Pact of Paris, discussed self-defence as a resort to war.[68] It understood the right of self-defence as the right of self-defence established in the inter-war period.[69] It is this that makes sense of Britain's distinguishing protection of nationals from self-defence.

(iii) *United States*

'Self-Defence' or 'Police Measures'?

As we have seen, both Japan and Britain considered use of force for protection of nationals justifiable under the Pact of Paris, but did so on very different grounds. Japan thought it justifiable by the right of self-defence, while Britain justified it as 'police measures' distinguished from the exercise of the right of self-defence. The views of the US government oscillated between these two polar approaches.

The Pact of Paris and Protection of Nationals Abroad

During the negotiations leading to the signing of the Pact, the US did not make clear its views on the status of protection of nationals. In Senate debates on ratification, however, whether protection of nationals would be permitted under the Pact became one of the most important questions at stake.[70]

---

65 'Treaty for renunciation of war, 27th June, 1928 [A4428/1/45]' in *PRO, FO 371/12794*.

66 Ibid.

67 'Foreign Office Memorandum, Treaty for renunciation of war, 18th June 1928 [A4462/1/45]' in *PRO, FO 371/12794*; 'Position created by treaty for renunciation of war, 11th Sept. 1928 [A6444/1/45]' (n 62).

68 It is unclear whether Britain's government was distinguishing the formal and substantive meanings of war. On this distinction, see Section B of this chapter.

69 'Treaty to outlaw war, 13th April 1928 [A2542/1/45]' in *PRO, FO 371/12790*. See also 'Sir C. Hurst to Sir Austen Chamberlain, 29th June, 1928 [A4478/1/45]' in *PRO, FO 371/12794*; 'Memorandum on the Draft Treaty for the Renunciation of War, with particular reference to the Question of the 'Special Regions' mentioned in Paragraph 10 of the British Note of May 19, 1928' in Adams (ed) (n 62) 164.

70 Treatment of the Monroe Doctrine was another.

While the chair of the Senate Foreign Relations Committee, Senator Borah, consistently maintained that such action would be permissible, he was less consistent in his theoretical grounds for this position. When the question was first raised in the Senate on 3 January 1929, Borah argued that the treaty renouncing war would not in any way restrict the state's actions; for 'so long as [a state's] action consists of defending and protecting the lives and property of [its] citizens it is not war'.[71] The next day, however, while continuing to maintain that protection of nationals was not war – 'A nation has a right to give protection to its citizens and their property, and this is not, in international law, war'[72] – he also argued that protection of nationals was covered by the right of self-defence: 'If a government were defending its citizens or protecting the property of its citizens, in my judgment such action would come under the principle of self-defence or under another principle which is kindred to self-defence'.[73] Further, on 7th January, when asked '[i]s the protection of the life or the property of an American citizen in a foreign country included in the right of self-defence?' Borah answered as follows: 'I stated on Friday … that I had no doubt it was. Assuming that life and property are in actual danger'.[74] Borah did not argue here that protection of nationals is not war. On 10th January, this assertion had returned:

> there is no rule of which I have knowledge in international law that is so thoroughly well established as that a nation has a right to protect its citizens in a foreign land against danger, against attack, against assault; in so doing it is acting in self-defense and under international law, and that in doing so it is not committing an act of war. It is not making war and it would not in so doing violate this treaty.[75]

On the one hand, then, Borah argued that protection of nationals was justified by the right of self-defence; and on the other he asserted that protection of nationals was not war. Not choosing between these two justifications in the end, but simply combining them in advocacy of ratification, he did not make clear the relationship between 'the right of self-defence' and acts of war.

71 [1928–1929] 70 Cong Rec 1068.

72 [1928–1929] 80 Cong Rec 1132.

73 [1928–1929] 70 Cong Rec 1131; see also [1928–1929] 70 Cong Rec 1125.

74 [1928–1929] 70 Cong Rec 1280.

75 [1928–1929] 70 Cong Rec 1471.

A Fluctuating Conception of the Right of Self-Defence

The lack of clarity in Borah's justification is a key to his understanding of 'self-defence'. The United States' working definition of 'self-defence' in relation to the Pact of Paris is generally sought in Kellogg's remark, 'Every nation is free at all times and regardless of treaty provisions to defend its territory from attack or invasion'.[76] This remark, however, identifies violations of territory as the threats against which the nation's right of self-defence may be invoked; it is difficult to see how it covers protection of nationals abroad. As the protection of nationals is not justified by the right of self-defence against invasion or attack, which would justify instead the resort to war, the need arose to emphasise the difference between protection of nationals and acts of war. In this respect, the US position was structurally similar to Britain's.

That the right of self-defence was nevertheless invoked to justify protection of nationals abroad signifies that 'self-defence' was not understood simply in the sense suggested by Kellogg's statement. Accordingly, it was emphasised that defence of territory was merely an example or illustration of self-defence.[77] Thus, Borah, challenged in the Senate on this point, insisted that '[i]f the Senator would read the entire communication of the Secretary of State he could not reach any other conclusion than that the Secretary of State stated the principle of self-defence in the very broadest terms'.[78] Indeed, Kellogg himself stated in the Senate:

> the right of self-defense is not limited to territory in the continental United States, for example. It means that this Government has a right to take such measures as it believes necessary to the defense of the country, or to prevent things that might endanger the country.[79]

It is in this sense that Borah asserted that 'the right of a nation to defend itself means the right to defend its citizens and their property'.[80]

Borah's understanding of self-defence seems to have been broader than the right of self-defence established in the inter-war period, such that any government 'has a right to take such measures as it believes necessary to the defense

76 'Note of the Government of the United States, June 23, 1928' (n 36) 57.

77 [1928–1929] 70 Cong Rec 1181, 1122–1123.

78 [1928–1929] 70 Cong Rec 1122.

79 *Hearings Before the Committee on Foreign Relations, United States Senate, Seventieth Congress, Second Session, on the General Pact for the Renunciation of War, Signed at Paris August 27, 1928* (Government Printing Office Washington 1928) 5.

80 [1928–1929] 70 Cong Rec 1280.

of the country, or to prevent things that might endanger the country'.[81] Regardless of how defensible we may consider Borah's understanding to have been, his moving between two different grounds of justification suggests that at the time of the Pact of Paris, two different notions of self-defence coexisted: a narrower conception of defensive war, and a conception justifying police measures by incorporating a still living right of self-defence from the 19th century.

(iv) *Conclusions*

While the US, Britain, and Japan all held that protection of nationals would be permitted under the Pact of Paris, they invoked different grounds to justify this claim. Their differing grounds reflected different understandings of what the right of self-defence entailed. Japan considered protection of nationals justified by the right of self-defence, under a conception of self-defence that comprehended the right of self-defence established in the inter-war period. Britain, in contrast, presented protection of nationals as not justified by the right of self-defence but as permissible in so far as it did not rise to the level of resort to war; the right of self-defence, for Britain, was precisely justification for resorting to war. The US moved between the two poles of justification presented by Japan and Britain.[82]

Doctrine of the time reflected the coexistence of alternative conceptions of 'self-defence'. Commenters who held protection of nationals to be justified by the right of self-defence understood 'self-defence' to carry its pre-War meaning;[83] those who sought other grounds for justifying protection of nationals understood 'self-defence' as the right of self-defence established in the inter-war period and accordingly believed that the right of self-defence would not justify protection of nationals.[84]

Behind the differing national and doctrinal views of the relation of protection of nationals to the Pact of Paris lie differing conceptions of the right of self-defence, or differing approaches to the status of the *Rechtsgüter* of protection of nationals' lives and property with respect to the right of self-defence. This in itself suggests that the outlawing of war under the Pact of Paris was not a complete renunciation of the 19th-century 'policing' conception of self-defence.

81 *Hearings Before the Committee on Foreign Relations* (n 79) 5.

82 The Japanese government, in a classified memorandum, referring to the US Senate's discussions, characterised the protection of nationals as 'not amounting to war and thus not prohibited by the treaty'. ('Senso Hoki ni kan suru Joyaku Setsumeishoan (Shumitsuin Haifuyo Genko) (Draft Explanation of the Treaty for Renunciation of War (Distribution Documents to the Privy Council))' in Yanagihara (n 40) 417 (*in Japanese*))

83 See the works cited at n 31.

84 See the works cited at n 32.

2 *The League of Nations Codification Conference*

Another source of direct evidence pertaining to the relationship between the 19th century right of self-defence and that established in the inter-war period is the League of Nations Conference for the Codification of International Law. How was the right of self-defence understood in the preparations for this Conference?

The League Codification Conference and the Right of Self-Defence

Pursuant to a resolution adopted by the Assembly in September 1927, the Conference was convened in 1930, following preparatory work undertaken in the interval.[85] One of the three issues considered by the conference was 'Responsibility of States for Damage Caused in their Territory to the Person or Property of Foreigners'.[86] Under this heading, self-defence was discussed as one of the circumstances 'in which a State is entitled to disclaim Responsibility'.[87]

Prior to the conference, a preparatory committee sent questionnaires to the participating states on legal questions related to the topics on the conference agenda to inform the work of drawing up 'bases of discussion'.[88] States' replies to the question on the right of self-defence, and the preparatory committee's comments on this issue, directly touched upon the relationship in the period of the League of Nations between the right of self-defence as established before World War I and the right of self-defence as it developed in the inter-war era.

Coexistence of the Two Conceptions

The question relating to the right of self-defence was: 'What are the conditions which must be fulfilled: "When the State claims to have acted in self-defence"?'[89] The replies made by states to it were so diverse that the preparatory committee observed, 'The replies do not all treat of the same case'.[90] Some replies 'appear[ed] to have in mind self-defence against acts occurring outside

85 S Rosenne 'The Hague Codification Conference of 1930' in S Rosenne (ed) *League of Nations Conference for the Codification of International Law* [*1930*] (Oceana New York 1975) vol 1, ix-xlvi; S Rosenne 'Codification of International Law' in Bernhardt (ed) (n 16) 636.

86 The others were 'Nationality' and 'Territorial Waters'.

87 League of Nations *Conference for the Codification of International Law, Bases of Discussion for the Conference Drawn up by the Preparatory Committee* vol 3 (Responsibility of States for Damage Caused in their Territory to the Person or Property of Foreigners) (C 75 M 69 1929 V), 125.

88 Ibid 5.

89 Ibid 125.

90 Ibid 127.

the national territory but capable of compromising its security (seizure of the *Caroline* in 1837)',[91] while others related to the 'question of legitimate defence against an aggressor State'.[92]

The two meanings assigned to the right of self-defence correspond respectively to the policing concept of the right that existed before World War I and the defensive war concept as it developed in the inter-war period. As discussed in Chapter 3 of this volume, one of the precedents for the pre-War right of self-defence was the *Caroline* incident; and 'acts occurring outside the national territory but capable of compromising its security (seizure of the *Caroline* in 1837)' were precisely the sort of action against which the pre-War right of self-defence could be invoked. That some respondents were discussing the pre-War right is made still clearer by the committee's reference to the danger 'with which the foreigner threatened the State or other persons'.[93] As for 'legitimate defence against an aggressor State', on the other hand, as discussed in Chapter 4, this was the right of self-defence established in the inter-war period.

The preparatory committee did not leave any sign of having reflected deeply on the relationship between these two conceptions of self-defence, and self-defence in the end was not even discussed at the Codification Conference.[94] It is noteworthy, nevertheless, that the preparatory committee indicated so clearly that respondent countries were working with two distinct conceptions of the right of self-defence. The preparatory committee did not refer to the right of defensive war against aggression, judging this topic to be outside the scope of the Conference's proper agenda.[95] Bases of discussion were drafted with particular reference to the other aspect, i.e. 'self-defence against acts occurring outside the national territory but capable of compromising its security'.[96] Thus, with respect to self-defence, we find only a reference to the danger 'with which the foreigner threatened the State or other persons'.[97]

---

91 Ibid.

92 Ibid 128.

93 Ibid 128.

94 League of Nations *Acts of the Conference for the Codification of International Law, Held at the Hague from March 13th to April 20th, 1930, Meetings of the Committees* vol 4 (Minutes of the Third Committee) (C 351(c) M 145(c) 1930 V), 15–197. This issue was not even dealt with by the three sub-committees established during the conference. (Rosenne (ed) (n 85 (*League of Nations* ...)) xxxiv)

95 It is not possible to trace the arguments on this point in the preparatory committee as no minutes of the committee meetings remain. (ibid vi)

96 League of Nations (n 87) 127.

97 The Basis of Discussion on this point was formulated as follows: 'A State is not responsible for damage caused to a foreigner if it proves that its act was occasioned by the immediate necessity of self-defence against a danger with which the foreigner threatened the State or other persons.

It is also worth noting that Denmark's reply to the questionnaire employed both conceptions of self-defence. In its reply, Denmark defined the right of self-defence as being against unlawful attack, and distinguished between an unlawful attack by a state and one by individual foreigners, giving an example of the latter type that is reminiscent of the *Virginius* incident, another precedent for the right of self-defence established before World War I:

> There cannot be lawful self-defence without unlawful attack ... In the relations between a State and individual foreigners, the question of self-defence could seldom arise, since unlawful acts committed by individuals cannot generally be regarded as constituting such an attack against the State as would justify self-defence. These persons might be punished under the ordinary laws of the country in question, so that the particular eventuality of self-defence would not arise. Only in exceptional cases when, for instance, from a vessel outside territorial waters acts are committed which constitute an unlawful attack and a danger to the security of the coastal State, would it be possible, in the relations between a State and private individuals, to adopt the particular plea of self-defence.[98]

3 *The US-Mexico Mixed Claims Commission*

An attempt to clarify the relationship between the pre-war and inter-war conceptions of self-defence need not rely only on sources that explicitly address that relationship. Any clear indication of the existence of the earlier right in inter-war period may provide indirect testimony on the state of the two rights' coexistence. The 1930 work of the US-Mexican Mixed Claims Commission is enlightening in this way.

The US-Mexico Mixed Claims Commission

In the Mexican Revolution of 1910–1920, foreigners in Mexico frequently incurred damage to their persons and their interests. Following the reopening of US-Mexico diplomatic relations in August 1923, the two states concluded a treaty on 9 September for the resolution of outstanding claims, under which a three-person claims commission was established.[99] Few of the cases considered by the commission reached questions of the right of self-defence under

Should the circumstances not fully justify the acts which caused the damage, the State may be responsible to an extent to be determined.' (ibid 128)

98 Ibid 126.

99 'Historical Note' in 4 RIAA xii. The treaty was extended in September 1929. (4 RIAA 547–550)

international law; the only case that demands our attention is that brought by Kelley against the Mexican state.[100]

The Kelley-Mexico Case

Kelley, who had signed an employment contract with Mexico's national railroad, was dismissed 1 May 1914 by order of Mexico's president, General Huerta. The previous month, the US Congress had called on the US president to 'use the armed forces of the United States in such ways and to such extent as may be necessary to obtain from General Huerta and his adherents the fullest recognition of the rights and dignity of the United States'.[101] Hostilities thereafter broke out between the US and Mexico, with Vera Cruz being occupied. In the case brought before the Commission, the US argued that Kelley's dismissal was unlawful and that damages should be paid.[102]

The Commission rejected the complaint, holding that whatever the proper legal assessment might be of the US-Mexican hostilities and the occupation of Vera Cruz, there were reasonable grounds for expecting at the time of Kelley's termination that hostilities would continue for some time and that his termination was therefore not an arbitrary act.[103]

The Right of Self-Defence in the *Caroline* Incident

It is noteworthy that the American side in this case invoked the so-called 'Webster formula', articulated in the precedent-setting *Caroline* incident. The Commission held that the *Caroline* incident was not a relevant precedent in this case, but not that the right of self-defence established in the incident no longer applied to international law:

> To be sure, the destruction of the *Caroline* might be regarded as a defensive measure. It involved hostile operations and an invasion of American sovereignty which, however, did not prompt the United States to go to war. The precise question which was discussed in connection with these

100 *ER Kelley* (*USA*) *v United Mexican States* (*October 8, 1930*) in 4 RIAA 608–615. It was not only this commission that almost never addressed issues of self-defence. A review of Reports of International Arbitral Awards also reveals almost no such cases.

101 *ER Kelley* (*USA*) *v United Mexican States* (n 100) 609.

102 H Lauterpacht (ed) *Annual Digest of Public International Law Cases* (Longmans, Green & Co London) Years 1929–1930, 480–481.

103 *ER Kelley* (*USA*) *v United Mexican States* (n 100) 608–615; JW Garner 'Decisions, Opinions, and Awards of International Tribunals: Decisions of the United States – Mexican Mixed Claims Commission' [1931] 12 BYIL 169; Lauterpacht (n 102) 481–482.

> incidents evidently pertained to the justification for a violation of sovereignty. Great Britain invoked the so-called right of self-defence[.][104]

The Commission accepted a conception of self-defence as policing measures.

To be sure, the case at hand raised no issue of violations of sovereignty, and the relevance of the Webster formula was denied for that reason; the Commission's remarks on the right of self-defence established in the *Caroline* were mere obiter dicta. It is nevertheless remarkable that as late as 1930 the conception of self-defence established by this 19th century precedent was clearly understood and articulated by a judicial tribunal. This is clear evidence that the 19th century right of self-defence survived well into the inter-war period.

B The Relationship between the Two Conceptions of Self-Defence

The Normative Relation

As noted in the introduction to this chapter, some advocates of the restrictive interpretation maintain that the scope of the 19th century right of self-defence was narrowed by the inter-war outlawry of war.[105] This view is based not on consideration of the normative relationship between the earlier and the later right, but on state practice. As we have seen throughout this chapter, however, inter-war state practice and nations' awareness of the right of self-defence as revealed by state practice do not support the view that the right of self-defence of the policing action type was in fact narrowed by the efforts to outlaw war.[106] State practice shows instead that this 19th century brand of self-defence coexisted in the inter-war period with the conception of self-defence established through those efforts.

By what normative relationship between the earlier and the later conceptions of self-defence was this coexistence made possible? Why were they able to coexist? If in the process of outlawry of war and establishment of a right of self-defence in the form of defensive war the right of self-defence in the

104 *ER Kelley* (USA) *v United Mexican States* (n 100) 614.

105 Other advocates of the restrictive interpretation, of course, deny even that a 19th century right of self-defence, properly speaking, existed, arguing that the right of self-defence in international law was established only with the outlawing of certain categories of war in the inter-war period. This second group of restrictive interpretation advocates accordingly have no reason to consider a possible relationship between the 19th century's and the inter-war period's conceptions of self-defence.

106 See also Chapter 2, Section C.2.

form of policing measures preserved its independent existence, how should the relationship between the outlawry of war and the policing conception of self-defence be characterised?

The normative relationship between the two distinct rights of self-defence has not received a great deal of attention. As we saw in our Chapter 2 consideration of doctrinal debate on the *Caroline* incident, it was not widely recognised, even at the time, that two distinct conceptions of self-defence were at play in the inter-war period. This is understandable given the over-riding preoccupation of the period. That is, the right of self-defence established in the inter-war period was initially discussed solely in the context of explaining the treaties that sought to prohibit resort to war; it was only with the Pact of Paris that the right of self-defence came to be discussed as an independent problem, rather than strictly in connection with each of the inter-war treaties.[107] The relationship between two distinct conceptions of self-defence, after all, cannot be discussed unless it is understood and accepted that two distinct conceptions in fact exist. Similarly, the need to discuss the relationship between two conceptions of self-defence could not arise for commenters who, even after the conclusion of the Pact of Paris, maintained that the right of self-defence recognised in international law was simply the right established in the inter-war period and who accordingly denied the existence of a pre-war right.[108]

Structure of this Section

While the problem of relating the two rights to each other was not widely taken up, some did in fact address it, either explicitly or implicitly. Approaches taken to the problem can be divided into those that focused on the two conceptions' sources of law (in Subsection 1) and those that focused on the conceptions' functions (in Subsection 2), though these two points of focus were closely interrelated.

Generally, these doctrinal approaches were developed by the mid-1930s and so did not take into account developments in the outlawry of war that appeared after that point. From the 1930s a shift occurred from 'outlawing war' to

107 Eg H Kelsen 'Unrecht und Unrechtsfolge im Völkerrecht' [1932] 12 Zeitschrift für Öffentliches Recht 562; R Ago 'Le délit international' [1939] 68 RCADI 538.

108 It was possible for such theorists to accept the existence of what I am calling the 19th century right of self-defence in the form of according special treatment to state of necessity. Such theorists treated the *Caroline* incident as such a case of necessity, and attempted to distinguish response to state of necessity from the exercise of self-defence by the lawfulness or unlawfulness of the precedent conduct. We can perhaps view such an approach as pointing out, in its own way, the differences between the notion of self-defence at work in the *Caroline* incident and that established by the inter-war treaties.

'prohibiting the use of force'; after looking into the two approaches described above, we will consider the influence this shift exerted on the conception of self-defence (in Subsection 3).

1 *The Right of Self-Defence in Customary International Law and Treaty Law*

Differentiation by Sources of Law

The two conceptions we have seen of the right of self-defence are understood to differ in source of law terms, both by those who assert their coexistence and by those who deny that the pre-war right of self-defence existed in the inter-war period. Commenters of the former category make the source of law distinction explicit while those of the latter rely on it implicitly.

Those who deny the survival of the pre-war right of self-defence define self-defence as resistance against unlawful attack. These commenters deny that this right of self-defence can be found in contemporary customary international law.[109] It was even argued in the inter-war period that '[n]e peuvent donc se justifier, *en droit international general,* les tentatives de certains auteurs, qui ont essayé de transplanter dans cet ordre juridique le principe de la légitime défense, en le présentant comme le droit de s'opposer par la force à une aggression injuste'.[110] On this view, the right of self-defence is recognized in international law only by virtue of the treaties outlawing war; it has no place in customary or general international law but is the creature of special or treaty law.

Jures Basdevant brought this distinction between the customary law right of self-defence and the treaty law right of self-defence into clearer relief through his critique of the doctrine denying the existence of the pre-war right of self-defence. Basdevant discussed the right of self-defence as established in the inter-war period:

> L'introduction dans le droit international de dispositions conventionnelles portant renonciation, plus ou moins large, au droit des Etats de recourir à la guerre ou de recourir à la force entre eux a attiré l'attention sur la notion de légitime défense et sur la possibilité de se fonder sur celle-ci pour mettre en échec l'obligation ainsi assumée par traité.[111]

---

109 Kelsen (n 107) 562.

110 Ago (n 107) 538. (emphasis added) See also D Anzilotti *Cours de Droit Internationational* (G Gidel (tr) Sirey Paris 1929) 506–507; A Cavaglieri 'Règles générales du droit de la paix' [1929] 26 RCADI 554–557.

111 Basdevant (n 30) 540.

Continuing directly, however, he contrasted that inter-war right with an earlier one: 'l'exception de la légitime défense est d'une origine antériure à ce droit conventionnel et peut se concevoir à l'encontre de certaines règles de droit international commun'.[112] Basdevant recognized the continuing validity of a 19th century right of self-defence by, for example, citing the *Caroline* incident as an instance of self-defence under customary international law.[113]

The 19th century and inter-war rights of self-defence, then, were distinguished on source of law grounds – whether explicity, as by Basdevant, or implicitly, as by Hans Kelsen and Ago. Further, while the 19th century right of self-defence was found by these commentators in the record of state practice, particularly in the *Caroline* incident, the right of self-defence established in the inter-war period was found in or in connection with the treaties and protocols of that period.

The Background to the Sources of Law Distinction

That the two rights were traced to different sources of law, however, reflects a more basic difference.[114] In the inter-war period, the two rights of self-defence were in fact understood *to justify different things*. The right of self-defence under treaty law was taken to justify the use of force, or 'resort to war',[115] prohibited

112 Ibid. Basdevant denied the existence of any special right of self-defence under treaty international law. He argued that the legal problem of responding to attacks in violation of the Pact of Paris required no formulation of a right of self-defence as the attacking country would, under general legal principles and the preamble of the Pact, forfeit its protected interests under that Pact, such that there could be no question of the actions of the counter-attacking country violating its treaty obligations. (ibid 544–545)

113 Ibid 540–541.

114 This is particularly important to bear in mind when presented with the argument that the outlawry of war and the prohibition of employing force became themselves part of customary law; if the two conceptions of self-defence are distinguished only by source of law, then the difference between them disappears once they are both taken to be incorporated in customary law. Brownlie does in fact contend that by 1939 a regime had been put in place, over and above the explicit obligations of the inter-war treaties, in which the right of self-defence as it developed in the inter-war period provided the only exception to the prohibition of the use of force. (Brownlie (n 6) 247–250)

115 Fierce debate surrounded the question of whether what was prohibited was only 'resort to war' or also uses of force not rising to the level of war. The narrower interpretation is found, eg, in L Oppenheim *International Law* (5th edn H Lauterpacht (ed) Longmans, Green & Co London 1935) vol 2, 155–157. JL Brierly 'Règles générales du droit de la paix' [1936] 58 RCADI 125–126 presents the broader interpretation. It is probably fair to say that the broader interpretation gained steadily in acceptance against the narrower throughout the period. See eg Q Wright 'The Meaning of the Pact of Paris' [1933] 27 AJIL 51–52;

by treaty. The customary international law right of self-defence, by contrast, justified violations of the customary law obligations to respect other states' territory and flag-state jurisdiction on the high-seas.[116]

2 *Violations of Territory and Resort to War*

Violations of Territory and War in Its Formal Meaning

If the 19th century and inter-war conceptions of self-defence were often distinguished in terms of their sources of law, some commenters also focused on the different functions of self-defence postulated by the two conceptions. As we have seen repeatedly, where self-defence in the pre-war period justified violations of territory and flag-state jurisdiction, the action justified by the right of self-defence established in the inter-war period was defensive war. When 'war' is given a formal, or legal, definition,[117] it becomes clear that these conceptions differ quite substantially. A good and representative formal definition was offered by Wright: 'a period of time during which the extraordinary laws of war and neutrality have superseded the normal law of peace in the relations of states'.[118] On this definition, a state of war did not exist unless the country committing acts of war or the country attacked declared its intention to create a state of war.[119] It was possible even for a country that had attacked another to deny that it had resorted to war as long as it had not made clear an intention to be at war; and violations of territory and flag-state jurisdiction were carried out amidst denials of such intention. It was thus possible clearly, and accurately, to distinguish such actions from war in 'formal' terms.

Change in the Conception of War

From the mid-1920s, the formalist or legalist understanding of war came under intense criticism; it was argued that 'war' should be understood in a material sense. Wright, for example, defined it as '*an act or series of acts of violence*

R Taoka 'Fusen Joyaku no Igi (Significance of the Pact of Paris)' [1932] 1–2 Hogaku (Journal of L & Political Science (Tohoku University)) 133–134 (*in Japanese*).

116 This is expressed particularly clearly by Basdevant ((n 30) 540–541), which posits a suspension of the treaty obligation not to resort to war or the use of force, on one hand, and on the other a relaxation of customary international law rules such as respect for territorial integrity.

117 This distinction was advanced by Brownlie (n 6) 84. Legal definitions were employed more often than formal definitions in the inter-war period.

118 Q Wright 'When Does War Exist?' [1932] 26 AJIL 363.

119 Ibid 365.

by one government against another'.[120] Though it was questioned whether the conception of war at work in the League Covenant and the Pact of Paris could be defined in this way,[121] state practice with respect to these treaties suggests that a material understanding of war was considered tenable.[122] Without a declaration of intent, Wright's 'act or series of acts of violence' would be regarded as a resort to war.[123]

Working with a material definition of war, can resort to war be distinguished from a violation of territory? On one hand, Oppenheim lists the following as hostile acts that might be construed as war: 'occupation of a part of foreign territory, an inroad into a foreign country, the blockade of a harbour, an attack on the frontier, an attack on a man-of-war, the capture of a merchantman, and the like'.[124] On the other, the same author categorizes as violation of territory a country's sending 'its troops, its men-of-war, and its police forces into or through foreign territory'.[125] It is not entirely clear how these two sets of enumerated acts differ. It is especially difficult to know what to make of the difference between 'an inroad into a foreign country' and the sending of 'troops ... into or through foreign territory'. In doctrinal terms, then, what basic

120 Q Wright 'Changes in the Conception of War' [1924] 18 AJIL 762; Q Wright *A Study of War* (University of Chicago Press Chicago 1942) vol 1, 8 n 1. See also JL Brierly 'International Law and Resort to Armed Force' [1932] 4 Cambridge LJ 314; JF Williams 'The Covenant of the League of Nations and War' [1933] 5 Cambridge LJ 14.

121 Brownlie (n 6) 84.

122 With respect to the Covenant, see Q Wright 'The Test of Aggression in the Italo-Ethiopian War' [1936] 30 AJIL 45, 50–51; H Lauterpacht '"Resort to War" and the Interpretation of the Covenant during the Manchurian Dispute' [1934] 28 AJIL 58–60. With respect to the Pact of Paris, see Brownlie (n 6) 87–88. Politis suggested that the material interpretation was well on its way to acceptance at the Disarmament Conference: 'The idea that a distinction no longer be made between war in the strict sense of the term and resort to force had gained a striking success during the present Conference'. (League of Nations *Records of the Conference for the Reduction and Limitation of Armaments, Series B (Minutes of the General Commission)*, vol 2 (December 14th, 1932–June 29th, 1933) (Series of League of Nations Publications, IX. Disarmament 1933 IX 10) 502)

123 Q Wright 'The Concept of Aggression in International Law' [1935] 29 AJIL 373, 376.

124 L Oppenheim *International Law* (Longmans, Green & Co London 1906) vol 2, 104. The second and later editions do not enumerate those acts. See eg Oppenheim (n 115) 249–250. While Oppenheim was committed to understanding of war in the legal sense, these examples are useful reference. See also Wright (n 120 ('Changes in the Conception of War')) 759.

125 Oppenheim (n 20) 173. See also L Oppenheim *International Law* (5th edn H Lauterpacht (ed) Longmans, Green & Co London 1937) vol 1, 236.

difference was there between war and lesser hostile acts? And how could the two conceptions of self-defence be kept distinct?

Doctrines

Hersch Lauterpacht is one of the few inter-war commenters who discussed the relationship between the two conceptions of self-defence. In the fifth edition of Oppenheim's *International Law*, he discussed both the conception surviving from the 19th century and the right established in the inter-war period.[126] The two conceptions, we should note, appear in different sections of that source. The former is discussed in volume 1 (on the law of peace), under the heading of 'self-preservation', the latter in volume 2 (on disputes, war and neutrality), in a chapter on 'renunciation of war'. We should also note that while Lauterpacht discussed the older right in the context of 'defence against *an act of individuals*',[127] in discussing the more recently established right he stated that the use of force '*in relations of States* may assume the form of war'.[128] In other words, Lauterpacht distinguished the two conceptions of self-defence by function, treating the earlier conception as pertaining to relations between a state and individuals and the inter-war conception as pertaining to relations among states.[129]

Sakutaro Tachi makes a similar distinction, between on the one hand, action in self-defence against individuals, which 'would violate the rights of another state were the right of self-defence denied', and on the other, 'action in self-defence against a nation or its institutions'.[130] Acts of self-defence here are clearly distinguished here by whether they are taken against individuals or foreign countries.[131]

126 Oppenheim (n 125) 242–248; Oppenheim (n 115) 157–160.

127 Oppenheim (n 125) 244 n 2. (emphasis added)

128 Oppenheim (n 115) 158. (emphasis added)

129 Where acts of an individual are attributed to a state, the matter becomes one of inter-state relations. This problem is treated in Subsection 3 of this section.

130 S Tachi *Heiji Kokusaihoron* (*Peacetime International Law*) (Nihonhyoronsha Tokyo 1930) 182 (*in Japanese*). Tachi employed a similar distinction in his earlier *Heiji Kokusai Koho* (*Peacetime Public International Law*) (n 50) 47. See also Verdross (n 31) 456. The distinction is also found in texts written at the inception of the United Nations era. (A Ross *A Textbook of International Law* (Longmans, Green & Co. London 1947) 244, 247–250; Fenwick (n 31) 230–231)

131 Tachi (n 50 (*Kokusai Koho* (*Public International Law*))) 255 adds emphasis to the distinction, insisting that 'where violence undertaken in self-defence on the territory of another state or on the high seas is taken directly against individuals, it constitutes a violation of the other state's independence only as an indirect result' and distinguishing such a case

Thomas Baty is still more emphatic on this distinction. 'Forcible acts of self-defence, as in the case of invasion to suppress border raids',[132] he argued, do not necessarily amount to war.[133] 'The question of whether [forcible acts of self-defence] constitute war will … depend to some extent on their magnitude, and, above all, on *the question of whether the force is exerted against private persons or against the public, the public authorities, and public rights*';[134] he maintained that acts taken under the right of self-defence dating from the pre-World War I period were directed against private persons and, therefore, did not 'appear to amount to war, or to be forbidden by the [Pact of Paris]'.[135]

Baty was not a formalist. He rejected the contention that 'there is no war unless there is an intention to make war'[136] as 'highly artificial'[137] and held that 'there is war whenever there is an invasion with the intention of imposing the invader's will by force'.[138] Thus, while espousing a material conception of war, he distinguished between resort to war and the exercise of the right of self-defence against individuals.

Inter-State Relations vs. Relations between a State and Individuals

Theorists thus differentiated the two conceptions of self-defence by the author of preceding acts and by the target against whom the right of self-defence was exercised.[139] For such theorists, the right of self-defence established in the inter-war period could be exercised where one state was attacked or threatened by another, and military action taken in self-defence was employed directly against the attacking state. In this scenario, the state is unquestionably both the author of the conduct that triggered the exercise of the right of self-defence, and the entity against which acts in self-defence are taken. Action taken in exercising the right of self-defence is action taken with hostile intent against another country.

In contrast, the 19th century right of self-defence is exercised where a country is attacked or threatened by individuals, and military force is employed

from that in which 'violence undertaken [in self-defence] directly against a state and directly violating that state's independence'.

132 Baty (n 31) 110.

133 Ibid 110–112.

134 Ibid 110. (emphasis added)

135 Ibid 111–112.

136 Ibid 91.

137 Ibid.

138 Ibid 94.

139 Ibid. See also Verdross (n 31) 481–486.

directly against those individuals. In the first instance, the exercise of this right of self-defence is a relation between a state and individuals. In this respect it was possible to speak of the right of the self-defence as a matter of police measures. As these measures were taken against individuals in foreign states, this earlier right also expresses a relationship among states; what the right of self-defence was used to justify, after all, were violations of territory and flag-ship jurisdiction. But the actions taken in self-defence were taken with hostile intent, not, strictly speaking, against a foreign state, but against individuals in the territory or under the jurisdiction of that state.[140]

The distinguishing of war from territorial violations by whether a use of force involves a state-state relationship or a relationship of a state to individuals, or by the presence or absence of hostile intent against a state, was hardly a novelty conceived by inter-war theorists. It can be seen, for example, as early as in Hall's treatise of 1884:

> a violation of [the territory of another state in self-defence] is not hostile in intention, it may indeed be committed with the express object of

140 Naoya Okuwaki finds that cases have arisen that call forth a distinction corresponding to that between *dominium* and *imperium*, turning on the dual nature of territorial sovereignty. 'Armed attack on another country's territory', he argues, may involve 'an intention to violate that country's territorial integrity' but in some cases 'amounts to no more than defiance of the primacy of the other country's effective territorial jurisdiction'. (N Okuwaki 'Ryoiki Shuken no Gainen wo megutte (On the Concept of Territorial Sovereignty)' in Kokusaiho Gakkai (Japanese Soc'y of Int'l L) (ed) *Riku, Sora, Uchu* (*Territory, Air Space, Outer Space*) (Sanseido Tokyo 2001) 13 (*in Japanese*)) Without entering into the question of when this distinction arose, we can note the consonance of Okuwaki's conception with the distinction under consideration here of the distinction between resort to war and violation of territory.

Those who deny the survival of the pre-World War I right of self-defence generally frame cases such as the *Caroline* incident as relevant precedent not for justification by a right of self-defence but rather for justification by emergency conditions. This approach assumes a special framework for excusing unlawful acts. At the same time, however, it can be seen as reflecting the fact that as the proximate action that makes the excuse legitimate is the action of individuals, rather than of a state, it does not contemplate prior state conduct such as would justify the exercise of the post-War right of self-defence.

If action taken in self-defence is to be distinguished based on whether the action is directed against a state or against individuals, then frontier incidents pose a particular difficulty. On one hand, the military force employed in a border incident is not directed against particular individuals. On the other, though the target of the action will be forces guarding a national border, action launched against those forces is not so much an employment of military force with hostile intent against the country they represent as a police measure against those subjectively held to have carried out an attack.

> preventing occurrences which would lead to war, and it is not directed against the state, or against persons or property belonging to it because they belong to it, but *against specific ill-doers because of their personal acts*; it therefore *differs in very important respects from ordinary acts of war*[.][141]

The distinction can also be found in state practice. We have already seen that the preparatory committee for the League Codification Conference, for example, distinguished the right to defend against harm 'with which the foreigner threatened the State or others' from 'legitimate defence against an aggressor State'[142] and that Denmark's reply to the preparatory committee explicitly referred to 'the relations between a State and individual foreigners'.[143]

3 *From Outlawry of War to Prohibition of the Use of Force*

Territorial Violations and Resort to Force

From the 1930s, a shift arose from the outlawing of war to the prohibition of the use of force. Was a distinction preserved between prohibited uses of force and violations of territory? To answer this question, we must try to identify a lower boundary of prohibited uses of force, or, in other words, to ask what uses of force were to be prohibited.

Contemporary understandings generally held that for violent or coercive action to amount, in a material sense, to war required the exercise of a considerable amount of military force.[144] Some held that 'the recourse to armed force', or resort to war in a material sense, differed from mere 'use of armed force' and 'measures of actual force'.[145]

We should be able to say something, however, about what the general term 'resort to force' meant or did not mean. How much armed force, or what kind of armed force, did the term designate? Taking the term at face value would suggest that any violation of one country's territory or flag-ship jurisdiction by a military contingent of another country would amount to a prohibited act. In that case, any difference would disappear between a right of self-defence formerly understood to justify certain territorial violations as police measures and a right of self-defence understood to justify resort to war or to any other use of force.

141 Hall (n 17) 245 n 1. (emphasis added)

142 League of Nations (n 87) 128.

143 Ibid 126.

144 Brownlie (n 6) 87.

145 Lauterpacht (n 122) 46, 58.

If some relationship other than identity is thought to exist between police measures taken in self-defence and self-defence in the form of defensive war, then we must have some idea of how far down the prohibition against the resort to force goes. Some clues to locating this lower boundary may be sought in discussions conducted in connection with the draft Act relating to the Definition of Aggressor, where this question was in fact addressed.

Absence of a Definition of 'Resort to Force'

The question of how to define 'resort to force' was not considered in any detail, however. In February 1933, at the Political Commission of the Conference for the Reduction and Limitation of Armaments, the British government proposed a draft declaration of non-resort to force, in which 'the Governments of Europe'[146] would 'solemnly undertake that they will not in any circumstances resort to force for the purpose of resolving any present or future differences between them'.[147] On the issue of what 'resort to force' meant, the British delegate explained that 'the expression "resort to force" was deliberately used to avoid subsequent controversy as to whether what might be done amounted or not to an actual state of war'.[148] The choice of expression was meant to avoid a formalist understanding that might have been invited by using the expression 'resort to war' instead. No definition was provided for the term, however, even by the British delegate, even by the discussion[149] through to adopting the resolution,[150] and even though some delegates pointed out that the term

146 The British delegate explained that this draft declaration was limited to European states because it was advanced in order to answer the French proposal of November, 1932, which intended to strengthen the regional security system in Europe. (League of Nations *Records of the Conference for the Reduction and Limitation of Armaments, Series D,* vol 5 (Minutes of the Political Commission, February 27th, 1932–March 10th, 1933) (Series of League of Nations Publications, IX. Disarmament 1936 IX 8), 11) As for the French plan, see 'Memorandum by the French Delegation dated November 14th, 1932. Plan for the Organisation of Peace (Conf.D.146)' in League of Nations *Conference for the Reduction and Limitation of Armaments, Conference Documents* vol 2 (Series of League of Nations Publications, IX. Disarmament 1935 IX 4), 435–439; T Ueda *Chiikiteki Anzenhosho no Shiteki Kenkyu* (*The Regional Security System under the League of Nations*) (Yamakawa Tokyo 1989) 89–92 (*in Japanese with English Summary*).

147 League of Nations *Records of the Conference for the Reduction and Limitation of Armaments, Series D,* vol 5 (Minutes of the Political Commission, February 27th, 1932–March 10th, 1933) (n 146), 12.

148 Ibid.

149 Ibid 5–30.

150 'Report of the Committee on Security Questions (Conf. D/C G 108)' in League of Nations *Conference for the Reduction and Limitation of Armaments, Conference Documents*, vol 2 (Series of League of Nations Publications, IX. Disarmament, 1935 IX 4), 679.

'resort to force' 'might be a little too vague, so that it might perhaps be desirable to define it clearly'.[151]

'Resort to Force' and the Definition of Aggression

The question of what 'resort to force' meant would be discussed after adoption of the resolution in the form of a related question: how to define aggression. In proposing a definition of aggression to the same Political Commission, the Soviet delegate explained that the definition was to be 'on the same plane as the "renunciation of the resort to force" that had been accepted by the Political Commission ... on March 2nd'.[152]

Based on their examination of the Soviet proposal, the Committee on Security Questions drafted the Act relating to the Definition of the Aggressor.[153] Most of the acts enumerated in the definition, regarded at the time as 'the most detailed which had as yet appeared',[154] were acts directed, with hostile intent, against countries, including the act most relevant to our investigation: 'Invasion by its armed forces, with or without a declaration of war, of the territory of another state'.[155]

Significance of 'Invasion of Territory'

The report on the draft act did not consider in any depth the significance of this crucial term. 'The act of invasion constitutes essentially an act of aggression, apart from any declaration of war',[156] is the report's full commentary on the matter. We should note, however, that when proposing the definition, the Soviet delegate stressed the inviolability of national borders.[157] The preamble to the Soviet proposal referred to 'the desire ... of safeguarding the security,

---

151 League of Nations *Records of the Conference for the Reduction and Limitation of Armaments, Series D* (Minutes of the Political Commission) vol 5 (February 27th, 1932–March 10th, 1933) (n 146), 20. See also ibid 16.

152 Ibid 48.

153 AN Mandelstam *Le Conflit Italo-Éthiopien devant la Société des Nations* (Recueil Sirey Paris 1937) 330–343; Wright (n 123) 385.

154 AVW Thomas and JAJ Thomas *The Concept of Aggression in International Law* (Southern Methodist University Press Dallas 1972) 19.

155 'Report of the Committee on Security Questions (Conf. D/C G 108)' (n 150) 683.

156 Ibid 681.

157 League of Nations *Records of the Conference for the Reduction and Limitation of Armaments, Series B* (*Minutes of the General Commission*) vol 2 (December 14th, 1932–June 29th, 1933) (n 122), 237–239.

independence and *complete territorial inviolability* of each State and its right to self-defence against attack or invasion from outside, *but only within its own frontiers*'.[158]

The preamble to the draft definition itself, moreover, announces a desire 'to ensure to all peoples *the inviolability of their territory*'.[159] Though it was sometimes pointed out, in Giraud's words, that '[*t*]*oute incursion d'une force armée sur le territoire d'un autre Etat ne constitue pas une invasion*',[160] the doctrine accepted that under the Draft Act, even the disembarkation of Marines and soldiers in another state would constitute an act of invasion.[161]

If the act of invasion is understood in this way, the violation of territory was, simply, aggression.

The Place of Police Measures in Self-Defence

With such a conception of aggression at work, was it conceivable that violations of territory might ever be justified by the right of self-defence? Put differently, how was the right of self-defence in the form of police measures understood within the operative conception of aggression?

The draft definition can be interpreted as permitting the exercise of self-defence, even if it does not contain that term. The forementioned report on the draft definition lays out the following narrow justification: 'these acts [of aggression] can only be justified by a State in the single hypothesis of that State having first been the victim of acts of this kind'.[162]

Whether the draft definition permitted self-defence in the form of police measures, however, is unclear. The report specified that a country might act in self-defence only if made the victim of any of its enumerated aggressive actions. Of these actions, one relates to conduct of individuals:

> Provision of support to armed bands formed in its territory which have invaded the territory of another State, or refusal, notwithstanding the request of the invaded State, to take in its own territory all the measures in its power to deprive those bands of all assistance or protection.[163]

---

158 Ibid 237 (emphasis added); B Broms 'The Definition of Aggression' [1977] 154 RCADI 309.

159 'Report of the Committee on Security Questions (Conf. D/C G 108)' (n 150) 683. (emphasis added) See also Wright (n 123) 385–386.

160 Giraud (n 32) 779.

161 Ibid 780.

162 'Report of the Committee on Security Questions (Conf. D/C G 108)' (n 150) 681.

163 Ibid 683.

Under this definition, however, it is not simply the conduct of individuals that constitutes aggression but conduct of individuals for which a state can be held responsible. At issue in this definition is the conduct of a state – provision of support – or the failure of a state to act as it should toward the armed bands.

Moreover, the report took pains to place some limits on the acts of armed bands for which a state might be held responsible:

> The committee, of course, did not wish to regard as an act of aggression any incursion into the territory of a State by armed bands setting out from the territory of another country. In such a case, aggression could only be the outcome of complicity by the State in furnishing its support to the armed bands or in failing to take the measures in its power to deprive them of help and protection. In certain cases (character of frontier districts, scarcity of population, etc.), the State may not be in a position to prevent or put a stop to the activities of these bands. In such a case, it would not be regarded as responsible, provided it had taken the measures which were in its power to put down the activities of the armed bands.[164]

This treatment of the conduct of individuals clearly fails to dispose of the right to take police measures in self-defence; for circumstances in which a state does not bear 'responsibility' for the actions of individuals under its jurisdiction are precisely the circumstances in which the 19th century had recognized the right to take police measures.[165] As we saw in Chapter 3, the 19th century precedents, in fact, typically stressed the very inability of the state with territorial jurisdiction to suppress the hostile acts as justification for the violation of sovereignty.

That a state unable to suppress acts of aggression proceeding from its territory should not be deemed an aggressor is a sensible proposition. In the context of the draft definition of aggression, however, it gives rise to a certain perversity. If the actions of armed bands are not in themselves aggression and a country attacked by such armed bands is accordingly not a victim of aggression, and if taking military action against individuals in another country requires being first made a victim of aggression, then the country responding with military force to an attack by armed bands outside the control of the state

164 Ibid 681.

165 To hold a state not 'responsible', in the sense that going to war against that state would not be permissible, does not address the question of whether that territorial state bears state responsibility for its inaction.

from whose territory they act will have committed aggression by virtue of having invaded that territory.[166]

Criticism of the Draft Definition

The understanding of the draft definition laid out by the Committee report was harshly criticised.[167] The report did not explicitly *deny* that a policing right of self-defence existed. On this point, the report is better understood as having neglected to consider the problem. Leaving out the 19th century conception of self-defence, however, did not insulate the draft definition from attack.

As we have seen, the draft was not adopted by the Disarmament Conference. Some conference delegates rejected the basic approach revealed by the committee report of enumerating specific acts constitutive of aggression and regarding as the aggressor whichever country first committed any of those acts.[168] As President of the Disarmament Conference Arthur Henderson recounted at the time,[169] the conference delegates were sharply divided on the question of whether a flexible approach or a detailed description of aggressive acts should be adopted.

The conception of aggression expressed by the draft definition clearly cannot be said to have gained general acceptance, even if full allowance is made for the treaties later concluded that did adopt it.[170] We clearly lack adequate grounds for concluding that by the time the draft definition and the treaties incorporating it were produced the customary international law right to take police measures in self-defence had ceased to be recognised.

How the draft definition related to the policing right of self-defence is unclear. In the following chapter, we will consider a number of questions raised by this indeterminacy, shifting our focus to the preparatory work to the United Nations Charter. Was the draft definition in later years effectively accepted? Should the principle of non-use of force incorporated in the UN Charter, in other words, be understood as recognising a similar definition? And what, after

166 Giraud (n 32) 784 n 1.

167 Ibid.

168 See n 102–104 of Chapter 4.

169 See Chapter 4.B.1.(g).

170 Particularly notable were the 'Convention de définition de l'agression (signé 3 Juillet 1933)' 147 LNTS 68; EA Korovine 'The U.S.S.R. and Disarmament' [1933] 292 Int'l Conciliation 351–354. See also 'Treaty of Arab Brotherhood and Alliance between the Kingdom of Saudi Arabia and Iraq (signed 2 April 1936)' 174 LNTS 132, 133; 'Traité de non-agression entre le Royaume d'Afghanistan, le Royaume de l'Irak, l'Empire de l'Iran et la République Turque (signé 8 Juillet 1937)' 190 LNTS 22, 24.

all, was the status assigned to the right of self-defence in the form of police measures?

C 'Outlawry of War' and the Two Conceptions of the Right of Self-Defence

As we have repeatedly found, two distinct conceptions of the right of self-defence coexisted in state practice and state awareness in the inter-war era: the right of self-defence in the form of police measures, and the right of defensive war. This coexistence rested on a normative relationship between the two rights: the two rights differed from each other, occupied different conceptual spaces, in terms of the author of the relevant precedent conduct, the target against whom action taken in self-defence was directed, and the presence or absence of hostile intent toward the country with jurisdiction over the site of hostile action. It is precisely because the two rights were in practice separated in this way that the right to take police measures in self-defence was not denied by the prohibitions of war attempted in the project of outlawing war.

However, with the move initiated in the 1930s from outlawry of war to prohibition of the use of force, the need arose to consider this normative relationship more carefully. The conception of the right of self-defence seen in the draft definition of aggression can be interpreted as denying the existence of the policing right of self-defence. This intent is certainly not made clear or explicit, however; and as the definition was bitterly contested and failed to be adopted, we should at the least be very cautious in declaring that the right of self-defence established in the inter-war period was meant to displace, or did displace, this earlier right of self-defence.

Now, the movement from outlawry of war to prohibition of the use of force culminated in the United Nations Charter's Article 2(4) principle of non-use of force. Within the context of the prohibition of the use of force, what became of the policing right of self-defence? Adequately addressing this question requires that we examine how the relationship between the non-use of force principle and the policing right of self-defence was treated in the process of formulating the UN Charter. This topic will be addressed in Chapter 6, Section B.

CHAPTER 6

The Right of Self-Defence in the *Travaux Préparatoires* of the United Nations Charter

Past Enquiries and Newly Released Documents

Many scholars, including such giants as Bowett[1] and Brownlie,[2] have discussed the preparatory work to the United Nations Charter in relation to the right of self-defence. Their studies, however, were hindered by the limitations of the documentation available to them.

The documents on which Bowett and Brownlie mainly relied in their debates of the 1950s and early 1960s were the public records of the San Francisco Conference,[3] at which the United Nations Charter was adopted. At the time, these records were among the most important of the few documentary records available. As we will see in Section C of this chapter, however, they offer almost no evidence on the formulation of the Charter's Article 51 on self-defence.

From the mid-1960s, US Department of State documents on the 1944 Dumbarton Oaks Conference and the San Francisco Conference came to be published,[4] and diplomatic papers held in other nations' repositories were also released. With these documents, in-depth research became possible.[5]

---

1 DW Bowett 'Book Reviews: International Law and the Use of Force by States. By Ian Brownlie' [1964] 13 ICLQ 1107. See also CHM Waldock 'General Course on Public International Law' [1962] 106 RCADI 234–236.

2 I Brownlie *International Law and the Use of Force by States* (Clarendon Press Oxford 1963) 265–270; I Brownlie 'Recent Appraisals of Legal Regulation of the Use of Force' [1959] 707, 717–719.

3 *Documents of the United Nations Conference on International Organization, San Francisco, 1945* (hereinafter UNCIO) (United Nations Information Organizations London 1945).

4 *Foreign Relations of the United States, Diplomatic Papers 1944* (Government Printing Office Washington DC 1966) vol I (General) (hereinafter [1944-I] FRUS), 614–959; *Foreign Relations of the United States, Diplomatic Papers 1945* (Government Printing Office Washington DC 1967) vol I (General: The United Nations) (hereinafter [1945-I] FRUS).

5 Among the recent studies of these documents are T Mori 'Shudanteki Jieiken no Tanjo (Birth of the Right of Collective Self-defence)' [2003] 102-1 Kokusaiho Gaiko Zassi (Journal of Int'l L & Diplomacy) esp 97–106 (*in Japanese with English Summary*); T Kearley 'Regulation of Preventive and Preemptive Force in the United Nations Charter: A Search for Original Intent' [2003] 3 Wyoming LR 663–733; F Nishizaki *Amerika Reisen Seisaku to Kokuren 1945–1950 (The United States, the United Nations and the Cold War 1945–1950)* (University of Tokyo Press

 DOI 10.1163/9789004355002_008

These documents, however, were not extensively used by Brownlie and Bowett, and have not been since. In recent years, especially, interest has focused on state practice since the inauguration of the United Nations, and the *travaux préparatoires* are seldom even noted. Christine Gray, one of the foremost authorities in the field, considers the subject not at all in her major work, *International Law and the Use of Force,*[6] and forthrightly announces her decision to focus elsewhere:

> the Charter system was a marked departure from that of the League of Nations, and the language of Articles 2(4) and 51 provides a new terminology and the first expression of the basic rules in their modern form ... This book will examine the use of force since the Charter; the focus will be on state and UN practice under the Charter.[7]

Those works that have made use of diplomatic papers released since the late 1960s, moreover, draw from them few new insights; where they consider the newly available documents, they do so within the framework established by the Bowett-Brownlie debates.[8] It is thus to be hoped that revisiting these documents may enable us to improve our understanding of the *travaux préparatoires*.

Structure of this Chapter

This chapter firstly seeks to make clear how the non-use of force principle was understood at the time of the Charter's adoption, by means of an examination of how the principle came to be formulated (Section A). We will see that in the process of its formulation the problem of the right of self-defence was a constant preoccupation, so much so that separating debate over the non-use

---

Tokyo 1992) 7–43 (*in Japanese*). R Yakemtchouk 'La légitime défense et l'Art. 51 de la Charte de l'O.N.U', [1954] 14-3 Annales de droit et de science politique (Annales de droit de Louvain) 57–70 is exceptionally notable for the author's having attained as deep an understanding as is found in recent studies based only on newspapers and other such materials available at the time.

6 C Gray *International Law and the Use of Force* (3rd edn OUP Oxford 2008).

7 Ibid 6–7.

8 Eg PL Zanardi *La Legittima Difésa nel Diritto Internazionale* (DA Giuffrè Editore Milano 1972) 192–204; LA Sicilianos *Les réactions décentralisées à l'illicite* (LGDJ Paris 1990) 299–300; SA Alexandrov *Self-Defense against the Use of Force in International Law* (Kluwer Law International The Hague 1996) 77–93; TM Franck *Recourse to Force* (CUP Cambridge 2002) 45–51. As stated plainly by Kearley ((n 5) 668), the focus of these scholars' interest was different from that of the drafters of the Charter.

of force principle and that over the right of self-defence is close to impossible. Nevertheless, we will treat the two problems separately for the sake of convenience in characterizing the drafters' deliberations.

As we have repeatedly noted, use of the term 'war' was intentionally avoided in the drafting of the Article 2(4) in order to make it quite clear that what was prohibited, both legally and formally, was not simply war but any use of force.[9] This poses the question of what 'use of force' means. In its relation to the status of the right of self-defence, this problem deals with the policing type of self-defence. In the terms introduced in Chapter 5, two questions are implied: Are 'uses of force' necessarily acts taken against another country with hostile intent? Or, is the violation by military forces of a state's territory in itself prohibited as a use of force? These questions are considered in Section A.2 below.

Now, it is often argued that as Article 2(4) requires that members 'refrain … from the threat or use of force … in any … manner inconsistent with the Purposes of the United Nations', no uses of force are lawful except those specifically enumerated as Article 2(4) exceptions to the general prohibition.[10] On this view, the only exceptions in which the use of force is justified, apart from measures against former enemies (Articles 53 and 107) are Chapter 7 collective security actions and self-defence against 'armed attack' (Article 51). How appropriate this view is will be considered as the second issue in this Chapter; as will be noted in Section A.3, this enquiry touches not only on the policing right of self-defence but also on the right of self-defence by defensive war.

After clarifying the process of the non-use of force principle's formulation and the meaning of the principle through a focus on such questions as those described above, this chapter will (in Sections B and C) seek to make clear how the policing and defensive war rights of self-defence were framed in the drafting of the UN Charter.

A Formulation of the Non-use of Force Principle

Arguments on the formulation of the non-use of force principle and the drafting of Article 2(4), in which the principle is expressed, were formerly constructed

9 LM Goodrich and E Hambro *Charter of the United Nations: Commentary and Documents* (World Peace Foundation Boston 1946) 69; Y Dinstein *War, Aggression and Self-Defence* (5th edn CUP Cambridge 2011) 88. On the distinction in legal and formal terms between war and the use of force, see Chapter 5, Section B.

10 A Randelzhofer and O Dörr 'Article 2(4)' in B Simma et al (eds) *The Charter of the United Nations: A Commentary* (3rd edn OUP Oxford 2012) vol 1, 216.

using as materials the Dumbarton Oaks proposals and discussions from the San Francisco Conference.[11] As is well known, Article 2(4) was produced through revision of a similar provision contained in the Dumbarton Oaks Proposals. In neither Article 2(4) nor the relevant Dumbarton Oaks Proposals provision, however, was it very clear what 'uses of force' meant or what was proscribed by the 'non-use of force principle'. It is often asserted that Article 2(4) prohibits, in Randelzhofer and Dörr's words, 'any possible kind of trans-frontier use of armed force'.[12] The basis for this contention is unclear.

If the meaning of the non-use of force principle is not to be found in discussions held in the process from the Dumbarton Oaks Proposals through the San Francisco Conference to the UN Charter, then we must search for the key to its meaning in discussions preceding the Dumbarton Oaks Proposals. In this section, we will first (in Subsection 1) review the process by which the non-use of force principle was formed and (in Subsection 2) try to make clear how the non-use of force principle was understood from the Moscow Declaration through the Dumbarton Oaks Proposals. In Subsection 3, we will use the discussions from the San Francisco Conference to explore the meaning of the Article 2(4) provisos.

1 *The Formulation Process*

Origins of the Non-use of Force Principle

The origins of the process of the formulation of the non-use of force principle which led to the Dumbarton Oaks Proposals can be characterized as follows.

The fourth of the Chapter 2 'Principles' of the Dumbarton Oaks Proposals provided that '[a]ll members of the Organization shall refrain in their international relations from the threat or use of force in any manner inconsistent with the purposes of the Organization'.[13] This is obviously the heart of the ultimate UN Charter Article 2(4). The only substantive alteration made in Article 2(4) is the addition of the qualification 'against the territorial integrity or political independence of any state'.

This Principle from Chapter 2 of the Dumbarton Oaks Proposals was created in the first phase of the Dumbarton Oaks Conference, in which the US, Britain, and the Soviet Union were the participants. The Principle was confirmed in second-phase discussions among the US, Britain, and China. The origin of the

11 Eg ibid.

12 Ibid.

13 Doc 1, G/1 in 3 UNCIO 3; R Russell *A History of the United Nations Charter* (Brookings Institution Washington DC 1958) 1019.

Principle, however, can be found in the US draft prepared for the stage one discussions,[14] Chapter 1 of which proposed that

> The organization should be empowered to make effective the principle that no nation should be permitted to maintain or use armed force in international relations in any manner inconsistent with the purposes envisaged in the basic instrument of the international organization or to give assistance to any state contrary to preventive or enforcement action undertaken by the international organization.[15]

A related provision of Chapter 6 of this same draft ('Determination of Threats to the Peace or Breaches of the Peace and Action With Respect Thereto') should also be noted: 'The executive council should be empowered to determine whether any condition, situation, or act involving an alleged threat to the peace or breach of the peace is of sufficient gravity to require action'. A note appended to this paragraph enumerating 'conditions, situations, and acts envisaged above' contains the following: 'employment of military forces by a state within the jurisdiction of another state not authorized by the international organization'.[16]

The direct source of these two provisions of the US draft were paragraph 6 of the Moscow Declaration issued by the US, the UK, the Soviet Union, and China: 'That after the termination of hostilities [of the World War II] they will not employ their military forces within the territories of other states except for the purposes envisaged in this declaration and after joint consultation'.[17]

The Process of Formulating the Non-use of Force Principle

The non-use of force principle presented in the Dumbarton Oaks Proposals can thus be traced to the October 1943 Moscow Declaration and further to the US Department of State's preparations for this four-country joint declaration. Following the Moscow Declaration, and particularly after December 1943, US Department of State internal deliberations looking toward the establishment

---

14 'Memorandum by the Assistant Chief of the Division of International Security and Organization (Greig) and the Executive Secretary of the Policy Committee (Yost)' [1944-I] FRUS 903.

15 See H Notter *Postwar Foreign Policy Preparation, 1939–1945* (Department of State Washington DC 1949 reprinted in 1975) 596.

16 Ibid 601.

17 See Russell (n 13) 977.

of a United Nations intensified.[18] In the deliberations leading to the Dumbarton Oaks Proposals prepared by the US on 18 July 1944 (the US draft), substantive discussions were carried out on the principle of non-use of military force.[19]

Thus, to see how the principle of non-use of force came to be formulated, it is of decisive importance to ask how the principle was understood in the formulation of the US draft, how paragraph 4 of Chapter 2 came to be shaped upon reception of the US draft by the UK and the Soviet Union, and how this work was in turn received by China in the second phase of the Conference. The significance of the San Francisco Conference deliberations must be approached on the basis of an understanding of this background. Accordingly, we proceed to lay out the process of the non-use of force principle's formulation by focusing primarily on the internal deliberations of the US State Department from the Moscow Declaration to the Dumbarton Oaks Conference.

2 *From the Moscow Declaration to the Dumbarton Oaks Proposals*

(a) Paragraph 6 of the Moscow Declaration

Preparations for the Moscow Conference

Paragraph 6 of the Moscow Declaration originated in the US Department of State and attained its final form after brief discussion at the Moscow Conference of US, UK and Soviet Union foreign ministers.

The basic conception of the Moscow Declaration, that for a transitional period the four great powers should maintain peace and security on their own, after which this function should rest with a permanent international organization in which the great powers would play the leading role, dates back to

18 Department of State preparations became concrete with the formation on 9 December 1943 of the Informal Agenda Group. On 29 December, the Plan for the Establishment of an International Organization for the Maintenance of International Peace and Security (hereinafter the December 1943 draft) was complete. This draft was little more than an outline of the organization, but the Informal Agenda Group's deliberations continued and deepened. On 24 April, it completed the Possible Plan for a General International Organization (hereinafter the April 1944 draft), which was revised somewhat through consultations with key senators to produce the Tentative Proposals for General International Organization (hereinafter the US draft) on 18 July. See H Uchida '"Kyohiken" no Kigen (Origin of "Veto")' [1964] 5-1 Tokyotoritsu Daigaku Hogaku Gakkai Zasshi (Tokyo Metropolitan University Journal of L & Politics) 109–111 (*in Japanese*).

19 While the US and Britain exchanged some information in the intervening seven months, there is no evidence that either country did anything to revise drafts prepared by the other, and at the Dumbarton Oaks Conference the participating countries offered their own respective drafts or memoranda (see Subsection 2.(c) below). On the preparations of the four countries, see Uchida (n 18) 111–112.

March, 1942.[20] Early in April, 1943, the Security Subcommittee of the Advisory Committee on Postwar Foreign Policy in the US State Department agreed that the declaration to be produced by the Moscow Conference should contain a provision by which 'the four powers should pledge themselves to refrain from the rise of force, except through joint agreement and as a police measure, for the extension of control over any territory in Europe after [Axis] unconditional surrender'.[21] This was perhaps the very first version of the provision concerning the non-use of force principle.

This issue would later be discussed in the context of 'limitation on employment of military forces within territories of other states',[22] and a number of drafts were produced.[23] It was emphasized at the time that the relevant provision would not improperly restrict the activities of the US military; to make this point clear, it was specified that 'military forces' did not cover naval forces, and in order not to restrict the actions of the navy, the text's reference to employment of military force outside a country's own territory was changed to refer rather to 'employment of military forces within territories of other states'.[24]

The Moscow Declaration draft resulting from these deliberations was approved at the First Quebec Conference[25] of August, 1943, and proposed at the Moscow Conference in October. In the relevant provision found in this draft, the four powers were to pledge that they would not 'employ their military forces within the territories of other states except for the purposes envisaged in this declaration and after joint consultation and agreement'.[26]

The Moscow Conference and Paragraph 6 of the Moscow Declaration

At the Moscow Conference, US Secretary of State Hull described this provision as 'in the nature of a self-denying ordinance', and intended 'to show that the four Powers did not have in mind the use of their military forces in territories of other countries, except for the purposes envisaged in the Declaration and

20 'The Drafting of the Four-Nation Declaration of October 30, 1943' in *National Archives at College Park, College Park, MD* (hereinafter *National Archives*), RG 79, *Notter File 498, Box 58, P/UND/23.*

21 Ibid.

22 Ibid.

23 Ibid. On the various drafts, see 'Background and Development of the Four-Nation Declaration, in the Light of Records in the Division of Political Studies' in *National Archives*, RG *59, Notter File 498, Box 58, P/UND/24.*

24 'The Drafting of the Four-Nation Declaration of October 30, 1943' (n 20).

25 Russell (n 13) 122–124.

26 'Tentative Draft of a Joint Four-Power Declaration' [1943-I] FRUS 523.

after joint consultation and agreement'.[27] Inclusion of such a statement was seen as the only way to allay small states' concerns about large-scale uses of force by the great powers.[28] Small states' fears that the great powers might use military forces in their territories after the conclusion of the war would only have been intensified by the general emphasis on the authority of the four powers to be found in a declaration issued in October 1943, precisely the period in which the powers were engaged in operations against the Axis in many countries.[29]

This general conception was accepted at the Moscow Conference almost without discussion. Participants' attention was focused rather on whether the four powers would need not merely to consult but to agree on the use of their military forces; and on this point the participants agreed that consensus should be made unnecessary.[30] Paragraph 6 of the Moscow Declaration accordingly referred only to 'consultation'. It has been noted that the Declaration's only safeguard against arbitrary action by the great powers was thus diluted to the general commitment to act in a manner consistent with the objectives of the Declaration.[31]

(b) US Department of State Internal Deliberations

The December 1943 Draft and 'Principal Obligations of a Member State'

Following the Moscow Declaration, deliberations intensified within the State Department on a United Nations organization. The December 1943 draft was prepared over ten meetings of the Informal Agenda Group between 9 December and 23 December and submitted to the President with a memorandum on the 29th.

27 'Oral Statement by Secretary Hull Regarding the Proposed Joint Declaration' [1943-I] FRUS 601.

28 'Summary of the Proceedings of the Eighth Session of the Tripartite Conference, October 26, 1943, 4 p.m.' [1943-I] FRUS 641–642. See also 'The Drafting of the Four-Nation Declaration of October 30, 1943' (n 20). See also 'S Minutes (Minutes of the Subcommittee on Security Problems) 44, June 10, 1943' in *National Archives, RG 59, Notter File 498, Box 76*; 'P Minutes (Summary Minutes of the Subcommittee on Political Problems) 1, March 7, 1942' in *National Archives, RG59, Notter File 498, Box 55*.

29 Similar concerns can also be seen at work in the later Tehran Conference. (Russell (n 13) 135–136)

30 'Summary of the Proceedings of the Eighth Session of the Tripartite Conference' (n 28) 641–642. See also 'Summary of the Proceedings of the Third Session of the Tripartite Conference, October 21, 1943, 4 p.m.' [1943-I] FRUS 599.

31 Russell (n 13) 135–136.

Chapter 1 of this draft proposed that a purpose of the Organization would be 'to prevent the use of force or of threats to use force in international relations except by authority of the international organization itself'.[32] The memorandum submitted to the President with the draft, moreover, contained a document entitled 'Principal Obligations of a Member State', which called on each member state to '[t]o refrain from use of force or threat to use force in its relations with other states and from any intervention in the internal affairs of other states, except in performance of its obligation to contribute to the enforcement procedures instituted by the Executive Council [of the Organization]'.[33]

The document 'Principal Obligations of a Member State' was proposed prior to the December 1943 draft. Its content was likely recast in the December 1943 draft as an enumeration of the purposes of the Organization. On December 17, at the fifth meeting of the Informal Agenda Group, State Department special advisor Pasvolsky, judging that the obligations of member states should be discussed before questions of design of the new organization, prepared a document entitled 'Principal Obligations of a Member State'. From the minutes of the meeting, however, it is not clear what sort of acts 'the use of force' was intended to refer to. When asked from where he had taken this conception, Pasvolsky emphasized that he had written the document in haste and stated only that some of the obligations had originated in 'the document prepared by Mr. Hudson's group of lawyers'.[34]

While Pasvolsky did not make it clear what this document was, he may have been referring to 'The International Law of the Future: Postulates, Principles and Proposals', which had been prepared by a group of mainly American and Canadian experts, including Judge of the Permanent Court of International Justice Manley O. Hudson.[35] This work is found in the Notter File of Department of State documents housed in the National Archives of the United States. Its issuance date there is recorded as 1 January 1944. It is not implausible, however, to imagine that Pasvolsky saw it the previous December.[36]

This document does bear a certain similarity to Pasvolsky's. Its Principle 7, for example, states: 'Each State has a legal duty to refrain from any use of force and from any threat to use force in its relations with another State, except as

32 Notter (n 15) 577.

33 Ibid 580.

34 'I.O. Minutes (Minutes of Informal Agenda Group) 5 Dec. 17, 1943' in *National Archives, RG 59, Notter File 502, Box 170.*

35 *National Archives, RG 59, Notter File 501, Box 158.*

36 The document is also found at [1944] 38 AJIL Suppl 41–139. The author thanks Professor Naoki Iwatsuki for bringing this to his attention.

authorized by the competent agency of the Community of States'.[37] Nothing in this document or in Pasvolsky's, however, gives us an indication of what 'use of force' meant or of its connection to paragraph 6 of the Moscow Declaration.[38]

From the April 1944 Draft to the US Draft

Thereafter, work on the non-use of force principle would head toward formulating it not as an obligation of member states but as a 'purpose' of the international organization to be created. In that process, however, while the expression of the principle would be altered, there is no sign that its meaning, or substantive content, was seriously discussed.[39] By this roundabout route, phrasing identical to that in the Dumbarton Oaks Proposals had already been formulated in the April 1944 draft.

The Meaning of the Conception of Use of Force

In the process by which Chapter 1, Section A, paragraph 3 of the April 1944 draft originated, it may not have been clear to the participants in that process how the 'use of force' was understood, or how the conception of the use of force was related to the Moscow Declaration's paragraph 6: non-employment of their military forces within the territories of other states.[40]

With respect to this relationship, however, it is worth noting the internal State Department memorandum of 14 July 1944.[41] While this memorandum was presented merely as a summary of official statements and views, it

37 Ibid 55.

38 The Hudson document states that the phrase 'use of force' was chosen in order to obviate the need for giving a definition of war. Both the Hudson and Pasvolsky documents, moreover, focus on the obligation of peaceful resolution of conflicts and on means by which one country forces its will on another. (ibid 84–86; 'I.O. Minutes 5' (n 34)) In this respect, both documents can be seen as extensions of the inter-war outlawry of war.

39 The most substantial revision of the relevant provision was the change of the December 1943 draft's 'except by authority of the international organization itself' to 'in any manner contrary to the authority of the international organization' and then 'in any manner inconsistent with the purposes envisaged in the basic instrument of the international organization'. ('I.O. Minutes 41, April 7, 1944' in *National Archives, RG 59, Notter File 502, Box 170*; 'I.O. Minutes 43, April 11, 1944' in ibid) This will be discussed at subsection 3.(b) of this section below.

40 The proposal to change 'authority' to 'purpose', however, did explicitly note the use of the word 'purpose' in paragraph 6 of the Moscow Declaration. ('I.O. Minutes 41' (n 39))

41 'Official Statements and Views Pertaining to Permanent International Organization' in *National Archives, RG 59, Notter File 498, Box 57, P/223d.* See also 'Summary of Official Statements and Views Pertaining to Permanent International Organization' in *National Archives, RG 59, Notter File 498, Box 58, P/250a.*

provided for a chapter on the 'Basic Principles of Organization' and a section on 'obligation to refrain from use of force', in which context was noted Hull's statement the previous April that the future international organization 'must be based upon firm and binding obligations that the member nations will not use force against each other and against any other nation except in accordance with arrangements made'.[42] The memorandum also contained a comment on this matter: 'While no comparable statement has been made by the Britain, Soviet or Chinese Government, the four Great Powers are committed, under the Moscow Declaration, not to employ, after the war, "their military forces within the territories of other states except for the purposes envisaged in this declaration and after joint consultation"'.[43] The non-use of force principle as a purpose of the Organization was thus linked to the non-employment of their military forces within the territories of other states, the conception shown in the Moscow Declaration.

In contrast, the relationship with the Moscow Declaration of Chapter 6, Section A, paragraph 2 of the April 1944 draft was clear from the beginning. Though originally advanced in connection with the problem of identifying aggression and later presenting the new conception of 'threats to or breach of the peace' when the difficulty of defining aggression had led to avoidance of that term,[44] 'employment of military forces by a state within the jurisdiction of another state' had been advanced as one of the actions to be taken into account in identifying an aggressor state.[45] It was, moreover, clearly recorded at the time of the memorandum that on this matter the April 1944 draft had 'adopted the language of the Moscow Declaration'.[46]

(c) The Dumbarton Oaks Conference

Perceptions of the Participant Countries

The other countries participating at Dumbarton Oaks also prepared drafts or memoranda in advance of the conference.

'Tentative Proposals by the United Kingdom for a General International Organization' contained no provisions directly corresponding to the non-use of force principle. These proposals comprise five memoranda, A through E. Memorandum A, 'Scope and Nature of the Permanent Organisation', in its

42 'Official Statements and Views Pertaining to Permanent International Organization' (n 41).

43 Ibid.

44 'I.O. Minutes 21, Feb. 16, 1944' in *National Archives, RG 59, Notter File 502, Box 170.*

45 Notter (n 15) 587. See also text to n 16.

46 'I.O. Minutes 17, Jan. 28, 1944' in *National Archives, RG 59, Notter File 502, Box 170.*

Chapter 1 ('The Principles and Objects of the Organization'), lays out principles pertaining to the obligations and legal status of member countries.[47] This section is thought to have been a model for Chapter 2 of the Dumbarton Oaks Proposals.[48] None of the principles laid out there, however, is related to the non-use of force principle.

The Soviet memorandum of 12 August is similarly not particularly explicit on this point.[49] By contrast, the Chinese proposals of 23 August, in Chapter 1 ('General Principles'), offered the following (at paragraph 4): 'The use of force as an instrument of national policy shall be absolutely prohibited. Any dispute between states, irrespective of its nature or origin, shall be settled only by pacific means'.[50] In its attempt at absolute prohibition, this Chinese proposal displays a strong continuity with the inter-war outlawry of war approach, and especially with the Pact of Paris. We must note, however, that the meaning of 'use of force' here is not entirely clear.

Phase One of the Dumbarton Oaks Conversations

The problem of the non-use of force principle was disposed of relatively quickly in the first phase of the Dumbarton Oaks Conversations, carried out among the US, the UK, and the Soviet Union between 21 August and 28 September. Consensus was reached on Chapter 2 on 29 August, a memorandum of that date noting agreement that '[t]he Organization will act in accordance with' the 'principle' of 'avoidance of the threat or use of force in any manner inconsistent with [the Organization's] purposes'.[51]

It is not entirely clear what discussions were held on this point. A State Department memorandum of 20 November 1944 on phase one of the conference, however, states:

---

47 'Tentative Proposals by the United Kingdom for a General International Organization [July 22, 1944]' [1944-I] FRUS 670–671.

48 'Memorandum by the Assistant Chief of the Division of International Security and Organization (Greig) and the Executive Secretary of the Policy Committee (Yost)' (n 14) 903.

49 'Memorandum on the International Security Organization, by the Soviet Union' [1944-I] FRUS 706.

50 'Tentative Chinese Proposals for a General International Organization' [1944-I] FRUS 719.

51 'Memorandum by the Under Secretary of State (Stettinius) to the Secretary of State, August 29, 1944' [1944-I] FRUS 747. Insofar as the principle is framed here as a matter of how the Organization should act, some conceptual shift seems to have taken place; Chapter 2, paragraph 4 of the Dumbarton Oaks Proposals frames the principle rather in terms of the obligations of member states. It is not clear how the conference participants saw the relationship between these two conceptions, or even whether the cited memorandum accurately portrayed the consensus accurately.

> The origin of this Chapter [Chapter II, 'Principles'] was largely British and was based upon their argument that it would give the smaller states some satisfaction to know that the action of the organization would be bound by certain stated principles, thus removing certain possible objections on their part that the principal states might act arbitrarily in exercising their far-reaching responsibilities for the maintenance of security.[52]

This memorandum also suggests that paragraph 4 originated in the US draft, that it was strongly supported by the British and Soviet delegations,[53] and that agreement was reached without much difficulty.

Less readily accepted was the US document's presentation of acts to be taken into consideration in designating threats to peace and breaches of peace (Chapter 6, A, paragraph 2 of the US document). Whether threats to peace, breaches of peace, or acts of aggression should be defined was discussed, and, as is well known, the attempt to provide such definitions was in fact abandoned.[54] The decision not to define such terms as aggression being accepted with little dispute, little discussion was devoted to particular acts. Accordingly, the status of the US draft's inclusion of 'employment of military forces by a state within the jurisdiction of another state' as conduct to be taken into account in the determination of aggression was not made clear.

Phase Two of the Dumbarton Oaks Conversations

The paragraph 4 principles of Chapter 2 of the Dumbarton Oaks Proposals were formulated in the course of the phase one discussions. Whether Britain and the Soviet Union, prior to or during the phase one discussions, had accepted the US conception of the non-use of force principle as a matter of 'employment of military forces within territories of other states' is unclear.

However, the matter would become clear in phase two, through an exchange between the Chinese and US delegates. China posed a hypothetical case:

> in which state A found that across the border in state B there was a threat of civil war and active preparations for it. Realizing the imminence of war, *state A took action to safeguard its frontier by crossing into state B* with

52 'Memorandum by the Assistant Chief of the Division of International Security and Organization (Greig) and the Executive Secretary of the Policy Committee (Yost)' (n 14) 903.

53 Ibid. Russell takes a different view of the intent of Britain's proposal, but agrees that agreement was reached on its content without much discussion. (Russell (n 13) 456–457)

54 'Memorandum by the Assistant Chief of the Division of International Security and Organization (Greig) and the Executive Secretary of the Policy Committee (Yost)' (n 14) 910.

> the idea of keeping the war from spreading. State A would claim that it was acting for the sake of peace. Under the Charter, would state A have to take the matter to the Council before it moved across the frontier?[55]

The US delegate responded as follows:

> If state A took action upon its own initiative, the Council would have to decide what to do about state A. In many cases in private life, for example, a person could not be prevented from taking action, but if he took unlawful action certain consequences followed, and he might be punished for his act.[56]

This US response seems clearly to assume that employment of military force within another state's territory was to be prohibited in principle. Precisely because this was prohibited in principle, the question could be posed whether in a particular case, where action was taken to defend national borders, the employment of military force in another state's territory would be permissible; and the understanding at work was that the permissibility of particular acts would be left to the judgment of the Council. This suggests that the principle of non-use of force was understood throughout the Dumbarton Oaks Conference to mean a prohibition against the use of military force in the territory of another state.

3 *Deliberations at the San Francisco Conference*

Chapter 2, paragraph 4 of the Dumbarton Oaks Proposals was one of the major points of focus during the San Francisco Conference, with many revisions proposed. Most notable in the discussions for our purposes are, first, that they resulted in the addition of reference to the 'territorial integrity or political independence of any state'; and, secondly, the questioning that took place concerning the implications of the language concerning the obligation to 'refrain ... from the threat or use of force ... in any ... manner inconsistent with the Purposes of the United Nations'. Focusing on these two elements of the deliberations, we will try to clarify how the non-use of force principle was understood.

55 'International Organisation Discussions: Second Meeting of the Joint Formulation Group, 6th October [U7995/180/70]' in *The National Archives, Kew* (formerly *Public Record Office, Kew*) (hereinafter PRO), FO 371/40721. (emphasis added)

56 Ibid.

(a) Against the Territorial Integrity and Political Independence of Any State

The Australian Amendment

The phrase in Article 2(4) of the UN Charter 'against the territorial integrity or political independence of any state' is generally interpreted as not intended to restrict the scope of the Charter's prohibition of the use of force.[57] Arguments in favor of this interpretation generally appeal to the drafting process of Article 2(4).[58] The corresponding paragraph of the Dumbarton Oaks Proposals, however, of course, contained no such phrase. Insertion of the phrase was proposed by the Australian delegation to the San Francisco Conference.[59]

Brownlie notes correctly that '[t]here is no indication in the records [of deliberations at the Conference] that the phrase was intended to have a restrictive effect'.[60] The British delegation's contemporary view of the Australian amendment, however, is worth noting:

> It was suggested that the Dumbarton Oaks document should be amended so as to debar members expressly from the use of force against one another's territorial integrity and political independence. Such words might do no harm, *though they are in fact a limitation on Principle 4*, and so far from adding anything to the protection of small states might possibly detract from it.[61]

This UK observation, as will be argued below, points to a discrepancy between the conception of 'employment of military forces within territories of other states' and that of 'territorial integrity'.

Meaning of the Australian Amendment

As is frequently noted,[62] the Australian amendment was but one of the amendments proposed to Chapter 2 of the Dumbarton Oaks Proposals seeking to

---

57 Randelzhofer and Dörr (n 10) 216; Oppenheim *International Law* (7th edn H Lauterpacht (ed) Longmans, Green & Co London 1952) vol 2, 124; N Ronzitti *Rescuing Nationals Abroad through Military Coercion and Intervention on Grounds of Humanity* (Martinus Nijhoff Publishers Dordrecht 1985) 8; A Verdross and B Simma *Universelles Völkerrecht* (3rd edn Duncker & Humblot Berlin 1984) 287.

58 Randelzhofer and Dörr (n 10) 216–217.

59 Doc 2, G/14(1) in 3 UNCIO 543; Doc 123/I/1/5 in 6 UNCIO 557.

60 Brownlie (n 2 (*International Law and the Use of Force by States*)) 267.

61 'San Francisco Conference: United Kingdom Delegation Document No. 1. [U3584/12/70]' in *PRO, FO 371/50709*. (emphasis added)

62 Eg Brownlie (n 2 (*International Law and the Use of Force by States*)) 266.

insert explicit guarantees of UN assurance of the territorial integrity and political independence of member states.[63] In the words of the UK delegate, '[s]ome governments, including those of New Zealand and Australia, are very anxious that the guarantee of Article 10 of the [League] Covenant should be renewed'.[64]

The silence of the Dumbarton Oaks proposals on the matter of guarantees of territorial integrity and political independence, however, was intentional.[65] Consideration of the reasons for this silence, in fact, brings into relief the significance, and limitations, of the assurance inserted.

Exclusion from the Dumbarton Oaks Proposals

The UK had given detailed consideration to the 'question of guarantees'[66] prior to the start of the Dumbarton Oaks Conference.[67] This problem was addressed in the 'Tentative Proposals by the United Kingdom for a General International Organisation', dated 22 July, 1944. Reviewing the history of Article 10 of the Covenant, this document presents the view that Article 10 was 'guarantee of frontiers',[68] or, in other words, that it was meant to 'prevent any change in frontiers being carried out'.[69] At the same time, however, the Tentative Proposals noted that such guarantees 'in themselves do little to prevent the invasion and occupation of territory by the armed forces of another State';[70] noting further that '[m]any other states would be likely to refuse to accept an Organisation which committed them to a guarantee of the territorial integrity of all

63 Doc 382, 1/1/19 in 6 UNCIO 304.

64 'San Francisco Conference: United Kingdom Delegation Document No. 1, [U3584/12/70]' (n 61). See also *A Commentary on the Dumbarton Oaks Proposals for the Establishment of a General International Organisation, Presented by the Secretary of State for Foreign Affairs to Parliament by Command of His Majesty, November 1944* (Cmd 6571 His Majesty's Stationery Office London 1944) 5.

65 'Minutes of the Eighteenth Meeting of the United States Delegation, Held at San Francisco, April 26, 1945, 9:30 a.m.' [1945-I] FRUS 423.

66 'Tentative Proposals by the United Kingdom for a General International Organization [July 22, 1944]' (n 47) 679.

67 The Dumbarton Oaks conversations among the UK, the US, and the Soviet Union were held from August 21 to September 28. The UK-US-China conversations were held from September 29 to October 7.

68 'Tentative Proposals by the United Kingdom for a General International Organization [July 22, 1944]' (n 47) 680.

69 *A Commentary on the Dumbarton Oaks Proposals* (n 64) 5.

70 'Tentative Proposals by the United Kingdom for a General International Organization [July 22, 1944]' (n 47) 680.

States', the Tentative Proposals 'suggested, therefore, that no such guarantee be included in the obligations undertaken by members of the Organisation'.[71] This understanding of the UK delegation was shared by the American delegation; and this is likely the reason why no such guarantee was written into the Dumbarton Oaks Proposals.[72]

The UK delegation maintained this stance on territorial integrity throughout the process of formulation of the UN Charter.[73] Indeed, at the San Francisco Conference, the UK delegation commented on the Australian amendment:

> there will be among some states a great demand that their territorial integrity and political independence should be guaranteed. The United Kingdom objections, which were strongly stated at Dumbarton Oaks and publicly put forward in the Commentary on the proposals, are that such a guarantee, if it is a real one, would amount to a guarantee of the *status quo*.[74]

Acceptance of the Australian Amendment

The US and UK thus both understood the conception of territorial integrity as implying that national borders were not to be altered, and opposed the insertion of language on territorial integrity on the grounds that an obligation to guarantee territorial integrity, understood in this sense, should not be placed on the United Nations or on its member states.[75] The US delegation judged the Australian amendment 'not too bad'[76] and accepted it without further discussion. This blithe acceptance, however, was due to the fact that the US did not consider the amendment as imposing an obligation to guarantee territorial

71 Ibid.

72 See also 'Minutes of the Eighteenth Meeting of the United States Delegation' (n 65) 625.

73 *A Commentary on the Dumbarton Oaks Proposals* (n 64) 5; 'World Organisation: Proposal by Australian Government that Security Council should guarantee the territory integrity of States [U2332/12/70]' in *PRO, FO 371/50692*; 'War Cabinet, World Organisation, Outstanding Points, Memorandum by the Secretary of State for Foreign Affairs, 31st March, 1945 [W.P. (45) 209]' in *PRO, CAB 123/237*.

74 'San Francisco Conference: United Kingdom Delegation Document No. 1. [U3584/12/70]' (n 61).

75 See esp 'Minutes of the Eighteenth Meeting of the United States Delegation' (n 65) 424; *A Commentary on the Charter of the United Nations, Signed at San Francisco on the 26th June, 1945, Presented by the Secretary of State for Foreign Affairs to Parliament by Command of His Majesty* (Cmd 6666 His Majesty's Stationery Office London 1945) 6.

76 'Minutes of the Thirty-Ninth Meeting of the United States Delegation, Held at San Francisco, Tuesday, May 15, 1945, 9 a.m.' [1945-I] FRUS 726.

integrity but simply viewed it as clarifying the obligation of member states not to use force against each other.[77]

The Meaning of 'Political Independence'

As for 'political independence', this was not clearly defined in the drafting of the Charter. The British government emphasized that the term was not easy to define,[78] but seems to have understood the concept as related to the status of a state in international relations.[79] This is suggested by the UK's Tentative Proposals:

> One State may control the actions of another State by indirect means. It is impossible to distinguish the line which divides actions from what is generally regarded as the legitimate influence which one State may exercise on the actions of another. The objection to any guarantee of "political independence", therefore is that it could only extend to external and legal forms. It could not take into account more indirect methods.[80]

Guarantees of political independence were left out of the Dumbarton Oaks Proposals because of such definitional difficulties. This does not mean, however, that the Proposals treated respect for states' political independence as unimportant. The UK's Tentative Proposals, in fact, stated that 'mutual respect for the political independence of its members is one of the essential principles of the Organisation'.[81] So it is that the US and UK delegations were willing to accept the Australian amendment without debate.[82]

---

77 Ibid; 'Minutes of the Fortieth Meeting of the United States Delegation, Held at San Francisco, May 16, 1945, 6 p.m.' [1945-I] FRUS 748.

78 'Tentative Proposals by the United Kingdom for a General International Organization [July 22, 1944]' (n 47) 681; 'War Cabinet, World Organisation, Outstanding Points, Memorandum by the Secretary of State for Foreign Affairs, 31st March, 1945 [W.P. (45) 209]' (n 73).

79 The British understanding was similar to that expressed in the German-Austrian customs union. *Customs Regime between Germany and Austria* (Advisory Opinion) PCIJ Rep Series A/B No 41, 45. See M Vierheilig 'Customs Regime between Germany and Austria (Advisory Opinion) in R Bernhardt (ed) *Encyclopedia of Public International Law* (Elsevier Amsterdam 1992) vol 1, 919–920.

80 'Tentative Proposals by the United Kingdom for a General International Organization [July 22, 1944] (n 47) 681; 'War Cabinet, World Organisation, Outstanding Points, Memorandum by the Secretary of State for Foreign Affairs, 31st March, 1945 [W.P. (45) 209]' (n 73).

81 'Tentative Proposals by the United Kingdom for a General International Organization [July 22, 1944]' (n 47) 681, 685. See also 'War Cabinet, World Organisation, Outstanding Points, Memorandum by the Secretary of State for Foreign Affairs, 31st March, 1945 [W.P. (45) 209]' (n 73).

82 Ibid.

Significance of the Insertion

While we can say that the phrase 'against the territorial integrity or political independence of any state' was not intended to limit the scope of the non-use of force principle, we can also say that it did not add to or alter the non-use of force principle articulated by the Dumbarton Oaks Proposals. It did not restrict the scope of the prohibition, but it did not expand it either.

(b) Or in Any Other Manner Inconsistent with the Purposes of the United Nations

Basis for Strict Interpretation of the Use of Force

Brownlie maintains that this phrase 'was not intended by the draftsmen to have a restrictive effect on paragraph 4 or on Article 51, and indeed it was probably meant to reinforce the prohibition of paragraph 4 and, perhaps, to refer to the legality of force when this took the form of enforcement action sanctioned by the Security Council'.[83] The phrase is also commonly made grounds for maintaining that 'the use of armed force is lawful only in those cases that are explicitly specified in the Charter as exceptions to Article 2(4)'.[84] On this view, the only such explicit exceptions (apart from Article 53 and Article 107 measures with respect to former enemy states) are collective security actions pursuant to Chapter 7 and self-defence against armed attack pursuant to Article 51.

Debate at the San Francisco Conference

Such assertions often cite the views of the US delegation to the San Francisco Conference. The US delegate to Commission I, Committee 1 said that 'the intention of the authors of the ... text [including the Australian amendment] was to state in the broadest terms an absolute all-inclusive prohibition; the phrase "or in any other manner" was designed to insure that there should be no loopholes'.[85] It is worth noting that the US view was offered in response to the position of the Norway delegation that 'it should be made very clear in the Report to the Commission that this paragraph 4 [of Article 2] did not contemplate any use of force, outside of action by the Organization, going beyond individual or collective self-defense'.[86]

From this exchange, it is natural to draw the conclusion that no use of force is lawful except pursuant to explicit exceptions in the Charter to the Article 2,

83 Brownlie (n 2 (*International Law and the Use of Force by States*)) 268.

84 Randelzhofer and Dörr (n 10) 216.

85 Doc 784, I/1/27 in 6 UNCIO 335.

86 Ibid 334. See also Doc 382, I/1/19 in 6 UNCIO 304.

paragraph 4 prohibition.[87] The Committee's report, informed by this exchange, provides further support for that conclusion: 'The use of force … remains legitimate only to back up the decisions of the Organization at the start of a controversy or during its solution in the way that the Organization itself ordains'.[88]

The US View

However, a broader view of the drafting process shows that the US understanding, at least, of the phrase in question was less restrictive: uses of force consistent with the purposes of the United Nations might be permissible, though this would require a judgment after the fact by the Security Council. To understand this, we need to follow the US position back to an earlier point, the preparatory work to the Dumbarton Oaks Conference.

Formulation of the US Draft

As we have noted in note 39 of this Chapter, the US drafting process in December 1943 had formulated as one of the purposes of the projected international organization 'to prevent the use of force or of threats to use force in international relations except by authority of the international organization itself'.[89] The phrase 'except by authority of the international organization itself', however, was changed, first to 'in any manner contrary to the authority of the international organization' and then to 'in any manner inconsistent with the purposes envisaged in the basic instrument of the international organization'. The change from 'authority' to 'purposes' of the organization was adopted notwithstanding observation in the working group that the provision was thereby greatly weakened.[90]

Dumbarton Oaks Conference

Moreover, the question was in fact raised at Dumbarton Oaks, by the Chinese representative, Koo, of how weak the prohibition described by the revised text actually was. The fourth principle under Chapter 2 of the Dumbarton Oaks Proposals read: 'All members of the Organization shall refrain in their international relations from the threat or use of force in any manner inconsistent

87 As maintained by Randelzhofer and Dörr (n 10) 216.

88 Doc 994, I/1/34(1) in 6 UNCIO 459.

89 Notter (n 15) 577.

90 See n 39 of this chapter. 'I.O. Minutes 41, April 7, 1944' (n 39); 'I.O. Minutes 43, April 11, 1944' (n 39).

with the purposes of the Organization'.[91] Koo asked whether this provision meant that 'a state might not use force except as expressly authorized by the Organization'.[92] Pasvolsky, the US representative, replied that that was precisely the intent of the principle.[93] Koo persisted in his questioning, however, whether 'a state could resort to force on the pretext that it was maintaining peace, contending that its action was consistent with the purposes of the Organization'.[94] Pasvolsky responded:

> in any case of the use of force, the Organization would be the final judge as to whether force had been used in a manner inconsistent with the purposes of the organization. A nation might take action which it claimed was consistent with the purposes of the Organization, but, if the state was confronted with a claim that its actions was not consistent with these purposes, the Organization would have to decide the question.[95]

Pasvolsky's reply indicates that a state's claims to have acted to keep the peace or in accordance with the purposes of the organization would not necessarily be rejected. Emphasising that the organisation would have to judge whether such uses of force were consistent with the organisation's purposes, he acknowledged the possibility that a use of force might be judged by the organisation after the fact to have been consistent with the organisation's purposes and, thus, permissible.

Further, as already noted, Koo pursued the issue by framing a hypothetical case of a state violating the territory of another state to prevent the widening of what the first state judges an imminent civil war. In this case, he noted, the invading state would likely claim to have acted to keep the peace. Would that state, he asked, be required by the Charter to submit the case to the Council prior to crossing the frontier?[96] This hypothetical case clearly is not covered by either of the exceptions explicitly provided by the Charter: the action

91 Doc 1, G/1 in 3 UNCIO 3. Note that the change from 'any manner inconsistent' to 'any other manner inconsistent' came about via acceptance of the Australian amendment. See Doc 2, G/14 (1) in 3 UNCIO 543; Doc 123, I/1/5 in 6 UNCIO 557.

92 'International Organisation Discussions: Second Meeting of Joint Formulation Group, 6th October [U7995/180/70]' (n 55).

93 Ibid. See also 'Memorandum by the Under Secretary of State (Stettinius) to the Secretary of State, October 2, 1944' [1944-I] FRUS 862.

94 'International Organisation Discussions: Second Meeting of Joint Formulation Group, 6th October [U7995/180/70]' (n 55).

95 Ibid.

96 Ibid.

described cannot be characterized as measures of collective security or as self-defence against armed attack. Pasvolsky was nevertheless unwilling to declare that any such use of force would be impermissible: as we have seen, he argued simply that should a state's actions be determined to have been unlawful it might face consequences.[97]

Pasvolsky clearly would not have welcomed action such as that presented by Koo's hypothetical, but he was unwilling to declare that such action would necessarily be unlawful by virtue of constituting neither enforcement measures sanctioned by the organisation nor self-defence.

Meetings of the US Delegation

There is good evidence that the US delegation maintained a consistent understanding of the phrase 'any other manner inconsistent with the Purposes of the United Nations' throughout the San Francisco Conference. From the start of the Conference until serious debate began on inserting text to the effect of Article 51, a proposal was debated within the US delegation to change the phrase in question to 'any manner inconsistent with the purposes *and principles* of the Organization *and the provisions of its Charter*'.[98]

Prior to deciding to seek insertion of an Article on self-defence,[99] the US delegation understood action in self-defence to be permissible as a matter of course, without explicit affirmation of the fact by the Charter. As a basis for this understanding, the consistency of self-defence with the purposes of the United Nations was cited: 'Since the prevention of aggression would be consistent with the purposes of the Organization, action by a state in self-defence would be in accord with the principles of the organization'.[100] As the Charter did not yet contain a provision on self-defence, the US delegation was reluctant to insert a reference to 'provisions of this Charter' into Article 2, paragraph 4, fearing that to do so would be to restrict the permissible use of force to conditions explicitly provided by the Charter.[101]

---

97 Ibid.

98 'Minutes of the Eighteenth Meeting of the United States Delegation' (n 65) 426. (emphasis added) This proposed amendment was in fact debated once before the San Francisco Conference. ('Minutes of the Twelfth Meeting of the United States Delegation, Held at Washington, Wednesday, April 18, 1945, 9:10 a.m.' [1945-I] FRUS 344)

99 This decision will be considered in Section C of this chapter.

100 'Minutes of the Twenty-Ninth Meeting of the United States Delegation, Held at San Francisco, Friday, May 4, 1945, 9:05 a.m.' [1945-I] FRUS 593. The relationship between self-defence and aggression raised here will be considered in Section C of this chapter.

101 'Minutes of the Eighteenth Meeting of the United States Delegation' (n 65) 426–427.

The problem of self-defence, however, was not the US delegation's only reason for not wanting to introduce any further restrictive language into Article 2, paragraph 4; the US was concerned about the effect of doing so on the general conditions for the use of force. One member of the delegation opposed such an addition on the grounds that should the Soviet Union, with its veto power, obstruct coercive UN measures, 'he wanted it to be possible for the United States to take *whatever action was necessary, consistent with the purposes of the Organization*'.[102] In this context, it was even argued that 'there was no prohibition on the individual use of force if it was done for the purposes of the Organization'.[103]

Debate at the San Francisco Conference and the Views of the US

A very different US understanding appears at the San Francisco Conference from that which we find expressed in the internal meetings of the US delegation.

When Article 2, paragraph 4, including the phrase reflecting Australia's proposed amendment – 'against the territorial integrity or political independence of any state' – was considered in Commission I, Committee 1, Brazil's delegate worried that the text might be interpreted as permitting unilateral uses of force, quite apart from legitimate self-defence, where a state claimed to be acting in accord with the purposes of the organization.[104] In response, Belgium's representative maintained that this danger was addressed by the 'in any other manner inconsistent' language.[105] This is the context in which the American argument quoted earlier, that the phrase 'in any other manner inconsistent with the Purposes of the Organization' was intended to foreclose any evasion of the absolute and comprehensive prohibition, was offered.[106]

Records of the Conference thus do indeed seem to lead to the conclusion that except in cases of self-defence a state cannot unilaterally decide to use force or assert the consistency of a unilateral use of force with the purposes of the United Nations. The very next day, however, the US delegation in an

102 Ibid 426. (emphasis added) See also 'Minutes of the Twelfth Meeting of the United States Delegation' (n 98) 344.

103 'Minutes of the Eighteenth Meeting of the United States Delegation' (n 65) 429. See also 'Minutes of the Thirty-Second Meeting of the United States Delegation, Held at San Francisco, Monday, May 7, 1945, 6:18 p.m.' [1945-I] FRUS 637; 'Minutes of the Sixty-Fourth Meeting of the United States Delegation, Held at San Francisco, Tuesday, June 5, 1945, 9:01 a.m.' [1945-I] FRUS 1162.

104 Doc 784, I/1/27 in 6 UNCIO 334.

105 Ibid.

106 Ibid 335.

internal meeting understood the prohibition of the use of the force more permissively.

In the next day's US internal meeting, a proposed amendment was discussed to change 'Purposes of the Organization' to 'provisions of this Charter'. Opposing this proposal, a member of the US delegation argued that 'the word[ing] should be retained as it was because the revision would constitute an unnecessary restriction upon the right of the member states to use force consistent with the purposes of the Organization'.[107] This was a consistent US position. It is particularly notable in this context, however: as we will note again in Section C of this chapter, this argument was made on 5 June 1945, after it had been decided to include in the Charter a provision on self-defence.[108] Had the US been concerned to maintain only its freedom of action in self-defence, it would not have had at this point any reason to oppose a reference to 'provisions of the Charter'. In the same meeting, the even more remarkable argument was made that '[t]he only restriction on the right of a member state to use force, in the wording under discussion [i.e. without a reference to 'provisions of this Charter'], would be that the use of force had to be consistent with the purposes of the Organization'.[109] This position seems not to have met much opposition within the delegation but to have been the common understanding.[110]

How are we to understand the apparently self-contradictory attitude of the US, or the relationship between the US delegation's consistently expressed understanding and the view it expressed in the public conference records and the subcommittee report considered above? One possible answer is that the US spoke with forked tongue. The US may have argued in open session, in order to contain the demands of smaller countries for clearer restrictions on the scope of the use of force,[111] that the current text contained no loopholes, while deliberating internally with the understanding that any use of force consistent with the UN's purposes was permissible, though subject to post hoc judgment by the Security Council. This account takes for granted that the US held contradictory

107 'Minutes of the Sixty-Fourth Meeting of the United States Delegation' (n 103) 1162.

108 The orginal form for the current Article 51 of the UN Charter was drafted in a five-power conference on 12 May, and on 23 May, inclusion of a provision almost identical to Article 51 was agreed in a meeting of Committee III/4.

109 'Minutes of the Sixty-Fourth Meeting of the United States Delegation' (n 103) 1162–1163.

110 Ibid 1163.

111 Attempts to make Article 2, paragraph 4 more clearly restrictive than it was made by the Australian amendment were supported by none of the five great powers. See 'Minutes of the Seventh Meeting, Committee of Five Deputies of the Heads of Delegations, Room 461, Fairmont Hotel, San Francisco, California, Tuesday, May 15, 1945, 10:40 a.m. to 1:00 p.m.' in *National Archives, RG 59, Notter File 504, Box 257.*

views and understands the US as having taken its stance in full knowledge of the contradiction it embodied.

We can also see the US as not considering its views mutually contradictory. As we have already noted, at the 5 June meeting of the US delegation, the wording of Article 2, paragraph 4 reflecting the Australian amendment was understood as recognizing 'the right of the member states to use force consistent with the purposes of the Organization'. Moreover, while the US delegation clearly opposed any further attempts to amend the paragraph, there is no evidence even of disapproving comment concerning either the amended wording, statements by other countries' representatives, or committee reports on the language in question. This suggests that, *as long as the Australian amendment was the provision in question*, the US saw its public and internal statements as mutually compatible expressions of its understanding of the paragraph's meaning.

The internally consistent US position can be discerned in the forementioned exchange at Dumbarton Oaks with the Chinese delegate. The apparent contradiction between saying that a state may not act without explicit authorization of the Organization and allowing that a state might permissibly resort to force which it claims is consistent with the Organization's purposes disappears if the necessary approval from the Organization is not assumed to be prior approval. For the US, the absence of prior approval was not sufficient reason for denying the lawfulness of unilateral action; the action would simply be permissible if the Organization judged it after the fact to be consistent with the Organization's purposes.

The same interpretation can be applied to the US-Brazilian exchange on the case in which a state unilaterally employs force while claiming to act in accord with the purposes of the Organization. The US can be taken as understanding the lawfulness of such action to be properly determined by a post hoc judgment of the Organization.[112]

4 *Conclusions of Section A*

When the non-use of force principle was formulated, 'employment of military forces within territories of other states' was understood to constitute

112 In US Senate debate on ratification of the Charter, it was maintained that the use of force to protect nationals abroad would be permitted after the Charter entered into force. ([1944–1945] 79 Cong Rec 8204, 8122, 8125, 8240) This too suggests that the US simply *did not believe* at the time of the Charter's adoption that the use of force was permissible only under the conditions explicitly provided for by the Charter.

the use of force to be prohibited. The relevant distinctions of the inter-war period – between force employed against a state and force employed against individuals, and between uses of force or violation of territory with hostile intent and such acts taken without hostile intent – were not part of the new understanding. We may see in this an intention of regulating the use of force without relying on subjective intentions but referring solely to objective standards for determining whether prohibited action had been taken.

It is questionable whether this conception, however, was as strict as, or fully consistent with, the view taken by Randelzhofer and many others that only such uses of force as explicitly provided for as exceptions to the UN Charter's Article 2, paragraph 4 are lawful. The US delegation to the San Francisco Conference, at least, consistently considered legitimate a use of force consistent with the purposes of the United Nations. This US view does not imply that the use of force based upon a state's subjective judgment is acceptable; that proposition was plainly rejected in San Francisco. The US delegation can be interpreted as having taken the position that objectivity was preserved by recognising the consistency of uses of force with the purposes of the United Nations as subject to after-the-fact judgment by the Security Council.

B The Perception of the Right of Self-Defence as Policing Measures

As we saw in Chapter 5, policing measures in self-defence were not constrained by the inter-war period's outlawry of war because they were considered territorial violations committed without hostile intent against the affected state and thus contrasted with war as such. The non-use of force principle, as articulated by Article 2, paragraph 4 of the UN Charter, did not preserve this distinction: 'employment of military force in the jurisdiction of another state' was prohibited. As we have seen, the stance behind the non-use of force principle is that which motivated the inter-war period's Draft Act Defining Aggression. Working with this conception, it is indeed possible to conclude that policing measures taken in self-defence are simply impermissible. In point of fact, however, what has become of the right of self-defence in this sense?

The UN Charter and the Right of Self-Defence as Policing Measures

In the drafting of the UN Charter, almost no attention was paid to the 19th century conception of self-defence as policing measures. Establishment of the UN Charter was intimately connected, as its Preamble puts it, to the searing experience of 'war, which twice in our lifetime has brought untold sorrow to mankind', and the very conception of a United Nations organization 'emanated from and was incorporated in the war aims of the Allied nations fighting the Axis Powers'.[113] In this context, it was natural in the preparatory work of the Charter for interest to focus on self-defence in terms of defensive war or resistance to aggression rather than the policing conception of self-defence, which after all had been articulated in the context of justifying violations of territory and flagship jurisdiction.

Discussion on this other conception of self-defence, however, was not completely absent from the *travaux préparatoires*. As we will see in Subsection 1 below, US State Department internal deliberations explicitly addressed the problems of defining invasion and breach of the peace and of formulating exceptions to the general definitions. In Subsection 2, we will touch on the relevance of these discussions to debate at Dumbarton Oaks and San Francisco on Article 2, paragraph 4 of the Charter. We will then be ready, in Subsection 3, to consider the theoretical status of policing-type self-defence in relation to the Charter's non-use of force principle.

1 *Internal Discussions of the US Department of State*

State Department Internal Deliberation

As we have noted, in State Department deliberations from the Moscow Declaration to the Dumbarton Oaks Conference, 'employment of military forces by a state within the jurisdiction of another state' was raised as conduct to be taken into account in the determination, first, of aggression, and later of threats to and breaches of peace. Within the delegation, it was accepted from the first and without dissent that activities performed in exercise of the right to take policing measures in self-defence were permissible.

When the concept of breach of the peace was raised in a meeting of the Informal Agenda Group, one of the participants asked 'whether the use of the National Guard across the Mexican boundary to keep a bandit, such as [Pancho] Villa, from menacing American territory would constitute a breach of the peace' as conceived by the proposal; the person who had proposed the concept replied that the breach of peace concept would not apply 'where military forces were used by a state to repel aggression before the International Organization had time to act'.[114] The responder added, moreover, that 'the use of forces outside the boundaries of the United States [supposed by the question] would he thought be incidental to driving out bandits who had encroached upon the territory of the United States' and that while military action in such

113 DE Khan 'Drafting History' in B Simma et al (eds) (n 10) 3.

114 'I.O. Minutes 17, Jan. 28, 1944' (n 46).

a case would be considered a use of force that use of force would be without question permissible.[115]

The Pancho Villa Expedition

In the 1910s, activity in the US-Mexico border area led by Pancho Villa was a matter receiving great attention in the United States. The 'Pancho Villa Expedition' arose against a backdrop of instability in this border region.[116] On 9 March 1916, the town of Columbus, New Mexico was attacked by a Villa-led force. Mexico at the time was in the midst of a civil war. The US government on 19 October 1915 had recognized the Carranza government, but Villa continued to resist this government's attempts to consolidate power. In the Columbus attack, American troops and civilians were killed, and most of the town's buildings burned. Though mindful of Mexican sovereignty, President Wilson immediately ordered a military contingent to cross into Mexico, with the limited objective of capturing Villa and preventing his forces from launching further attacks.

On 10 March, Carranza's foreign minister argued to the US special envoy that in the hunt for Pancho Villa America, whose forces had immediately crossed into Mexico, should likewise allow Mexican forces to enter US territory. On 13 March, the US Secretary of State approved this. On 18 March, however, the Carranza government's representative in the US stated that terms on which the two states' military forces would be allowed to enter each other's territory had not been agreed and that the Mexican government's stated agreement to the crossing of the border by American forces had been misconstrued as permission to enter Mexico to pursue Villa. Thereafter, the Mexican foreign ministry demanded withdrawal of US forces on the grounds that basing US troops in Mexico without an agreement on reciprocal border crossing was unacceptable.

Meanwhile, another attack by Mexican bands was launched, in Texas this time, on 5 May 1916. US forces immediately pursued, crossing into Mexican territory. On 22 May, Mexico's foreign ministry protested to the Department of State, calling the crossing of troops into Mexico a violation of Mexican sovereignty and demanding immediate withdrawal and restraint in future cross-border action. At the same time, Mexico's foreign ministry appealed for US understanding of the difficulty of policing the border.

115 Ibid.

116 Unrest and instability in the border region dated back to the first half of the 19th century. HW Baade 'American-Mexican Boundary Disputes and Cooperation' in R Bernhardt (ed) (n 79) 136–144. See Chapter 3, Section A.1.(a) above on the 1836 incident heralding the border issues of the 20th century.

While diplomatic negotiations between the US and Mexico continued, Mexican and US forces on 22 June clashed about 100 miles south of the border, with fatalities on both sides, and 17 US soldiers were captured.[117] Wilson immediately called for the captured soldiers to be released, and they were on 28 June. The release of the prisoners eased tensions, and an American-Mexican Joint Commission was established. While the Commission did not reach a permanent resolution of outstanding Mexican-US disputes, the incident passed away with the withdrawal of all US forces by 6 February 1917.[118]

Justification for Violation of Territory

The issue at stake in this incident was the US violation of Mexican territory, the incursion by US forces and their continued presence on Mexican soil.[119] In this respect, the Pancho Villa incident is similar to other cases in which the right to take police measures in self-defence was exercised through violations of another state's territory. On what basis, though, did the United States claim justification for its actions?

US Secretary of State Lansing argued that Mexico's government had signally failed to prevent incursions from Mexican territory against persons in the US, noting that 'it was well known that the forces of the *de facto* government in Mexico had not carried on a vigorous pursuit of the remaining bandits and that no proper distribution of forces had been made to prevent the invasion of American territory'.[120] This US presentation rests on a conception, not explicitly mentioned, of 'self-defence' or 'an obligation of self-preservation' with respect to US nationals. The Mexican government, unable or unwilling to prevent incursions on people in the United States, Lansing said, '[sought] to

117 An alternative account has the clash occurring on the 21st, with twelve US soldiers killed and fourteen captured. See JB Scott 'The American-Mexican Joint Commission of 1916' [1916] 10 AJIL 891.

118 For fuller accounts of the incident, see GH Hackworth *Digest of International Law* (Government Printing Office Washington DC 1941) vol 2, 291–298; Scott (n 117) 890–896; CC Clendenen *The United States and Pancho Villa: A study in Unconventional Diplomacy* (Cornell University Press Ithaca 1961) 234–269. Also see JB Scott 'The American Punitive Expedition into Mexico' [1916] 10 AJIL 337–340. Another incident of US forces crossing into Mexico in pursuit of Villa occurred following an attack by Villa on El Paso on June 16, 1919. (AS Hershey 'Incursions into Mexico and the Doctrine of Hot Pursuit' [1919] 13 AJIL 557)

119 In connection with the proposed convening of a Joint Commission, the Carranza government described 'the two points which constitute the true causes of the conflict' as 'the insecurity of [the] frontier' and 'the presence of American troops on Mexican territory'. (Cited in Scott (n 117) 893)

120 Hackworth (n 118) 296.

absolve itself from the first duty of any Government, namely, the protection of life and property'. 'This', Lansing continued, 'is the paramount obligation for which governments are instituted, and governments neglecting or failing to perform it are not worthy of the name'.[121]

The Pancho Villa Incident in Later State Department Thinking

The US position on this incident was clearly that the actions of its military forces were a permissible exercise of the (policing) right of self-defence for the protection of nationals' life and property. As we have noted, in later State Department deliberations which played a major role in the formulation of the non-use of force principle, explicit reference was made to the permissibility under this principle of the US military's actions in the Pancho Villa Expedition. This fact clearly indicates that, at least at some stage of the preparatory work that produced the UN Charter's non-use of force principle, activities amounting to the exercise of the right of self-defence in a policing measures sense were understood to be consistent with the non-use of force principle being formulated. We must note, however, that in neither the Pancho Villa incident nor the State Department debates preparatory to the UN Charter, was the expression 'right of self-defence' used in this connection. This point will be explored in Subsection 3 of this section below.

2 *From Dumbarton Oaks to San Francisco*

If the right of self-defence in a policing-measures sense was clearly recognized at some point in the State Department, what became of this right in the drafting of the UN Charter? Did the State Department reaffirm the right? Or did it come to reject it?

The subject was not explicitly discussed, either at Dumbarton Oaks or in San Francisco. As we have noted, deliberations on drafting the Charter focused almost entirely on the defensive war conception of self-defence. Debate on the crucial phrases 'against the territorial integrity or political independence of any state' and 'in any other manner inconsistent with the Purposes of the Organization' simply did not cover the 19th century notion of self-defence. This fact, however, does not tell us whether these refinements to the non-use of force principle, or the principle in any of its forms, altered the status of this self-defence right.

---

121 Ibid 297. On the treatment of protection of its nationals' life and property as a 'duty of self-preservation' which a state bears toward its people, and on the relation of this 'self-preservation' to the right of self-defence, see n 37 of Chapter 3.

Against the Territorial Integrity or Political Independence of Any State

As we have noted, the notion of territorial integrity was understood at the time as implying a guarantee of current borders. The right of self-defence as exercised through policing measures was seen as an exception to the prohibition of the employment of military force in the territory of another state, and thus as not involving a question of altering borders. Likewise, the exercise of this right of self-defence was not understood as touching on a state's political independence. Reference in Article 2, paragraph 4 of the Charter to states' territorial integrity and political independence thus had no bearing on the question of the post-Charter status of the 19th century right of self-defence.

Any Other Manner Inconsistent with the Purposes of the United Nations

As we have seen, this phrase is often taken to imply that only those uses of force explicitly designated as exceptions to the Article 2, paragraph 4 prohibition can be lawful. If this proposition is accepted, then policing measures in self-defence, for which the Charter provides no explicit exception, are not permissible. As we have seen, however, the US delegation, at least, did not take this position.

Phase Two of the Dumbarton Oaks Conference

The hypothetical case posed by China's representative at Dumbarton Oaks, which we saw in Section A.2.(c) of this Chapter, obviously presents a use of force not amounting to action taken for collective security or self-defence as explicitly provided for by the UN Charter. It is also not entirely clear, however, whether it was framed with the policing conception of self-defence in mind; the threat of civil war in one country does not necessarily imply any injury to another. This makes it particularly notable that Pasvolsky was unwilling to declare any such use of force impermissible under the fourth principle of Chapter 2 of the Dumbarton Oaks Proposals. As we have seen, Pasvolsky simply insisted that whether the hypothetical use of force was inconsistent with the Purposes of the United Nations should be determined by the Security Council. If Pasvolsky did not later change his position in later debates, it seems safe to say that in his understanding there was room for lawful uses of force in exercise of the policing-type right of self-defence.

3 *Theoretical Status of the Policing Conception of Self-Defence*

If it was accepted within the US delegation that policing measures taken in self-defence were compatible with the non-use of force principle's prohibition of the employment of military force within the territory of another state, this proposition was not explicitly or clearly affirmed in international law. Such action, that is to say, was not explicitly treated as self-defence.[122]

That it was effectively considered self-defence is suggested by the view from the Informal Agenda Group, already quoted, that the conception of breaches of the peace would not apply to a state's employing military force prior to action of the United Nations in order to repel invasion. US debates on self-defence in connection with the founding of the United Nations date back to discussions in the Informal Agenda Group of early 1944; from that point through the San Francisco Conference it was consistently affirmed that the right of self-defence would be recognized by the Charter.[123] The logic of this position was that while the member states under today's Article 2, paragraph 4 would commit not to use force in a manner inconsistent with the purposes of the United Nations, preventing aggression was itself a purpose of the United Nations and where the Security Council did not act to prevent aggression, the use of force for this purpose was consistent with the UN's purposes and thus not prohibited by Article 2, paragraph 4.[124]

This logic, of course, fit nicely with the US view of cross-border uses of force for the purpose of repelling bandits. Treating such uses of force as self-defence, however, is problematic. What was meant by 'aggression' in the cases at hand was incursions by bandits, territorial violations by non-state actors. It was far from universal practice in the international jurisprudence of the time to

---

122 Ambiguity on this point corresponds well to the oscillation we have described in the US position on the relationship between the Pact of Paris and the protection of nationals abroad. See Chapter 5, Section A.1.(b).

123 See eg 'I.O. Minutes 41, April 7, 1944' (n 39); 'I.O. Minutes 70, July 8, 1944' in *National Archives, RG 59, Notter File 502, Box 170*; 'Memorandum by the Under Secretary of State to the Secretary of State, October 2, 1944' (n 93); *A Commentary on the Dumbarton Oaks Proposals* (n 64) 5; 'Minutes of the Sixth Meeting of the United States Delegation, Held at Washington, Tuesday, April 10, 1945, 10:15 a.m.' [1945-I] FRUS 229–230.

124 See eg 'Memorandum by the Under Secretary of State to the Secretary of State, October 2, 1944' (n 93) 862; 'Minutes of the Eighteenth Meeting of the United States Delegation' (n 65) 426–429; 'Minutes of the Thirty-Second Meeting of the United States Delegation' (n 103) 637; 'Minutes of the Sixty-Fourth Meeting of the United States Delegation (n 103) 1162–1163; 'Report to the President on the Result of the San Francisco Conference by the Chairman of the United States Delegation, the Secretary of State, June 26, 1945' in *Hearings before the Committee on Foreign Relations, United States Senate, Seventy-Ninth Congress, First Session, on the Charter of the United Nations for the Maintenance of International Peace and Security, Submitted by the President of the United States on July 2, 1945* (1945) 55.

conceive of such violations perpetrated by non-state actors as 'aggression'.[125] Analogous arguments notwithstanding, we should not conclude hastily that policing measures were in fact understood as self-defence in the drafting of the Charter.

The lack of theoretical clarity on conduct that had heretofore been regarded as an exercise of the policing right of self-defence is related to the abandonment, in the formulation of the Charter's non-use of force principle, of the distinction between uses of force carried out with hostile intent against a state and violations of territory committed without such intent. As we have seen, the fundamental differences between the defensive war and policing measures types of self-defence recognized in the inter-war period were differences in the agent to whom prior conduct was attributed and in the target against whom action taken in self-defence was directed. The non-use of force principle formulated in the UN Charter reflects a loss of the latter basis of distinction: uses of force carried out in self-defence seem equally subject to censure insofar as they are conducted in territory under another state's jurisdiction, regardless of whether they are taken against states or against individuals.

The attempt to regulate the use of force in international society on the basis of the objective criterion of employment of military force in another state's territory, forsaking the attempt to distinguish uses of force from violations of territory on the basis of the presence or absence of hostile intent, makes sense from a certain legislative standpoint. Activity that had to that point been carried out against individuals as an exercise of the right of self-defence could be placed within a framework of a general prohibition on the use of force; whether any such activity was or was not permissible might theoretically be considered without an assumption made that the activity constituted self-defence.

This was not the approach taken, however. It was not made clear whether policing measures were permissible as self-defence; nor was any other basis of evaluation offered. We should be clear, nevertheless, that such measures are in fact not covered by the non-use of force principle as defined by Article 2, paragraph 4. This is not to say that any such measure is justifiable as an exercise of the right of self-defence; which such actions the right of self-defence might justify is beside the point. Put bluntly, if they are not self-defence, then they are not prohibited by Article 2, paragraph 4; and if they are self-defence, the insertion of Article 51 was not needed to establish them as not prohibited: irrespective of the conditions for invoking Article 51, the activities, insofar as

---

125 See Chapter 4, Section B.1.(f) on discussions held in connection with the Draft Act Defining Aggressor concerning the attribution of aggression to states in cases where states, by active support or complicity, bore responsibility for activity of non-state actors.

they are consistent with the purposes of the United Nations, are not violations of Article 2, paragraph 4.

C 'Insertion' of the Right of Self-Defence as Defensive War

As noted in Section B above, the self-defence focus in the process of constructing the UN Charter was on the right of self-defence established in the inter-war period. In this section, we will consider how the defensive-war conception of self-defence was discussed in the *travaux préparatoires*, and the process by which the preconditions provided by Article 51 were created.

The Process by Which Article 51 was Inserted

The Dumbarton Oaks Proposals contained no provisions concerning self-defence. The provisions that would become Article 51 of the UN Charter were added during the San Francisco Conference. The process by which these provisions came to be added is generally understood as follows.[126] Chapter 8, Section C.(2) of the Dumbarton Oaks Proposals provided that 'no enforcement action should be taken under regional arrangements or by regional agencies without the authorization of the Security Council'.[127] It should be noted that at the time of the Dumbarton Oaks Conference agreement had not been reached on the voting procedures by which the Security Council would authorize such action. It was at Yalta in February, 1945 that it was agreed that such Security Council authorization would require a unanimous vote of the permanent members of the Security Council.[128] With this, each permanent member of the Security Council acquired the power to veto an enforcement action decided by a regional authority to which that state was not itself a concluding party. The countries of Latin America strongly opposed the possibility of a Security Council state exercising such a veto. Shortly before the opening of the San Francisco Conference, they had concluded the Act of Chapultepec,[129] a treaty providing for measures of collective defence. A new article on self-defence (Article 51)

126 See eg Russell (n 13) 688–706; Goodrich and Hambro (n 9) 175–177; CHM Waldock 'The Regulation of the Use of Force by Individual States in International Law' [1952] 81 RCADI 496–497; DW Bowett *Self-Defence in International Law* (Manchester University Press Manchester 1958) 182–184.

127 Doc 1, G/1 in 3 UNCIO 19.

128 Uchida (n 18) 120–124.

129 <http://www.yale.edu/lawweb/avalon/intdip/interam/chapul.htm>.

was incorporated to address the resistance of the Latin American countries to a possible veto on the measures to be taken under the Act of Chapultepec.

The Process of Article 51's Formulation

The foregoing account of how Article 51 came to exist is correct but incomplete. Most notably, it offers no hint, as to why armed attack became the criterion for the exercise of the right of self-defence. As Bowett indicates, 'though the reasons for the insertion of Art. 51 are tolerably clear, there is no explanation of this curious proviso "if an armed attack occurs"'.[130]

As with other provisions of the UN Charter, discussion of how Article 51 was formulated has been based on the public records of the San Francisco Conference. These records, however, offer almost no material on this question.[131] For this silence, moreover, there may be a simple explanation: it has been reported that Committee III/4 of the San Francisco Conference, which dealt with the issue of self-defence, met only six times – fewer than any other committee – for the simple reason that the major decisions on this subject had been taken over a long string of informal meetings of US, UK, Soviet, Chinese, and French representatives, leaving almost nothing for this committee to do.[132]

The formulation process of Article 51, however, can be made clearer by consideration of other documents concerning informal discussions, which have been made public since the mid-1960s. Through the remainder of this section, we will use these documents, focusing on the significance of Article 51's criteria for the exercise of the right of self-defence, to clarify the position of defensive war within the drafting of the Charter.

1 *From Dumbarton Oaks to San Francisco: The Two Contexts in Which the Right of Self-Defence was Discussed*

Perceptions of the Right of Self-Defence Prior to the San Francisco Conference

While the Dumbarton Oaks Proposals contained no provisions on the right of self-defence, it was thought, during the Dumbarton Oaks Conference and

130 Bowett (n 126) 184; Waldock (n 126) 497; W Tsutsui *Jieiken* (*Right of Self-defence*) (Yuhikaku Tokyo 1980) 84–85 (*in Japanese*).

131 A Cassese 'Article 51' in JP Cot et al (eds) *La Charte des Nations Unies* (3rd edn Economica Paris 2005) vol 1, 1331.

132 BE Schmitt *The United Nations Conference on International Organization, San Francisco, California, April 25–June 26, 1945* (provisional, Department of State Washington DC 1949) vol 3, 1139–1140 in *National Archives, RG 59, Notter File 504, Box 261.*

earlier, that states had a right to use force in self-defence.[133] This point, which the present work has made more than once, is important to bear in mind; it serves as a starting point to an enquiry into the status of the right of defensive war in the drafting of the Charter.

When China's representative during the second phase of the Dumbarton Oaks conversations questioned whether measures taken in self-defence would be permitted under the Dumbarton Oaks Proposals, the US representative stated that 'a state had the inherent right to act in self-defence'.[134] This view was shared by the UK representative, who stated that 'it was self-evident that a state could and would employ force in self-defence and that therefore this had not been written into the document'.[135] The British government's commentary on the Dumbarton Oaks Proposals, moreover, pointed out that '[t]he right of self-defence would of course remain to all members if they were suddenly attacked by another State'.[136] The understanding that action in self-defence was permitted under the Dumbarton Oaks Proposals was also clearly presented in a meeting of the US delegation immediately prior to the San Francisco Conference.[137]

The first thing to note concerning these affirmations of the legitimacy of the right of self-defence is that they were made in discussions not on Chapter 8 of the Charter (Regional Arrangements) but on the provisions concerning the non-use of force principle (the current Article 2, paragraph 4). The Chinese representative's question noted in the preceding paragraph was precisely 'whether measures of self-defense by a state that was invaded, taken prior to action by the [Security] Council, would be consistent with the purposes of the organization'.[138] Similarly, the statements cited in the preceding paragraph

---

133 On this belief prior to the Dumbarton Oaks Conference, see text to n 123.

134 'Chronological Notes of the Second Plenary Session, Assembly Hall, Dumbarton Oaks, 10:40 a.m.–11:50 a.m. [Conv. B, Plenary Record 2, October 2, 1944]' in *National Archives, RG 59, Notter File 502, Box 185*. See also Russell (n 13) 465–466; 'Memorandum by the Under Secretary of State to the Secretary of State, October 2, 1944' (n 93) 862; 'International Organisation Discussions: Second Meeting of Joint Formulation Group, 6th October [U7995/180/70]' (n 55).

135 'Chronological Notes of the Second Plenary Session [Conv. B, Plenary Record 2, October 2, 1944]' (n 134).

136 *A Commentary on the Dumbarton Oaks Proposals* (n 64) 5.

137 'Minutes of the Sixth Meeting of the United States Delegation' (n 123) 229–230; 'Memorandum by the Secretary of State to President Truman, [Washington] April 19, 1945' in [1945-I] FRUS 355; Russell (n 13) 599.

138 'Chronological Notes of the Second Plenary Session [Conv. B, Plenary Record 2, October 2, 1944]' (n 134).

from the British commentary on the Dumbarton Oaks Proposals and the meeting of the US delegation were both made in connection with the text corresponding to Article 2, paragraph 4 of the Charter.

The Chinese question, and the British and American statements, then, pertained quite simply to the individual right of self-defence.

The Right of Self-Defence at the San Francisco Conference

In stark contrast to this, discussion on the right of self-defence at the San Francisco Conference was focused on the matter of 'regional arrangements'. The relationship between such regional arrangements and the international organization, in turn, was discussed in two distinct contexts. The first of these, allowing for bilateral treaties between various European countries directed against their World War II enemies, was brought up, with strong French support,[139] by the Soviet Union. On this European question, the five great powers agreed to accept 'measures against [the World War II] enemy states' taken under regional arrangements as an exception to the general rule on authorization of enforcement measures.[140]

Discussion in this first context gave rise to the second: Latin American states' demand for autonomy of their regional arrangement from the Security Council's veto power. The amendment accepted at the behest of the victorious European countries gave 'a considerable number of the Latin American delegations the impression that European regional arrangements were being removed from the control of the Security Council whereas the much older and better-established regional system of the Western Hemisphere would be subjected to the domination of that Council'.[141] In order to deal with the firm demand of some Latin American states of similar exemption from Security Council control for enforcement measures under the Act of Chapultepec,[142] it was proposed in a meeting of the US delegation 'that it might be best to spell out in the Charter the right of self-defence'.[143] What the Charter should provide concerning the right of self-defence thereafter became the subject of intense

---

139 Doc 2, G/7(o) in 3 UNCIO 379, 387.

140 'The Acting Secretary of State to Diplomatic Representatives in the American Republics, Washington, May 21, 1945–10:40 a.m.' [1945-I] FRUS 832. Also see Article 53, paragraph 1 of the Charter of the United Nations, and Russell (n 13) 688–692.

141 'The Acting Secretary of State to Diplomatic Representatives in the American Republics' (n 140) 832–833.

142 Ibid. See also Russell (n 13) 693; Nishizaki (n 5) 27–30.

143 'Minutes of the Thirty-Fifth Meeting of the United States Delegation, Held at San Francisco, Thursday, May 10, 1945, 6:30 p.m.' [1945-I] FRUS 659.

debate within the US delegation and among the five powers, from which would emerge Article 51.

Article 2, Paragraph 4 and the Right of Self-Defence

As the generally accepted interpretation holds, then, the immediate reason for inserting Article 51 was provided by the demands of Latin American states. Throughout the Charter drafting process, however, the US delegation had discussed the right of self-defence, not only in connection with the question of inserting new provisions to deal with regional arrangements, but also with what is now Article 2, paragraph 4.

The US delegation, as we have seen, had always seen the right of self-defence as a right that would be respected under the international organization, since before the Dumbarton Oaks Conference and right up to the imminent start of the San Francisco Conference. And after the San Francisco Conference began, the US delegation continued to maintain this view. As we have noted, this understanding was based on the argument that as preventing aggression was consistent with the purposes of the organization, state actions in self-defence were in accord with those purposes.[144] The relevant text, for this delegation, was Article 2, paragraph 4.[145]

The San Francisco Conference did not alter this position. The delegation's report to the President after the Conference stated that '[u]nder Article 51, force may … be used in self-defence before the machinery of the Organization can be brought into action, since self-defence against aggression would be consistent with the purposes of the Organization'.[146] Though this statement does mention Article 51, it appears in commentary on Article 2, paragraph 4.[147] Article 51 is discussed in detail elsewhere in this report, in connection with 'regional arrangements'.[148]

Two Contexts

In the drafting of the Charter, then, self-defence was discussed both in relation to Article 2, paragraph 4 and in relation to Article 51. Discussion in the

144 'Minutes of the Twenty-Ninth Meeting of the United States Delegation' (n 100) 593; 'Minutes of the Eighteenth Meeting of the United States Delegation' (n 65) 426–429; 'Minutes of the Thirty-Second Meeting of the United States Delegation' (n 103) 636–637. Also see the sources cited at n 124 of this chapter.

145 'Minutes of the Sixty-Fourth Meeting of the United States Delegation' (n 103) 1162–1163.

146 'Report to the President on the Result of the San Francisco Conference by the Chairman of the United States Delegation' (n 124) 55.

147 Ibid.

148 Ibid 87, 97–101.

former context concerned the right of individual self-defence, discussion in the latter the right of collective self-defence. Moreover, in the former context, self-defence was consistently framed as a use of force against aggression. How were individual and collective self-defence discussed once the decision had been made to draft Charter text on self-defence?

2 *The Birth of Article 51*

The judgment that it was best to include text on self-defence in the Charter was presented in the US Delegation meeting of 10 May 1945.[149] From that point, deliberation on this matter proceeded rapidly.

A first US draft of the relevant language was discussed in a meeting of the US delegation the next day,[150] and informal discussions held with the UK delegation that afternoon.[151] On the morning of the 12th, a draft revised in light of the UK delegation's comments was presented to the US delegation, which was revised further through debate there.[152] This draft, in turn, was considered on the afternoon of the 12th in an informal meeting of the five powers.[153] While the five-power meeting was adjourned for several hours, the US and UK delegations met informally and produced a new draft,[154] which was presented that evening to the reconvened five-power meeting.[155] This US-UK draft became the basis for five-power negotiations and, notwithstanding some amendments made in further negotiations, was almost identical to today's Article 51. As Kearley has said, 'If May 10 was the date of conception for the right of self-defence, May 12 was its birthday'.[156]

Understanding how Article 51 took its ultimate form thus requires some examination of the discussions held in the rapid series of informal meetings that

---

149 'Minutes of the Thirty-Fifth Meeting of the United States Delegation' (n 143) 659–660.

150 'Minutes of the Thirty-Sixth Meeting of the United States Delegation, Held at San Francisco, Friday, May 11, 1945, 2:30 p.m.' [1945-I] FRUS 664–674.

151 'Minutes of the Thirty-Seventh Meeting of the United States Delegation, Held at San Francisco, Saturday, May 12, 1945, 9 a.m.' [1945-I] FRUS 676–677.

152 Ibid 674–677, 680–686.

153 'Minutes of the Third Five-Power Informal Consultative Meeting on Proposed Amendments (Part I), Held at San Francisco, Saturday, May 12, 1945, 2:30 p.m.' [1945-I] FRUS 691–698.

154 'Memorandum by Mr. Robert Hartley of the United States Delegation of a Conversation Held at San Francisco, Saturday, May 12, 1945, 3:30 p.m.' [1945-I] FRUS 698–704; 'Minutes of Informal Drafting Session, by Mr. Robert W. Hartley' [1945-I] FRUS 705–706.

155 'Minutes of the Third Five-Power Informal Consultative Meeting' (n 153) 706–707.

156 Kearley (n 5) 696. On the joint US-UK draft, see 'Minutes of Informal Drafting Session' (n 154).

created it, especially the afternoon US-UK meeting of 12 May. These discussions, as we will see, show clearly what the criterion of 'armed attack' meant.

Collective Measures as the Focus of Interest

The US draft presented to the other powers on 12 May read as follows:

> Should the Security Council not succeed in preventing aggression, and should aggression occur by any state against any member state, such member state possesses the inherent right to take necessary measures for self-defense. The right to take such measures for self-defense against armed attack shall also apply to understandings or arrangements like those embodied in the Act of Chapultepec, under which all members of a group of states agree to consider an attack against any one of them as an attack against all of them. The taking of such measures shall be immediately reported to the Security Council and shall not in any way affect the authority and responsibility of the Security Council under this Charter to take at any time such action as it may deem necessary in order to maintain or restore international peace and security.[157]

Britain's Foreign Minister Anthony Eden condemned this draft quite harshly, saying that it 'would result in regionalism of the worst kind' and by encouraging the formation of regional arrangements undermine the basic purpose of creating a world organization.[158] Indeed, he went so far as to say that the amendment, 'clearly of Latin American origin', would render the document 'a regional agreement'.[159] The intention of the American draft, he argued,[160] was adequately served by France's proposed amendment to Chapter 6, Section C,

---

157 'Minutes of the Third Five-Power Informal Consultative Meeting' (n 153) 691–692.

158 Ibid 692–696, esp 692. This British denunciation of 'regionalism' cannot be taken at face value. The British fear was that in referring to the Act of Chapultepec, the draft posed a risk of limiting collective measures recognized as legitimate by the Charter to those uniting states within a particular region or bound by a formal treaty and thus denying British rights to engage in such operations as mutual defence among Commonwealth states and immediate action to counter an invasion of Turkey by the Soviet satellite Bulgaria. (Cf 'Amendments of Dumbarton Oaks Proposals, 15th May, 1945 [U3692/12/70]' in *PRO, FO 371/50710*; 'Memorandum by Hartley' (n 154) 700–703) In declaring itself satisfied with the joint US-UK draft, Britain cited both the preservation of the necessary authority in the international organization and the assurance of adequate British freedom of action. ('Amendments of Dumbarton Oaks Proposals' (n 158))

159 'Minutes of the Third Five-Power Informal Consultative Meeting' (n 153) 692.

160 Ibid 696.

paragraph 1 of the Dumbarton Oaks Proposals (Article 27 of the UN Charter): 'Should the Council not succeed in reaching a decision, the members of the Organization reserve to themselves the right to act as they may consider necessary in the interest of peace, right and justice'.[161]

The US noted that it had used the French proposal as a basis for its own,[162] but argued that the French proposal would 'give all member states complete freedom of action' and thus 'smash ... the entire international organization'.[163]

It was thus clearly and acutely perceived that allowing member states to engage in collective action without Security Council approval, whether under the US proposal or under the French proposal preferred by Britain, was strongly in tension with the purpose of putting in place a global collective security system.[164] For this reason, the US and UK delegations in their meeting on the afternoon of the 12th faced the task of coming up with a formula that would allow for automatic measures of collective defence without impairing the global system of collective security.[165] Efforts to work through this problem were naturally focused on collective measures.

Formulation as the Right of Collective Self-Defence

Having strongly criticized the French amendment for affording member states too much freedom of action,[166] the US in its draft of the 12th sought to limit this freedom of action by appealing to the conception of collective self-defence.[167] The restrictive effect was to work both through the preconditions for taking collective measures and through the function of such measures.

---

161 Doc 2, G/7 (o) in 3 UNCIO 385.

162 'Minutes of the Third Five-Power Informal Consultative Meeting' (n 153) 691.

163 'Memorandum by Hartley' (n 154) 702–703.

164 It must be noted that on the right of individual self-defence, there was no dispute whatever.

165 Ibid 703. This same worry, of course, was revealed in the inter-war discussions on the precursor to the right of collective self-defence. See Chapter 4, Section B.4.

166 The US also rejected a British amendment proposed in the US-UK informal meeting of the 12th as effectively the same as the French amendment, '[s]hould a breach of the peace arise out of a dispute or situation still under consideration by the Security Council or shall a sudden and unforeseen breach of the peace occur, any member state has the right to take measures of self-defense. If the Security Council should be unable to take a decision on the measures to be undertaken to restore the situation, the members of the organization reserve to themselves the right to take such action as they shall consider necessary for the maintenance of right and justice.' (ibid 699–700)

167 Ibid 702.

Collective measures under the French amendment were completely unrelated to the conception of self-defence, the only precondition of their implementation being the failure of the Security Council to reach a decision.[168] The US proposal, by contrast, though based on the French amendment,[169] added the criteria of aggression and armed attack.[170] Further, it was repeatedly pointed out that the French amendment, in permitting member states 'to act as they may consider necessary in the interest of peace, right and justice', was an attempt to incorporate in the UN Charter the reservation of individual states' right provided by Article 15, paragraph 7 of the Covenant of the League of Nations:[171] 'If the Council fails to reach a report which is unanimously agreed to by the members thereof … the Members of the League reserve to themselves the right to take such action as they shall consider necessary for the maintenance of right and justice'. This provision, allowing League member states to make war on their own, was one of the 'gaps' that plagued the Covenant,[172] and its reintroduction was at the core of the US concern over 'giv[ing] all member states complete freedom of action'.[173]

In terms of function, the US proposal sought to limit collective action by incorporating the conception of self-defence. It defined as 'measures for self-defence' the collective measures which states could take, and while it was not made clear, either in the proposal itself or in the meeting of the 12th, what 'measures for self-defence' meant in concrete terms, it was clear that these measures were contrasted with 'such action as [the Security Council] may deem necessary in order to maintain or restore international peace and security'.[174]

---

168 See text to n 160 and n 161 of this chapter.

169 'Minutes of the Third Five-Power Informal Consultative Meeting' (n 153) 691. The US draft, like the French, was intended to deal with the case of a member of the Security Council exercising its veto. (See eg 'Minutes of the Thirty-Second Meeting of the United States Delegation' (n 103) 636; 'Minutes of the Thirty-Seventh Meeting of the United States Delegation' (n 151) 677) That France and the US shared this starting point is indicated by the first words of the US proposal: 'Should the Security Council not succeed in preventing aggression, and should aggression occur …'.

170 'Memorandum by Hartley' (n 154) 702.

171 'Minutes of the Third Five-Power Informal Consultative Meeting' (n 153) 706; 'Minutes of the Thirty-Seventh Meeting of the United States Delegation' (n 151) 677.

172 See Chapter 4, Section A.

173 In light of its experience of the two great wars of the 20th century, France was bound to be wary of entrusting its security to a system of collective security which did not even exist yet, and the sufficiency of the functions of which remained unclear. On Foreign Minister Bidault's remarks in the Constituent Assembly, see Yakemtchouk (n 5) 57–58. The French amendment was an expression of the same French perspective.

174 See text to n 157 of this chapter.

The Joint US-UK Draft

The US and UK agreed on the following joint proposal to resolve their differences over competing drafts:

> Nothing in this Charter impairs the inherent right of self-defense, either individual or collective, in the event that the Security Council has failed to maintain international peace and security and an armed attack against a member state has occurred. Measures taken in the exercise of this right shall be immediately reported to the Security Council and shall not in any way affect the authority and responsibility of the Security Council under this Charter to take at any time such action as it may deem necessary in order to maintain or restore international peace and Security.[175]

Defining the measures allowed to states as measures of self-defence, and distinguishing them from the broader set of measures to be taken by the Security Council,[176] this proposal was a rejection of the 'complete freedom of action' which the French amendment would have granted states.

3 *Collective Self-Defence against Armed Attack and Individual Self-Defence against Aggression*

Where the joint US-UK draft[177] provided that '[n]othing in this Charter impairs the inherent right of self-defence, either individual or collective, in the event that ... an armed attack against a member state has occurred', the Article 51 text

175 'Minutes of Informal Drafting Session' (n 154) 705.

176 The relationship between measures of self-defence and action to be taken by the Security Council was made clearer in later discussions. In the five-power meeting of 16 May, the US representative stated that 'the right of self-defence still existed under the provisions of the Charter, and that right could be exercised until the Security Council took the necessary measures in order to maintain or restore peace and security'. ('Minutes of the Ninth Meeting, Committee of Five Deputies of the Heads of Delegations, May 16, 1945, 5:10 p.m. to 7:10 p.m.' in *National Archives, RG 59, Notter File 504, Box 257*) This understanding was progressively reflected in the proposed amendment text. ('Minutes of the Sixth Five-Power Informal Consultative Meeting on Proposed Amendments, Held at San Francisco, May 19, 1945' [1945-I] FRUS 812; 'Minutes of the Fourteenth Meeting, Committee of Five Deputies of the Heads of Delegations, May 19, 1945, 3:45 p.m. to 6:40 p.m.' in *National Archives, RG 59, Notter File 504, Box 257*; 'Minutes of the Fifteenth Meeting, Committee of Five Deputies of the Heads of Delegations, May 20, 1945, 5:00 p.m. to 5:45 p.m.' in ibid) The right of self-defence can accordingly be seen as a provisional measure within the UN collective security system.

177 See text to n 175 of this chapter.

ultimately adopted provides that '[n]othing in the present Charter shall impair the inherent right of individual or collective self-defence if an armed attack occurs against a member of the United Nations'. In both cases, armed attack is made a precondition for the exercise of both the individual and the collective right of self-defence.

Inter-war discussions on the precursor to the collective right of self-defence (covered in Chapter 4, Section B.4) did recognize a certain difference between collective and individual self-defence in terms of the preceding acts thought to justify their exercise. No such distinction seems to be recognized in the UN Charter. This raises the question of how the distinction was treated, if at all, in the drafting of the Charter.

Distinct Preconditions

The US draft submitted to the morning five-power informal meeting of 12 May did in fact present two distinct preconditions. Where its first sentence provides that '... should *aggression* occur by any state against any member state, such member state possesses the inherent right to take necessary measures for self-defence', its second sentence refers instead to 'the right to take measures for self-defence against *armed attack*'.[178]

The distinction here between aggression and armed attack 'was made deliberately',[179] such that the individual right of self-defence would be exercised by countries subjected to aggression while the second sentence of the proposal clearly pertained to the collective right of self-defence. Aggression, in other words, was the precondition for individual self-defence, armed attack the precondition for exercising the right of collective self-defence.[180]

178 'Minutes of the Thirty-Fifth Meeting of the United States Delegation' (n 143) 691. (emphasis added)

179 'Minutes of the Thirty-Sixth Meeting of the United States Delegation' (n 150) 667. In the US draft of the 11th, 'attack' appeared in the first sentence where 'aggression' appeared in the draft of the 12th. The view was expressed in the delegation that the distinction between 'attack' and 'armed attack' would be difficult to explain to the other powers; 'attack' was accordingly changed to 'aggression'. (ibid 670, 672) The original distinction between 'attack' and 'armed attack' was intended 'to cover the Monroe Doctrine which has two parts – the case of an overt attack and that of political efforts from outside the [American] continent to overthrow the political institutions of the American Republics'. While it was recognized that the word 'attack' could cover both cases, it was explained that 'armed attack' 'has specific reference to collective action under the Act of Chapultepec'. (ibid 667)

180 Kearley (n 5) 700. See eg 'Minutes of the Thirty-Sixth Meeting of the United States Delegation' (n 150) 667; 'Minutes of the Thirty-Eighth Meeting of the United States Delegation, Held at San Francisco, Monday, May 14, 9:05 a.m.' [1945-I] FRUS 710.

Aggression and Armed Attack

The aggression-armed attack distinction in the US draft of the 12th was a major point of discussion in the US-UK informal meeting of that day. As we have seen, collective self-defence, rather than individual self-defence, was the problem on which this meeting focused. Interestingly, while the US draft's criterion for exercising the former was not 'aggression' but 'armed attack', the UK delegation was concerned with the word 'aggression', which the US draft proposed as the criterion for exercising the individual right of self-defence. The UK delegation noted the difficulty of defining 'aggression',[181] Foreign Minister Eden complaining that 'no one had been able to define aggression in thirty years'.[182]

The US delegation actually shared the UK's sense of the difficulty of defining aggression. The Charter does not in fact define the term. Definition was intentionally avoided, the idea being that as it was impossible for a definition of the term to cover all instances of aggression, attempting to define it would result in genuine acts of aggression being committed that did not fit the terms of the definition.[183]

In response to the UK criticism on 'aggression', the US delegation emphasized the significance of defining armed attack as the precondition for the exercise of the collective right of self-defence: 'the right of collective or group action only comes into operation in the event of an armed attack';[184] and 'the United States proposal attempted to define aggression in terms of "armed attack" to avoid the problem of defining aggression as such'.[185] The scope of 'armed attack' was taken to be narrower than that of 'aggression', and armed attack was to be understood as 'a clear case of aggression'.[186]

Making armed attack, rather than aggression, the precondition for exercising the collective right of self-defence, then, was an attempt to make the conditions for action in collective self-defence more restrictive than those for exercising the individual right. The distinction operating here between collective and individual self-defence overlaps quite broadly with the inter-war distinction between the precursor to collective self-defence and individual self-defence, which we considered in Chapter 4, Section B.4. In other words, the conditions under which the individual right of self-defence could be exercised were thought to be broader than armed attack.

---

181 'Minutes of the Third Five-Power Informal Consultative Meeting' (n 153) 692; 'Memorandum by Hartley' (n 154) 700.

182 'Minutes of the Third Five-Power Informal Consultative Meeting' (n 153) 692.

183 Doc 881, III/3/46 in 12 UNCIO 505; Goodrich and Hambro (n 9) 157.

184 'Minutes of the Third Five-Power Informal Consultative Meeting' (n 153) 694.

185 'Memorandum by Hartley' (n 154) 700.

186 'Charter of World Organization, 12th May, 1945 [U3646/12/70]' in *PRO, FO 371/50709*.

Erasure and Latency of the Distinction

The distinction between an individual right of self-defence against aggression and a collective right of self-defence against armed attack was lost in the US-UK joint proposal, as armed attack was understood as the precondition for the exercise of either right. Within the US delegation, there was opposition to dropping the term 'aggression'. Dulles, for example, complained of the deletion and 'thought that the individual right should not be curtailed in any way'.[187] Such opposition was not thoroughly discussed at the time. This does not mean, however, that such opposition was considered off the mark. What happened, rather, is that Secretary of State Stettinius moved to wrap up the meeting at which that objection, among others, was raised, saying 'that there would be many refinements of language before a document was finally agreed upon'.[188]

Moreover, the US delegation seems to have maintained the distinction between an individual right of self-defence against aggression and a collective right against armed attack until the Charter was adopted. As we have noted, the delegation's report submitted to the president after the conclusion of the San Francisco Conference discussed the right of self-defence in two contexts. In connection with Article 2, paragraph 4, the report stated that 'force may … be used in self-defence before the machinery of the Organization can be brought into action, since self-defence *against aggression* would be consistent with the purposes of the Organization'.[189] Regarding Article 51, the report commented:

> In thus recognizing the paramount authority of the world organization in enforcement action as well as *the inherent right of self-defence against armed attack* pending the time when the Security Council undertakes such action, this Article [51], with the other relevant provisions of the

---

187 'Minutes of the Thirty-Eighth Meeting of the United States Delegation (n 180) 710. Removal of 'aggression' suggests that the US agreed to wording reflecting the UK stance on the difficulty of defining that term. The draft on which the joint US-UK proposal was based was composed by a single member of the UK delegation, and did not contain the word 'aggression'. ('Memorandum by Hartley' (n 154) 704) In light of this, it is not entirely clear that removal of the term implied a narrowing of the preconditions for exercising the individual right of self-defence from 'aggression' to 'armed attack'.

188 'Minutes of the Thirty-Eighth Meeting of the United States Delegation (n 180) 710. In the event, there is no record that the matter was discussed again, either in the five-power meetings or in the public meetings of the Conference.

189 'Report to the President on the Result of the San Francisco Conference by the Chairman of the United States Delegation' (n 124) 55. (emphasis added)

> Charter, makes possible a useful and effective integration of regional systems of cooperation with the world system of international security.[190]

Where the right of self-defence is discussed in connection with Article 2, paragraph 4, the focus is on individual self-defence; and where self-defence is discussed in connection with Article 51, the focus is rather on collective self-defence. This framing of the Charter's provisions on self-defence reflects the understanding held by the US delegation throughout the drafting process.

Nor was this the understanding only of the US delegation. It was never entirely ruled out in the San Francisco Conference negotiations that followed the proposal of Article 51. The report of the Subcommittee I/1/A rapporteur to Committee I/1 stated that 'it was clear to the subcommittee that *the right of self-defence against aggression* should not be impaired or diminished'.[191] The report contains no commentary on this sentence, and it is not easy to divine all of its implications. It can be noted, however, that this report is dated 1 June. On 23 May it had been decided in Committee III/4 to insert provisions nearly identical to the current Article 51.[192] It is unlikely that the rapporteur for Subcommittee I/1/A did not know how Article 51 defined the preconditions for action in self-defence. If he did know, it is notable that he nevertheless refers to 'self-defence against aggression'.[193]

The Status of the Individual Right of Self-Defence against Aggression

As we have seen, in the drafting of Article 51, an individual right of self-defence against aggression was mentioned along with the more restrictively conceived collective right of self-defence against armed attack. Article 51 as ultimately adopted names only armed attack as a criterion for the exercise of the right of self-defence, whether individual or collective. The original distinction may nevertheless be thought to lurk in the background, present though unnamed.

---

190 Ibid 100. (emphasis added)

191 Doc 739, I/1/A/19(a) in 6 UNCIO 721. (emphasis added)

192 Doc 576, III/4/9 in 12 UNCIO 680.

193 The statement of the Commission I, Committee I *Rapporteur's* report concerning Article 2, paragraph 4 should probably be understood in the same way: 'The use of arms in legitimate self-defence remains admitted and unimpaired'. (Doc 944, I/1/34 (1) in 6 UNCIO 459) This single sentence of the Commission I, Committee I *Rapporteur* report has been for some time the subject of, unfortunately unproductive, interpretative debate. See Bowett (n 126) 182; Waldock (n 1) 234–235; Brownlie (n 2 (*International Law and the Use of Force by States*)) 269–270.

Our discussion to this point brings us to the question: how to view the status of the individual right of self-defence against aggression not amounting to armed attack. We can note first that this right is not denied by Article 51. The phrasing of Article 51, 'Nothing in the Charter shall impair the inherent right of individual or collective self-defence if an armed attack occurs against a member of the United Nations', does not imply that no inherent right of self-defence against aggression not amounting to armed attack can be recognized.

Further, it is worth recalling that the exercise of the individual right of self-defence was considered permissible under the Article 2, paragraph 4 non-use of force principle. Article 2, paragraph 4 prohibits any use of force not consistent with the purposes of the United Nations, but as we have noted repeatedly, it was thought that '[s]ince the prevention of aggression would be consistent with the purposes of the Organization, action by a state in self-defense would be in accord with' those principles.[194]

D The Meaning of the Right of Self-Defence in the Drafting Process of the UN Charter

In light of the foregoing considerations, we can summarize the right of self-defence in the drafting process of the UN Charter as follows.

Right of Self-Defence in Terms of Policing Measures

That little attention was paid in the drafting of the UN Charter to the policing conception of the right of self-defence is not particularly surprising given the intimate connection of that project to the experience of the Second World War and the war aims of the Allies.[195] As the conception of use of force embodied in Article 2, paragraph 4 of the Charter was understood to cover the employment of military force within the jurisdiction of another state, territorial violations came under the non-use of force principle. This fact would naturally have consequences for the status of policing measures in self-defence under the Charter. However, the question of whether such actions as had been understood to be permissible in exercise of the policing-type right of self-defence were permissible under the non-use of force principle was not discussed in the multinational meetings through which the Charter was formulated, and its

194 'Minutes of the Twenty-Ninth Meeting of the United States Delegation' (n 100) 593. See also 'Minutes of the Eighteenth Meeting of the United States Delegation' (n 65) 426–429; and text to n 124.

195 Khan (n 113) 3.

answer is not obvious. It is worth noting that in US State Department internal deliberations such actions were thought to be permissible, and if we view the debates of the San Francisco Conference through the lens of US delegation understandings, it is difficult to think that such actions were thought to be prohibited.

Self-Defence in Terms of Defensive War

In contrast to the 19th century right of self-defence, that established in the inter-war period attracted great interest. As is generally accepted, the immediate spur to insertion of Article 51 was the demand by Latin American states for excluding from Security Council control enforcement actions taken under the Act of Chapultepec. The inter-war right of self-defence, however, had already been debated, in connection with what would become Article 2, paragraph 4 of the Charter, at Dumbarton Oaks. At that time, the right of self-defence was understood as the individual right of self-defence and was thought to be lawfully exercised against aggression. While uses of force not consistent with the purposes of the world organization were prohibited by Article 2, paragraph 4 of the Charter, it was not thought necessary to provide explicitly that self-defence against aggression was permissible, the prevention of aggression being itself a purpose of the organization.

That the individual right of self-defence was thought to be legitimately exercised not against armed attack but against aggression has gone all but unnoted in studies to date of the preparatory work to Article 51. Awareness of this fact is essential to understanding how the preconditions specified in Article 51 for exercising the right of self-defence attained their current form. The US draft of 12 May presented for five-power consultation made armed attack the precondition for collective self-defence and aggression the precondition for individual self-defence. It goes without saying that the scope of armed attack was understood to be narrower than the scope of aggression; armed attack was characterized as 'a clear case of aggression'.[196]

The distinguishing of preconditions arose from concern over regionalism and collective action, the same concern revealed by records of inter-war debate on the precursor to the collective right of self-defence.[197] Distinguishing the individual and collective rights of self-defence by the preconditions for their exercise was intended to address these concerns by restricting the use of force in collective self-defence more than the use of force in individual self-defence.

196 'Charter of World Organization, 12th May, 1945 [U3646/12/70]' (n 186).

197 See Chapter 4, Section B.4.

Article 51, formulated through vigorous debate on the US draft, did not preserve the draft's different preconditions for individual and collective self-defence. The drafting process of Article 51, however, does not show the distinction to have been rejected. The US Secretary of State's report to the President on the results of the San Francisco Conference, moreover, clearly shows that the US delegation, at the time of the Charter's adoption, considered the preconditions for individual self-defence as differing from those for collective self-defence.

This is not to say that this US understanding, which was not presented in open session at San Francisco, should be considered the definitive interpretation of the Charter's relevant provisions. Whether this line of the thought deserves greater emphasis than any opposing current in the *travaux preparatoires* to the Charter is an open question. Moreover, interpretation of the Charter is beyond the goals of this study, as this would require analysis of state practice since 1945. Further, since the UN came into existence, the US itself has not maintained the validity of this framework distinguishing the individual from the collective right of self-defence based on the preconditions of their exercise, at least not in a clear and unmistakable form. Nevertheless, if we wish to understand the conception of the right of self-defence current at the time of the Charter's adoption, it is surely worth knowing that the available documentary evidence shows key drafters of the Charter, at the time of its adoption, to have held the distinction to be valid.

The *Rechtsgüter* and Legal Status of the Right(s) of the Self-Defence

Finally, I would like to note what the drafting process of the UN Charter shows us concerning the *Rechsgüter* and the legal status of the policing and defensive war rights of self-defence.

The *Rechtsgut* of the defensive war right of self-defence was simply the security of the state. At the same time, while it was clear that the *Rechsgüter* of the collective right of self-defence comprised international peace and security, this was also a *Rechtsgut* of the individual right of self-defence, as is indicated by the frequent insistence that as preventing aggression was a purpose of the United Nations, action taken by a state in self-defence against aggression was in accord with the organization's purposes.[198] Further, with respect to the legal status of such action, as under the inter-war treaties, such action was clearly recognized as constituting a permissible use of force. As resistance to

198 'Minutes of the Twenty-Ninth Meeting of the United States Delegation' (n 100) 593. See also 'Minutes of the Eighteenth Meeting of the United States Delegation' (n 65) 426–429.

aggression was consistently seen as in accord with the UN's purposes, the use of force in self-defence was understood not to be prohibited by the Charter.

What, then, of the policing right of self-defence? As the Charter did not explicitly recognize such a right, the question arises whether it is appropriate to see policing actions as comprehended within the right of self-defence recognized at the time of the Charter's adoption. To address this question, we must note that in the cases presented which we would recognize as policing action, the *Rechtsgut* cited was the protection of the life and property of nationals. Actions taken for that purpose fall within the exception to the non-use of force principle. That is, it seems appropriate to view them not as excusable violations of that principle, but more simply as not violating it.

Conclusion

The Origins of the Right of Self-Defence

This book has been dedicated to a consideration of the development of conceptions of the right of self-defence from the mid-19th century to 1945. In following this development, we have seen two basic conceptions of this right to have been recognized over this period: a right of 'policing-type' self-defence and a right of self-defence as 'defensive war'. The latter conception can be subdivided into that of a right of collective self-defence and that of a right of individual self-defence, giving us three conceptions that together form a bedrock of the right of self-defence in our current international law. Let us briefly review what we have learned about each.

The Policing-Type and Defensive War Rights of Self-Defence

The policing-type right of self-defence justifies the violation by one state of another state's territory or flag-ship jurisdiction for the purpose of defending itself from attack by private persons. A country can exercise this right of self-defence only when attacked or threatened by such individuals as paramilitaries or insurgents, operating from the territory of another country or on the high-seas under the flag-ship jurisdiction of another country (as in the *Caroline* Incident and *Virginius* Incident respectively), and only where the state with territorial or flag-ship jurisdiction was unable to prevent the behavior in question (see Chapter 3). In contrast, the defensive-war right of self-defence justified a war of self-defence or the countering of aggression in order to repel attack by another country (see Chapter 4).

The policing-type right of self-defence was established in international law in the mid-19th century and thus can be described as a survival from the 19th century. The defensive war right of self-defence, in contrast, came to be recognized with the development of the outlawry of war in the interwar period and thus can be termed 'the right of self-defence established in the interwar period'. It must be noted, however, that in the interwar period, the two rights of self-defence, as indicated by state practice in that period, coexisted. The basis of their coexistence lay in their normative relations to each other: they were distinguished from each other in terms of the actor against whom action in self-defence could be taken, in terms of the actions that could be taken in self-defence, and in terms of the scope of the *Rechtsgüter* invoked.

Military action undertaken in the exercise of the policing-type right of self-defence was directed not against a state with territorial or flag-state jurisdiction, but against individuals operating under that jurisdiction. In international

 | DOI 10.1163/9789004355002_009

relations, the military action in question was understood as violation of a state's territory or flag-ship jurisdiction and the function of the right of self-defence invoked was to justify such violation. The *Rechtsgut* was typically the lives and property of nationals, and under certain conditions might extend to national safety; and in any case the scale of the military action justified typically was comparatively small, as the actions occasioning the exercise of the right of self-defence were actions of individuals.

In the case of defensive war, military action was taken against another state *per se*. Accordingly, the military action justified by the right of self-defence was actual war or counterattack against aggression, and the *Rechtsgut* nothing less than national security. The scale of action taken in self-defence might thus be limited to a border incursion or extend to resistance to a war of aggression (see Chapter 5).

The Policing Right of Self-Defence and the Establishment of the Non-use of Force Principle

If the two rights of self-defence thus coexisted and were distinct from each other in the interwar period, the distinction between them was complicated by the adoption of the UN Charter and establishment of the non-use of force principle. In the drafting process of the Charter, the category 'use of force' was understood to include employment of military forces within the territory of other states. Thus, while actions justified by the policing right of self-defence included both violations of territory and violations of flag-state jurisdiction on the high seas, the former can be said to have fallen within the scope of the 'use of force', directed strictly against individuals though they might be.[1]

This raises the question of whether action of this type, which came under the heading of uses of force and had been justified as an exercise of the policing-type right of self-defence, was permissible. At least in US State Department internal deliberations, it was taken to be so. This indicates deep-rooted US support for action that had been justified by the policing-type right of self-defence.

If such action was thus clearly held to be permissible, however, its theoretical status was not clear, and almost no attention was devoted to clarifying it. Where it was recognized as permissible, the term 'self-defence' was not used

1 Actions of the latter type can be thought not to be 'uses of force' under the non-use of force principle. This provides a basis for treating certain employments of force recognized under the law of the sea as uses of force not covered by Article 2(4) of the Charter (A Randelzhofer and N Dörr 'Article 2(4)' in B Simma et al (eds) *The Charter of the United Nations: A Commentary* (3rd edn OUP Oxford 2012) vol 1, 217) – a topic requiring further study.

to describe it. In so far as we consider this silence significant, we may see such action as an exception to the non-use of force principle not covered by the right of self-defence. However, if we focus instead on the fact that, referring to the case of Pancho Villa, such action had been treated as repelling invasion before the operation of international organizations, it seems more natural to characterize it as an exercise of the right of self-defence. The theoretical place of policing action, even within the US position that held it clearly to be permissible, is thus uncertain.

The Legal Status of the Two Rights of Self-Defence

In terms of legal status, too, there was a contrast between the two types of self-defence. Defensive war, both in the process of the interwar outlawry of war and in the drafting of the Charter, was understood to be a permitted use of force, rather than a circumstance excusing a use of force that would otherwise be unlawful. Defensive war constituted the exercise of a genuine *right* of self-defence, even if it was not entirely clear what the conception of such a right entailed. In contrast, policing-type self-defence, regarded as a basic right of states in the mid-19th century, would thereafter assume the status of an excuse for violating the territory of another state. Its legal status, however, would again change greatly in the drafting of the UN Charter: an exception to the non-use of force principle, action taken under the policing-type right of self-defence was treated as permissible in its own right. As indicated in Chapter 6 of this book, however, the drafting of the UN Charter left such ambiguities in the legal status of policing-type self-defence as how its recognition as an exception to the non-use of force principle was related to its status as condition excusing the violation of territory.

Collective Self-Defence

The defensive-war right of self-defence can be divided into a collective right and an individual right. The right of collective self-defence is often considered a new concept, first established in international law with the adoption of the Charter. A precursor of the right of collective self-defence, however, can be found in the interwar period. In that period, the precursor of the right of collective self-defence was understood to differ from the individual right of self-defence not only in terms of function but also in terms of preconditions.

The collective right, permitting the use of force by a country not directly attacked in aid of another country that has been, obviously differs in function from the right of an individual state directly attacked. In addition, the preconditions for exercising the right of collective self-defence were more restrictively defined than those of the individual right. In the interwar period, it was seen as essential to distinguish the precursor of the collective right in this way in light of the perceived danger that it would cause a world war. This fear was born of the consideration that, given the difficulty of defining aggression, the precursor to the collective right of self-defence would essentially be a justification for collective military measures in the absence of designation of an aggressor by a system of collective security. The fear was that if collective military action could be justified against a country that cannot legitimately be considered an aggressor, nothing would stand in the way of world war. The danger of subjective judgment causing war applies to the individual right of self-defence as well, but the prospect of such judgment justifying collective action was seen to heighten that danger and thus the importance of restricting the preconditions (see Chapter 4).

The UN Charter, interestingly, did not explicitly distinguish the preconditions of the exercise of a collective from those of the individual right of self-defence. A distinction can be found, however, in the *travaux préparatoires*. The intention of the Charter's drafters can be understood as restricting the conditions for exercising the collective right, not as limiting the right of individual self-defence to cases of armed aggression (see Chapter 6).

The Charter's Silence

As we have seen, the right of self-defence that existed in 1945 was actually three rights: the policing-type right of self-defence and the individual and collective rights of defensive war. The Charter, however, provides explicitly only for the defensive war rights and makes only armed attack a condition for exercising either the individual or the collective right. In other words, the Charter makes clear neither the status of the policing-type right of self-defence nor the distinction between the preconditions of the collective and individual rights of defensive war. Whether this implies a denial of either the policing-type right of self-defence or the distinction between the prerequisites of the individual and collective self-defence rights is unclear. On these matters, the Charter's silence is complete.

•••

The Relationship between this Work's Argument and the Traditional Theoretical Framework

How does our argument fit into the framework established by the Bowett-Brownlie debate?

Scope of *Rechtsgüter* and Preceding Acts

As noted in Chapter 1, the first issue to address in this connection is how to characterize the *Rechtsgüter* and scope of preceding acts of the right(s) of self-defence that existed in 1945. Was the precondition for exercising the right of self-defence limited to cases of armed attack? Or could it be exercised against aggression other than armed attack? That the right of defensive war in the interwar period could be exercised against aggression is clear. Defining aggression or the conditions for defensive war, however, posed tremendous difficulties. Now, Article 51 of the UN Charter specified only armed attack as a condition enabling the exercise of the right of self-defence. In the *travaux préparatoires*, however, the broader category of aggression was understood as a sufficient condition for exercising the individual right of self-defence (see Chapters 4, 5, and 6). With respect to the *Rechtsgüter*, we must bear in mind that the policing right of self-defence, which concerned the lives and property of nationals, continued to exist in the interwar period (see Chapters 3 and 5).

What Self-Defence is Taken to Mean

In situating this work with respect to Bowett and Brownlie, we must next address the basic question of what self-defence is taken to mean. As noted in Chapter 1, Bowett offered a general formula which he intended to cover the whole of self-defence from the mid-19th century to 1945, or even to the present day: 'The essence of self-defence is a wrong done, a breach of a legal duty owed to the state acting in self-defence'.[2] Brownlie objects that 'this definition of self-defence in such a way as to include the protection of certain rights makes it difficult and probably impossible to distinguish it from self-help'.[3] Brownlie argues further that Bowett's 'concept of the defence of essential rights seems in the last resort to differ little from the concept of self-preservation'.[4] Based on this understanding, Brownlie argues that self-help and self-preservation came to be prohibited in the interwar period, and that the conception of the right of self-defence established in the 19th century accordingly was unrelated to contemporary international law's right of self-defence, the origin of which is to be found in the interwar period.

We have seen, however, that the 19th century right of self-defence should not be equated with self-help or self-preservation. The 19th century conception of the right of self-defence has its own meaning and function, distinct from

2 DW Bowett *Self-Defence in International Law* (Manchester University Press Manchester 1958) 9. See also ibid 269.

3 I Brownlie 'Recent Appraisals of Legal Regulation of the Use of Force' [1959] 8 ICLQ 715–716.

4 Ibid 716.

those of self-preservation and self-help (see Chapter 3). To say that the right of self-defence has roots in the 19th century implies no general acceptance of the use of force for self-help or self-preservation. In this respect, the traditional framework, which poses a choice between holding that Article 51 restricted the right of self-defence to cases of armed attack and holding self-help to be generally permitted, is clearly in need of rethinking.

This is not to say that Bowett's general definition is appropriate. His formula is overly broad, and Brownlie's reformulation not so very wide of the mark. In aiming for a general formulation to cover both the policing-type and the defensive war right of self-defence while recognizing a distinction between self-defence and self-preservation, Bowett can be thought to have settled on 'the essence of self-defence [as] a wrong done' as capturing their common element. On the other hand, to be criticized for conflating self-defence and self-preservation must have been great disappointment to Bowett.

Dichotomous Argument

As noted in Chapter 1, Brownlie's and Bowett's contending characterizations of the 19th century right of self-defence are related to their differing views of whether developments before or after the First World War deserve the greater emphasis. Bowett emphasized continuities between the prewar and interwar periods, Brownlie the importance of interwar development. Both, however, took self-defence as a single conception justifying uses of force by states and accepted the task of arguing whether it was the earlier or the later period that deserved the greater emphasis – as do many today. This practice of treating two conceptions as one is an invitation to the '*grande confusion*' that reigns on the subject of self-defence.

That post-World War II theorists should view the right of self-defence as a single concept is perhaps only natural. If self-defence is a matter of interpretation of the UN Charter provisions, which is to say a state's use of force covered by an exception to the general prohibition, then it only makes sense for analysis to focus on the necessary conditions for justified invocation of that exception. Does not treating the right of self-defence as a single, unified conception, however, give an overly narrow view of the problem? In order to understand the entirety of the conception of the right of self-defence existing in international law, or at least to understand its historical development, we must bear in mind that the right of self-defence had been understood to justify violations of territorial and flag-state jurisdiction.

To be sure, with the prohibition of military operations in the territory of another state by the non-use of force principle under the Charter, the policing-type right of self-defence, at least in so far as it justified violations of territory, did come within the ambit of justification of 'uses of force'. In that respect, we may think it not greatly mistaken to treat the right of self-defence simply as justification for 'the use of force'. However, to do so means reframing the *Caroline* incident, for example, as a precedent for the right of self-defence understood as an exception to the present-day non-use of force principle. And if we confine ourselves to discussing the right of self-defence solely as justification for the use of force in this sense, we must nevertheless recognize that the policing-type right of self-defence is distinct from the right of defensive war in terms of preceding act, action to be taken in exercise of the right, and the *Rechtsgüter*. If our analysis of cases is to take such distinctions into account, then the approach typically followed in the past, disputing whether the prewar or interwar period deserves the greater emphasis, will prove too crude.

Commonalities and Differences between the Two Rights of Self-Defence

We have to this point emphasized differences between the two types of self-defence. In a broad sense, the two are obviously unified on protection of the state against invasion. Overemphasis of this commonality, however, invites the Brownlie critique of a conception that would make permissible any action taken for the safety of the nation. On this point, the argument of this book has been that the two types of self-defence against invasion of the nation that have historically been recognized can be formulated as the policing-type self-defence and defensive war.[5] It is thus not only the commonalities of the two

5 In contemporary international law, moreover, it is not disputed that the right of self-defence is constrained by the principles of necessity and proportionality. The concrete meaning of these constraints, however – particularly the relationship between the conditions establishing necessity and the Article 51 criterion of 'armed attack' – has not been made entirely clear. (See J Gardam *Necessity, Proportionality and the Use of Force by States* (CUP Cambridge 2004) 149) Excessive reliance on these two principles as means of defining the meaning of the right of self-defence, moreover, may easily result in such unhelpful formulations as that where action is necessary, action within the limit of what is necessary should be taken. (I Brownlie 'The Use of Force in Self-Defence' [1961] BYIL 265)

Our study has shown that such principles have been refined and given categorical forms through a process of argumentation on specific cases and treaties. 'Occurrence of armed attack' is nothing more or less than a formulation describing the case in which it is necessary to exercise the right of defensive war. Likewise, 'aggression' is a formulation describing conditions of exercising the individual right of defensive war. The constraints developed for the policing-type right of self-defence can be described as attack or threat of attack from individuals such as paramilitaries or groups in rebellion, operating from territory or ships under the jurisdiction of another state, where the state with such jurisdiction cannot prevent such individuals' actions. This is not to say that where these conditions are satisfied no further attention to the question of necessity is required; the principle of necessity can be understood

conceptions of self-defence but also the differences of which we need to be aware.

•••

Origins of the Right of Self-Defence and the Right of Self-Defence in Current International Law

Can the categories presented in this study be applied to the contemporary right of self-defence in international law? The question obviously requires further study. The unique precondition given for an exercise of self-defence given by the Charter is the occurrence of an armed attack, and not only academic argument but state practice and court judgments have proceeded since on that basis. Given this limitation of the terms of reference, our three conceptions of self-defence are not to be found, neatly laid out in the terms in which we have discussed them here, in current international law. Approaching the current state of law from the perspective of our categories, however, may help us make our contemporary law a bit more orderly. The discussion that follows is decidedly tentative, but indicates some lines of analysis worth pursuing.

Collective and Individual Self-Defence

A distinction noted in this work between collective self-defence, exercised against armed attack, and individual self-defence, which was exercised against 'aggression', a category broader than armed attack, appears also in the ICJ judgement in *Nicaragua v. United States of America*. The ICJ in this case contrasted armed attack with 'a use of force of a lesser degree of gravity', which might justify only 'proportionate countermeasures on the part the State which had been the victim'.[6]

Christine Gray has spotted the significance of this contrast:

> At first sight it might seem that the distinction drawn in a sketchy way in the *Nicaragua* case between armed attacks and lesser incursions such as frontier incidents was illogical and unnecessary … But it is clear, despite the criticisms of the *Nicaragua* case, that there were nevertheless serious

as having developed further to constrain the actions of the state acting in self-defence. (See *Case concerning Oil Platforms* (*Islamic Republic of Iran v United States of America*) (Merits) [2003] ICJ Rep 198. See also C Greenwood 'The Relationship between Ius ad Bellum and Ius in Bello' [1983] Rev Int'l Studies 222) This is a subject requiring further study.

6 *Case concerning Military and Paramilitary Activities in and against Nicaragua* (*Nicaragua v United States of America*) (Merits) [1986] ICJ Rep 127.

> reasons for the Court's distinction between armed attacks and mere frontier incidents. Its concern was with *collective* self-defence; it wanted to limit *third state* involvement. Its insistence on a high threshold for armed attack would serve to limit third party involvement. If there was no armed attack, there could be no collective self-defence.[7]

As Gray makes clear, the difference in preconditions between the exercise of the right of collective self-defence and the action undertaken by a single state (putting aside the question of whether the latter should be called self-defence) springs precisely from the same deep unease with collective self-defence revealed in the interwar period and the drafting of the UN Charter.

Policing-Type Self-Defence

It is worth noting that recent years have seen numerous instances of action ostensibly justified by the policing-type right of self-defence: the Thai army's 1995 attack on guerrillas in Myanmar, campaigns by Senegal in Guinea Bissau in 1992 and 1995, the Tajikistan campaign in Afghanistan, Turkish operations against Kurdish groups in Iraq, and so forth.[8] The so-called 'war on terror', can also be discussed from this perspective, though only with great caution.[9]

It may be asserted that what this work has termed instances of 'policing-type self-defence' are not self-defence at all, but rather examples of the 'state of necessity'. This position is presented with particular clarity by Robert Ago, who led the formulation of the UN International Law Commission's First Reading Draft on State Responsibility.

As we noted in Chapter 2, Ago distinguished self-defence and state of necessity by whether a wrong has been committed.[10] Ago himself acknowledged, however, that

> A survey of practice shows that States engaging in some action involving the use of force have sometimes pleaded that they had a duty to protect, by such action, a vital interest which was threatened by a grave danger,

---

7 C Gray *International Law and the Use of Force* (3rd edn OUP Oxford 2008) 179–181.

8 Ibid 140–143.

9 See ibid 193–253. Also, on Colombia's campaign against terror groups in Ecuador's territory, see T Waisberg 'Colombia's Use of Force in Ecuador against a Terrorist Organization' [2008] 12–17 ASIL Insight <http://www.asil.org/insights080822.cfm>.

10 R Ago 'Addendum to the Eighth Report on State Responsibility: The Internationally Wrongful Act of State, Source of International Responsibility (Part 1) (Concluded)' [1980] 2–1 Yb Int'l L Comm'n 53–54.

> but that they have not expressly invoked as a justification the ground of necessity[11]

and that in these cases

> The concept of state of necessity was neither mentioned nor taken into consideration, even though some of the alleged facts stated by those who spoke of 'self-defence' and who were contested on that point by their opponents may have borne more relation to state of necessity than to self-defence.[12]

The Articles on State Responsibility were adopted by the International Law Commission in 2001. In the Second Reading on State Responsibility, Special Rapporteur James Crawford denied that unlawful uses of force were excusable by a state of necessity.[13] This does not quite mean, however, that such uses of force with which Ago struggled are impermissible under international law.

Starting from the presumption that any act in violation of Article 2(4) violates obligations derived from peremptory norms (*jus cogens*) of international law, Crawford rejects the argument that a state of necessity can be invoked to excuse unlawful acts in violation of *jus cogens*.[14] In this, Crawford contrasts sharply with Ago, who cited the *Caroline* incident in allowing that unlawfulness of an act violating Article 2(4) but not *jus cogens*, might be precluded under a state of necessity.[15] For Crawford, no appeal to a state of necessity will avail to excuse a use of force in violation of Article 2(4), and as a use of force that does not violate Article 2(4) is lawful, no claim of a state of necessity is needed.[16] Crawford suggests here a different conception of the use of force to

---

11 Ibid 42.

12 Ibid 44. See JJA Salmon 'Faut-il codifier l'état de nécessité en droit international?' in L Makarczyk (ed) *Essays in International law in Honour of Judge Manfred Lachs* (Nijhoff The Hague 1984) 237. See also J Crawford *The International Law Commission's Articles on State Responsibility* (CUP Cambridge 2002) 178–186. In more recent cases, too, 'a certain tendency to claim self-defence' has been noted by, for example, T Yamada 'Kokusaiho ni okeru Kinkyujotai Riron no Rekishiteki Tenkai to Jisshosei (The Doctrine of Necessity in International Law: Its Historical Development)' [2006] 105–3 Kokusaiho Gaiko Zassi (Journal of Int'l L & Diplomacy) 39–44 (*in Japanese with English Summary*).

13 Yamada (n 12) 35.

14 J Crawford 'Second Report on State Responsibility: Addendum' (A/CN.4/498/Add. 2) (1999) 30–31 para 287.

15 Ago (n 10) 39–43.

16 Crawford (n 14) 30–31 para 287.

Ago's, under which certain uses of force may simply be lawful as a matter of primary norms. In other words, though he does so in the context of denying that the unlawfulness of a use of force may be precluded by a state of necessity, he makes the question of whether a use of force is unlawful largely a matter of primary norms.

The ILC commentary on the 2001 Articles makes the point more plainly: 'a State exercising its inherent right of self-defence as referred to in Article 51 of the Charter is not, even potentially, in breach of Article 2 (4)'.[17] Again, it thereby indicates an understanding that the unlawfulness of the use of force in this case is not precluded as a matter of secondary norms, but permitted as a matter of primary norms.

True, the ILC commentary treats the *Caroline* incident as a case pertaining to the state of necessity. It fails to make clear, however, what the precluded unlawfulness is thought to be, and, more importantly, how the case relates to present-day international law.[18] In light of Crawford's remarks noted above on the relationship between Articles 2(4) and 51 of the Charter, however, we can state that the commentary considers the UK activities in the *Caroline* incident not a use of force in violation of Article 2(4) of the Charter. In this respect, its view agrees with the reading of the right of self-defence which this work finds justified in the historical record.

The question of what to make of cases in which a policing-type right of self-defence is claimed is thus deeply tied up with the problem of how self-defence and state of necessity are respectively understood, and this problem in turn with the task of defining the status of uses of force justified by either. Such cases present us, in other words, with the unresolved question of the status of the policing-type right of self-defence in present-day international law.

This Work's Contribution, and Future Tasks

The objective of this work has been to shed light on the historical development of the conception of self-defence. By inquiring into what the term was understood to mean when the Charter was adopted, we have attained a key to

17 Crawford (n 12) 166.

18 The commentary argues, '[t]he "*Caroline*" incident of 1837, though frequently referred to as an instance of self-defence, really involved the plea of necessity at a time when the law concerning the use of force had quite different basis than it now has'. (ibid 179) Whether the unlawfulness of similar action might today be precluded on state of necessity grounds it leaves unclear. Further, though the *Caroline* incident is cited in a footnote to a discussion of rules governing the use of force, within a section on state of necessity, no view of the merits of any such claim is offered. (ibid 185)

resolving the '*grande confusion*' that reigns on the question of what it means today.

Without examining the conception's historical development, it is not possible to interpret accurately what self-defence entails in present-day international law. This is not to say, of course, that clarifying the conception that operated in and before 1945 can substitute for an examination of what the term means now; the meaning of self-defence since 1945 must be discovered through study of state practice in this current era. But the conception operative in the present day cannot be perceived accurately if the historical development of the conception, upon which the present-day conception has been formed by a process of addition and amendment rather than of wholesale replacement, remains obscure.

It is often claimed that the law of the Charter is dead or has been transformed. Such a claim can be neither upheld nor rejected unless we know what that law of the Charter actually was. And we do not know the law of the UN Charter on self-defence if we cannot characterize the conception of self-defence recognized at the time of the Charter's adoption. It is an historical awareness that must provide the basis for analysing state practice since 1945; by its consideration of the development of the right of self-defence from the mid-19th century, this book is intended to provide just that.

Bibliography

I Documents

1 *International Judgments and Advisory Opinions*

Permanent Court of International Justice

Customs Régime between Germany and Austria (Advisory Opinion) (1931).

International Court of Justice

Case concerning Corfu Channel (*United Kingdom of Great Britain v People's Republic of Albania*) (Merits) (1949).

Case concerning Military and Paramilitary Activities in and against Nicaragua (*Nicaragua v United States of America*) (Merits) (1986).

Case concerning Oil Platforms (*Islamic Republic of Iran v United States of America*) (Merits) (2003).

Advisory Opinion concerning the Legal Consequences of the Construction of a Wall on the Occupied Palestinian Territory (Advisory Opinion) (2004).

Case concerning Armed Activities on the Territory of the Congo (*Democratic Republic of Congo v Uganda*) (Merits) (2005).

Arbitration

Fur Seal Arbitration (*USA v Great Britain*) (1893).

Mixed Claims Commission (*Mexico-United States*)

ER Kelley (*USA*) *v United Mexican States* (1930).

Eritrea-Ethiopia Claims Commission

Partial Award, Jus Ad Bellum (*Federal Democratic Republic of Ehiopia v State of Eritria*) (2005).

2 *Treaties*

Treaty of Amity, Settlement and Limits between Spain and the United States (Washington, 22 February 1819).

Treaty of Limits between Mexico and the United States (Mexico City, 12 January 1828).

Treaty of Amity, Commerce and Navigation between Mexico and the United States (Mexico City, 5 April 1831).

Covenant of the League of Nations (Versailles, 28 June 1919).

Traité de garantie mutuelle entre l'Allemagne, la Belgique, la France, la Grande-Bretagne et lÍtalie (Locarno, 16 Octobre 1925).

Convention d'Arbitrage entre l'Allemagne et la Belgique (Locarno, 16 Octobre 1925).
Convention d'Arbitrage entre l'Allemagne et la France (Locarno, 16 Octobre 1925).
Traité d'Arbitrage entre l'Allemagne et la Pologne (Locarno, 16 Octobre 1925).
Traité d'Arbitrage entre l'Allemagne et la Tchécoslovaquie (Locarno, 16 Octobre 1925).
Traité de garantie mutuelle entre la France et la Pologne (Locarno, 16 Octobre 1925).
Traité de garantie mutuelle entre la France et la Tchécoslovaquie (Locarno, 16 Octobre 1925).
Treaty for the Renunciation of War (Pact of Paris) (Paris, 27 August 1928).
Convention de définition de l'agression (Londres, 3 Juillet 1933).
Treaty of Arab Brotherhood and Alliance between the Kingdom of Saudi Arabia and Iraq (Bagdad, 2 April 1936).
Traité de non-agression entre le Royaume d'Afghanistan, le Royaume de l'Irak, l'Empire de l'Iran et la République Turque (Téhéran, 8 Juillet 1937).
Inter-American Reciprocal Assistance and Solidarity (Act of Chapultepec) (Mexico City, 6 March 1945).
Charter of the United Nations (San Francisco, 26 June 1945).

3 *Diplomatic and Congressional Records*

(1) International Law Digests

Wharton, F., *A Digest of the International Law of the United States, Taken from Documents Issued by Presidents and Secretaries of State, and from Decisions of Federal Courts and Opinions of Attorney-General* (2nd edn Government Printing Office Washington DC 1887) vols 1 & 3.
Moore, J.B., *A Digest of International Law* (Government Printing Office Washington DC 1906) vols 1 & 2.
Hackworth, G.H., *Digest of international Law* (Government Printing Office Washington DC 1941) vol 2.

(2) US–Mexico Border Incident

Manning, W.R. (ed) *Diplomatic Correspondence of the United States: Inter-American Affairs 1831–1860* (Carnegie Endowment for World Peace Washington DC 1937) vol 8 (Mexico 1831–1848 (Mid-Year)).
'Memorandum of a Conference between John Forsyth, Secretary of State of the United States, and Mauel Eduardo de Gorostiza, Mexican Minister to the United States, April 20, 1836'.
'Manuel Eduardo de Gorostiza, Mexican Minister to the United States, to John Forsyth, Secretary of State of the United States, April 23, 1836'.
'John Forsyth, Secretary of State of the United States, to Manuel Eduardo de Gorostiza, Mexican Minister to the United States, May 3, 1836'.

'Manuel Eduardo de Gorostiza, Mexican Minister to the United States, to John Forsyth, Secretary of State of the United States, September 10, 1836'.

'Manuel Eduardo de Gorostiza, Mexican Minister to the United States, to Asbury Dickins, Acting Secretary of State of the United States, September 27, 1836'.

'Asbury Dickins, Acting Secretary of State of the United States, to Manuel Eduardo de Gorostiza, Mexican Minister to the United States, October 13, 1836'.

'Manuel Eduardo de Gorostiza, Mexican Minister to the United States, to Asbury Dickins, Acting Secretary of State of the United States, October 15, 1836'.

'John Forsyth, Secretary of State of the United States, to Powhatan Ellis, United States Chargé d'Affairs at Mexico City, December 10, 1836'.

(3) *Caroline* Incident

Bourne, K. (ed) *British Documents on Foreign Affairs: Reports and Papers from the Foreign Office Confidential Print, Part I From the Mid-Nineteenth Century to the First World War, Series C North America, 1837–1914* (University Publications of America, Maryland, 1986) vol 1 (McLeod and Maine, 1837–1842).

'Sir Francis Head to Mr. Fox, Jan. 8, 1838'.

'Mr. Fox to Viscount Palmerston, Jan. 13, 1838'.

'Mr. Stevenson to Viscount Palmerston, May 22, 1838'.

'Mr. Fox to Viscount Palmerston, January 10, 1841'.

'Mr. Webster to Mr. Fox, April 24, 1841'.

'Viscount Palmerston to Mr. Stevenson, August 27, 1841'.

'Mr. Webster to Lord Ashburton, July 27, 1842'.

'Lord Ashburton to Mr. Webster, July 28, 1842'.

'Mr. Webster to Lord Ashburton, Aug. 6, 1842'.

Manning, W.R. (ed) *Diplomatic Correspondence of the United States; Canadian Relations 1784–1860* (Carnegie Endowment for International Peace Washington DC 1943) vol 3 (1836–1848).

'John Forsyth, Secretary of State of the United States, to Henry S. Fox, British Minister to the United States, Jan. 5, 1838'.

'Sir Francis Head, Lieutenant Governor of Upper Canada, to Henry S. Fox, British Minister to the United States, January 8, 1838, annexed to the letter from Henry S. Fox, British Minister to the United States, to John Forsyth, Secretary of State of the United States, February 6, 1838'.

'Henry S. Fox, British Minister to the United States, to John Forsyth, Secretary of State of the United States, Feb. 6, 1838'.

'Andrew Stevenson, United States Minister to Great Britain, to Daniel Webster, Secretary of State of the United States, April 7, 1841'.

'Andrew Stevenson, United States Minister to Great Britain, to Daniel Webster, Secretary of State of the United States, June 18, 1841'.

'Deposition of J. Radenhurst, Aide-de-Camp to Colonel Allen N. MacNab, Canadian Commander, Enclosed with the Letter from Lord Palmerston, British Secretary of State for Foreign Affairs, to Andrew Stevenson, United States Minister to Great Britain, August 27, 1841'.
'Lord Ashburton, British Secretary of State for Foreign Affairs, to Lord Ashburton, British Special Envoy to the United States, Feb. 8, 1842'.
'Lord Ashburton, British Special Envoy to the United States, to Lord Aberdeen, British Secretary of State for Foreign Affairs, April 25, 1842'.
Lord McNair (ed) *International Law Opinions* (Cambridge University Press Cambridge 1956) vol 2 (Peace).
'Reports of the British Law Officers, Oct. 31, 1838'.
Phillimore, R.J., *A Letter to the Right Honourable Lord Ashburton, Suggested by the Question of International Law, Raised in the Message of the American President* (J Hatchard & Son, London 1842).
'Extract from Message of President, at the close of the year 1841'.

(4) *Virginius* Incident

British and Foreign State Papers (William Ridgway London 1881) vol 65 (1873–1874). ([1873–1874] 65 BFSP)
Foreign Relations of the United States 1875 (US Government Printing Office Washington DC 1875) vol 2. ([1875–2] FRUS)
'Admiral Polo de Bernabé to Mr. Fish, February 2, 1874'.
'Mr Fish to Admiral Polo de Bernabé, April 18, 1874'.

(5) *Bering Sea* Arbitration

Proceedings of the Tribunal of Arbitration, Convened at Paris under the Treaty between the United States of America and Great Britain Concluded at Washington February 29, 1892, for the Determination of Questions Between the Two Governments concerning the Jurisdictional Rights of the United States in the Waters of Bering Sea (Government Printing Office Washington DC 1895).
'Award of the Tribunal of Arbitration Constituted under the Treaty Concluded at Washington, the 29th of February, 1892, between the United States of America and Her Majesty the Queen of the United Kingdom of Great Britain and Ireland'. (vol 1)
'Opinion of Mr. Justice Harlan'. (vol 1)
'Case Presented on behalf of the Government of Her Britannic Majesty to the Tribunal of Arbitration'. (vol 4)
'Argument of the United States'. (vol 9)
'Oral Arguments of James C. Carter Esq., on Behalf of the United States'. (vol 12)
'Oral Argument of Sir Charles Russell, Q.C.M.P., Her Britannic Majesty's Attorney-General, on Behalf of Great Britain'. (vol 13)

'Oral Argument of Hon. Edward J. Phelps, on Behalf of the United States'. (vol 15)

British Foreign State Papers (Harrison & Sons London 1889) vol 86 (1893–1894). ([1893–1894] 86 BFSP)

'M. Chichkine to Sir R. Morier, Le 6/18 Avril, 1893'.

'The Earl of Rosebery to Sir R. Morier, March 17, 1893'.

(6) Draft Treaty of Mutual Assistance

League of Nations *Official Journal, Special Supplement* No 13 (1923).

'Report Submitted by the Third Committee to the Assembly'.

League of Nations *Official Journal, Special Supplement* No 16 (1923).

'Report of the Temporary Mixed Commission for the Reduction of Armaments'.

'Commentary on the Definition of a Case of Aggression, Drawn up by a Special Committee of the Temporary Mixed Commission'.

League of Nations *Official Journal, Special Supplement* No 26 (1924).

'Treaty of Mutual Assistance: Replies from Governments'.

'Replies of the Governments on the Subject of the Draft Treaty of Mutual Assistance'.

(7) Geneva Protocol: Protocol for the Pacific Settlement of International Disputes

League of Nations *Official Journal, Special Supplement* No 23 (1924).

'Protocol for the Pacific Settlement of International Disputes'.

League of Nations *Official Journal, Special Supplement* No 24 (1924).

'Protocol for the Pacific Settlement of International Disputes'.

'Arbitration, Security and Reduction of Armaments: General Report submitted to the Fifth Assembly on behalf of the First and Third Committees by M. Politis (Greece), Rapporteur for the First Committee, and M. Benes (Czechoslovakia), Rapporteur for the Third Committee'.

League of Nations *Official Journal* 6th Year (1925)

'Statement by the representative of Great Britain'.

(8) Rheinland Pact (Locarno Treaties)

The National Archives, Kew (formerly *Public Record Office, Kew*) (*PRO*)

'French views regarding British draft of mutual guarantee, 10th July, 1925 [C9216/459/18]' (FO 371/10736).

'Anglo-French negotiations regarding proposed treaty of mutual guarantee, 23rd July, 1925 [C9801/459/18]' (FO 371/10736).

'Anglo-French negotiations regarding proposed draft Treaty of Mutual Guarantee, 11th August, 1925: Notes of a Conversation which took place at the Foreign Office on August 11 1925, at 3 p.m., between Representatives of Great Britain and France [C10610/459/18]' (FO 371/10738).

'Anglo-French negotiations regarding proposed draft Treaty of Mutual Guarantee, 11th August, 1925: Annex (A) Proposed Treaty of Mutual Guarantee, Original British Text, July 3, 1925 [C10610/459/18]' (FO 371/10738).

'Anglo-French negotiations regarding proposed draft Treaty of Mutual Guarantee, 12th August, 1925: Notes of a Conversation which took place at the Foreign Office on August 12, 1925, at noon, between Representatives of Great Britain and France [C10611/459/18]' (FO 371/10738).

'Anglo-French negotiations regarding proposed draft Treaty of Mutual Guarantee, 12th August, 1925: Annex (C) Proposed Treaty of Mutual Guarantee (including the Amendments provisionally agreed upon by Mr. Chamberlain and M. Briand on August 12, 1925 [C10611/459/18]' (FO 371/10738).

Medlicott, W.N. and Dakin D. (eds) *Documents on British Foreign Policy 1919–1939*, First Series (Her Majesty's Stationary Office London 1986) vol 27.

'Draft Security Pact suggested by Sir C. Hurst, May 12, 1925'.

'Draft suggested by Central Department as basis for a Security Pact, May 13, 1925'.

'Notes by Sir C. Hurst on the Revised Draft Security Pact, June 17, 1925'.

'Draft Security Pact, June 17, 1925' (enclosure in 'Notes by Sir C. Hurst on the Revised Draft Security Pact, June 17, 1925').

'Report by Sir C. Hurst on the Proceedings of a Meeting of Jurists held at the Foreign Office, September 1–4, 1925, in connection with the proposed Treaty of Mutual Guarantee'.

'Proceedings of the Conference of Locarno and Records of Conversations connected therewith, October 5–16, 1925'.

'Notes by Sir C. Hurst on the Revised Draft Security Pact, June 17, 1925'.

(9) Treaty for the Renunciation of War (Pact of Paris)

National Archives at College Park, College Park, MD, RG 59, Decimal File 1910–1929, Box 6514.

'Latin America and the Renunciation of War, Sept. 12, 1928 [711.0012 Anti-War/440]'.

The National Archives, Kew (formerly *Public Record Office, Kew*) (*PRO*).

'United States arbitration treaties etc., Jan. 30th, 1928 [A691/1/45]' (FO 371/12789).

'Franco-United States proposals for treaty to outlaw war, 5th March 1928 [A1815/1/45]' (FO 371/12790).

'Treaty to outlaw war, 13th April 1928 [A2542/1/45]' (FO 371/12790).

'Foreign Office Minute, Proposed treaty for renunciation of war, 7th June, 1928 [A3886/1/45]' (FO 371/12793).

'Treaty for renunciation of war, 27th June, 1928 [A4428/1/45]' (FO 371/12794).

'Foreign Office Memorandum, Treaty for renunciation of war, 18th June, 1928 [A4462/1/45]' (FO 371/12794).

'Sir C. Hurst to Sir Austen Chamberlain, June 29, 1928 [A4478/1/45]' (FO 371/12794).

'Position created by treaty for renunciation of war, 11th Sept. 1928 [A6444/1/45]' (FO 371/12800).

League of Nations *Official Journal, Special Supplement* No 94 (1931).

'Amendment of the Covenant of the League of Nations in Order to Bring It into Harmony with the Pact of Paris (Report Submitted by the Sub-Committee)'.

Department of State *Treaty for the Renunciation of War; Text of the Treaty, Notes Exchanged, Instruments of Ratification and of Adherence and Other Papers* (Government Printing Office Washington DC 1933).

'Draft of Pact of Perpetual Friendship between France and the United States, Submitted June 20, 1927'.

'The Secretary of State (Kellogg) to the French Ambassador (Claudel), December 28, 1927'.

'The French Ambassador (Claudel) to the Secretary of State (Kellogg), le 5 janvier, 1928'.

'The Secretary of State (Kellogg) to the French Ambassador (Claudel), January 11, 1928'.

'The Secretary of State (Kellogg) to the French Ambassador (Claudel), February 27, 1928'.

'The Japanese Minister for Foreign Affairs (Tanaka) to the American Ambassador (MacVeagh)'.

'The British Secretary of State for Foreign Affairs (Chamberlain), on behalf of the Union of South Africa, to the American Chargé (Atherton)'.

'Note of the Government of the United States to the Governments of Belgium, Czechoslovakia, France, Germany, Great Britain, Irish Free State, Italy, Japan and Poland, Delivered at the Respective Foreign Offices, June 23, 1928'.

'Notes Exchanged between the United States and the Governments which were Invited to Adhere – Instruments of Adherence'.

Congressional Records (Government Printing Office Washington DC 1929) vol 70 Part 1 (1928–1929).

Hearings Before the Committee on Foreign Relations, United States Senate, Seventieth Congress, Second Session, on the General Pact for the Renunciation of War, Signed at Paris August 27, 1928 (Government Printing Office Washington DC 1928).

Ministère des Affaires Étrangères, *Pacte general de renonciation à la guerre comme instrument de politique nationale; trente pieces relatives à l'élaboration et à la conclusion du traité signé à Paris, le 27 Août 1928 (5 Avril – 27 Août 1928)* (Imprimerie des journaux officials Paris 1928).

'Texte de l'avant-projet de traité soumis, à titre de suggestion, par le Gouvernement de la République française aux Gouvernements de Grande-Bretagne, d'Allemagne, d'Italie et du Japon'.

Adams, D.K. (ed) *British Documents on Foreign Affairs: Reports and Papers from the Foreign Office Confidential Print, Part II From the First to the Second World War, Series*

C North America, 1919–1939 (University Publications of America Maryland 1995) vol 18 (Arbitration, Arms Control and Pact of Paris, 1927–1929).

'Memorandum by the Secretary of State for Foreign Affairs: The Franco-American Draft Pact of Perpetual Friendship'.

'Sir Austen Chamberlain to Mr. Houghton, May 19, 1928'.

'Memorandum on the Draft Treaty for the Renunciation of War, with particular reference to the Question of the "Special Regions" mentioned in Paragraph 10 of the British Note of May 19, 1928'.

Yanagihara, M. (ed) *Kokusaiho Senrei Shiryoshu (1) Fusen Joyaku* (*Document Collection of International Law Precedents (1) Pact of Paris*) (Shinzansha Tokyo 1996) vol 1 (*in Japanese*).

'Dai-ichiji Teian nitaisuru Kaitoan (Dai-ichi-an – Dai-juyon-an) (Draft Reply to the First Proposal (1st – 14th Draft))'.

'Jieiken nitsuite (1929 (Showa 4-nen) Ajia-kyoku Dai-ichi-ka) (On Right of Self-defence (1929) Asian Affairs Bureau 1st Devision))'.

'Gimon Gito (Simulation Questions and Answers)'.

'Senso Hoki ni kan suru Joyaku Setsumeishoan (Shumitsuin Haifuyo Genko) (Draft Explanation of the Treaty for Renunciation of War (Distribution Documents to the Privy Council))'.

(10) League of Nations Codification Conference

League of Nations *Conference for the Codification of International Law, Bases of Discussion for the Conference Drawn up by the Preparatory Committee* vol 3 (Responsibility of States for Damage Caused in their Territory to the Person or Property of Foreigners) (C 75 M 69 1929 V) (Series of League of Nations Publications, V. Legal, 1929 V 3).

League of Nations *Acts of the Conference for the Codification of International Law, Held at the Hague from March 13th to April 20th, 1930, Meetings of the Committees* vol 4 (Minutes of the Third Committee) (C 351(c) M 145(c) 1930 V) (Series of League of Nations Publications, V. Legal, 1930 V 17).

(11) Draft Act Defining Aggressor

League of Nations *Records of the Conference for the Reduction and Limitation of Armaments, Series B (Minutes of the General Commission)* vol 2 (December 14th 1932 – June 29th 1933) (Series of League of Nations Publications, IX. Disarmament, 1933 IX 10).

League of Nations *Conference for the Reduction and Limitation of Armaments, Conference Documents* vol 2 (Series of League of Nations Publications, IX. Disarmament 1935 IX 4).

'Report of the Committee on Security Questions (Conf. D/C G 108)'.

'Memorandum by the French Delegation dated Novermber 14th, 1932. Plan for the Organisation of Peace (Conf. D 146)'.

League of Nations *Conference for the Reduction and Limitation of Armaments, Preliminary Report on the Work of the Conference, Prepared by the President, Mr. Arthur Henderson* (Conf D 171 (I)) (Series of League of Nations Publications, IX. Disarmament, 1936 IX 3).

League of Nations *Records of the Conference for the Reduction and Limitation of Armaments, Series D (Minutes of the Political Commission)* vol 5 (February 27th 1932 – March 10th 1933) (Series of League of Nations Publications, IX. Disarmament, 1936 IX 8).

Beck, P.J. (ed) *British Documents on Foreign Affairs: Reports and Papers from the Foreign Office Confident Print, Part II From the First to the Second World War, Series J The League of Nations, 1918–1941* (University Publications of America Maryland 1992) vol 4 (The Question of Disarmament, 1932–1933).

'Provisional Minutes of the Sixty-Fifth Meeting, Geneva, May 25, 1933 – (Received in Foreign Office, June 7)'.

(12) Manchurian Incident

League of Nations *Official Journal* 12th Year (1931).

'Text of Memorandum Sent from the Japanese to the Chinese Government, dated October 9th, 1931 (C 690 M 296 1931 VII)'.

'Letter from the Japanese Delegation to the Secretary-General of the league of Nations regarding the Incident at Chinchow, October 12th, 1931 (C 704 M 310 1931 VII)'.

League of Nations, *Appeal by the Chinese Government, Report of the Commission of Enquiry* (C663 M320 1932 VII) (Series of League of Nations Publications, VII. Political, 1932 VII 12).

League of Nations *Official Journal, Special Supplement* No 111 (1933).

'Records of the Special Session of the Assembly Convened in virtue of Article 15 of the Covenant at the Request of the Chinese Government, Vol. III'.

'Observations of the Japanese Government on the Report of the Commission of Enquiry Constituted under the Council's Resolution of December 10th, 1931 (C775 M366 1932 VII)'.

League of Nations *Official Journal, Special Supplement* No 112 (1933).

'Report Provided for in Article 15, Paragraph 4, of the Covenant, Submitted by the Special Committee of the Assembly in Execution of Part III (Paragraph 5) of the Resolution of March 11th, 1932, and Adopted by the Assembly on February 24th, 1933 (A (Extr.) 22 1933 VII)'.

(13) Italo-Ethiopian War

League of Nations *Official Journal* 16th Year (1935).

'Dispute between Ethiopia and Italy: Report of the Council Committee, October 7th, 1935 (C 417 1935 VII)'.

'Telegram, Dated September 25th, 1935, from His Majesty the Emperor of Ethiopia to the Secretary-General (C 384 M 192 1935 VII)'.

'Telegram, Dated September 28th, 1935, from His Majesty the Emperor of Ethiopia to the President of the Council (C 400 M 197 1935 VII)'.

'Telegram, Dated October 3rd, 1935, from the Italian Government to the Secretary-General, October 3rd, 1935 (C 404 M 200 1935 VII)'.

(14) Marco Polo Bridge Incident

League of Nations *Official Journal, Special Supplement* No 169 (1937).

League of Nations *Official Journal, Special Supplement* No 177 (1937).

'First Report of the Sub-Committee of the Far-East Advisory Committee, Adopted by the Committee on October 5th and by the Assembly on October 6th, 1937 (A 78 1937 VII)'.

'Report of the Far-East Advisory Committee and Resolution Adopted by the Assembly on October 6th, 1937 (A 79 1937 VII)'.

Kampo (*Official Gazett*) (Extra News 6th September 1937 (The 72nd Shorthand Report of Parliamentary Proceedings of Empire Council, the Lords of Peers, vol 2)) (*in Japanese*).

(15) Charter of the United Nations

Documents of the United Nations Conference on International Organization, San Francisco, 1945 (United Nations Information Organization London 1945). (UNCIO).

Doc 1, G/1 in 3 UNCIO.

Doc 2, G/7 (o) in 3 UNCIO.

Doc 2, G/14 (1) in 3 UNCIO.

Doc 123, I/1/5 in 6 UNCIO.

Doc 382, I/1/19 in 6 UNCIO.

Doc 576, III/4/9 in 12 UNCIO.

Doc 739, I/1/A/19(a) in 6 UNCIO.

Doc 784, I/1/27 in 6 UNCIO.

Doc 881, III/3/46 in 12 UNCIO.

Doc 944, I/1/34 (1) in 6 UNCIO.

Foreign Relations of the United States, Diplomatic Papers 1943 (United States Government Printing Office, Washington D.C., 1963) vol I (General). ([1943-I] FRUS)

'Tentative Draft of a Joint Four-Power Declaration'.

'Summary of the Proceedings of the Third Session of the Tripartite Conference, October 21, 1943, 4 p.m.'.

'Oral Statement by Secretary Hull Regarding the Proposed Joint Declaration'.

'Summary of the Proceedings of the Eighth Session of the Tripartite Conference, October 26, 1943, 4 p.m.'.

Foreign Relations of the United States, Diplomatic Papers 1944 (United States Government Printing Office Washington 1966) vol I (General). ([1944-I] FRUS)

'Tentative Proposals by the United Kingdom for a General International Organization [July 22, 1944]'.

'Memorandum on an International Security Organization, by the Soviet Union'.

'Tentative Chinese Proposals for a General International Organization'.

'Memorandum by the Under Secretary of State (Stettinius) to the Secretary of State, August 29, 1944'.

'Memorandum by the Under Secretary of State (Stettinius) to the Secretary of State, October 2, 1944'.

'Memorandum by the Assistant Chief of the Division of International Security and Organization (Greig) and the Executive Secretary of the Policy Committee (Yost)'.

Foreign Relations of the United States, Diplomatic Papers 1945 (United States Government Printing Office Washington 1967) vol I (General: The United Nations). ([1945-I] FRUS)

'Minutes of the Sixth Meeting of the United States Delegation, Held at Washington, Tuesday, April 10, 1945, 10:15 a.m.'.

'Memorandum by the Secretary of State to President Truman, [Washington,] April 19, 1945'.

'Minutes of the Eighteenth Meeting of the United States Delegation, Held at San Francisco, April 26, 1945, 9:30 a.m.'.

'Minutes of the Twelfth Meeting of the United States Delegation, Held at Washington, Wednesday, April 18, 1945, 9:10 a.m.'.

'Minutes of the Twenty-Ninth Meeting of the United States Delegation, Held at San Francisco, Friday, May 4, 1945, 9:05 a.m.'.

'Minutes of the Thirty-Second Meeting of the United States Delegation, Held at San Francisco, Monday, May 7, 1945, 6:18 p.m.'.

'Minutes of the Thirty-Fifth Meeting of the United States Delegation, Held at San Francisco, Thursday, May 10, 1945, 6.30 p.m.'.

'Minutes of the Thirty-Sixth Meeting of the United States Delegation, Held at San Francisco, Friday, May 11, 1945, 2:30 p.m.'.

'Minutes of the Thirty-Seventh Meeting of the United States Delegation, Held at San Francisco, Saturday, May 12, 1945, 9 a.m.'.

'Minutes of the Third Five-Power Informal Consultative Meeting on Proposed Amendments (Part I), Held at San Francisco, Saturday, May 12, 1945, 2:30 p.m.'.

'Memorandum by Mr. Robert W. Hartley of the United States Delegation of a Conversation Held at San Francisco, Saturday, May 12, 1945, 3:30 p.m.'.

'Minutes of Informal Drafting Session, by Mr. Robert W. Hartley'.

'Minutes of the Thirty-Eighth Meeting of the United States Delegation, Held at San Francisco, Monday, May 14, 1945, 9:05 a.m.'.

'Minutes of the Thirty-Ninth Meeting of the United States Delegation, Held at San Francisco, Tuesday, May 15, 1945, 9 a.m.'.

'Minutes of the Fortieth Meeting of the United States Delegation, Held at San Francisco, May 16, 1945, 6 p.m.'.

'Minutes of the Sixth Five-Power Informal Consultative Meeting on Proposed Amendments, Held at San Francisco, May 19, 1945'.

'The Acting Secretary of State to Diplomatic Representatives in the American Republics', Washington, May 21, 1945 – 10:40 a.m.'.

'Minutes of the Sixty-Fourth Meeting of the United States Delegation, Held at San Francisco, Tuesday, June 5, 1945, 9:01 a.m.'.

National Archives at College Park, College Park, MD (hereinafter *National Archives*), *RG 59, Notter File*

'P Minutes (Summary) (Summary Minutes of the Subcommittee on Political Problems) 1, March 7, 1942' in *National Archives, RG 59, Notter File 498, Box 55.*

'Official Statements and Views Pertaining to Permanent International Organization' in *National Archives, RG 59, Notter File 498, Box 57, P/223d.*

'Summary of Official Statements and Views Pertaining to Permanent International Organization' in *National Archives, RG 59, Notter File 498, Box 58, P/250a.*

'The Drafting of the Four-Nation Declaration of October 30, 1943' in *National Archives, RG 59, Notter File 498, Box 58, P/UND/23.*

'Background and Development of the Four-Nation Declaration, in the Light of Records in the Division of Political Studies' in *National Archives, Notter File 498, Box 58, P/UND/24.*

'S Minutes (Minutes of the Subcommittee on Security Problems) 44, June 10, 1943' in *National Archives, RG 59, Notter File 498, Box 76.*

'I.O. Minutes (Minutes of Informal Political Agenda Group) 5, Dec. 17, 1943' in *National Archives, RG 59, Notter File 502, Box 170.*

'I.O. Minutes 17, Jan. 28, 1944' in ibid.

'I.O. Minutes 21, Feb. 16, 1944' in ibid.

'I.O. Minutes 41, April 7, 1944' in ibid.

'I.O. Minutes 43, April 11, 1944' in ibid.

'I.O. Minutes 70, July 8, 1944' in ibid.

Chronological Notes of the Second Plenary Session, Assembly Hall, Dumbarton Oaks, 10:40 a.m. – 11:50 a.m. [Conv. B, Plenary Record 2, October 2, 1944]' in *National Archives, RG 59, Notter File 498, Box 185.*

'Minutes of the Seventh Meeting, Committee of Five Deputies of the Heads of Delegations, Room 461, Fairmont Hotel, San Francisco, California, Tuesday, May 15, 1945, 10:40 a.m. to 1:00 p.m.' in *National Archives, RG 59, Notter File 498, Box 257.*

'Minutes of the Ninth Meeting, Committee of Five Deputies of the Heads of Delegations, May 16, 1945, 5:10 p.m. to 7:10 p.m.' in ibid.

'Minutes of the Fourteenth Meeting, Committee of Five Deputies of the Heads of Delegations, May 19, 1945, 3:45 p.m. to 6:40 p.m.' in ibid.

'Minutes of the Fifteenth Meeting, Committee of Five Deputies of the Heads of Delegations, May 20, 1945, 5:00 p.m. to 5:45 p.m.' in ibid.

Schmitt B.E., *The United Nations Conference on International Organization, San Francisco, California, April 25 – June 26, 1945* (provisional, Department of State 1949) vol. 3, 1139–1140, in *National Archives, RG 59, Notter File 498, Box 261.*

The National Archives, Kew (formerly *Public Record Office, Kew*) (*PRO*)

'War Cabinet, World Organisation, Outstanding Points, Memorandum by the Secretary of State for Foreign Affairs, 31st March, 1945 [W.P. (45) 209]' (CAB 123/237).

'International Organisation Discussions: Second Meeting of Joint Formulation Group, 6th October [U 7995/180/70]' (FO 371/40721).

'World Organisation: Proposal by Australian Government that Security Council should guarantee the territorial integrity of States [U 2332/12/70]' (FO 371/50692).

'San Francisco Conference: United Kingdom Delegation Document No. 1. [U 3584/12/70]' (FO 371/50709).

'Charter of World Organization, 12th May, 1945 [U 3646/12/70]' (FO 371/50709).

'Amendments of Dumbarton Oaks Proposals, 15th May, 1945 [U 3692/12/70]' (FO 371/50710).

Command Papers

A Commentary on the Dumbarton Oaks Proposals for the Establishment of a General International Organisation, Presented by the Secretary of State for Foreign Affairs to Parliament by Command of his Majesty, November 1944 (Cmd. 6571 His Majesty's Stationery Office London 1944).

A Commentary on the Charter of the United Nations, Signed at San Francisco on the 26th June, 1945, Presented by the Secretary of State for Foreign Affairs to Parliament by Command of His Majesty (Cmd. 6666 His Majesty's Stationery Office London 1945).

Congressional Records (Government Printing Office Washington DC 1945) vol 79 Part 1 (1944–1945).

Hearings before the Committee on Foreign Relations, United States Senate, Seventy-Ninth Congress, First Session, on the Charter of the United Nations for the Maintenance of International Peace and Security, Submitted by the President of the United States on July 2, 1945 (1945).

'Report to the President on the Result of the San Francisco Conference by the Chairman of the United States Delegation, the Secretary of State, June 26, 1945'.

4 *Others*

'Proclamation by the Commanders in Chief of His Majesty's Forces by Sea and by Land, 16th August 1807' in *Papers Presented to the House of Commons, Relating to the Surrender of the Danish Fleet & c.* (1808 London). (Danish Fleet Incident)

Lawrie, W. and Franklin, W.S., *American State Papers: Documents, Legislative and Executive, of the Congress of the United States from the First Session of the Fourteenth to the First Session of the Seventeenth Congress, Inclusive: Commencing March 4, 1815, and Ending May 8, 1822* (Gales and Seaton Washington 1834) vol 4. (Amelia Island Incident)

Regulations for the Government of the Navy of the United States (Government Printing Office Washington DC 1909). (Protection of Nationals Abroad)

League of Nations *Monthly Summary of the League of Nations* vol 6 (1926).

League of Nations *Official Journal* 8th Year (1927). (Greco-Bulgarian frontier incident)

'Report by M. de Brouckère on Point 1(b) of the Proposal Laid before the Preparatory Commission for the Disarmament Conference by the French Delegation' in League of Nations *Reports and Resolutions of the Subject of Article 16 of the Covenant (Memorandum and Collection of Reports, Resolutions and References prepared in Execution of the Council's Resolution of December 8th, 1926)* (A 14 1927 V).

'Report of the Council, Provided for in Article 15, Pragraph 4, of the Covenant, Submitted by the Committee of the Council' [1933] 14 League of Nations OJ. (Leticia Incident)

'Report of the Assembly, Provided for in Article 15, Paragraph 4 and 10, of the Covenant, Submitted by the Special Committee of the Assembly' [1939] 20 League of Nations OJ. (Finn-Soviet War)

UNGA Res 3314 (XXIX) (14 December 1974).

Ago, R., 'Addendum to the Eigth Report on State Responsibility: The Internationally Wrongful Act of State, Source of International Responsibility (Part I) (Concluded)' [1980] 2–1 Yb Int'l L Comm'n 53.

Crawford, J., 'Second Report on State Responsibility: Addendum' (A/CN.4/498/Add.2) (1999).

'Letter Dated 20 August 1998 from the Permanent Representative of the United States of America to the United Nations Addressed to the President of the Security Council' S/1998/780 (20 August 1998).

'Letter Dated 21 August 1998 from the Minister of State at the Ministry of Foreign Affairs of the Sudan Addressed to the President of the Security Council' S/1998/786 (21 August 1998).

'Letter Dated 7 October 2001 from the Permanent Representative of the United States of America to the United Nations Addressed to the President of the Security Council' S/2001/946 (7 October 2001).

II Books and Articles

Ago, R., 'Le délit international' [1939] 68 RCADI.

Akande, D. and Lifländer, T., 'Clarifying Necessity, Imminence, and Proportionality in the Law of Self-Defense' [2013] 107 AJIL.

Alexandrov, S.A., *Self-Defense against the Use of Force in International Law* (Kluwer Law International The Hague 1996).

Anzilotti, D., *Cours de droit international* (Gidel G. (tr) Sirey Paris 1929).

Arai-Takahashi, Y., 'Shifting Boundaries of the Right of Self-Defence' [2002] 36 Int'l Lawyer (American Bar Ass'n).

Asada M., 'Nihon to Jieiken (Japan and Right of Self-defence)' in Kokusaiho Gakkai (Japanese Soc'y of Int'l L) (ed) *Anzen Hosho (International Security)* (Sanseido Tokyo 2001) (*in Japanese*).

Baade, H.W., 'American-Mexican Boundary Disputes and Cooperation' in Bernhardt R. (ed) *Encyclopedia of Public International Law* (Elsevier Amsterdom 1992) vol 1.

Baker, P.J.N., *The Geneva Protocol for the Pacific Settlement of International Disputes* (PS King London 1925).

Basdevant, J., 'Règles générales du droit de la paix' [1936] 58 RCADI.

Baty, T., *The Canons of International Law* (John Murray London 1930).

Becker, T., *Terrorism and the State* (Hart Oxford 2006).

Benedek, W., 'Drago-Porter Convention (1907)' in Bernhardt R. (ed) *Encyclopedia of Public International Law* (Elsevier Amsterdam 1992) vol 1.

Bethlehem, D., 'Principles of Self-Defense – A Brief Response' [2013] 107 AJIL.

Bethlehem, D., 'Self-Defense against an Imminent Attack or Actual Armed Attack by Nonstate Actors' [2012] 106 AJIL.

Bisschop, W.R., 'The Locarno Pact' [1925] 11 Transactions of the Grotius Society.

Borchard, E.M., *The Diplomatic Protection of Citizens Abroad or the Law of International Claims* (Banks Law Publishing New York 1915).

Bourquin, M., 'Le problème de la sécurité internationale' [1934] 49 RCADI.

Bourquin, M., 'Règles générales du droit de la paix' [1931] 35 RCADI.

Bowett, D.W., 'Book Reviews: International Law and the Use of Force by States. By Ian Brownlie' [1964] 13 ICLQ.

Bowett, D.W., *Self-Defence in International Law* (Manchester University Press Manchester 1958).

Bowett, D.W., 'The Use of Force for the Protection of Nationals Abroad' in Cassese A. (ed) *The Current Legal Regulation of the Use of Force* (Martinus Nijhoff Publishers Dordrecht 1986).

Bowett, D.W., 'The Use of Force in the Protection of Nationals' [1962] 43 Transactions of the Grotius Society.

Brierly, J.L., 'Règles générales du droit de la paix' [1936] 58 RCADI.

Brierly, J.L., *The Law of Nations* (4th edn Oxford University Press Oxford 1949).

Brierly, J.L., *The Law of Nations* (6th edn Waldock H. (ed) Oxford University Press Oxford 1963).

Broms, B., 'The Definition of Aggression' [1977] 154 RCADI.

Brown, P.M., 'The Geneva Protocol' [1925] 19 AJIL.

Brownlie, I., *International Law and the Use of Force by States* (Clarendon Press Oxford 1963).

Brownlie, I., '*International Law and the Use of Force by States* Revisited' [2000] 21 Australian Yb Int'l L.

Brownlie, I., 'International Law at the Fiftieth Anniversary of the United Nations' [1995] 255 RCADI.

Brownlie, I., *Principles of Public International Law* (6th edn Oxford University Press Oxford 2003).

Brownlie, I., 'Recent Appraisals of Legal Regulation of the Use of Force' [1959] 8 ICLQ.

Brownlie, I., 'The United Nations Charter and the Use of Force, 1945–1985' in Cassese A. (ed) *The Current Legal Regulation of the Use of Force* (Matinus Nijhoff Publishers Dordrecht 1986).

Brownlie, I., 'The Use of Force in Self-Defence' [1961] 37 BYIL.

Bryde, B-O., 'Self-Defence' in Bernhardt R. (ed) *Encyclopedia of Public International Law* (Elsevier Amsterdam 2000) vol 4.

Byers, M., 'Terrorism, the Use of Force and International Law after 11 September' [2002] 51 ICLQ.

Byers, M., 'The Shifting Foundations of International Law: A Decade of Forceful Measures against Iraq' [2002] 13 EJIL.

Callahan, J.M., *American Foreign Policy in Mexican Relations* (Macmillan Company New York 1932).

Calvo, C., *Le droit international théorique et pratique* (2nd edn A Durand et Pedone-Lauriel Paris 1870) vol 1.

Calvo, C., *Le droit international théorique et pratique précédé d'un exposé historique des progrès de la science du droit des gens* (3rd edn Guillaumin et Cie Paris 1880) vol 1.

Cassese, A., 'Article 51' in Cot J-P. et al (eds) *La Charte des Nations Unies* (3rd edn Economica Paris 2005).

Cavaglieri, A., 'Règles générales du droit de la paix' [1929] 26 RCADI.

Charney, J.I., 'The Use of Force Against Terrorism and International Law' [2001] 95 AJIL.

Cheng, B., *General Principles of Law as Applied by International Courts and Tribunals* (Stevens & Son London 1953).

Clendenen, C.C., *The United States and Pancho Villa: A Study in Unconventional Diplomacy* (Cornell University Press Ithaca 1961).

Combacau, J., 'The Exception of Self-Defence in U.N. Practice' in Cassese A. (ed) *The Current Legal Regulation of the Use of Force* (Matinus Nijhoff Publishers Dordrecht 1986).

Couveinhes-Matsumoto, F., 'Les travaux préparatoires' in Kolb R. (ed) *Commentaire sur le Pacte de la Société des Nations* (Bruylant Bruxelles 2014).

Crawford, J., *The International Law Commission's Articles on State Responsibility* (Cambridge University Press Cambridge 2002).

Curtis, G.T., *The Case of the Virginius, Considered with Reference to the Law of Self-Defence* (Baker, Voorhis & Co New York 1874).

Delbrück, J., 'Collective Self-Defence' in Bernhardt R. (ed) *Encyclopedia of Public International Law* (Elsevier Amsterdam 1992) vol 1.

Delivanis, J., *La légitime defense en droit international public moderne* (JGDJ Paris 1971).

Department of State *Memorandum on the Monroe Doctrine, Prepared by J Reuben Clark, Undersecretary of State, December 17, 1928* (Government Printing Office Washington DC 1930).

Descamps, M., 'Le droit international nouveau: l'influence de la condamnation de la guerre sur l'évolution juridique internationale' [1930] 31 RCADI.

Despagnet, F., *Cours de droit international public* (2nd edn Sirey Paris 1899).

Despagnet, F., *Cours de droit international public* (3rd edn Sirey Paris 1905).

de Visscher, C., 'Les lois de la guerre et le théorie de la nécessité' [1917] 24 Rev Gén D I Pub.

Dinstein, Y., *War, Aggression and Self-Defence* (5th edn Cambridge University Press Cambridge 2011).

Dunn, F.S., *The Protection of Nationals* (Johns Hopkins Press Baltimore 1932).

Dupuy, P-M., 'L'Invocation de la légitime defénse dans la justification des états' in Guilhaudis J-F. and Torrelli M. (eds) *Force armée et diplomatie* (Nijhoff Dordrecht 1985) vol 2.

Eagleton, C., 'The Attempt to Define Aggression' [1930] 264 Int'l Conciliation.

The Earl of Birkenhead *International Law* (6th edn Moelwyn-Hughes Ronw (ed) JM Dent London 1927).

European Journal of International Law Discussion Forum 'The Attack on the World Trade Center: Legal Responses' <http://www.ejil.org/forum_WTC/index.html>.

Fauchille, P., *Traite de droit international public* (Rousseau Paris 1922) vol 1.

Fenwick, C.G., *International Law* (Century New York 1924).

Fenwick, C., 'The Legal Significance of the Locarno Agreements' [1926] 20 AJIL.

Ferencz, B.B., *Defining International Aggression* (Oceana New York 1975) vol 1.

Fiore, P., *Nouveau droit international public suivant les besoins de la civilisation moderne* (2nd edn Antoine C. (tr) A Durand et Pedone-Lauriel Paris 1885) vol 1.

Fitzmaurice, G.G., 'The Definition of Aggression' [1952] 1 ICLQ.

Franck, T., *Recourse to Force* (Cambridge University Press Cambridge 2002).

Franck, T.M., 'Terrorism and the Right of Self-Defense' [2001] 95 AJIL.

Franck, T.M., 'Who Killed Article 2(4)?' [1970] 64 AJIL.

Gardam, J., *Necessity, Proportionality and the Use of Force by States* (Cambridge University Press Cambridge 2004).

Garner, J.W., 'Decisions, Opinions, and Awards of International Tribunals: Decisions of the United States – Mexican Mixed Claims Commission' [1931] 12 BYIL.

Garner, J.W., 'The Geneva Protocol for the Pacific Settlement of International Disputes' [1925] 19 AJIL.

Gathorne-Hardy, G.M., *A Short History of International Affairs 1920–1939* (4th edn Oxford University Press Oxford 1950).

Gazzini, T., *The Changing Rules on the Use of Force in International Law* (Manchester University Press Manchester 2005).

Geck, W.K., 'Diplomatic Protection' in Bernhardt R. (ed) *Encyclopedia of Public International Law* (Elsevier Amsterdam 1992) vol 1.

Genoni, M.A.M., *Die Notwehr im Völkerrecht* (Schulthess Polygraphischer Verlag Zürich 1987).

Gidel, G., 'Droits et devoir des nations' [1925] 10 RCADI.

Giraud, É., 'La théorie de la légitime défense' [1934] 49 RCADI.

Glennon, M.J., 'Why the Security Council Failed' [2003] 82(3) Foreign Affairs.

Goodrich, L.M. and Hambro, E., *Charter of the United Nations: Commentary and Documents* (World Peace Foundation Boston 1946).

Gray, C., *International Law and the Use of Force* (3rd edn Oxford University Press Oxford 2008).

Gray, C., 'The Use of Force and the International Legal Order' in Evans M.D. (ed) *International Law* (4th edn Oxford University Press Oxford 2014).

Greenwood, C., 'International Law and the "War against Terrorism"' [2002] 78 Int'l Affairs.

Greenwood, C., 'The Relationship between Ius ad Bellum and Ius in Bello' [1983] 9 Rev Int'l Studies.

Gregg, R.D., *The Influence of Border Troubles on Relations between the United States and Mexico 1876–1910* (Johns Hopkins Press Baltimore 1937).

Grob, F., *The Reality of War and Peace* (Yale University Press New Haven 1949).

Gross, L., 'Was the Soviet Union Expelled from the League of Nations?' [1945] 39 AJIL.

Hall, W.E., *A Treatise on International Law* (2nd edn Clarendon Press Oxford 1884).

Halleck, H., *International Law; or, Rules Regulating the Intercourse of States in Peace and War* (HH Bancroft & Co San Francisco 1861).

Heffter, A.W., *Das Europäische Völkerrecht der Gegenwart* (Berlag von EH Schroeder Berlin 1844).

Heffter, A.G., *Le droit international de l'Europe* (4th edn Heinrich Geffcken F. (ed) Bergson J. (tr) HW Müller Berlin 1883).

Henkin, L., 'The Reports of the Death of Article 2(4) Are Greatly Exaggerated' [1971] 65 AJIL.

Hershey, A.S., 'Incursions into Mexico and the Doctrine of Hot Pursuit' [1919] 13 AJIL.

von der Heydte, F.A.F., 'Geneva Protocol for the Pacific Settlement of International Disputes (1924)' in Bernhardt R. (ed) *Encyclopedia of International Law* (Elsevier Amsterdam 1995) vol 2.

Higgins, R., *Problems and Process* (Oxford University Press Oxford 1994).

Higgins, R., *The Development of International Law through the Political Organs of the United Nations* (Oxford University Press Oxford 1963).

Hmoud, M., 'Are New Principles Really Needed? The Potential of the Established Distinction between Responsibility for Attacks by Nonstate Actors and the Law of Self-Defense' [2013] 107 AJIL.

Hudson, M.O., *The Verdict of the League: China and Japan in Manchuria* (World Peace Foundation Boston 1933).

The Institute of World Polity *The Law of Limited International Conflict* (Georgetown University Washington DC 1965).

Jennings, R. and Watts, A. (eds) *Oppenheim's International Law* (9th edn Longman London 1996) vol 1.

Jennings, R.Y., 'The *Caroline* and McLeod Cases' [1938] 32 AJIL.

Jinks, D. 'State Responsibility for the acts of Private Armed Groups' [2003] 4 Chicago J Int'l L.

Kammerhofer, J., 'The Armed Activities Case and Non-State Actors in Self-Defence Law' [2007] 20 Leiden J Int'l L.

Kaufmann, E., 'Règles générales du droit de la paix' [1935] 54 RCADI 579–580.

Kearley, T., 'Raising the *Caroline*' [1999] 17 Wisc Int'l LJ.

Kearley, T., 'Regulation of Preventive and Preemptive Force in the United Nations Charter: A Search for Original Intent' [2003] 3 Wyoming LR.

Kelsen, K., 'Unrecht und Unrechtsfolge im Völkerrecht' [1932] Zeitschrift für Öffentliches Recht.

Kennan, G.F., *Realities of American Foreign Policy* (Oxford University Press London 1954).

Khan, D.E., 'Drafting History' in Simma B. et al (eds) *The Charter of the United Nations; A Commentary* (3rd edn Oxford University Press Oxford 2012).

Klein, A., 'Finland' in Toynbee A. and Toynbee V.M. (eds) *The Initial Triumph of the Axis* (Oxford University Press London 1958).

Klüber, J.L., *Droit des gens moderne de l'Europe* (JG Cotta Stuttgart 1819) vol 1.

Klüber, J.L., *Droit des gens moderne de l'Europe* (new edn Ott M.A. (ed) Librairie de Guillaumin et Cie Paris 1861).

Knipping, F., von Mangoldt H. and Rittberger V., *The United Nations System and Its Predecessros* (Oxford University Press Oxford 1997) vol 2.

Kolb, R., 'De la S.D.N. à l'O.N.U. en matière de maintien de la paix' in Kolb R. (ed) *Commentaire sur le Pacte de la Société des Nations* (Bruylant Bruxelles 2014).

Kolb, R., 'La légitime défense des états au XIXe siècle et pendant l'époque de la Société des Nations' in Kolb R. (ed) *Commentaire sur le Pacte de la Société des Nations* (Bruylant Bruxelles 2014).

Komarnicki, M.W., 'La définition de l'agresseur dans le droit international moderne' [1949] 75 RCADI.

Korovine, E.A., 'The U.S.S.R. and Disarmament' [1933] 292 Int'l Conciliation.

Kosaka, M., 'Shudan Anzen Hosho to Domei no Hensen (Transition of Collective Security and Alliance)' [1981] 258 Kokusai Mondai (International Affairs) (*in Japanese*).

Lauterpacht, H., *The Function of Law in the International Community* (Clarendon Press Oxford 1933).

Lauterpacht, H. (ed) *Annual Digest of Public International Law Cases* (Longmans, Green & Co London) Years 1929–1930.

Lauterpacht, H., '"Resort to War" and the Interpretation of the Covenant during the Manchurian Dispute' [1934] 28 AJIL.

Le Fur, L.E., 'Le développement historique du droit international, de l'anarchie internationale à une communauté internationale organisée' [1932] 41 RCADI.

League of Nations *Ten Years of World Co-operation* (Secretariat of the League of Nations Geneva 1930) 55–65.

Lowe, A.V., 'Peace without Justice' in Butler W.E. (ed) *Perestroika and International Law* (Nijhoff Dordrecht 1990).

von Liszt, vF., *Das Völkerrecht* (O Haering Berlin 1898).

Macdonald, R.St.J., 'The Nicaragua Case: New Answers to Old Questions?' [1986] 24 Canadian Yb Int'l L.

Malanczuk, P., 'Countermeasures and Self-Defence as Circumstances Precluding Wrongfulness in the International Law Commission's Draft Articles on State Responsibility' in Spinedi M. and Simma B. (eds) *United Nations Codification of State Responsibility* (Oceana Publications New York 1987).

Malanczuk, P., 'Monroe Doctrine' in Bernhardt R. (ed) *Encyclopedia of Public International Law* (Elsevier Amsterdam 1997) vol 3.

Mandelstam, A.N., *Le conflit Italo-Éthiopien devant la Société des Nations* (Sirey Paris 1937).

de Martens, G.F., *Précis du droit des gens moderne de l'Europe fondé sur les traités et l'usage* (2nd edn Dietrich Gottingue 1801).

de Martens, G.F., *Précis du droit des gens moderne de l'Europe* (New edn Vergé M.C. (ed) Guillaumin et Cie Paris 1858) vol 1.

Matsuda, T., 'Sensou-Ihouka to Nihon (Outlawry of War and Japan)' [1981] 79 Kokusaiho Gaiko Zassi (Journal of Int'l L & Diplomacy) (*in Japanese*).

Matsui, Y., *Gendai Nihon no Kokusai Kankei: Anpo Taisei no Hoteki Hihan* (*International Relations of Contemporary Japan: Legal Criticism to the Japan-US Security Alliance*) (Keisoshobo Tokyo 1978) (*in Japanese*).

Matsui, Y., 'Nihon Gunkokushugi no Kokusaihöron (International Law Theory under Japanese Militarism)' in Kenkyujo Tokyo Daigaku Shakai Kagaku (Institute of Social Science, University of Tokyo) (ed) *Senji Nihon no Hotaisei* (*Legal System of Japan in Time of War*) (University of Tokyo Press Tokyo 1979) (*in Japanese*).

Meng, W., 'The Caroline' in Bernhardt R. (ed) *Encyclopedia of Public International Law* (Elsevier Amsterdam 1992) vol 1.

Mérignhac, A., *Traité de droit public international* (Librairie Générale de Droit & de Jurisprudence Paris 1905).

Miller, H., *The Drafting of the Covenant* (GP Putman's Sons New York 1928).

Miller, D.H., *The Geneva Protocol* (Macmillan Company New York 1925).

Moore, J.B., *History and Digest of the International Arbitrations to Which the United States Has Been a Party* (Government Printing Office Washington DC 1898) vol 1.

Morgenthau, H.J., 'Diplomacy' [1946] 55 Yale LJ.

Morgenthau, H.J., *Politics Among Nations* (5th edn Knopf New York 1973).

Mori T., 'Italia-Echiopia Senso (Italo-Ethiopian War)' in Kokusaiho Gakkai (Japanese Soc'ty of Int'l L) (ed) *Kokusai Kankeiho Jiten* (*Encyclopedia of International Law*) (2nd edn Sanseido Tokyo 2005) (*in Japanese*).

Mori, T., 'Karoraingo Jiken ni okeru Jieiken no Kino (The "Right of Self-Defence" in the *Caroline* Case)' [2002] 53 Shakai Kagaku Kenkyu (Journal of Social Science (University of Tokyo)) 69–101 (*in Japanese*).

Mori, T., 'Shudanteki Jieiken no Tanjo (Birth of the Right of Collective Self-Defence)' [2003] 102 Kokusaiho Gaiko Zassi (Journal of Int'l L & Diplomacy) (*in Japanese with English Summary*).

Morison, S.E., *The Oxford History of the American People* (Oxford University Press Oxford 1965).

Morris, R.S., 'The Pact of Paris for the Renunciation of War: Its Merits and Effect in International Law' [1929] 23 Proc Am Soc'y IL.

Morvay, W., 'Locarno Treaties (1925)' in Bernhardt R. (ed) *Encyclopedia of Public International Law* (Elsevier Amsterdam 1997) vol 3.

Murphy, S.D., 'Terrorism and the Concept of Armed Attack in Article 51 of the UN Charter' [2002] Harvard J Int'l L.

Nagy, K., *Le problème de la légitime défense en droit international* (Acta Universitatis Szegediensis Szeged 1992).

Nakanishi, H., 'Kokusai Chitsujo wo meguru Ho to Seiji ni kansuru Ikkosatsu (A Study about Law and Politics over the International Order)' in *Kyoto Daigaku Hogakubu Soritsu Hyakushunen Kinen Ronbunshu* (*A Festschrift in Celebration of Kyoto University Faculty of Law's Centennial Anniversary of Foundation*) (Yuhikaku Tokyo 1999) vol 2 (*in Japanese*).

Nemoto, K., 'Jieikenkoshi ni okeru Hitsuyosei-Kinkyusei Gensoku (Nessesity and Proportionality Principles of Self-Defence)' in Murase S. (ed) *Jieiken no Gendaiteki Tenkai* (*The Right of Self-defence in the Contemporary Context*) (Toshindo Tokyo 2007) 59–87 (*in Japanese*).

Neuhold, H., Hummer, W. and Schreuer, C. (eds) *Österrichisches Handbuchs des Völkerrechts* (Manzsche Verlags- und Universitätsbuchhandlung Wien 1983) vol 1.

Nishizaki, A., *Amerika Reisen Seisaku to Kokuren 1945–1950* (*The United States, the United Nations and the Cold War 1945–1950*) (University of Tokyo Press Tokyo 1992) (*in Japanese*).

Notter, H., *Postwar Foreign Policy Preparation, 1939–1945* (Department of State Washington DC 1949 reprinted in 1975).

Nussbaum, A., *A Concise History of the Law of Nations* (2nd edn Macmillan Company New York 1962).

Occelli, M.B., '"Sinking" the Caroline: Why the Caroline Doctrine's Restrictions on Self-Defense Should Not Be Regarded as Customary International Law' [2003] 4 San Diego Int'l LJ.

O'Connell, D.P., *International Law* (Stevens & Sons London 1965) vol 1.

Offutt, M., *The Protection of Citizens Abroad by the Armed Forces of the United States* (John Hopkins Press Baltimore 1928).

Okuwaki, N., 'Ryoiki Shuken no Gainen wo megutte (On the Concept of Territorial Sovereignty)' in Kokusaiho Gakkai (Japanese Soc'y of Int'l L) (ed) *Riku, Sora, Uchu* (*Territory, Air Space, Outer Space*) (Sanseido Tokyo 2001) (*in Japanese*).

Onuma, Y., *Senso Sekininron Josetsu* (*Introduction to the Issues of Responsibility for War*) (University of Tokyo Press Tokyo 1975) (*in Japanese*).

Oppenheim, L., *International Law* (Longmans, Green & Co New York 1905) vol 1.

Oppenheim, L., *International Law* (Longman, Green & Co London 1906) vol 2.

Oppenheim, L., *International Law* (5th edn Lauterpacht H. (ed) Longmans, Green & Co London 1937) vol 1.

Oppenheim, L., *International Law* (5th edn Lauterpacht H. (ed) Longmans, Green & Co London 1935) vol 2.

Oppenheim, L., *International Law* (7th edn Lauterpacht H. (ed) Longmans, Green & Co London 1952) vol 2.

Paust, J., 'Use of Armed Force against Terrorists in Afghanistan, Iraq, and Beyond' [2002] 35 Cornell Int'l LJ.

Phillimore, R., *Commentaries upon International Law* (WG Benning London 1854) vol 1.

Phillimore, W.G.F, 'Droits et devoirs fondamentaux des états' [1923] 1 RCADI.

Pittard, E., *La protection des nationaux à l'étranger* (Imprimerie W Kündig & Fils Genève 1896).

Potter, P.B., 'L'Intervention en droit international moderne' [1930] 32 RCADI.

Pradier-Fodéré, P., *Traité de droit international public* (A Durand et Pedone-Lauriel Paris 1885) vol 1.

Randelzhofer, A., 'Article 2(4)' in Simma B. (ed) *The Charter of the United Nations: A Commentary* (2nd edn Oxford University Press 2002) vol 1.

Randelzhofer, A., 'Article 51' in Simma B. (ed) *The Charter of the United Nations: A Commentary* (2nd edn Oxford University Press Oxford 2002) vol 1.

Randelzhofer, A., 'Use of Force' in Bernhardt R. (ed) *Encyclopedia of Public International Law* (Elsevier Amsterdam 2000) vol 4.

Randelzhofer, A. and Dörr O., 'Article 2(4)' in Simma B. et al (eds) *The Charter of the United Nations: A Commentary* (3rd edn Oxford University Press 2012) vol 1

Randelzhofer, A. and Nolte, G., 'Article 51' in Simma B. et al (eds) *The Charter of the United Nations: A Commentary* (3rd edn Oxford University Press Oxford 2012) vol 2.

Ray, J., *Commentaire du Pacte de la Société des Nations selon la politique et la jurisprudence des organs de la Société* (Sirey Paris 1930).

Reisman, W.M., 'In Defense of World Public order' [2001] 95 AJIL.

Richardson, J.D., *A Compilation of the Messages and Papers of the Presidents 1789–1897* (Government Printing Office Washington DC 1896) vol 2.

Rifaat, A.M., *International Aggression* (Almqvist & Wiksell International Stockholm 1979).

Right to Protect Citizens in Foreign Countries by Landing Forces (Memorandum by the Solicitor) (Department of State, Division of Information, Series M, No 14, Printed and distributed October 5, 1912).

'Rights and Duties of States in Case of Aggression: Draft Convention, with Comment, Prepared by the Research in International Law of Harvard Law School' [1939] 33 AJIL Suppl Sec.

Rivier, A., *Principes du droit des gens* (Rousseau Paris 1896) vol 1.

Rodick, B.C., *The Doctrine of Necessity in International Law* (Columbia University Press New York 1928).

Ronzitti, N., *Rescuing Nationals Abroad through Military Coercion and Intervention on Grounds of Humanity* (Martinus Nijhoff Publishers Dordrecht 1985).

Root, E., 'The Basis of Protection to Citizens Residing Abroad' [1910] 4 AJIL.

Rosenne, S., 'Codification of International Law' in Bernhardt R., (ed) *Encyclopedia of Public International Law* (Elsevier Amsterdam 1992) vol 1.

Rosenne, S., 'The Hague Codification Conference of 1930' in Rosenne, S. (ed) *League of Nations Conference for the Codification of International Law [1930]* (Oceana New York 1975) vol 1.

Ross, A., *A Textbook of International Law* (Longmans, Green & Co London 1947).

Rousseau, C., *Le droit des conflits armés* (Pedone Paris 1983).

Russell, R., *A History of the United Nations Charter* (Brookings Institution Washington DC 1958).

Ruys, T., *'Armed Attack' and Article 51 of the UN Charter* (Cambridge University Press Cambridge 2010).

Ruys, T. and Verhoeven, S., 'Attacks by Private Actors and the Right of Self-Defence' [2005] 10 J Conflict & Security L

Salmon, J.J.A., 'Fant-il codifier l'état de nécessité en droit international?' in Makarczyk L. (ed) *Essays in International Law in Honour of Judge Manfred Lachs* (Nijhoff the Hague 1984).

Schachter, O., *International Law in Theory and Practice* (Kluwer Law International Boston 1995).

Schlochauer, H.J., 'Bryan Treaties (1913/1914)' in Bernhardt R. (ed) *Encyclopedia of Public International Law* (Elsevier Amsterdam 1992) vol 1.

Scott, J.B., 'The American-Mexican Joint Commission of 1916' [1916] 10 AJIL.

Scott, J.B., 'The American Punitive Expedition into Mexico' [1916] 10 AJIL.

Sefériadès, S., 'Principes généraux du droit international de la paix' [1930] 34 RCADI.

Serup, A., *L'Article 16 du Pacte et son interprétation dans le conflit Italo-Ethiopien* (Rousseau Paris 1938).

Sicilianos, L.A., *Les réactions décentralisées à l'illicite* (LGDJ Paris 1990).

Sogawa, T., 'Karu Shumitto ni okeru "Senso Kannen no Tenkan" ni tsuite (Carl Schmitt's "Shift of Theory of War") (1)' [1953] 17–2 Hogaku (Journal of L & Political Science (Tohoku University)) (*in Japanese*).

Sogawa, T., 'Shudanteki Jiei: Iwayuru US Formula no Ronriteki Kozo to Genjitsuteki Kino (Collective Self-Defence: Logical Structure and Actual Function of So-Called US Formula)' in Sogawa T. (ed) *Kokusai Seiji Shiso to Taigai Ishiki* (*International Political Thought and Foreign Consciousness*) (Sobunsha Tokyo 1977) (*in Japanese*).

Stevens, K.R., *Border Diplomacy* (University of Alabama Press Tuscaloosa 1989).

Stone, J., 'Book Review (reviewing I Brownlie *International Law and the Use of Force by States* (1963))' [1965] 59 AJIL.

Stratis, S.C., *Le Pacte Général de Renonciation à la Guerre* (M Riviere Paris 1931).

Stromseth, J., 'Law and Force after Iraq: A Transitional Moment' [2003] 97 AJIL.

Strüpp, K., *Das Völkerrechtliche Delikt* (W Kohlhammer Stüttgart 1920).

Tabata, S., *Kokusaiho* (*International Law*) (2nd edn Iwanamishoten Tokyo 1966) (*in Japanese*).

Tabata, S., *Kokusaiho* (*International Law*) (new edn Yuhikaku Tokyo 1973) vol 1 (*in Japanese*).

Tachi, S., *Heiji Kokusaiho Ron* (*International Law in Peacetime*) (Nihonhyoronsha Tokyo 1930) (*in Japanese*).

Tachi, S., *Heiji Kokusai Koho* (*Public International Law in Peacetime*) (Chuo University Tokyo unknown) (*in Japanese*).

Tachi, S., *Nairan to Kokusaiho* (*Internal Strife and International Law*) (Nihon University Tokyo 1912) (*in Japanese*).

Takano, Y., *Kokusaiho Gairon* (*Treatise on International Law*) (rev edn Kobundo Tokyo 1985) vol 1 (*in Japanese*).

Tams, C., 'Note Analytique: Swimming with the Tide or Seeking to Stem It' [2005] 18 Revue québécoise de droit int'l.

Taoka, R., 'Fusen Joyaku no Igi (Significance of the Pact of Paris)' [1932] 1–2 Hogaku (Journal of L & Political Science (Tohoku University)) (*in Japanese*).

Taoka, R., *Kokusaihojo no Jieiken* (*Right of Self-defense under International Law*) (2nd edn Keisoshobo Tokyo 1981) (*in Japanese*).

Taoka, R., *The Right of Self-Defence in International Law* (Institute of Legal Study, Osaka University of Economics and Law Osaka 1978).

Thomas, A.V.W. and Thomas, J.A.J., *The Concept of Aggression in International Law* (Southern Methodist University Press Dallas 1972).

Tladi, D., 'The Nonconsenting Innocent State: The Problem with Bethlehem's Principle 12' [2013] 107 AJIL.

Toynbee, A.J., *Abyssinia and Italy* (*Survey of International Affairs* 1935 Vol 2) (Oxford University Press London 1936).

Travalio, G. and Altenburg, J., 'Terrorism, State Responsibility and the Use of Military Force' [2003] 4 Chicago J Int'l L

Treves, T., 'High Seas' in Berbhardt R. (ed) *Encyclopedia of public International Law* (Elsevier Amsterdam 1995) vol 2.

Tsutsui, W., *Jieiken* (*Right of Self-Defence*) (Yuhikaku Tokyo 1980) (*in Japanese*).

Twiss, T., *The Law of Nations Considered as Independent Political Communities* (Longman, Green, Longman & Roberts London 1861).

Uchida, H., '"Kyohiken" no Kigen (Origin of "Veto")' [1964] 5–1 Tokyotoritsu Daigaku Hogaku Gakkai Zasshi (Tokyo Metropolitan University Journal of L & Politics) (*in Japanese*).

Ueda, T., *Chiikiteki Anzenhosho no Shiteki Kenkyu* (*The Regional Security System under the League of Nations*) (Yamakawa Tokyo 1989) (*in Japanese with English Summary*).

de Vattel, M., *Le droit des gens ou principes de la loi naturelle* (edn of 1758 Carnegie Institute Washington DC 1916) vol 1.

Verdross, A., 'Règles générales du droit international de la paix' [1929] 30 RCADI.

Verdross, A. and Simma B. *Universelles Völkerrecht* (3rd edn Duncker & Humblot Berlin 1984).

Vierheilig, M., 'Customs Régime between Germany and Austria (Advisory Opinion)' in Berbhardt R. (ed) *Encyclopedia of public International Law* (Elsevier Amsterdam 1992) vol 1.

Waisberg, T., 'Colombia's Use of Force in Ecuador Against a Terrorist Organization' [2008] 12–17 ASIL Insight <http://www.asil.org/insights080822.cfm>

Waldock, C.H.M., 'General Course on Public International Law' [1962] 106 RCADI.

Waldock, C.H.M., 'The Regulation of the Use of Force by Individual States in International Law' [1952] 81 RCADI.

Walters, F.P., *A History of the League of Nations* (Oxford University Press Oxford 1952).

Wedgwood, R., 'Responding to Terrorism' [1999] 24 Yale J Int'l L.

Wehberg, H., 'Le problème de la mise de la guerre hors la loi' [1928] 24 RCADI.

Wehberg, H., 'Le Protocole de Genève' [1925] 7 RCADI.

Westlake, J., *Chapters on the Principles of International Law* (Cambridge University Press Cambridge 1894).

Westlake, J., *International Law* (Cambridge University Press Cambridge 1904) part I.

Wheaton, H., *Elements of International Law with a Sketch of the History of the Science* (Carey, Lea & Balnchard Philadelphia 1836).

Wheaton, H., *Wheaton's Elements of International Law* (5th English edn Phillipson C. (ed) Stenvens & Sons London 1916).

Williams, J.F., 'The Covenant of the League of Nations and War' [1933] 5 Cambridge LJ.

Williams, W., 'Reminiscences of the Bering Sea Arbitration' [1943] 37 AJIL.

Willoughby, W.W., *The Sino-Japanese Controversy and the League of Nations* (Greenwood Press New York 1935).

Woolsey, L.H., 'The Leticia Dispute between Colombia and Peru' [1933] 27 AJIL.

Woolsey, L.H., 'The Leticia Dispute between Colombia and Peru' [1935] 29 AJIL.

Wright, Q., *A Study of War* (University of Chicago Press Chicago 1942) vol 1.

Wright, Q., 'Changes in the Conception of War' [1924] 18 AJIL.

Wright, Q., 'The Concept of Aggression in International Law' [1935] AJIL.

Wright, Q., 'The Meaning of the Pact of Paris' [1933] 27 AJIL.

Wright, Q., 'The Test of Aggression in the Italo-Ethiopian War' [1936] 30 AJIL.

Wright, Q., 'When Does War Exist?' [1932] 26 AJIL.

Yakemtchouk, R., 'La légitime defense et l'Art. 51 de la Charte de l'O.N.U.' [1954] 14–3 Annales de Droit et de Science Politique (Annales de droit de Louvain).

Yamada, T., 'Kokusaiho ni okeru Kinkyujotai Riron no Rekishiteki Tenkai to Jisshosei (The Doctrine of Necessity in International Law: Its Historical Development)' [2006] 105–3 Kokusaiho Gaiko Zassi (Journal of Int'l L & Diplomacy) 39–44 (*in Japanese with English Summary*).

Yamamoto, S., *Kokusaiho* (*International Law*) (2nd edn Yuhikaku Tokyo 1994) (*in Japanese*).

Yamamoto, Y., 'Shudan Anzen Hosho (Collective Security)' in Kokusaiho Gakkai (Japanese Soc'y of Int'l L) (ed) *Kokusai Kankeiho Jiten* (*Encyclopedia of International Law*) (2nd edn Sanseido Tokyo 2005) (*in Japanese*).

Yanagihara, M., 'Iwayuru "Musabetsu Sensokan" to Senso no Ihoka' (The "Idea of Non-Discriminating War" in Japan and the Doctrine of Carl Schmitt) [2001] Sekaiho Nenpo (Yearbook of World Law) (*in Japanese*).

Yanagihara, M., 'Senso no Ihoka to Nihon (Outlawry of War and Japan)' in Kokusaiho Gakkai (Japanese Soc'y of Int'l L) (ed) *Anzen Hosho* (*International Security*) (Sanseido Tokyo 2001) (*in Japanese*).

Yokota, K., *Jieiken* (*Right of Self-Defence*) (Yuhikaku Tokyo 1951) (*in Japanese*).

Zanardi, P.L., *La Legittima Difésa nel Diritto Internazionale* (DA Giuffrè Editore Milano 1972).

Zimmern, A.E., *The League of Nations and the Rule of Law 1918–1935* (Mcmillan London 1936).

Žourek, J., 'La notion de légitime défense en droit international' [1975] 56 Annuaire (Institut de Droit Interntional).

Index

Act of Chapultepec 214, 217
Ago, Roberto 1, 32, 168, 240, 241
aggression 15, 33, 83, 89–110, 118, 128–138, 176–180, 191, 193, 202, 212, 218, 224–226
  definition of aggression 97–104, 107–110, 125, 129–131, 225, 235
  flagrant aggression 103, 104, 130–136
  indirect aggression 16–18
  simple aggression 103, 104, 134
aggressive war 89, 105, 106, 137
aggressor (state) 96, 99, 106, 108, 162, 179
  determination of aggressor (state) 99, 101–104, 107, 108, 110, 125, 128, 130–132, 135, 191, 193, 235
alliance 129, 130
Amelia Island incident 43, 63
armed attack 4, 5, 7, 8, 11, 12, 15, 17, 18, 20, 21, 23, 83, 96, 223–228, 236, 239
  occurrence of an armed attack 4, 12, 82, 236
Articles on Responsibility of States for Internationally Wrongful Acts 1, 240, 241

Basdevant, Jules 167, 168
Baty, Thomas 172
Bering Sea (*Fur Seal*) Arbitration 60–69
Bowett, Derek William 11–19, 22–24, 34, 83, 181, 182, 215, 235–237
Brierly, James Leslie 35, 122
Brownlie, Ian 11–13, 17–24, 30, 37–39, 54, 70, 83, 95, 96, 142, 181, 182, 235–238

Caroline incident 25–39, 50–55, 63, 65–67, 70–74, 76, 78–80, 162, 164, 165, 241, 242
Chamberlain, Austen 92, 106
Chamberlain Doctrine 125, 126, 156
collective security system 89, 127–129, 131, 136
customary right of self-defence *see* right of self-defence

Danish fleet incident 76, 77
defensive war 87, 90, 137, 160
defensive war conception of self-defence *see* self-defence
de Visscher, Charles 4, 22
Draft Act Defining Aggressor 107, 110, 176, 180
Draft Treaty of Mutual Assistance 88, 98–101, 110, 128–131, 134–136
Dumbarton Oaks Conference 184–186, 191–194, 200–202, 210, 211, 214, 215
Dumbarton Oaks Proposals 194–196, 214, 215

Eden, Anthony 220
employment of military forces by a state within the jurisdiction of another state 185, 191, 193
employment of military forces within territories of other states 187, 190, 191, 194, 205, 228, 237
excuse 78, 234

Franck, Thomas 2, 14
freedom to wage war 126, 127
frontier incidents 119, 121, 173, 239, 240
fundamental rights of States 30, 71, 78
  theory of fundamental rights of States 78, 80

Geneva Protocol (Protocol for the Pacific Settlement of International Disputes) 88–90, 101–103, 110
Gray, Christine 6, 14, 22, 182, 239, 240

Hall, William Edward 69, 76, 77, 146, 173
hostile intent 69, 173, 183, 206, 213

intervention 18, 19, 23, 35, 147, 149
invasion of territory *see also* violation of territory 66, 100, 176, 179, 183, 213
Italo-Ethiopian War 114, 118

just war doctrine 26

Kellogg-Briand Pact *see* Pact of Paris
Kellogg, Frank 92–94, 105, 106, 150, 159
Kelsen, Hans 168

Lauterpacht, Hersch 171
League of Nations
  Council of the League of Nations 98, 99, 101–104, 112, 131–135
  Covenant of the League of Nations 85–87, 97
    Article 8 88
    Article 10 85, 97, 98, 120, 196
    Article 11 112, 120
    Article 12 111, 113, 115, 116
    Article 12(1) 86
    Article 13(4) 86
    Article 15 116
    Article 15(7) 86, 91, 222
    Article 16 88, 91, 98
  League of Nations Codification Conference 161–163, 174
Locarno Treaties *see also* Rhineland Pact 85, 90, 103, 106, 123, 132
Lytton Commission 112
Lytton Report 112–114

Manchurian incident 111–114, 118
Marco Polo Bridge incident 116, 118
Monroe Doctrine 125, 126
Moscow Conference 186–188
Moscow Declaration 185, 186, 188, 191

necessity *see* state of necessity

Oppenheim, Lassa 77, 78
outlawry of war 85–87, 166, 174, 180

Pact of Paris (Treaty for Renunciation of War) 31, 87, 92–94, 105–107, 113, 125–127, 150, 151, 154, 156–160
Phillimore, Robert 51, 73, 76
policing conception of self-defence *see* self-defence
political independence 15, 198, 199
principle of non-use of force 2, 183–186, 192, 205–207, 213, 234
principle of proportionality 122–124
principles of necessity and proportionality 238
proportionate countermeasures 239
protection of nationals (abroad) 4, 15, 18, 19, 44, 144–160
Protocol for the Pacific Settlement of International Disputes *see* Geneva Protocol

Rhineland Pact *see also* Locarno Treaties 90, 91, 103–105, 110, 127, 132–136
resort to force 83, 174–176
resort to war 169, 170
right of resort to war 26, 36, 44, 85
right of self-defence *see also* self-defence
  coexistence of the two conceptions of the right of self-defence 143, 161, 165, 180, 232
  customary right of self-defence *see also* right of self-defence in customary international law 12, 24, 141
  function of the right of self-defence 35, 37, 38, 40, 65, 69, 80, 82, 83, 90, 93, 95, 136, 137, 148, 150, 169, 233
  legal status of the right of self-defence 137, 230, 234
  19th century right of self-defence *see also* policing conception of self-defence, right of self-defence that existed before World War I 96, 148, 172, 232, 236, 237
  prerequisites for the right of self-defence 4, 7, 8, 11, 17, 20, 22, 24, 40, 95, 107, 118, 138, 213, 215, 220, 222, 229, 230, 234, 235
    permissive interpretation of the prerequisites for the right of self-defence 4, 5, 11, 16, 23, 28, 40, 82, 141, 144
    restrictive interpretation of the prerequisites for the right of self-defence 4–6, 14, 23, 29, 40, 82–84, 141, 142, 144, 145, 165
  Rechtgut (Rechtsgüter) of the right of self-defence 15, 18, 20, 49, 54, 55, 58, 59, 67–69, 95, 131, 134–136, 160, 230–233, 236
  right of collective self-defence 124, 125, 219, 224, 234, 235, 239, 240
    precursor of the right of collective self-defence 96, 110, 124, 125, 127, 135, 136, 234, 235
  right of individual self-defence 217, 219

right of self-defence (cont.)
prerequisites for the right of individual self-defence 224, 229, 234, 235
right of self-defence established in the inter-war period *see also* defensive war conception of self-defence 23, 39, 40, 44, 82–84, 136–138, 159, 161, 162, 172, 229, 232
right of self-defence in customary international law *see also* customary right of self-defence 11, 13, 14, 18
right of self-defence that existed before World War I *see also* 19th century right of self-defence, policing conception of self-defence 23, 24, 39, 40, 43–45, 79–81, 83, 136, 141, 142, 145, 148, 150, 160, 161, 168
right to territorial inviolability 72, 78, 136

San Francisco Conference 194–206, 217, 219
self-defence *see also* right of self-defence
anticipatory self-defence 4, 15, 20
defensive war conception of self-defence *see also* right of self-defence established in the inter-war period 136–138, 229, 230, 233–238
duty of self-defence 51
necessity of self-defence 27, 50, 51, 54, 55, 57–59, 64, 67
policing conception of self-defence *see also* 19th century right of self-defence, right of self-defence that existed before World War I 79, 136, 137, 177–180, 206, 207, 209–213, 228, 230–232, 234, 235, 237, 238, 240
principle of self-defence 46–49
self-help 18–21, 23, 24, 38, 39, 236
self-preservation 19, 20, 36, 67, 78, 79
duty of self-preservation 48, 210
necessity of self-preservation 27, 58
principle of self-preservation 46, 48, 76
right of self-preservation 16, 20, 29–31, 37, 38, 57, 58, 70–80, 236, 237
state of necessity 29–32, 95, 240–242

Tachi, Sakutaro 154–156, 171
Taoka, Ryoichi 36, 43
territorial integrity 15, 121, 196–198
threats to or breach of the peace 191, 193
Twiss, Travers 73, 76

United Nations Charter
Article 2(4) 1, 2, 11, 34, 182–184, 195, 199, 200, 202–206, 212–214, 216–218, 227–229, 241, 242
Article 51 2, 4, 11, 12, 20–22, 181–183, 213–215, 218, 226–230, 242
Chapter VII 2, 183, 199
joint US-UK draft 223
travaux préparatoires 6, 181–231
US draft of 12 May 220, 221, 225
use of force 2, 184, 190, 191, 193, 194, 212, 233
prohibition of the use of force 2, 174, 180
use of force short of armed attack 8, 15, 17, 239
US-Mexico border incident 45, 47

Verdross, Alfred 149, 171
violation of territory *see also* invasion of territory 48, 49, 52–55, 65, 66, 69, 169, 170, 174, 177, 209, 213, 228, 233, 237
violation of the flag-state jurisdiction 57–59, 65, 67, 68, 232, 233, 237
Virginius incident 55–59, 74, 76, 78, 163

war
formal definition of war 169
legal definition of war 169
material definition of war 169, 170, 172, 174
see also aggressive war
see also defensive war
see also freedom to wage war
see also resort to war
see also right of resort to war
Webster, Daniel 25, 53, 54
Webster Formula 25, 53, 54, 67, 74, 113, 164, 165
Westlake, John 75, 77, 78, 146

Yalta Conference 214

www.ingramcontent.com/pod-product-compliance
Lightning Source LLC
LaVergne TN
LVHW020634300926
849161LV00004B/702